Praise for
ATD's Handbook for Measuring and Evaluating Training

"*ATD's Handbook for Measuring and Evaluating Training* is essential for talent development professionals seeking to demonstrate the true impact of their work. With its clear methodologies and actionable insights, it transforms training evaluation into a strategic tool for driving measurable business success."

—Abdulrahman Alsheail, Director General of Human Resources, The Institute of Public Administration, Saudi Arabia

"Whether you are new to ROI or an experienced ROI practitioner, the second edition of *ATD's Handbook for Measuring and Evaluating Training* is a must-read that you will use as a reference guide over and over. The wealth of knowledge contained between the pages is phenomenal!"

—Ida Dalessandro-Felix, EMOD, CPC, ACC, CRP, Education Program Director, US Office of Personnel Management

"Patti's knowledge about measuring learning programs is second-to-none and this book helps the talent development professional understand how to put together the puzzle of measurement and evaluation. Using her process and measurement strategy has helped us evaluate and validate our learning programs with our senior leaders to place talent development as a top pillar of our enterprise business strategy."

—Kristine M. Ellis, MEd, MPC, PCC, Director, Talent Development, Florida Blue; A GuideWell Company

"It's more critical than ever to elevate our business partnerships with enablement impact mapped to business goals. Patti Phillips, a prominent measurement and evaluation leader, delivers a step-by-step guide that is compelling, comprehensive, and credible. If you invest in one evaluation resource for your L&D strategy, make it this one."

—Jaimie Krause, PhD, Director of Learning and Development, Indeed

Patricia Pulliam Phillips, Editor

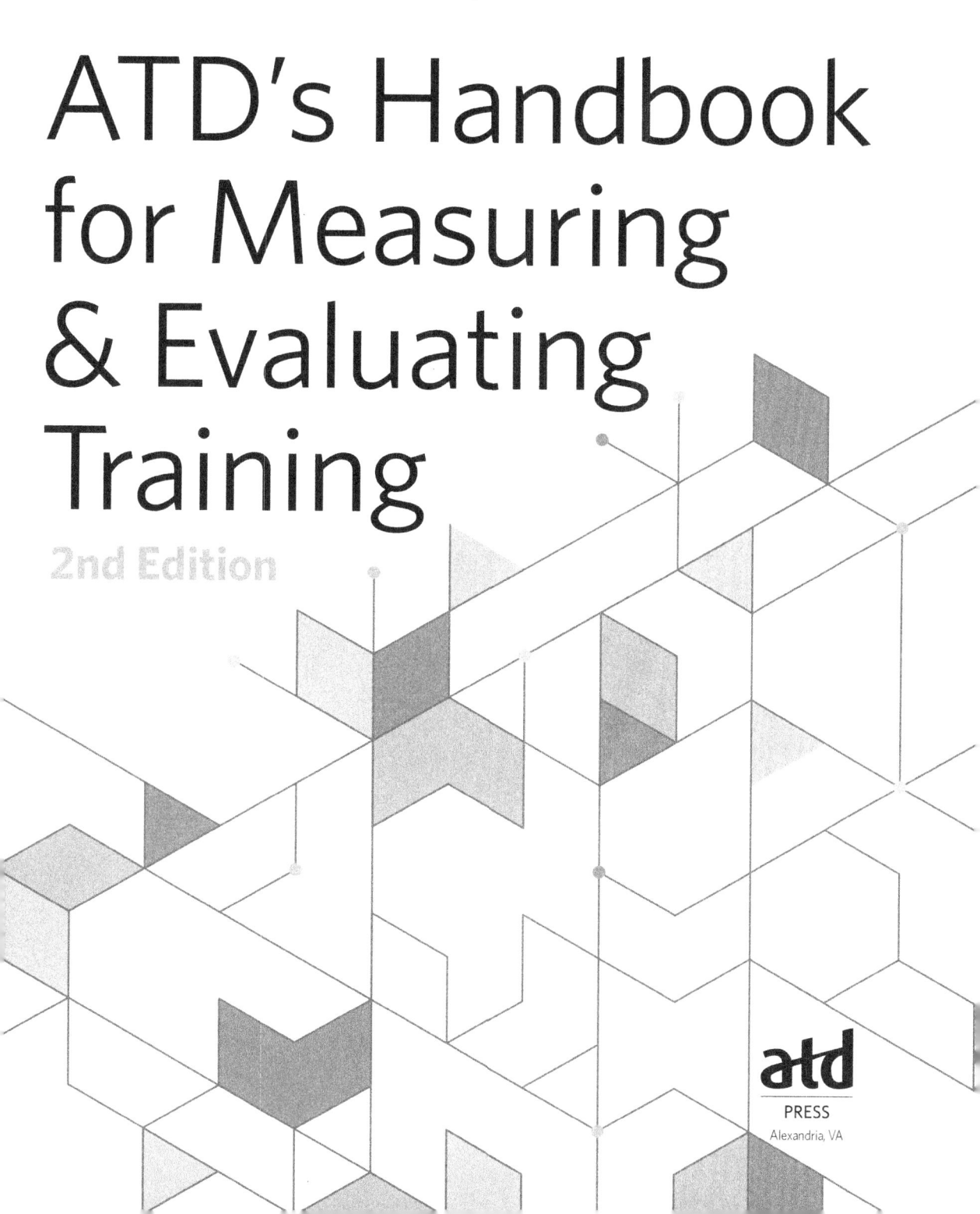

ATD's Handbook for Measuring & Evaluating Training

2nd Edition

atd PRESS
Alexandria, VA

© 2025 ASTD DBA the Association for Talent Development (ATD)
All rights reserved. Printed in the United States of America.

28 27 26 25   1 2 3 4 5

No part of this publication may be reproduced, distributed, or transmitted in any form or by any means, including photocopying, recording, information storage and retrieval systems, or other electronic or mechanical methods, without the prior written permission of the publisher, except in the case of brief quotations embodied in critical reviews and certain other noncommercial uses permitted by copyright law. For permission requests, please go to copyright.com, or contact Copyright Clearance Center (CCC), 222 Rosewood Drive, Danvers, MA 01923 (telephone: 978.750.8400; fax: 978.646.8600).

ATD Press is an internationally renowned source of insightful and practical information on talent development, training, and professional development.

ATD Press
1640 King Street
Alexandria, VA 22314 USA

Ordering information: Books published by ATD Press can be purchased by visiting ATD's website at td.org/books or by calling 800.628.2783 or 703.683.8100.

Library of Congress Control Number: 2024952089

ISBN-10: 1-960231-24-3
ISBN-13: 978-1-960231-24-6
e-ISBN: 978-1-960231-25-3

ATD Press Editorial Staff
Director: Sarah Halgas
Manager: Melissa Jones
Content Manager, Learning & Development: Bianca Woods
Developmental Editor: Jack Harlow
Production Editor: Katy Wiley Stewts
Cover Designer: Shirley E.M. Raybuck

Text Layout: PerfecType, Nashville, TN

Printed by BR Printers, San Jose, CA

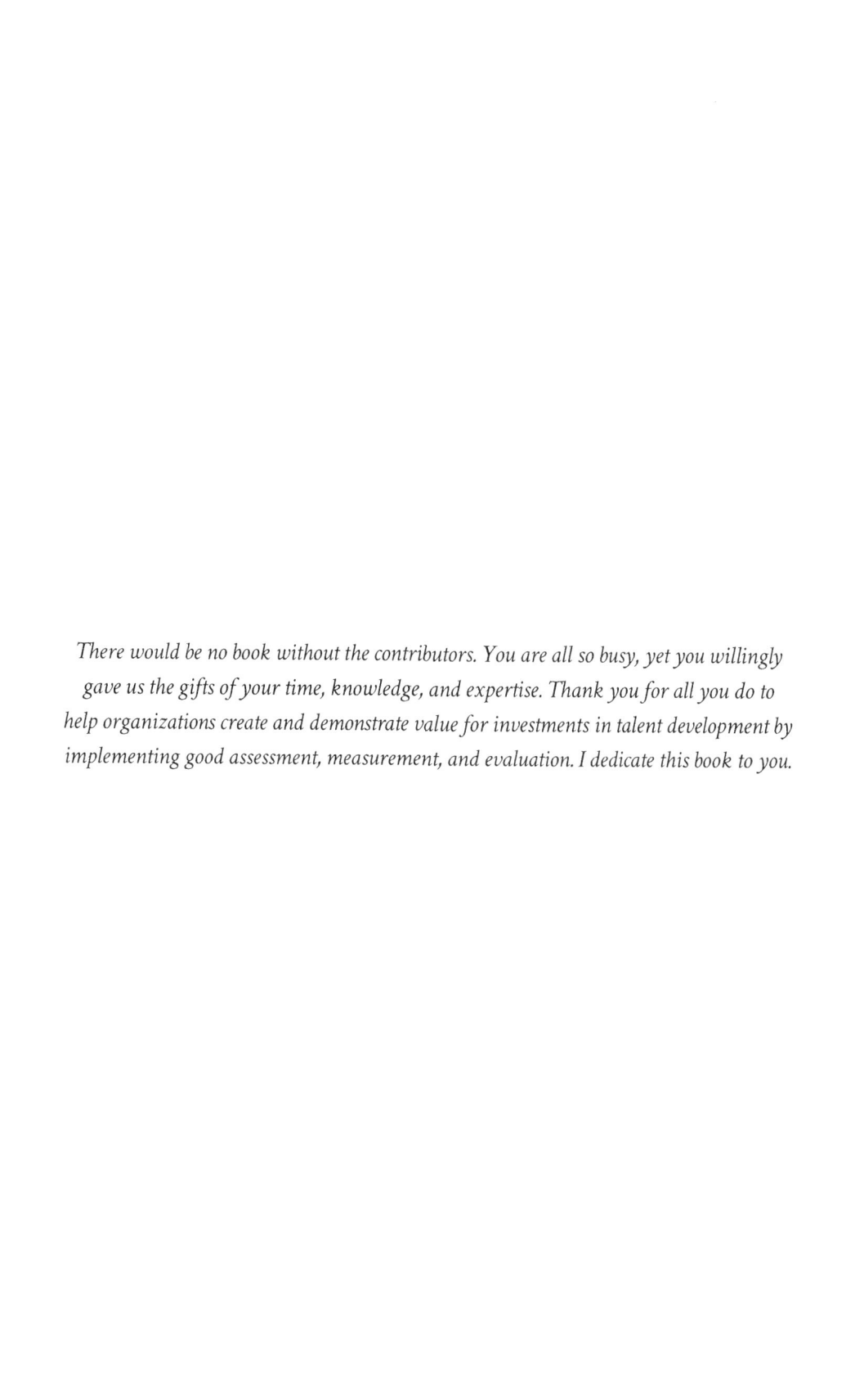

There would be no book without the contributors. You are all so busy, yet you willingly gave us the gifts of your time, knowledge, and expertise. Thank you for all you do to help organizations create and demonstrate value for investments in talent development by implementing good assessment, measurement, and evaluation. I dedicate this book to you.

Contents

Foreword *by Jack J. Phillips* xi
Foreword *by Courtney Vital Kriebs* xvii
Introduction *by Patti P. Phillips* xxv

Part 1. Evaluation Planning

1. Aligning Training to the Needs of the Business 3
   by Faith Krebs
2. Analyzing Performance Gaps 19
   by Sardék Love
3. Developing Powerful Program Objectives 33
   by Katharine Aldana
4. Planning Your Evaluation Project 49
   by Kaycee Buckley

Part 2. Data Collection

5. Designing Learner Surveys 65
   by Will Thalheimer
6. Designing Questionnaires and Surveys for Follow-Up Evaluation 79
   by Caroline Hubble
7. Designing and Delivering Tests 97
   by Cindy L. Hill and Eric T. Vincent
8. Conducting Interviews 111
   by Henri van den Idsert
9. Conducting Focus Groups 125
   by Katinka Koke

CONTENTS

10. Using Action Planning as a Measurement and Transfer Strategy 139
    by Emma Weber

Part 3. Data Analysis

11. Using Statistics in Evaluation 157
    by Timothy R. Brock
12. Analyzing Qualitative Data 171
    by Damien M. Sanchez
13. Isolating the Effects of the Program 185
    by Jack J. Phillips and David Maddock
14. Converting Measures to Monetary Value 199
    by Patti P. Phillips
15. Identifying Program Costs 215
    by Judith Cardenas
16. Calculating the Return on Investment 223
    by Beryl Oldham
17. Measuring Intangible Benefits 235
    by Nader Bechini
18. Forecasting ROI 249
    by Suzanne Schell

Part 4. Results Optimization

19. Telling the Story 265
    by Kevin M. Yates
20. Visualizing Data 279
    by Peggy Parskey
21. Implementing the ISO Standards for L&D Metrics 301
    by David Vance
22. Using Black Box Thinking to Optimize Training Outcomes ... 315
    by Rachell Baghelai
23. Using Financial Analysis to Compare OJT and S-OJT 325
    by Ronald L. Jacobs

Part 5. Make Measurement and Evaluation Work

24. Implementing a Sustainable Measurement Practice 337
    by Holly Burkett
25. Getting Stakeholder Buy-In for Measurement and Evaluation 355
    by Brenda Sugrue
26. Developing and Using Professional Standards for Evaluation............. 367
    by Michael A. Lawson
27. Leveraging Artificial Intelligence 387
    by Trish Uhl
28. Building a Measurement and Evaluation Strategy: A Real-Life Example
    at ASML... 405
    by Robin Dijke and Klaas Toes

Acknowledgments 419
Appendix A. Evaluation Planning Workbook.............................. 421
Appendix B. Answers to Knowledge Checks 439
References 455
Additional Resources... 467
About the Contributors... 471
Index 483
About the Editor.. 495
About ATD 497

Foreword

JACK J. PHILLIPS

Many books about training measurement and evaluation have hit the market since I wrote the first book on this topic, *Handbook of Training Evaluation and Measurement Methods*, in 1983 with Gulf Publishing. Since then, I have authored or co-authored more than 30. With this in mind, one might wonder: "Do we need another book (or new edition) about measuring, evaluating, and analyzing the training and talent development profession?" My response: Yes!

Complex and persistent problems require multiple solutions, and demonstrating the value of learning investments is a persistent problem. A few years ago, *TD* magazine's editors wrote a retrospective article examining how the topics highlighted by the magazine had changed over time. They found that one important topic in particular—proving the worth of training—had not changed. Much of the continued interest in this topic is driven by senior executives in organizations seeking data on the value of their investments. Unfortunately, many practitioners do not fully understand why this is an issue or how to address it. We need multiple solutions with a variety of techniques, approaches, and models to motivate practitioners to step up to the measurement challenge.

Learning is an important activity that's central to building organizations, driving operational excellence, building important relationships, and ensuring innovative and sustainable performance. It is through learning that organizations advance from good to great and achieve outstanding results—and it doesn't stop with organizations. Our communities, states, and nations are all by-products of learning, whether it occurs individually, collectively, or collaboratively. Executives, administrators, and leaders will invest more in learning when they fully understand its value. This book will help you do just that.

FOREWORD

What Are the Challenges?

Concerns that surround proving the value of learning rest within five issues. These are not new concerns, and we are making progress, but the issues persist:

1. **Learning is rarely measured at the levels desired by organizational executives.** As studies clearly show, executives want to see how learning programs connect to the business—and that desire spans across government, nonprofit, for-profit, and nongovernmental organizations. The good news is that it is possible to achieve this, and this book will show you how.

2. **Most learning isn't aligned to the business.** This is unfortunate because the business connection should be the starting point of any investment, including learning programs. (All organizations have business measures of output, quality, costs, and time.) Some learning teams understand this and approach learning with business needs in mind; most do not. Additionally, while learning is frequently proposed, it's not always the most effective solution. Other solutions could contribute more. Or, maybe learning is the right solution, but the program is subpar. This book will help with the alignment issue.

3. **Much of learning is wasted.** We hear a lot about scrap learning, which occurs when someone learns knowledge or skills to use on the job but doesn't actually use it. Research suggests that the amount of learning waste can range from 60 to 90 percent. While we are making some progress in this area, much more is needed and this book will help.

4. **Talent development professionals are not prepared to tackle measurement issues.** Whether they landed their jobs through academic preparation or a rotational assignment, the majority of L&D team members have no formal preparation for evaluation, measurement, analytics, or return on investment (ROI). I landed my first learning job as an instructor based on my engineering education. And while this is changing, it's not happening fast enough. This book will help you build this capability.

5. **Talent development professionals are not motivated to pursue evaluation.** Evaluation is not restricted to people with full-time evaluation responsibilities—it is the responsibility of every stakeholder. However, if evaluation is not your full-time job, it is easy to let the other activities you have to do get in the way of designing for and delivering results. TD professionals may not pursue evaluation because they

aren't sure if they really need it or they think it is too complex, too confusing, or too difficult. As the cartoon character Pogo so appropriately said, "We have met the enemy, and he is us." This book will help motivate the team to pursue evaluation.

What's Needed

We need to make important changes to our learning systems. The issues we are facing are not new—seasoned professionals have been discussing and addressing them for years. Progress is being made, but more is needed. Following these steps will help:

1. **Start with why.** The beginning of a learning solution should be a business measure that represents why you are implementing the solution. Specifically defining the why ensures that every stakeholder understands the reasons behind developing the program or solution. Stakeholders should not have to wonder why they are making this investment. There should be at least some level of discussion about the business need for every program. Some organizations won't even implement a new program unless the business measure is identified, and an impact objective is written to describe the impact it will deliver.

2. **Think about measurement in the beginning.** Evaluation is usually stuck at the end of the ADDIE (analyze, design, develop, implement, and evaluate) model, which causes the misperception that evaluation only happens after it is all over. Unfortunately, evaluation needs to be addressed early and often—from the initial analysis through every phase of the process—so you can adjust the program as needed. Also, you need processes that drive the desired results and create expectations for those results. If you think about measurement only at the end, you are at a disadvantage because it will take more time and data will be difficult to capture.

3. **Take measurement beyond content delivery.** There is a lingering perception that you can only measure what you can control. You may control the learning content when the learner is captive because you can require them to provide data and measure their success. Unfortunately, if they do not use what they have learned, it's all a waste, and the program you thought was successful is actually a failure. Push the evaluations to Level 3 Application, Level 4 Impact, and yes, occasionally, Level 5 ROI. The data at these levels may be a bit more challenging to capture, but it tells the real story about the value of the learning investment.

4. **Focus on process improvement.** One of the greatest barriers to evaluation is a fear of the outcomes. If a program is not working and the results are trending negative, those involved may not want to know. After all, they supported, designed, facilitated, and implemented the program. We suggest approaching your evaluation from the perspective of process improvement—you're improving the program, not the individuals. With this approach, you stand a much better chance of collecting credible data, gaining acceptance for adjustments, and taking some of the fear out of any negative results.

5. **Manage the measurement and evaluation resources.** No organization has an unlimited budget, which means that any money allocated to measurement and evaluation, is taking away from design, development, and delivery. Unfortunately, many talent development functions have underinvested in measurement and evaluation (averaging around 1 percent of the TD budget). Best practice is to invest around 3 to 5 percent of the budget in measurement and evaluation, but that's still a lot of money for some large organizations. You can also spend more than you should. This book will help you manage your resources, particularly when using technology, to keep the investment in measurement, evaluation, and analytics at an amount that's suitable for most budgets.

6. **Share the joy.** Measurement, evaluation, and analytics are not just for those who have evaluation or analytics in their job title. It is everyone's responsibility, including analysts, designers, developers, facilitators, program owners, participants, and managers of participants. The entire team has a role in making it work, and all stakeholders must understand their roles and how they can influence the ultimate outcomes.

7. **Be proactive.** Anticipate outcomes. As Peter Drucker stated so eloquently, "It's a manager's job to anticipate the future." You have to anticipate the type of data you may need in the future because you can't assume that your funding stream will always exist. Constantly ask, "Are we providing enough evidence, data, and hard facts to convince the individuals who are funding these programs that this is a good investment?" If not, then something may need to change. And if you wait for them to request more data, it will be too late. You need to drive evaluation and analytics, not wait for others to push it. You want to be proactive by playing on the offense rather than the defense when it comes to measuring the learning investment.

8. **Leverage the results.** Process improvement positions the next program or project to be more successful than the previous. In essence, you are optimizing the return on investment to influence the allocation of funds in the future. You might make the case that a project or program needs additional funding because it yields a better return on the investment. But without the data, it is difficult to make that argument. For example, in our work at ROI Institute, we have seen that properly aligned, implemented, and supported soft skills programs can yield very high ROIs—much higher than hard skills programs. These results enable us to make a compelling argument to allocate large portions of the TD budget to soft skills programs.

The good news is that this book provides helpful advice to make these steps come to life and is filled with examples and case studies of practitioners doing just that.

Call to Action

You can't just read this book—you need to put the content into action. The key is to recognize the need for change. Wherever you are along the evaluation maturity continuum, there is always room for improvement.

This book offers several options, approaches, and actions. Make plans to implement smart action steps and check your progress. Consider creating a discussion group with colleagues as you read certain sections or chapters of this book. Rethink your strategy and make necessary adjustments. Reach out to the chapter authors for amplification, clarification, and additional assistance.

And remember, when it comes to showing the value of your programs, hope is not a strategy, luck is not a factor, and doing nothing is not an option. When it comes to accountability requirements for talent development, change is inevitable; progress is optional. Take the lead and use this book to make it work.

Good luck on your journey.

Jack J. Phillips, PhD
Chairman and Co-Founder, ROI Institute
Recipient of ATD's 2022 Thought Leader Award
Author, Co-Author, or Editor of more than 100 books including *Show the Value of What You Do: Measuring and Achieving Success in Any Endeavor*

Foreword
Measurement, Evaluation, and ATD's Talent Development Capability Model

COURTNEY VITAL KRIEBS

The Association for Talent Development's mission for more than 80 years has been to share knowledge, foster community, and establish standards for the field we now know as talent development, with a goal of educating professionals on the capabilities they need to perform in their roles and positively influence individual and organizational performance. Aspiring and current practitioners look to ATD for research, information, and practical wisdom on how to develop others in the workplace.

ATD has been developing competency models since 1978 to highlight the specific technical skills required of those in talent development, which in turn helps build a solid foundation of skills for TD professionals. ATD's newest model, the Talent Development Capability Model, was released in 2019 following an extensive occupational research study informed by more than 3,000 professionals from diverse roles, experience levels, geographies, and industries. The Talent Development Capability Model contains three domains of practice—personal, professional, and organizational—comprising 23 capabilities and 188 knowledge and skill statements that reflect the many skills and functions of our field (Figure F-1).

Both practical and future-focused, the goal of the Capability Model is to ensure TD professionals are able to equip their workforces to drive their workplaces and organizations forward and become more adaptable, strategic, and future-ready workers. When we do this, we elevate ourselves, our profession, and our society by making the world work better. The model also serves as the basis for professional credentialing through the ATD Certification Institute's

FOREWORD

Associate Professional in Talent Development (APTD) and Certified Professional in Talent Development (CPTD) certifications.

Figure F-1. ATD's Talent Development Capability Model

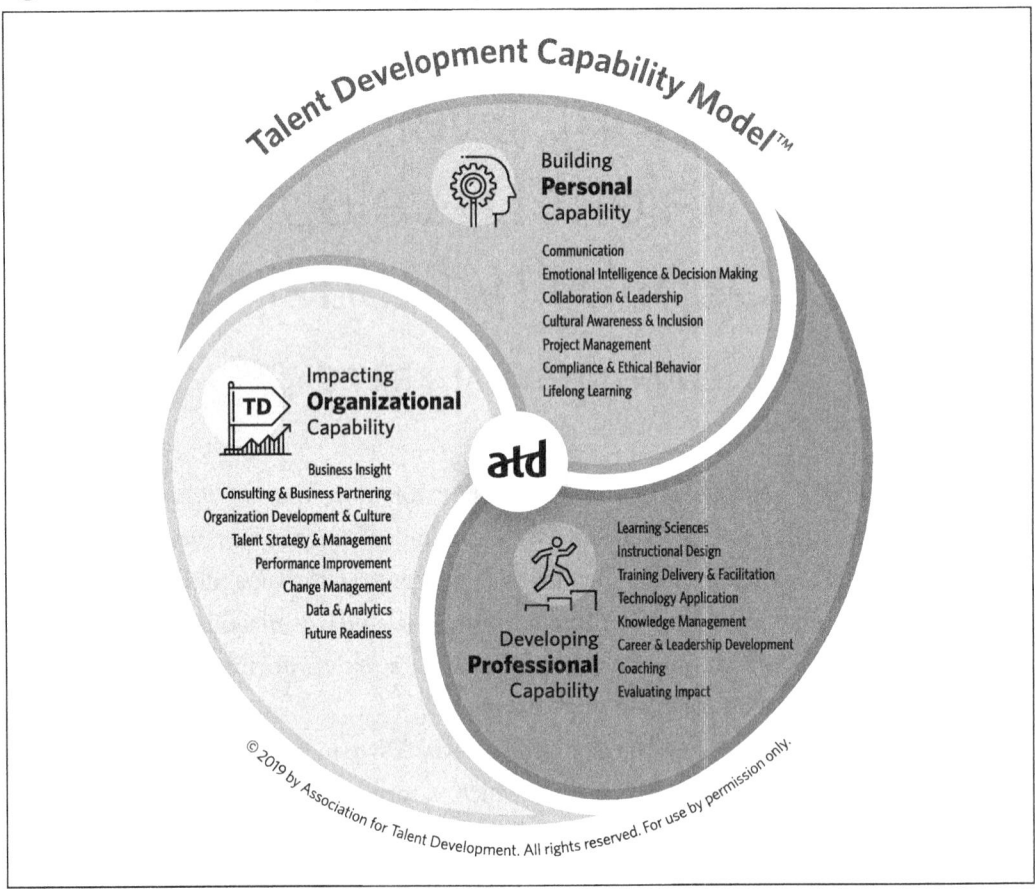

[Talent Development Capability Model™

Building Personal Capability
- Communication
- Emotional Intelligence & Decision Making
- Collaboration & Leadership
- Cultural Awareness & Inclusion
- Project Management
- Compliance & Ethical Behavior
- Lifelong Learning

Impacting Organizational Capability
- Business Insight
- Consulting & Business Partnering
- Organization Development & Culture
- Talent Strategy & Management
- Performance Improvement
- Change Management
- Data & Analytics
- Future Readiness

Developing Professional Capability
- Learning Sciences
- Instructional Design
- Training Delivery & Facilitation
- Technology Application
- Knowledge Management
- Career & Leadership Development
- Coaching
- Evaluating Impact

© 2019 by Association for Talent Development. All rights reserved. For use by permission only.]

While the Capability Model is aspirational and forward-looking, you can use it in your day-to-day life as a practitioner as you seek to:

- **Understand the field.** Comprehend the full scope of what TD covers, identify what's beyond training, and learn how cross-functional competencies are integrated to execute learning and performance solutions.
- **Create a development plan.** Build learning plans for yourself and your TD team, explore the areas in which you want to focus your development, and plan your upskilling and professional development journey.

- **Engage your leaders.** Better understand and align to business strategies, become a strategic partner and advisor, build business cases for TD investments, and help your organization become more innovative and competitive.
- **Increase your relevance.** Be a resource to your learners, colleagues, and leaders, position yourself as a champion of the highest standards, and remain competitive in today's challenging labor market.

You wouldn't be reading this book if you didn't see value in demonstrating the results of your work—results that reflect meaningful improvements in the effectiveness of your programs, employee performance, and organizational outcomes. However, this requires more than simply measuring how many courses you delivered, Level 1 satisfaction scores, and the number of learners you reached. It requires a true evaluation mindset and starting with the desired outcome or result you want to generate instead of focusing on the activity. For example, creating a training program is an activity, whereas outcomes reflect the deeper concerns driving that activity, such as the skills you need to develop, the performance that needs to improve, the business measures that need to change, and the value (ROI) the program will need to deliver back to the business.

ATD's Capability Model can help you grow this mindset and shift your approach from activity-based to results-based. Understanding all that's within our field and how one discipline connects to another provides a more strategic view into the levers we can pull to influence the organization's people, processes, and systems. And this is precisely what measurement and evaluation efforts seek to reveal. Further, the Capability Model states that we should always be connecting the work we do—whether designing courses, facilitating programs, implementing a new LMS, or coaching employees—to organizational strategy. When we align what we do to business goals, we become better positioned to assess and communicate the strategic impact of that work.

The heart of what we do as TD professionals is to listen to our stakeholders' needs and provide mechanisms for learning, support, and growth. Using the underlying connection points among the hundreds of individual activities we do to assess gaps, identify solutions, and enable learning and performance improvement in our jobs is critical to becoming the most strategic partner possible to our organizations. Our business leaders aren't concerned with the minutiae of how we approach instructional design, training, and performance improvement. They simply want a workforce that's prepared, engaged, and equipped to achieve business goals in an environment that's continually changing and increasingly complex.

FOREWORD

An evaluation mindset ensures that you will be in lockstep with your leaders and set up for more fruitful needs assessment conversations, opportunities to be a part of important discussions related to people investments, and trusted strategic partnerships.

Practitioner's Tip

As talent development professionals and leaders, it is our job to act as trusted advisors and thought partners within our sphere of influence. Our clients, be they internal or external, look to us to make decisions that will build and sustain successful workforce strategies. We are stewards, and to be successful, we need to demonstrate accountability, discretion, and sound judgment when using our organization's tangible and intangible resources. How can we do that without having strong learning evaluation knowledge? We need to ensure that the decisions that we make and recommend use resources in the most effective ways and continue to add value for our clients to ensure their future readiness."

—Angela L.M. Stopper, PhD, Chief Learning Officer and Director, People and Organization Development, University of California, Berkeley

Feeling overwhelmed by the weight of responsibility you've been gifted as a TD professional? The Capability Model can help you plan, organize, and develop your approach with an evaluation mindset and business impact lens. Let's review some of the many ways evaluation shows up across the spectrum of talent development roles:

- **Instructional designers** apply systematic methodologies rooted in adult learning principles and instructional theories and models to design and develop content, experiences, and other solutions that support the acquisition of new knowledge or skills. They need to be able to identify desired outcomes for learning, application, and business impact to develop objectives and build a measurement and evaluation plan for the programs they design.
- **Trainers and facilitators** facilitate learning in a traditional or virtual classroom, one-on-one, or on-the-job in an organization to help individuals improve their performance. They seek to understand and align the learning experience audience and organizational goals to ensure the training evaluation matches the intended outcome.
- **E-learning professionals** serve in a range of roles that support the creation of structured courses or learning experiences delivered electronically, including

online or computer-based learning, virtual classrooms, performance support materials, and digital collaboration and knowledge sharing. They use effective design strategies to embed evaluation into the course experience and connect individual courses to overall program outcomes.
- **Coaches** are qualified professionals who partner with individuals or teams to maximize their potential through a process that involves establishing goals, using strengths, pursuing development, and achieving results. They establish development plans to track movement toward agreed upon goals and identify mechanisms for evaluating the impact of the coaching solution upon completion.
- **HR and OD professionals** serve in roles aimed at optimizing talent and organizational processes or systems toward the achievement of business goals. They continually look for ways to uncover organizational requirements and goals and assess the results of development and performance-related initiatives.
- **Learning technologists** manage and execute the technology infrastructure necessary to enable an organization's talent development strategy. They work with stakeholders to uncover the gap between the current and desired future state that the technology needs to close and establish analytics and success measures to enable continuous improvement.
- **Training or talent development coordinators** plan, administer, and implement internally and externally developed learning programs that foster employee performance, development, and growth. They are responsible for collecting and analyzing evaluation data and executing the evaluation strategy to ensure consistency across in-house and vendor programs.
- **Talent development managers** supervise the work of a group of people and the processes responsible for fostering learning and employee development to drive organizational performance, productivity, and results. They may serve as a department of one in small organizations. They also determine what to measure and how evaluation data should be collected and reported and identify recommended improvements to TD solutions based on the results.
- **Talent development directors or executives** lead and set the strategy for a talent development unit within an organization. This unit may be composed of multiple functional areas with broad responsibility for developing talent in the workplace. They engage with evaluation data to identify how talent development

is contributing, how strategies should be adjusted, and what level of funding or investment is required.
- **Chief talent development officers** (also known as chief learning officers) represent the talent development function at the organization's executive level and typically report directly to the CEO. They establish the vision for how the talent development function should support organizational strategy, which provides a basis for how all TD initiatives should be evaluated.
- **Independent consultants** help teams and organizational leaders assess employee learning and performance gaps and recommend or create solutions to address those gaps. They uncover and recommend success metrics for the identified solution and champion the development and communication of a formal evaluation plan.
- **Professors and educators** are responsible for teaching learners through an academic institution or course of study. This role encompasses those who work in primary education, secondary education, higher education, and executive academic education. They look at a variety of data and analytics to identify course and program level metrics that need to be measured.

While measurement and evaluation is and should continue to be a component of every talent development role, it's increasingly becoming a defined and dedicated role; learning analytics leader, director of learning analytics, director of assessment and evaluation, and director of measurement and evaluation are just a few examples. Digitization, new technologies, and global scale are driving a need for learning measurement data and analytics specialists.

Measurement and evaluation is a lifelong practice—there is no destination and the more you learn, the greater your impact will be. But getting started doing something is the key and there are many practical approaches in this book that you can implement immediately. Other things you can do to mature your evaluation practice include:
- **Seek to understand the big picture.** Avoid a narrow focus on the role you have today. Instead, you need to get up to speed on your profession as a whole. As you explore this book, consider how to increase your evaluation capability and capacity across the full scope of work your TD team is engaged with, not just training.
- **Learn M&E terminology, models, and methodologies.** Expanding your acumen will contribute to a greater evaluation mindset, lead to ideas for how to improve your evaluation strategy and position you as a knowledgeable resource for your

team. ATD and ROI Institute offer a suite of foundational to advanced professional education programs on measurement and evaluation.
- **Put a learning plan together.** Evaluating learning impact and data and analytics are the TD capabilities most aligned to this topic. Other aligned areas include performance improvement, business insight, and consulting and business partnering. Dive into the specific knowledge and skills needed to perform these capabilities and grow your proficiency using books, courses, conferences, and communities of practice.
- **Engage your stakeholders and business leaders.** When you champion a measurement and evaluation–focused approach to training and talent development, it not only helps your organization, but positions you as a strategic, mission-focused professional. In other words, elevating your M&E practice isn't just good for your people and your organization—it's good for your career.

As you use this book, consider how each concept relates to this bigger picture of why our profession exists, what it is responsible for influencing, and how you can best align your work to the standards to create maximum impact. Quite simply, there is no greater way to improve your results than being able to identify the right development solutions to achieve the greatest business outcomes. Weaving measurement and evaluation into everything you do is the key to doing this. As your practice matures, these actions will position you as a champion for furthering your team's or organization's evaluation approaches. Remember, evaluation is not always the first thing on a stakeholder's mind. Let this book provide the information, data, and justifications you need to continue to bring visibility to and elevate evaluation.

Introduction

PATTI P. PHILLIPS

Much has been and continues to be written and spoken about measuring and evaluating training. And it should be so. Through good assessment, measurement, and evaluation, talent development professionals can intentionally create, deliver, and demonstrate value for investments in training. This is also how talent development professionals can improve their programs and processes, including their evaluation approach, and build relationships with those who have offered little support in the past. Good assessment, measurement, and evaluation can lead to increased budgets, expansion of programs, and, yes, the elimination of programs that need to go.

The Benefits of Measurement and Evaluation

When the training function uses evaluation to its fullest potential, the benefits grow exponentially. Some of the advantages of measuring and evaluating training include:

- Giving senior executives the information they need
- Justifying budgets
- Improving program design
- Identifying and improving dysfunctional processes
- Enhancing the transfer of learning
- Eliminating unnecessary or ineffective projects or programs
- Expanding or implementing successful programs
- Satisfying client needs
- Enhancing the respect and credibility of the training staff
- Increasing support from managers
- Strengthening relationships with key executives and administrators
- Setting priorities for training
- Reinventing training
- Altering management's perceptions of training
- Achieving a monetary payoff for investing in training

These key benefits, inherent with almost any type of impact evaluation process, make measurement and evaluation an attractive challenge for the training function.

INTRODUCTION

Unfortunately, this abundance of information about measurement and evaluation also means that it's easy to overlook the fundamentals amid the allure of shiny distractions, misinformation, and the urge to increase followership by writing and saying what will sell.

The fundamentals are what ensure the sustainable growth and long-term success of any endeavor. Those who play sports or a musical instrument understand the critical importance of mastering the fundamentals before advancing to more complex maneuvers. The same is true for measurement and evaluation. Sound practice is the foundation for more advanced techniques. So, what are the components of a sound practice?

The Measurement and Evaluation Puzzle

A sound measurement and evaluation strategy has five parts: an evaluation framework, process model, standards or guiding principles, case application and practice, and an implementation strategy (Figure I-1).

Figure I-1. Evaluation Puzzle

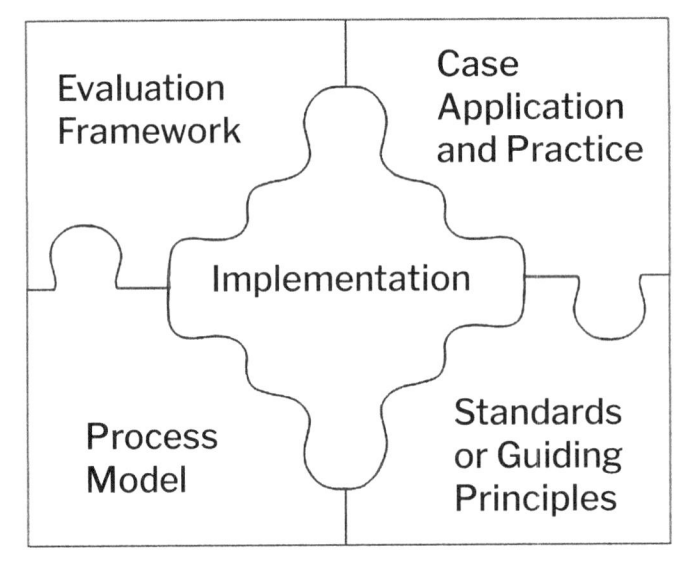

Evaluation Framework

An evaluation framework is not itself a process or a methodology, but merely a data (or measurement) categorization scheme. Most talent development professionals categorize evaluation results using the Phillips's five levels of evaluation (Table I-1).

Table I-1. Evaluation Framework

	Levels of Evaluation	Measurement Focus	Typical Measures
0	Input and Indicators	The input into the project in terms of scope, volume, efficiencies, and costs	Participants, hours, costs, and timing
1	Reaction and Planned Action	Measures participant satisfaction and captures planned actions (if appropriate)	Relevance, importance, usefulness, appropriateness, intent to use, and motivation to act
2	Learning	Measures changes in knowledge, skills, and attitudes	Skills, knowledge, capacity, competencies, confidence, and contacts
3	Application and Implementation	Measures changes in behavior or actions	Extent of use, task completion, frequency of use, actions completed, success with use, barriers to use, and enablers to use
4	Business Impact	Measures changes in business impact variables	Productivity, revenue, quality, time, efficiency, customer satisfaction, and employee engagement
5	Return on Investment	Compares project benefits to the costs	Benefit-cost ratio (BCR), ROI, and payback period

Source: ROI Institute. Used with permission.

Level 0, while not a category of results, is the beginning point. These measures indicate the activity or input into a training investment. Results begin with Level 1, Reaction and Planned Action, which uses measures to determine participant satisfaction with a program's content, the content delivery, and their overall experience. Specific measures that are predictive of application include content relevance and importance, the amount of new information, participant commitment to apply what they learn, and participant willingness to recommend the training to others in similar roles. Level 2, Learning, measures focus on what participants learned during the program, which may include the acquisition of new knowledge, skills, information, and insights, or increased confidence based on newly acquired knowledge. This level of data may also include new connections, or the people participants meet.

Level 3, Application and Implementation, measures indicate the extent to which participants apply what they now know—through behavior change, process change, action steps, frequency of use, or other actions—and if that knowledge is being applied routinely. They also indicate the extent to which barriers and enablers are inhibiting or supporting the transfer of learning to actual application. This requires measuring the support that the organization as a system is giving to participants when they use newly acquired knowledge, skills, insights, and information. At Level 4, Business Impact, the measurement focuses on the changes in the impact measures as a direct result of the program. Typical Level 4 measures represent output, quality, costs, time, employee satisfaction, and customer satisfaction, and may also include work habits and innovation. Impact measures represent the consequence of people applying the knowledge, skills, information, and insights they've gained through training and performance improvement programs.

> **Practitioner's Tip**
>
> Measures within each level may be further categorized to ensure alignment with critical issues. For example, The Conference Board's ROI in Inclusion Toolkit offers three categories of impact data: representation measures, preventative measures, and value-add measures (Table I-2).

Table I-2. Sample Impact Measures Diversity, Equity, and Inclusion Investments Influence

Representation Measures	Preventive Measures	Value-Add Measures
• Age or generation • Disability • Gender • Level of education • National origin • Race or ethnicity • Religious affiliations • Tenure within organization • Veteran status • LGBTQ+	• Absenteeism • Complaints • Conflicts • Employee engagement • Employee mobility • Employee turnover • Inclusion • Job satisfaction • Lawsuits • Transfers	• Brand • Cost • Customer satisfaction • Efficiencies • Innovation • Productivity • Quality • Sales • Societal impact • Time

Source: Sabattini and Phillips (2021)

Level 5, Return on Investment (ROI), measurement compares the program's monetary benefits with the program costs. Often considered the ultimate measure of success, this metric demonstrates the magnitude of the benefits resulting from the program as compared with the program costs. The ROI formula is:

$$\text{ROI} = \frac{\text{Program benefits} - \text{Program costs}}{\text{Program costs}} \times 100$$

Regardless of your preferred evaluation approach, the results of your evaluation fall into one of these five categories; hence, the framework is universal.

Process Model

The second component of a sound practice is the process model, which shows the steps required to ensure reliable results and consistent implementation. These models are also helpful for explaining how each step of an evaluation is conducted. The ROI Methodology—the most applied and documented process model for evaluating training—consists of four stages: Plan the evaluation, collect data, analyze data, and optimize results (Figure I-2).

Standards or Guiding Principles

Standards or guiding principles help with replication because standards ensure that there is consistency in the evaluation process and that a conservative approach is taken. Standards also help manage the subjectivity inherent in measures and methods, keep evaluation credible, help ensure that data is reliable, enable benchmarking against best practices and industry norms, and help ensure evaluation meets an agreed upon level of quality and rigor.

Table I-3 summarizes the 12 Guiding Principles that support implementation of the ROI Methodology. ROI Institute developed these standards over the past four decades in partnership with academics, practitioners, and C-suite executives, and they serve evaluation professionals well as they defend their results. Other measurement and evaluation standards such as those from the American Evaluation Association (AEA), International Organization of Standardization (ISO), Joint Commission on Standards for Evaluation Education (JCSEE), US Office of Personnel Management (OPM), and other standard setting organizations further support sound evaluation practice.

INTRODUCTION

Figure I-2. ROI Methodology Process Model

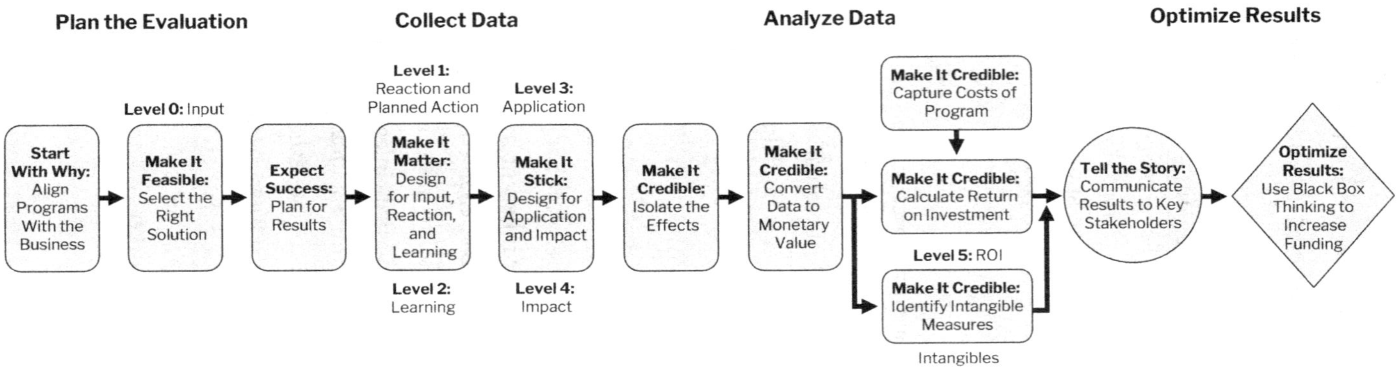

Plan the Evaluation

- **Start With Why:** Align Programs With the Business — Level 0: Input
- **Make It Feasible:** Select the Right Solution
- **Expect Success:** Plan for Results

Collect Data

- Level 1: Reaction and Planned Action
- **Make It Matter:** Design for Input, Reaction, and Learning
- Level 2: Learning
- **Make It Stick:** Design for Application and Impact
- Level 3: Application
- Level 4: Impact

Analyze Data

- **Make It Credible:** Isolate the Effects
- **Make It Credible:** Convert Data to Monetary Value
- **Make It Credible:** Capture Costs of Program
- **Make It Credible:** Calculate Return on Investment — Level 5: ROI
- **Make It Credible:** Identify Intangible Measures — Intangibles

Optimize Results

- **Tell the Story:** Communicate Results to Key Stakeholders
- **Optimize Results:** Use Black Box Thinking to Increase Funding

Source: ROI Institute. Used with permission.

Table I-3. ROI Methodology Guiding Principles and Their Meaning

Guiding Principle	Meaning
1. When conducting a higher level of evaluation, collect data at lower levels.	Tell the complete story of program success.
2. When planning a higher-level evaluation, the previous level of evaluation is not required to be comprehensive.	Conserve resources for higher-level evaluations.
3. When collecting and analyzing data, use only the most credible sources.	Use the most credible sources.
4. When analyzing data, select the most conservative alternative for calculations.	Choose the most conservative alternative.
5. Use at least one method to isolate the effect of the solution.	Give credit where credit is due.
6. If no improvement data is available for a population or from a specific source, assume that no improvement has occurred.	Make no assumptions for non-respondents.
7. Adjust estimates of improvement for the potential error in the estimates.	Adjust estimates for error.
8. Avoid the use of extreme data items and unsupported claims when calculating ROI.	Omit the extremes.
9. Use only the first year of annual benefits in the ROI analysis of short-term solutions.	Report only first-year benefits for short-term programs.
10. Fully load all costs of the solution, project, or program when analyzing ROI.	Account for all program costs.
11. Define intangible measures as measures that are purposely not converted to monetary values.	Report intangible benefits.
12. Communicate the results of the ROI Methodology to all key stakeholders.	Communicate and use your evaluation data.

Case Application and Practice

While a framework, process model, and standards are important, it is imperative to put these theoretical elements to work. The fourth component—case application and practice—represents using a framework for evaluation that includes the measures important to all stakeholders, as well as a process model supported by agreed upon standards. This step moves what is theoretical to what is actionable.

Since 1994, case studies published by ATD demonstrate the efficacy, feasibility, and credibility of sound measurement and evaluation, while also giving practitioners models to follow. However, nothing is more important than the measurement and evaluation that occurs in the workplace and the lessons learned from those case studies. This is where evaluation creates real value.

Implementation

The fifth and final component of a sound evaluation practice is an implementation strategy that helps grow and sustain the measurement practice. Even the best tool, technique, or model must become a routine part of the operations process before it can be successful. As with any change, those who resist the implementation will be the people affected by a comprehensive measurement and evaluation process, including the talent development team and other stakeholders. Part of that resistance will be based on realistic barriers. The other part, however, will be based on misunderstandings and perceived problems. In both cases, the organization must work to overcome resistance by carefully, methodically, and proactively implementing robust evaluation.

About This Handbook

This handbook aims to provide talent development professionals with a resource they can use to build their measurement and evaluation practice. Its contributors—experts from corporations, nonprofits, government entities, academic institutions, and a broad range of other organizations—address each step in the training evaluation process. You will have the opportunity to learn, reflect upon, and practice using key concepts as you:
- Plan an evaluation project, beginning by identifying stakeholder needs.
- Identify appropriate data collection methods, given the data type, resources, constraints, and conveniences.
- Analyze data using quantitative and qualitative methods.
- Communicate results to various audiences to address their data needs.
- Use data to improve programs and processes and ensure the correct data is available at the right time.
- Develop an evaluation strategy that aligns learning programs with the organization's needs and delivers results that matter.

This handbook covers a variety of aspects of training measurement and evaluation, providing readers with a broad look at different elements. And, while the ROI Methodology framework and model serve as the basis for the outline, this book has a broader focus—strategies to make measurement and evaluation work for any type of organization, regardless of its adopted approach. Let's review what's covered in each part.

Part 1. Evaluation Planning

Planning evaluation upfront yields better programming and superior results. Clarifying the organization's needs—beginning with the business needs—ensures the program aligns with those needs and that there is a clear road map for design and delivery. This road map shows how to incorporate measurement into the program rather than leaving it on the side of the road in hopes someone will find it.

Successful measurement and evaluation processes begin by identifying stakeholder needs. Answers to the following questions clarify expectations about business impact, job performance, and knowledge acquisition:

- What is the opportunity for the organization?
- Is the opportunity worth pursuing?
- What specific business measures need to improve to be successful with this opportunity?
- What is or is not happening on the job (or in a system) that, if changed, would contribute to improving business measures?
- What do people need to know to create and sustain that change?
- What specific measures should we track?

Once you have defined the program's needs and expectations, it becomes easier to develop specific, measurable objectives and the likelihood of program success increases. With defined objectives in hand, the next step is to plan the evaluation project. By planning the evaluation upfront, you can determine which measures the program should target, what data to collect, and when to collect it. The more detailed the planning, the easier the execution.

In part 1, you will learn how to:

- Align training to the business.
- Analyze performance gaps.
- Develop powerful objectives.
- Plan an evaluation project.

Part 2. Data Collection

All too often, we make decisions based on data that we believe is accurate, but that we've derived from asking the wrong questions or using the wrong measures. Or, if they were the right questions, they were framed in a way that made an objective response impossible.

Data collection involves asking questions to get the answers you need to measure the progress and success of your programs. What those questions are, how you should ask them, whom you should ask, and when you should ask all depends on the objectives you set during the planning phase. There is no one best way to collect evaluation data; however, by considering program objectives, type of data, time requirements, resource constraints, cultural constraints, and convenience, you'll be able to find the best way for your evaluation project.

In part 2, you will learn how to:
- Design surveys to collect participant reaction.
- Design questionnaires and surveys for follow-up evaluation.
- Design and deliver tests.
- Conduct interviews.
- Conduct focus groups.
- Use action planning as a learning transfer strategy.

Part 3. Data Analysis

Without appropriate data analysis, stakeholders can't make good decisions from the information they are given through the evaluation process. But what is proper data analysis? Well, it depends. You'll need to take into account the population size, acceptable error, and type of measures, as well as the considerations that influenced your method of data collection.

Good analysis balances the experimental context with the organizational context. Program participants, supervisors, peers, and direct reports do not function in a lab—they work in dynamic organizations and make quick decisions, sometimes with minimal information. So, it's necessary to provide the best data possible, given the constraints. To succeed, you must know how to analyze data and balance accuracy with costs to ensure results reflect the proper context.

In part 3, you will learn how to:
- Use basic statistical techniques.
- Analyze qualitative data.

INTRODUCTION

- Isolate the effects of the program.
- Convert measures to monetary value.
- Capture program costs.
- Calculate the ROI.
- Measure intangible benefits
- Forecast ROI.

Part 4. Results Optimization

The benefits of measuring and evaluating training depend on whether people use the insights from the process. However, those communicating evaluation results often focus too heavily on the numbers or metrics (rather than the story behind the numbers) or share only what a handful of sources say without balancing the narrative with numbers.

Measurement and evaluation results are best shared through a good story that is compelling, logical, and credible. It must include quantitative, qualitative, financial, and nonfinancial data and follow a standard that makes it easy for audiences to consume. Most importantly, a good story leads to action that delivers an impact.

Good evaluation also provides insights that inform decisions for improving programs and the system that supports them. Black box thinking harnesses our curiosity and desire to learn from the mistakes or failures of a program. It requires an environment that enables program owners, managers, and participants to learn from errors and embrace potentially negative ROI results.

In part 4, you will learn how to:
- Tell the story of the results.
- Visualize and display data.
- Implement International Organization of Standardization (ISO) standards for L&D metrics.
- Use black box thinking.
- Use financial analysis to compare unplanned on-the-job training (OJT) to structured OJT.

Part 5. Make Measurement and Evaluation Work

To effectively use evaluation data, systems must be in place to support its implementation and sustainability. This begins in part by getting stakeholder buy-in and focusing on standards to ensure consistency, reliability, and credibility. In addition, to make measurement and evaluation work for the long-term, it is important to at least understand, if not embrace, technology. The use of generative artificial intelligence (AI) as an enabler is growing at a rapid speed, so it is important that this handbook represents that technological advancement. Last, making measurement and evaluation work requires a clear strategy and robust capability.

In part 5, you will learn how to:
- Implement and sustain the measurement and evaluation practice.
- Get stakeholder buy-in for measurement and evaluation.
- Follow evaluation standards.
- Leverage AI.
- Create a measurement and evaluation strategy.

What's New and Different in the Second Edition

ATD published the first edition of the *Handbook of Measuring and Evaluating Training* in 2010. In addition to the contributions of experts, practitioners, and academics, the book included a part referred to as Voices, which included transcripts of interviews with training evaluation trailblazers. These true thought leaders in the field are Robert O. Brinkerhoff, Mary L. Broad, Jac Fitz-enz, Roger Kaufman, Donald L. Kirkpatrick, Jack J. Phillips, Dana Gaines Robinson, and William J. Rothwell. We've opted not to revise this section for the new edition, instead replacing it with a new part 5 focused on strategies for seamless integration and techniques, as well as the technologies that are advancing the practice of measuring and evaluating training.

Contributors

This handbook's contributors all are experts in their content areas. In this book, we define expertise based on what contributors are doing with training evaluation and how they contribute to the evaluation practice of others.

You will learn from external consultants who touch many organizations, internal consultants who focus on training evaluation within a specific organization, individuals with experience as both internal and external consultants, and professors who hone and share their expertise through research. Some of the contributors are ATD Education certificate program facilitators and conference presenters, and they're all practitioners of the work they describe in their chapter. Additionally, our contributors work in organizations worldwide, ensuring we cover issues relevant to all types of practitioners.

Target Audience

Four groups serve as the target audience for this book. First, this handbook is a reference that all talent development professionals need for their resource library. This book will serve managers responsible for a training, learning, or talent development team as they support evaluation within their function. Professors who teach training measurement and evaluation will find this book to be an excellent resource for addressing all elements of the evaluation process. The exercises and references will help them develop coursework, challenge their students' thinking, and assign application projects. Finally, training evaluation students can use this book to learn more about evaluation and how it drives excellence in program implementation.

How to Get the Most From This Book

This handbook provides a learning experience as well as information. Each chapter begins with key learning objectives. Throughout each chapter, you'll find references to real-life application, practitioner tips from individuals applying the concepts, additional resources, and knowledge checks to assess your understanding of the chapter content. Some knowledge checks have specific correct answers that can be found in appendix B; others offer an opportunity for you to reflect and discuss with your colleagues. To get the most out of the book, you should:

- Review the table of contents to see what areas are of most interest.
- Read the chapter objectives and work through the knowledge checks after reading the chapter.
- Follow up on prescribed actions steps, references, and resources.
- Connect with the contributors through LinkedIn and other social outlets.

Outside the book, you might:

- Access additional resources through ATD or your local chapter.
- Engage in conversation through other networks such Cognota's LearnOps Community, the American Evaluation Association, Center for Talent Measurement Reporting, and the ROI Network.
- Participate in ATD's Evaluating Learning Impact Certificate program and Measuring Return on Investment Certificate program.

- Join ROI Institute's ROI Certification Program.
- Experience other conferences, workshops, and academic courses.

I hope you find this second edition of *ATD's Handbook for Measuring and Evaluating Training* a useful resource full of relevant and timely content. I'd love to know if you have any suggestions for additional information, workshops in content areas, or supporting material. You can reach me at patti@roiinstitute.net, and I will work with ATD to help ensure talent development and learning professionals get the information they need to build a successful training measurement and evaluation practice.

PART 1
Evaluation Planning

It is well-established that planning evaluation up front yields superior results. Early planning for evaluation ensures that:
- Programs align with the needs of the business.
- Instructional designers focus design on the outcomes that matter most.
- Data collection is seamless throughout the program.
- Stakeholders agree on the approach, including analysis.
- Reporting design and strategy are ready regardless of results.
- Time is managed appropriately.

Yet, practitioners worldwide still wait to think about evaluation, particularly the higher levels of evaluation, until the program is over—or worse, until someone asks. Waiting for the request results in unnecessary costs, resources, time, and pressure. And it places program results at risk.

Successful measurement and evaluation processes begin during the initial stakeholder conversation—when their needs are being established. Answers to the following questions clarify expectations about business impact, job performance, knowledge acquisition, and approach to delivering content:
- What is the opportunity for the organization?
- Is the opportunity worth pursuing?
- What are the specific business measures that need to improve for this opportunity to be successful?
- What is happening or not happening on the job (or with a system) that, if it changed, would contribute to the improvement in the business measures?

- What are the specific performance gaps?
- What do people need to know how to do so the business measures will improve?
- How best can the knowledge, skill, or information be delivered so participants perceive it as relevant to their jobs?

With needs well-defined, the specific, measurable objectives representing these needs are developed to position the program for success. Program objectives are the architectural blueprint for program design. Well-written objectives serve as the basis for measures taken during the evaluation, establish targets for success, establish the timing of data collection, and, in many cases, inform how best to incorporate data collection and analyze the data. From there, it is important to develop a data collection plan and an analysis plan so all parties are in sync with the reason for the program, the purpose of evaluation, and how success is defined and will be reported. The more detailed the planning, the easier the evaluation execution.

In this part, you will learn how to:
- Align training to the needs of the business.
- Analyze performance gaps.
- Develop powerful objectives.
- Plan an evaluation project.

CHAPTER 1

Aligning Training to the Needs of the Business

FAITH KREBS

IN THIS CHAPTER

This chapter explores the importance of aligning training programs to the needs of the business. After reading it, you will be able to:

- Describe why it's critical to align training solutions to business needs and the potential payoff for addressing those needs.
- Recall the important reasons for showing the value that training solutions produce.
- Discover how to use the Business Alignment Model with your clients.

Why Align Training Solutions to the Business?

The quest to show training programs' effectiveness is not a new concept. According to Will Thalheimer's chronological history of methods for measuring and evaluating training programs, the first efforts began in 1948 (Thalheimer 2018). Fast forward to today and you'll find that many organizations still struggle to align, measure, and evaluate their talent solutions. LinkedIn's *2023 Workplace Learning* report found that the number 1 priority of learning professionals is to "map learning to business goals." Yet linking business results to training doesn't even rank in the top five ways talent development departments measure results (Table 1-1).

CHAPTER 1

Table 1-1. Top Ways L&D Measures Success

	● Vanity Metric	Business Metrics
1. Employee satisfaction, measured via survey		
2. Employee satisfaction, informal or qualitative feedback		
3. Number of employees taking courses or trainings		
4. Employee performance on post-learning quizzes or assessments		
5. Number of courses or trainings each employee has completed		
6. Improved performance reviews		
7. Team or org business metrics		
8. Improved employee productivity		
9. Improved employee retention		
10. Number of hours spent learning		
11. Progress toward closing workforce skill gaps		
12. Number of new skills learned per learner		

Source: LinkedIn (2023)

In 2009, the Association for Talent Development (ATD) and ROI Institute studied how CEOs perceive the learning investment and found a gap between what CEOs wanted to know and what they were currently receiving (Phillips and Phillips 2009). Of the 96 Fortune 500 CEOs participating in the study, 96 percent wanted to see the impact data, yet only 8 percent received it. And, while 74 percent of CEOs wanted to see ROI data, only 4 percent received that information. Of all the data items investigated, impact and ROI ranked first and second out of eight, respectively, in terms of importance; vanity metrics such as employee reaction to and satisfaction with training programs, on the other hand, ranked eighth out of eight (Table 1-2).

Since then, other studies have demonstrated similar findings. A 2015 study by *Chief Learning Officer*'s Business Intelligence Board reported that 58 percent of senior leaders were dissatisfied with the training measurement that occurs in their organization. Approximately 71 percent of CLOs responding to the survey were either using ROI when reporting to company executives to demonstrate the impact of training or planned to use it in the future (HCM Advisory Group 2015). A 2019 EY study reported that 53 percent of chief executives and 89 percent of CLOs believed the impact of learning should be measured (Vona, Woolf, and Sugrue 2019). Watershed's 2022 report *Adopting Learning Analytics, Closing the C suite/L&D Language Gap* found that learning leaders believe the C-suite wants to see a relationship between learning performance and business measures (72.4 percent; Table 1-3).

Table 1-2. What CEOs Want

ROI Institute and ATD research show that the data CEOs receive do not reflect what they want out of their talent investment. (n=96)

Measures	Currently Measure	Should Measure	Importance
Inputs and Indicators	94%	86%	6
Efficiency	78%	82%	7
Reaction	53%	22%	8
Learning	32%	28%	5
Application	11%	61%	4
Impact	8%	96%	1
ROI	4%	74%	2
Awards	40%	44%	3

Source: Phillips and Phillips (2009)

Table 1-3. Learning Leaders' Perception of What the C-Suite Wants

	Current	Wished For	Difference
Correlate learning performance with skills data	26.4%	63.0%	+36.6%
Learning program analytics—use advanced analysis to optimize future learning pathways	33.2%	70.3%	+37.1%
Correlate learning performance with business KPIs to measure effectiveness	37.2%	72.4%	+35.2%
Performance and learning—individual and group KPIs and competencies	42.4%	71.5%	+29.1%
Compliance reporting	56.0%	37.0%	-19.0%

Source: Watershed (2022)

Now that we've established (or reaffirmed) that it's important to align training results to the business, the question we must ask ourselves is, why does the misalignment still exist and how can we correct it? A place to begin answering this question is understanding why senior leaders want this data.

Executives ask for impact and ROI numbers so they can make data-driven decisions about investments within their organizations, weighing the benefits, costs, and risks associated with them. They must understand how the allocated funds and resources drive improvements toward their strategic goals. The C-suite views functions that can link and measure their programs to business results as credible, accountable, and valuable. And these functions are more likely to secure the funds and resources requested during the budget cycle. Watershed's 2022 study highlighted the language gap between talent development and executives due to an inconsistency between the qualitative data that L&D presents to executives, and the quantitative data they need to justify their budget allocations and make sound financial investments.

Another Watershed report, *Measuring the Business Impact of Learning 2022,* found that, in the six years prior to the report's release, there had been minimal progress demonstrating the impact and ROI of training. This was due to several reasons, including:

- Capability of the team.
- Budget for measurement.
- Competing priorities.
- It takes too much time.
- Negative results will be devastating.
- No one is asking for it.

These perceived barriers, most of which are based on misinformation, stifle organizations from moving forward. Organizations can align training to the business—even with small budgets and limited capability—by:

- Being proactive rather than waiting for a request to show the impact of training
- Building assessment, measurement, and evaluation into program design
- Conducting impact and ROI studies on select programs
- Partnering with others in the organization who have the capability to measure impact
- Recognizing that negative results can offer positive benefits
- Developing a growth mindset and embracing the challenge and opportunity evaluation brings
- Building capability through the many resources available to the training industry

If delivering meaningful value for investments in training is important, we must view potential barriers as surmountable and plan accordingly.

> **Practitioner's Tip**
>
> Many talent development professionals shy away from measurement and evaluation because they fear the process will reveal zero impact on business outcomes or a negative ROI. But it's important to remember that a negative ROI can have positive benefits.
>
> Kaycee Buckley, a director of global commercial talent, has more than 25 years of experience in the L&D industry. She works with organizational leaders to define talent development strategies, develop and deploy learning events, and measure the business impact for these initiatives. Here's an excerpt from an email she wrote to Patti Phillips, CEO of ROI Institute, the day after presenting a negative ROI in a coaching solution:
>
> "Just wanted to let you know that I presented the coaching ROI results to my DVP and the area commercial directors last Thursday. It was amazing! They were surprised and not surprised by the results. That is, they were not surprised that the ROI was negative because they are all aware that the sales managers are not coaching and agreed with the barriers I had outlined in the study. They were surprised at what a negative impact not applying coaching was having on the business, which sparked a very productive conversation as to what to do to fix it. Wow... such positive outcomes from my stakeholders... and with a negative ROI!"

Benefits of Aligning Training to the Business

The benefits of overcoming barriers to alignment far outweigh the costs. Let's review a few of the benefits to aligning training with the business.

Executive Commitment

The sustained success of the learning function depends on executive commitment, support, and involvement (Phillips and Phillips 2009). Commitment is increased when executives see routine data showing that the training process is working effectively and delivering value. Commitment shows up in resource allocation; personal time devoted to the function; and in the attitudes, behaviors, and support for the function. Without commitment, the training function will not flourish as a value-added part of the organization. To gain commitment, executives must recognize training as a necessity to fuel growth and enable the organization to remain competitive. This requires a connection between the investments in training and improvement in business measures that indicate the organization is growing.

CHAPTER 1

Manager Support

Let's turn our focus to the learner's manager. Mary L. Broad and John W. Newstrom's seminal work on learning transfer, as well as other research, has shown that 50 to 90 percent of what an employee is expected to learn during a program is not used on the job (Broad and Newstrom 1992). One of the key roles in this learning transfer process is the learner's manager. However, the learner's manager may not support learning if they don't see a connection to business results or are concerned about their employees taking time off or being away from their jobs to attend training. Therefore, it's imperative to provide every learner's manager with data that links training back to their business goals and outcomes. They must see this alignment to influence their engagement and support their employees throughout the learning process.

Practitioner's Tip

The learner's manager plays an instrumental role in the learning transfer process. They use business and organizational data to assess each team member's performance to determine who needs development and what kind. Managers who have a clear understanding of the performance outcomes from the learning solutions can leverage this information with their employees to enhance the transfer process.

The manager's responsibilities before and after their employee participates in training are critical. They can actively engage in meeting with their employee before the training to establish specific performance expectations, collect baseline performance data, take part in the employee's needs assessment, provide guidance on planning development activities, brief employees on the importance of on-the-job application, and offer ongoing feedback. After the training program, once the employee is back on the job applying their new skills, managers can use individual performance data to measure and track improvements, offer coaching to encourage behavioral changes, meet regularly with their employee to reinforce application, remove barriers impeding performance change, and provide recognition when positive performance change occurs. Managers who don't know how learning is linked to the performance outcomes of their business may not be equipped to help employees during the transfer process to optimize their investments in learning.

Incorporating learning transfer strategies that engage the learner's manager in ensuring alignment exists will increase the likelihood of a successful program and increase the chances participants apply what they learn. And, in doing so, will deliver the business impact and ROI that senior leaders want.

Improved Business Partnership

Focusing on the alignment of training to the business will help business unit leaders perceive the training function and its team members as partners contributing to their unit's and the broader organization's strategic objectives and key results. Stakeholders seek innovative, agile, and efficient talent solutions that close skills gaps, improve performance, and lead to outcomes that give the organization a competitive advantage. Managers and team leaders want partners to help them solve problems and leverage opportunities. To become a valued business partner, you need to speak the language of the business, asking pertinent questions and collaborating with business unit leaders to identify the most feasible solution for problems and opportunities.

Better Programs—Better Results

When aligned with the business, training programs will be designed to deliver business results—and they will. Program objectives are the architectural blueprint for program design, representing the intended outcomes of a program. Objectives are a central element of the alignment process.

When business alignment is the focus, the call for training begins with the business need and potential payoff for addressing that need. From there, the assessment looks at the existing performance gaps that, if closed, will address the business need. Solutions begin to surface and learning needs are established. From there, objectives are defined. By designing programs around objectives that clearly define the why for a program, there is a much greater likelihood results will occur.

Less Costly and Time-Consuming Evaluation

Business alignment leads not only to better programs and better results, but also less costly evaluation. When evaluation is an afterthought, it becomes costly, time consuming, and stressful, and the results are often unreliable and less than desirable. And this happens all too often. When the programs are aligned with the business, the measures that matter are defined. Program objectives reflect those measures. By incorporating ways to collect data during and after the program into the program's design, the evaluation becomes more straightforward.

CHAPTER 1

Start by Changing the Conversation With Your Client

Clients often approach TD professionals with a request to develop a specific kind of training. Has this happened to you? What was your reaction? If you typically provide the requested program, you might respond by asking questions like:

1. How many managers will attend this training?
2. How long can this training be?
3. How do you want it to be delivered? Virtually or in person?

While necessary for defining project scope, these questions are not the most important ones to ask when your client comes to you with a request. Instead, you should begin your dialogue by asking open-ended probing questions to understand your client's needs. Let's now review a proven approach to help you start the conversation!

The Business Alignment Process: V Model

The classic framework by which talent development professionals categorize their results includes five levels: reaction, learning, application, impact, and ROI. This five-level framework provides a process for aligning conversations called the Alignment Process: V Model (Figure 1-1).

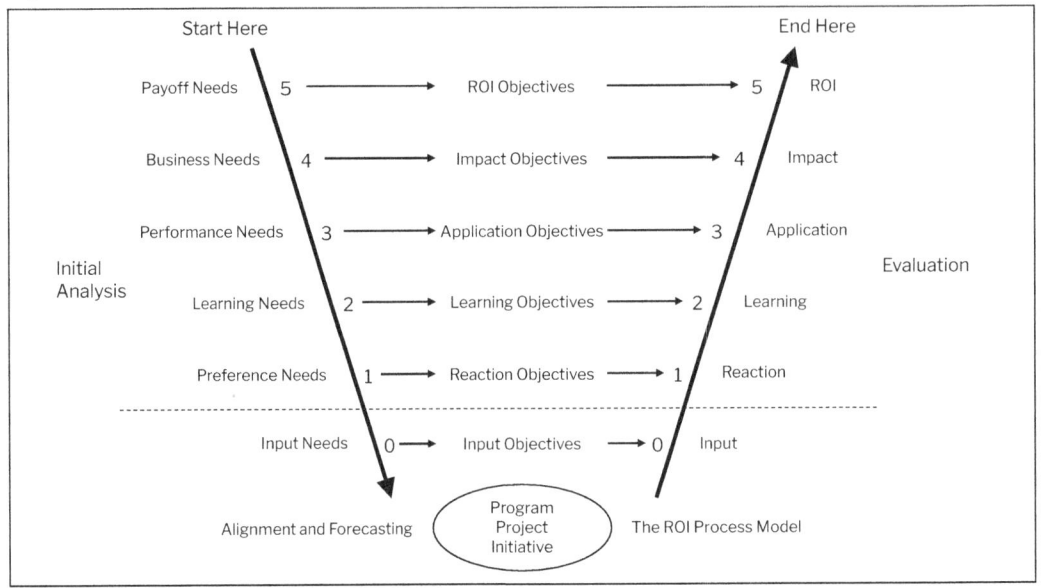

Figure 1-1. The Alignment Process: V Model

Payoff Needs

The first step in aligning training to the business is determining the payoff opportunity for the organization, or the payoff needs. This is where you identify the problems or opportunities that, if addressed, will lead to revenue generation, cost savings, or cost avoidance, along with contribution to the business in other ways. Here the overarching question is the problem or opportunity the client wants to address. You might begin by asking an open-ended question, such as "What area of the business is underperforming?" The client might respond with concerns about the need to increase sales, improve profits, or reduce costs by improving employee productivity. They might add that reducing employee turnover and the associated cost is imperative. Maybe they want to enhance brand image or improve customer satisfaction.

Now that the client has identified the problem or opportunity, ask them to describe the current state as it compares with the ideal future state, as well as the value of closing this gap. Identifying this performance gap provides tangible information that helps:

- **Describe the magnitude of the problem or opportunity.** How encompassing is it within the organization?
- **Assess the value.** How much does the gap in performance represent in monetary terms, such as revenue, profits, or costs? Is the problem worth pursuing?
- **Determine the level of urgency.** How quickly should the problem be resolved?

By starting with the payoff needs, you change the conversation from one that focuses on the activity of training to one that focuses on problem resolution. You are asking the client to think strategically and share how this problem or opportunity affects their business results.

Business Needs

Next, define the *business needs*. You can ask the client, "What business measures, if improved, would indicate the problem or opportunity is being addressed?" These key performance indicators (KPIs) represent quantitative (hard) and or qualitative (soft) data. Hard data measures represent output, quality, cost, and time. Soft data measures might include job satisfaction, customer satisfaction, and innovation.

During this step, it is meaningful to link the measures back to their payoff needs. For example, if the client's payoff need is that the current year's sales are trending lower than the previous year, you could ask them to provide the specific business measures that define their sales goals. You might then review quantitative data to support their sales goals, such as the number of products sold each month, the amount of time it takes for a sales employee to close a sale, average sales dollars generated for each sale, and the productivity of each sales employee. Another example of a payoff need is addressing an increase in customer complaints. The business measures could be the specific type of complaint, such as complaints from new customers about poor service or from existing customers about product quality. Or, if your organization is facing high rates of turnover, the business need would define the type of turnover, such as turnover of customer service representatives in the bank branches.

In general, most clients will have access to this type of data, although they may need to gather it from other sources that support their business such as marketing, finance, data insights, operations, and HR functions. Once the data is collected, agree on the specific business measures (quantitative or qualitative) to focus on improving. You'll use these measures to track progress toward the goal established during the payoff needs, which will serve as your basis for program design and evaluation.

By adding business needs to the conversation, you define the problem or opportunity in measurable terms. This step ensures you're focused on the client's needs, which will increase your credibility and, in time, contribute to your position as a trusted business partner.

Performance Needs

Once you define the business needs, you can determine the performance needs. This process answers questions such as:

- What specific performance change must occur to improve the business measures?
- What behaviors, processes, or tasks do you want employees to start doing?
- What behaviors, processes, or tasks do you want them to stop doing?
- What barriers could be influencing your employees' performance?
- What solutions have you tried to improve performance?
- What results did the previous solutions produce?

It can be easy to assume that business measures are not performing as they should due to a lack of training. Asking the client questions about performance needs will help provide a better preliminary diagnosis to aid you in your analysis. Other techniques to determine performance gaps include statistical process control, brainstorming, problem analysis, cause-and-effect diagrams, force-field analysis, mind mapping, affinity diagrams, simulations, diagnostic instruments, focus groups, probing interviews, job satisfaction surveys, engagement surveys, exit interviews, exit surveys, and nominal group techniques.

Chapter 2 describes the process for determining performance gaps in more detail. Once you have determined those gaps, and considered possible solutions, it is time to assess what is required to ensure change in performance occurs. This is the next step of the V-model: defining the learning needs.

Learning Needs

Learning needs may consist of offering employees the opportunity to receive new information, master new knowledge, build new skills, and develop new attitudes to perform their jobs. It's imperative to continue asking your client open-ended questions so you can better understand what different audiences need to learn. "What information, knowledge, skills, and attitudes are required to address the performance change?" is a good opening question to ask.

Let's walk through an example. A new technology application is being implemented to automate several processes to improve productivity and reduce errors. Here are some potential open-ended questions you could ask the client:
- What audiences will be affected by this new technology change?
- What specific positions or roles will need to learn how to use this new technology?
- What new knowledge is needed to operate this technology?
- What new skills are needed to successfully use this technology?
- What type of information or data will this new technology provide?
- What specific behaviors need to change because of the newly acquired information, knowledge, and skills?

These types of open-ended questions will help you determine the necessary scope required by the solution for the learning need.

Preference Needs

With payoff, business, performance, and learning needs in hand, it is time to focus on the best ways to deliver the content employees need to acquire new information, knowledge, and skills. During this step, consider the audiences who will be changing their performance, including how they prefer to learn. Questions you could ask include:
- What will employees need to learn that they don't already know?
- How much practice time do you think is needed to learn how to use the new technology application during the training course?

CHAPTER 1

- What level of proficiency is needed for each audience to successfully apply the new knowledge on the job?
- What blend of learning approaches will be most effective for each audience?
- How do you envision testing each audience to ensure they know how to use the new technology application?

Input Needs

The final step is gathering information from the client to help you design a solution. These are the input needs. Types of open-ended questions you could ask include:

- What are the guardrails (such as time, costs, resource allocation, and culture) that you need to consider when designing, developing, and implementing the learning solution?
- What are the actual number of users in each audience group that need this content?
- When do you need to start this program? When does it need to be completed?
- What other considerations could influence the solution design, development, or implementation?

Case Study: Alignment At Work

SECOR Bank, a midsize regional bank, was suffering from changes in the banking industry. Mergers and acquisitions were taking place, reducing the number of competitors. SECOR's customers were leaving, with satisfaction scores at an all-time low. Additionally, employee turnover was 57 percent across the enterprise. Digging deeper into the relationship between customer departure and employee turnover, leaders discovered the most significant turnover was at the branch level—71 percent or 336 employees were leaving per year. Cost per departure was $16,650 or $5,594,400 per year. SECOR had a problem worth solving.

Rather than rely solely on exit survey data to understand the performance gap, they conducted a series of focus groups and used a process called *nominal group technique*. Through this process, they heard from employees in the same positions as those departing. In the focus group setting, employees were asked a simple question: "Why are your colleagues leaving?"

Then, they ranked the given reasons and weighted them using a 10-point system. The top five findings were lack of opportunity to advance, lack of opportunity to learn, inadequate pay, little autonomy, and lack of recognition. Leadership decided that implementing a skills-based pay program could address all five reasons.

To ensure the process worked, the team knew that branch employees involved in the program as well as their managers and other employees would have to know why the initiative was taking place, as well as their role in the process. Participating employees would acquire certain knowledge and skills so they could advance, and managers needed to learn how to coach their employees to performance. The program would launch within each of the branches and be designed so those not participating were not penalized.

In addition to assessing the needs, leaders wanted to understand the potential payoff for investing in this program. They estimated the initial investment would be about $800,000. Based on what they knew, branch managers and employees estimated the program would prevent 60 turnovers in the first year. This would reduce costs of $999,000 and provide a forecasted ROI of 25 percent.

Table 1-4 summarizes the results of SECOR's alignment process.

Table 1-4. SECOR's Alignment Process

Payoff Need	• Mergers and acquisitions taking out the competition. • Financial institution facing operational issues. • Customer service scores at an all-time low. • Overall turnover 57% compared with 26% for the industry. • Cost of turnover ranges from 110% to 125% of salary.
Business Need	• Voluntary turnover in branches is the biggest problem. • Turnover is 71% or 336 employees voluntarily leaving each year. • This contributes to the customer service problem. • Cost of turnover per job is $16,650 per person.

Performance Need	• Exit interviews offered limited perspective.
	• Nominal group technique used to discover cause of turnover.
	• Results indicated the top 5 reasons for departure were:
	  1. Lack of opportunity for advancement
	  2. Lack of opportunity to learn new skills and new product knowledge
	  3. Inadequate pay level
	  4. Not enough responsibility and autonomy
	  5. Lack of recognition and appreciation

Table 1-4. (continued)

	Solution: Skills-Based Pay Program
Learning Needs	• Why the initiative is underway • Role of branch employees • How the process works • Target staff acquire certain knowledge and skills • Managers learn how to coach to performance
Preference Needs	• Launch within each of the branches • Ensure those who do not participate are not penalized
Input Needs	• Estimate the program will prevent 60 turnovers in the first year, leading to a cost avoidance of $999,000 • Initial investment of $800,000 • Target ROI for year one is 25%

How to Conduct an Alignment Conversation

It's important to prepare questions for each step of the alignment process before engaging with a client. Having an agenda and a plan to facilitate the conversation will help you gather relevant information and data. Do your homework—find out all you can about your client, including their position and how their function contributes to the organization's results.

You might role play with someone acting as the client. This allows you to try out the flow, pilot your questions, and practice your active listening skills. If you haven't done this type of intake meeting before, ask to observe a seasoned consultant first.

The alignment conversation can take place over several meetings, either in person or virtually. It can be beneficial if two people can attend the client sessions. That way one person can facilitate the meeting and ask the client the questions, while the other person takes notes.

Practitioner's Tip

It was vital to make metrics approachable when developing our annual BOLD Leadership Institute. When a senior leader said, "We need to make it real back at work," in the early design phases, this bridged learning to performance and created a compelling sense of shared ownership and accountability. "Make it real" became a common language and brand that resonated across levels. We engaged "make it real" champions and motivators to share the business case for learning and stories to support the transfer of learning beyond BOLD. This catchphrase made metrics an easier conversation between leaders, trainers, and learners.

—Lynne Daley, Talent Development Manager, Virginia Department for Aging and Rehabilitative Services

Summary

By conducting a productive alignment conversation with your client, you can begin to build stronger relationships and change how you engage with them to create meaningful performance solutions that improve their business results. To start the journey to align training to the needs of your organization, complete these two actions:
1. **Assess your function's current state.** Use the "Training and Development Programs Assessment: A Survey for Managers" tool in appendix A to establish your baseline score. This will help you identify, prioritize, and establish a plan to improve your organization's overall measurement and evaluation system.
2. **Identify one client to conduct an alignment conversation using the Business Alignment: V Model.** Capture the information gathered as the first step in developing your program's evaluation plan.

In the upcoming chapters, you will explore how alignment leads to measurable objectives and how those objectives guide the development of the evaluation plan. The next chapter dives deeper into performance gaps, which ties into the first step of the Business Alignment Process: V Model—payoff needs.

Knowledge Check

Here are a few questions to test your comprehension of the content in this chapter. After completing the knowledge check, review your answers in appendix B:

1. According to *Adopting Learning Analytics, Closing the C-Suite/L&D Language Gap*, what type of information do CEOs most want to receive?
    A. Learner's satisfaction with the program
    B. Correlate learning performance with skill data
    C. Correlate learning's performance with business KPIs to measure effectiveness
    D. Compliance reporting
    E. Net promoter score
2. Based on research, what percent of training doesn't stick once a learner goes back to apply what they learned on the job?
    A. 10–20 percent
    B. 20–30 percent
    C. 30–40 percent

CHAPTER 1

   D. 50–90 percent
   E. 100 percent
3. Choose the three factors that are key for the sustainable success of the learning function.
   A. Executive commitment
   B. Executive involvement
   C. Executive knowledge
   D. Executive preference
   E. Executive support
4. In which step in the Business Alignment Process: V Model do you ask the client questions regarding the problem or opportunity they need help improving?
   A. Business needs
   B. Learning needs
   C. Payoff needs
   D. Performance needs
   E. Preference needs
5. Where during the Business Alignment Process: V Model do you ask the client, "What business measures, if improved, would indicate the problem or opportunity is being addressed"?
   A. Business needs
   B. Learning needs
   C. Payoff needs
   D. Performance needs
   E. Preference needs
6. List the benefits that can be achieved when you link learning content to the learner's performance outcomes.
   A. They understand why the program is designed to support their outcomes.
   B. They can connect their behaviors to drive improvements in their performance.
   C. They can measure the change of their KPIs to their results.
   D. It can increase the learner's accountability for training.
   E. It can increase the likelihood the learner will apply what they've learned back on the job.
   F. All of the above.

CHAPTER 2

Analyzing Performance Gaps

SARDÉK LOVE

IN THIS CHAPTER

This chapter provides the steps for analyzing performance gaps. After reading it, you will be able to:

- Conduct interviews of top performers and standard performers.
- Identify the six factors that influence employee performance.
- Calculate the performance gap at the business and employee level.

Performance Gaps Defined

Performance gaps exist whenever performance does not meet desired expectations; they occur on two levels within an organization. In the first—the organizational or business level—metrics used to manage the business are not being met. Metrics at this level are typically well defined and regularly shared within the organization. The second is the individual performer level. Employees are commonly given a set of KPIs to manage and evaluate their performance.

As simple as defining performance gaps may appear, it can be quite challenging to analyze them. In this chapter, you will learn steps to minimize the complexity of this very important process.

CHAPTER 2

The Importance of Analyzing Performance Gaps

When performance gaps exist, the need to conduct an analysis is often overlooked or dismissed by stakeholders. This resistance is more likely to occur for any performance gap that is:

- **Urgent**—the pressure to resolve the gap is increasing over time.
- **Pervasive**—the gap has a widespread influence on the team, business unit, or organization.
- **Expensive**—the cost is increasing as time passes.

Without assessing this gap, talent development professionals run the risk of tackling symptoms but failing to address their root causes. Doing so can damage their credibility, significantly reduce their influence, and relegate them to "order taker" status.

Analyzing the performance gap establishes a baseline for measuring the impact of training. This analysis also enables talent development professionals to identify nontraining-related solutions that are necessary but not accounted for in the business impact phase of evaluation.

The Performance Gap Analysis Process

A performance gap analysis follows a six-step process beginning at the organizational level and methodically drilling down to the individual employee level. It provides a comprehensive view of performance data on two levels, which is then used to make recommendations (often including training). Here are the six steps of the process:

1. Defining organizational goals
2. Hosting stakeholder project planning meetings
3. Assessing employee performance
4. Assessing the six factors that influence employee performance
5. Involving key stakeholders in the analysis
6. Summarizing the performance gap

These steps ensure the process reveals the information needed to make the data-driven recommendations designed to close the performance gap. Let's explore them in greater detail.

Defining Organizational Goals

When you receive a request for training, it is tempting to begin asking questions focused on the individual performer level. Instead, you should step back and initiate the project request intake process. The initial questions in the project intake process focus on the organizational or business-level goals and metrics. This begins an organizational analysis, which offers insight into what needs to change to address the business-level goals and metrics. It also creates a structured flow as you define the project needs, scope, and results. You can then combine these details into a project plan summary.

Preparing the Project Needs, Scope, and Results

While the list of items in a project request intake form can vary, the most requested data typically includes:

- Department
- Project requestor
- Business goals and metrics
- Initial statement of need or request (What's the issue?)
- Project scope (How wide or narrow is the focus of the project need?)
- Job titles of roles being evaluated
- Desired performance results from the job titles being evaluated
- Desired timeline
- Budget

It is important to keep the initial discussion focused on defining the organizational goals, which helps keep the project requestor from prescribing a solution, such as training. This can be difficult because stakeholders often view training as the quickest and easiest solution for solving a performance gap. By maintaining an initial focus on key business goals, you plant the seeds needed to get agreement and avoid accepting a prescribed solution without conducting an analysis of the situation.

Preparing the Project Plan Summary

The next step is to create a summary of the project request. This provides a historical agreed upon accounting of the initial project, its purpose, and metrics for project success. An example of a project plan summary appears in Table 2-1.

CHAPTER 2

Table 2-1. The Project Plan Summary

Project Overview

Project name	
Department	
Start date	
End date	
Project sponsor (name and email)	
Project manager (name and email)	

Project Purpose

Business goal / metrics	
Initial statement of need	
Project scope (project deliverables and key tasks)	
Job titles of roles being evaluated	
Desired performance results from the job titles	
Metrics for project success	
Budget	

Stakeholders

Stakeholder Name	Role	Contact Information (email and phone)

Project Plan Summary Approval

Project Approval	Signature and Date
Project sponsor	
Project manager	

Once the project plan summary is in place, it's time to establish agreements and obtain commitments from key stakeholders.

Hosting Stakeholder Project Planning Meetings

Schedule a meeting with the project sponsor and other key stakeholders to review the project plan summary and obtain their agreement and commitment to the project. The list of attendees should include the project sponsor, project manager, subject matter experts (as needed), and any other key stakeholders you want to attend.

During the meeting, provide an overview of the performance gap analysis process and emphasize the outcome-based, not behavior-based, approach. Failure to do so may result in stakeholders advocating for a solution (such as training) that may not close the performance gap. Review the project plan summary to obtain agreements and sign-off on the project. If anyone disagrees with the plan, facilitate the meeting to obtain acceptable revisions for moving forward with the analysis. Once the project plan summary is approved, send copies to the attendees and prepare to begin assessing employee performance.

Assessing Employee Performance

Assessing employee performance is an essential task for developing targeted initiatives for enhancing employee and organizational productivity. There are a multitude of assessment approaches available, and they all require the assessor to use systems thinking to consider the factors that influence performance. Here are the critical steps in assessing employee performance:
- Defining KPIs
- Defining outcomes, work routines, and tasks
- Selecting and interviewing top and standard performers

Defining Key Performance Indicators

Every job role being evaluated should have a set of specific, measurable performance metrics that are aligned with the organization's goals and objectives. These KPIs, may include productivity targets, quality of work standards, and customer satisfaction scores. KPIs describe how the organization, function, and employees are doing, and without them, teams risk lack of direction, inefficiencies, poor decision making, and an inability to identify problems and opportunities. In addition, employees won't know how their performance is being evaluated. KPIs for each employee are obtained from the employee's immediate manager, HR, or the performance appraisal system.

KPIs should define three categories of performance for the job role: low performance, standard performance, and top performance. This range of performance is vital to performance analysis because you will want to interview top performers to discover what they are doing differently.

Defining Outcomes, Work Routines, and Tasks for a Job Role

When collecting data at the individual employee level, managers and employees will work toward defining three types of performance data: outcomes, work routines, and job tasks. Let's review each type:

- **Outcomes** are three to seven major things an employee produces as the output of a work process or work routine in their job role. For example, when a salesperson completes a series of work routines to produce a sale, the sale is the outcome. An instructional designer designs training courses; therefore, the training course is the outcome. A cashier at a fast-food restaurant completes orders; therefore, the order is the outcome.
- **Work routines** are the processes individuals repeatedly complete to produce outcomes. For the salesperson, work routines to produce a sale may include the prospecting process, the lead management (follow-up) process, and the closing the sale process.
- **Tasks** are the individual actions an employee completes. Work routines are simply a collection of tasks that produce outcomes. For example, a salesperson may complete the following tasks during the prospecting work routine:
    - Add the prospect to the customer relationship management software.
    - Contact the prospect.
    - Assign a potential sales score to the prospect.

The key to understanding the difference between an outcome, work routine, and task is simple. Outcomes are at the top of the performance hierarchy. Drill down to the next level to get to work routines, and another to get to the task level.

Selecting and Interviewing Top and Standard Performers

The next step is to use interviewing to gather performance trend data from employees. First, select individuals from the target work group to interview, ensuring that you're working with both top performers and standard performers. Use performance appraisals, which provide a structured framework for assessing performance against predetermined criteria, to determine who to include in your interview pool. Remember, your goal is to identify performance trends, which requires interviewing a sufficient number of top and standard performers. If there aren't enough top and standard performers, focus on relative performance—comparing employees against one another rather than an absolute standard.

Table 2-2 (which is adapted from ATD's Master Performance Consultant program) provides a guide for calculating how many top performers to interview.

Table 2-2. Calculating the Number of Top Performers to Interview

What is the total number of employees in the job role? Enter the answer in box A.	A.
For example, if there are 200 sales reps in the company, you would enter 200.	
How many employees are in the work group you are evaluating? Enter the answer in box B.	B.
If you are not evaluating the entire population, this would show the subset you're targeting for evaluation. For example, you would enter 100 here if you were only evaluating the 100 sales reps in the North American business unit.	
Calculate the number of top performers you need to interview by multiplying the answer in box B by 2 percent. Enter the answer in box C.	C.
For example, 2 percent of 100 sales reps is two sales reps. Note: If your answer in box B is 300 or less, it's best to interview at least five top performers. Otherwise, you won't have enough data to identify trends.	

Based on the size of the targeted work group, interview one to three standard performers, which will help confirm and validate your top performer data.

Interviewing Performers

Conducting interviews yields rich data that is particularly useful for identifying barriers and enablers to performance success in a job. When interviewing an employee, it is important to ask questions that reveal how they do their work. Using a consistent interview template helps ensure you're collecting cleaner and more easily comparable data. The interview's initial questions should focus on identifying the primary job responsibilities, while the next set is designed to obtain detailed insights about each major job responsibility. Table 2-3 contains a sample interview worksheet.

CHAPTER 2

Table 2-3. Interview Worksheet

Employee Information

Check one	☐ Top performer ☐ Standard performer
Date	
Name	
Job title or position	
Time in job or role	

Major Job Responsibility

What is produced or created?		
% of total job time	Level of Importance	Level of Difficulty
	Circle one: 1 2 3 4 5 (1 = low and 5 = high)	Circle one: 1 2 3 4 5 (1 = low and 5 = high)
Metrics that define standard performance		
What job aids, tools, or resources do you use to successfully complete this responsibility?		
Barriers to performance success		
Key tasks		

Major Job Responsibility

What is produced or created?		
% of total job time	Level of Importance	Level of Difficulty
	Circle one: 1 2 3 4 5 (1 = low and 5 = high)	Circle one: 1 2 3 4 5 (1 = low and 5 = high)
Metrics that define standard performance		
What job aids, tools, or resources do you use to successfully complete this responsibility?		
Barriers to performance success		
Key tasks		

Use additional copies of the interview worksheet as necessary to document the answers for each major job responsibility.

After completing all interviews, review the worksheets for trends in these specific data points:

- Level of importance
- Level of difficulty

- Job aids and resources that enable successful performance
- Barriers to performance

By interviewing mostly top performers, you will discover the workarounds and other tactics they use to perform at a high level. The insights gathered from interviews with standard performers also enable you to determine what top performers do differently to outperform standard performers. You can also use all the trend data acquired to calculate the performance gap.

Assessing Six Factors That Influence Performance

According to the ATD Master Performance Consultant program, you should consider six factors after completing your initial data collection: workplace structure and environment, training and development, talent acquisition, management structure and support, personal motivation, and technology.

Depending on what you learn during the interviews, you may want to explore these other factors to determine what, if any, influence they are having on performance. It is important to note that conducting an assessment on any of the six factors is optional. Thus, assessments should only be done if there is evidence the factor is contributing to a performance gap.

Workplace Structure and Environment

The work environment can have an outsized influence on performance. Look for evidence that any of the following exist:
- Poor working conditions
- Inefficient equipment
- Safety issues
- Poor ergonomics and workspace layout
- Poor collaboration or a lack of teamwork

Training and Development

Access to and the quality of training can vary. Look for evidence of:
- Availability of training (bad, good, or great)
- Employees never receive training
- Employees lack the knowledge or skills to perform the job tasks

Talent Acquisition

Hiring and retaining talent is one of the greatest challenges organizations experience. Look for evidence of the following:
- A lack of specific skills requirements for the job
- A lack of new-hire orientation and support
- Inadequate compensation

Management Structure and Support

Due to a lack of development, managers are a common source of performance gaps. Look for evidence of:
- Lack of manager availability
- Poor manager communication and interpersonal skills
- Span of control issues
- Ineffective at removing barriers for direct reports
- Unclear or undocumented performance expectations
- Lack of regular performance feedback to direct reports

Personal Motivation

A lack of personal motivation is common in the modern workplace. What is not-so-common is understanding its root causes. To uncover the reasons for a lack of motivation, look for evidence of:
- Heavy workloads
- Jobs not seen as meaningful
- Repetitive and boring job tasks
- Lack of discretionary authority adversely influencing performance

Technology

The impact of using technology to complete jobs and tasks cannot be underestimated. To discover technology challenges, look for evidence of:
- Poorly designed technology-driven work processes
- Access issues
- Technology infrastructure not matching the job or task requirements
- Usability issues with the technology

Document the influence of each factor that is confirmed to be contributing to the performance gap in the appropriate major job responsibility section of the interview worksheet. Before calculating the performance gap, you'll also need to obtain insights from a few stakeholders.

Involving Key Stakeholders in the Analysis

The manager interview is a critical data gathering tool for developing an understanding of management support in relation to the performance gaps being evaluated. You may also interview other stakeholders to acquire further information. When preparing to conduct a manager interview, follow these recommendations:

- Select the manager of a top performer for your interview.
- Complete at least two interviews with top performers before interviewing their managers.
- Collect data during the interview—don't provide a project status update. Resist requests by managers for preliminary information.

Prepare a standard set of interview questions to ensure consistency in the data gathering process. Here are some questions to ask during manager interviews:

- How is employee performance measured?
- How do you link the employee's role to the team's, department's, or organization's goals?
- How frequently do you provide performance feedback to the employee?
- What reward systems (formal and informal) are used?
- What do top performers do differently to achieve that level of performance?
- What specific knowledge or skills lead to successful performance on the job?
- What are the barriers to performance success?
- What workarounds, job aids, and other tools and resources do top performers use?

You may also want to interview other stakeholders, including HR, subject matter experts, internal and external customers, and peers, to obtain their insights.

At this point, you have completed an organizational analysis, a performance analysis, and a performer analysis. It's time to use the trends from this data to calculate the performance gap.

Summarizing the Performance Gap

The final step in the process is to review the data collected from performers, managers, and stakeholders. Then, you'll summarize the current versus desired state of performance and calculate the performance gap. Table 2-4 presents a completed example of the performance gap summary worksheet.

Table 2-4. Example Performance Gap Summary Worksheet

Original problem or request	Sales are not meeting target.
Business goal	Increase overall sales in the southern region by 10% in the next 12 months.
Desired state	Increase sales for each retail location in the southern region by 7% in the next 12 months.
Current state	All retail locations are missing their respective sales target.
Target work group being evaluated	Sales reps in the southern region
Barriers contributing to the performance gap	• Sales reps lack product knowledge due to ineffective product training. • Inefficient sales software is causing an increase in quote delivery time by 25%. This opens the door for competitors to steal sales by closing prospects faster. • Poor product knowledge leads to the wrong product offer to prospects. • The turnover of experienced sales reps is higher than expected. Exit interviews support data heard in top-performer interviews that sales managers are rarely available to provide approvals for pricing discounts when needed at close of sale. This lack of responsiveness to create competitive pricing at close appears to be causing the sales rep to lose 5% to 10% of their new business sales.
The performance gap	Currently, all retail locations in the southern region are missing their annual sales target by an average of 1.5%. In total, the southern district sales are missing the target by 2%. Sales reps have an annual sales revenue target of $300,000. The desired state is to increase overall sales for the southern region by 10%. **The Performance Gap** **Business-level gap:** To increase overall sales in the southern region, each retail location will need to increase sales by 7%. **Sales rep-level gap:** Sales reps will need to increase sales over their current target of $300,000 by 7% over the next 12 months. The new annual sales rep revenue target is $321,000. All top performers were already meeting or exceeding the new $321,000 annual revenue target.

Case Study: Digital Tool Utilization Performance Gap

Laurel, a senior manager for a large global enterprise resource planning organization, leads a team of internal consultants who support various sales teams. She's an experienced assessor in conducting performance gap analysis. Her team member, Alejandro, received a request from a senior leader focused on digital strategy and innovation. The senior leader wanted them to create an internal digital product certification program for his account executives. Because the request was framed as a solution, Alejandro knew that he needed to first schedule a meeting to go through the proper project intake process. During the meeting, he learned that the business goals were to use three digital tools to increase sales productivity, scale, and shorten the sales cycle time. The client believed that each of these digital tools were of equal value, so he expected account executives to master all three.

Alejandro resisted the temptation to be an order taker and convinced the senior leader to grant him access to top-performing account executives so he could conduct an analysis on their performance. Using the interview worksheet, Alejandro met with several top performers and discovered something quite stunning—the distinguishing factor for a top account executive was the use of a specific tool (not all three).

The key to top performance in the account executive role was found by obtaining answers to three questions: What is the level of importance? What is the level of difficulty? What tools were used to close sales? Alejandro also found other previously unknown influence factors that were adversely influencing sales and sales cycle times.

Armed with this knowledge, the project team set out to address the nonlearning issues that were affecting performance while also designing a learning initiative that was better tailored to the specific behavior changes the sales leader was looking to influence. Alejandro shared the results with his client, who was blown away by the results and recognized Alejandro publicly with an internal award. The senior leader was able to take qualitative feedback from Alejandro's research and align it with the internal quantitative metrics to co-develop a new, improved approach. Laurel's team garnered massive internal publicity, and they are now attending meetings with senior leaders and consulting on initiatives that are more strategic in nature.

CHAPTER 2

Summary

Analyzing performance gaps is a dynamic and multifaceted process that promotes organizational success. By defining organizational goals and assessing employee performance and six factors that influence performance, talent development professionals can identify performance gaps and diagnose underlying causes. Once complete, the most appropriate solutions can be identified. When delivered as part of the solution, training can be evaluated to determine the business impact.

Knowledge Check

For each of the questions listed here, select true or false. After completing the knowledge check, review your answers in appendix B:

1. Stakeholders are likely to resist requests to conduct a performance gap analysis if the gaps are urgent, pervasive, and expensive.
2. Performance gaps occur on two levels: the business level and the performer level.
3. When interviewing performers, you should include poor performers.
4. When analyzing performance gaps, consider six influence factors.
5. When interviewing managers, speak with managers of standard performers.

CHAPTER 3

Developing Powerful Program Objectives

KATHARINE ALDANA

IN THIS CHAPTER

This chapter explores the importance, use, and development of program objectives. After reading it, you will be able to:
- Explain the benefits of developing and communicating program objectives.
- Use objective criteria to write, assess, and improve objectives.
- Identify and avoid common pitfalls in developing powerful objectives.

The Value of Objectives

Organizational priorities and high-level goals serve to create a common destination, providing rallying points within nearly every organization. They excite and inspire people by creating an energy and palpable buzz. But the creation of a common destination often leaves a gap in its wake—an abyss between the current state (point A) and the desired state (point B). Navigating this void is called "execution," and objectives are the enablers of execution.

In the book *Measure What Matters*, John Doerr (2018) calls out this timeless challenge—programs "get people whipped up with enthusiasm, but they don't know what to do with it." Powerful objectives channel this enthusiasm with clarity and precision. They narrow program focus to actionable, measurable building blocks of success, serving as the road map to program design while facilitating alignment with organizational needs. Objectives define desired results and serve as the starting point for developing data collection and evaluation plans.

Despite the importance of program objectives, many TD professionals continue to overlook them when designing and developing training programs. Program outcomes with less than desired results, including negative ROIs, frequently result from inadequacies in alignment, program design, and evaluation planning that could have been prevented by the creation and communication of powerful program objectives.

The Chain of Impact

The outcome of any initiative can be measured along five levels—reaction, learning, application, impact, and ROI. These levels represent a chain of impact that occurs when participants attend a program, learn, apply their new knowledge, and improve impact measures.

The chain of impact begins with participant involvement and describes what must occur at each level to enable program success at the following level (Table 3-1). This interconnected sequence of desired events and outcomes provides layers of direction (objectives) and enables the collection of evidence (evaluation) in support of program success.

The chain of impact begins when the target audience completes the intended experience (Level 0 objectives are met). If participants react to the program in the desired way, acquire skills and knowledge associated with the program, and apply what they learned in a variety of ways—and this application results in a measurable, positive impact in the work unit or individual performance—then Levels 1 through 4 have been met. Once project leaders determine whether the program benefits exceed the costs at an acceptable rate of return, Level 5 objectives are met. When evaluating Level 5 objectives, always use either the ROI or BCR formulas:

$$BCR = \frac{\text{Program benefits}}{\text{Program costs}}$$

$$ROI = \frac{\text{Program benefits} - \text{Program costs}}{\text{Program costs}} \times 100$$

Table 3-1. Levels of Objectives

Level of Objectives	Measurement Focus	Typical Measures
0 – Input and indicators	The input into the project in terms of scope, volume, efficiencies, and costs	• Participants • Hours • Costs • Timing
1 – Reaction and perceived value	Reaction to the project or program, including the perceived value	• Relevance • Importance • Usefulness • Appropriateness • Intent to use • Motivation to take action
2 – Learning and confidence	Learning to use the content and materials, including the confidence to use what was learned	• Skills • Knowledge • Capacity • Competencies • Confidence • Contacts
3 – Application and implementation	Use of content and materials in the work environment, including progress with actual items and implementation	• Extent of use • Task completion • Frequency of use • Actions completed • Success with use • Barriers to use • Enablers to use
4 – Impact and consequences	The consequences of using the content and materials expressed as business impact measures	• Productivity • Revenue • Quality • Time • Efficiency • Customer satisfaction • Employee engagement
5 – ROI	Comparison of the monetary benefits of the program to its costs	• Benefit-cost ratio (BCR) • ROI (%) • Payback period

For a program to yield a positive ROI, the chain of impact must be present and maintain continuity (Phillips and Phillips 2008). This logical progression provides a comprehensive, credible narrative culminating in the ultimate measure of program success.

CHAPTER 3

Powerful Objectives

Objectives should be created in response to the needs defined along the left side of the alignment model (Figure 3-1). Consider what success looks like when those requirements are met; these desired outcomes populate the middle of the V model. The more clearly and objectively you define program needs, the more efficiently you can create objectives. Powerful objectives make it easy to populate the measurement plan on the right side of the V Model. To be considered powerful, they must include:

- One area of focus per objective
- An observable outcome
- Applicable conditions and criteria

Figure 3-1. The Alignment Process: V Model

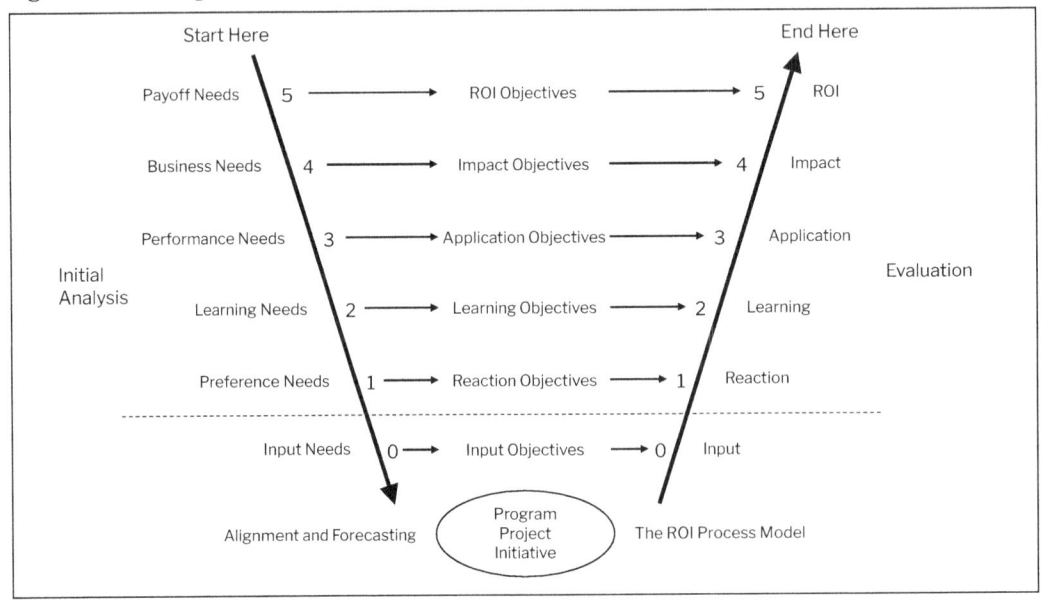

	Initial Analysis				Evaluation
Start Here					End Here
Payoff Needs	5	→ ROI Objectives →	5	ROI	
Business Needs	4	→ Impact Objectives →	4	Impact	
Performance Needs	3	→ Application Objectives →	3	Application	
Learning Needs	2	→ Learning Objectives →	2	Learning	
Preference Needs	1	→ Reaction Objectives →	1	Reaction	
Input Needs	0	→ Input Objectives →	0	Input	
Alignment and Forecasting		Program Project Initiative		The ROI Process Model	

After developing the initial iterations of objectives at each level, share them with key stakeholders and seek final approval from program sponsors. This step promotes vital alignment and provides an opportunity for stakeholders and sponsors to confirm whether objectives accurately capture their envisioned outcomes as discussed during the needs analysis.

While not every objective has a condition or criterion, considering these elements is essential:

- *Conditions* refer to the circumstances under which the performance should occur.

- *Criteria* specify acceptable degrees of performance, providing measurable standards of evaluation.

Table 3-2 provides examples of condition and criterion clauses that might appear in a program objective. Table 3-3 illustrates the difference between ineffective, mediocre, and powerful objectives. In the case of Levels 0 (Input), 1 (Reaction), and 5 (ROI), something is better than nothing. It's hard to be completely ineffective because you can achieve mediocre alignment and clarity simply by calling attention to these areas. Levels 2 (Learning), 3 (Application), and 4 (Impact) are more complex. Writing an objective at these levels without specificity won't yield alignment, clarity, or execution enablement.

Table 3-2. Conditions and Criteria for Objectives

Conditions	
Considerations	**Example**
What are the conditions in which program participants should be able to demonstrate their learning?	• Upon completion of the program, … • Given any reference of the participant's choice, … • With the aid of software, …
What are the conditions in which participants should apply what they have learned?	• When a customer becomes angry, … • When a transaction is initiated, … • During peak hours, … • When delivering feedback, …
Criteria	
Considerations	**Example**
When?	• Within six months of program completion • In 90 days • Within 30 minutes
How often?	• In 95% of occurrences • Every interaction • Quarterly
What level of performance?	• 10% increase in productivity • 15% increase in sales revenue • 10% reduction in handing time • 13% reduction in turnover
What level of proficiency?	• With an 80% accuracy level • Within 10 minutes • With a minimum quality score of 85 • Without error

In most cases, you should write all objectives at each level prior to program development. This enables you to leverage them to promote things like effective planning, participant and leadership motivation and accountability, and measurement and evaluation planning—all of which increase likelihood of success. However, there are some instances in which it is appropriate to have participants create their own application and impact objectives during or immediately following the program. This can be facilitated in numerous ways, like part of an action-planning exercise, a debrief with their leader, or a follow up session. This works well for programs that require each participant to apply content differently to achieve different business impact measures (such as KPIs). Keep in mind, for participants to create their own powerful application and impact objectives, they will need guidance to ensure the necessary specificity. When collected, compiled, and measured, these objectives and subsequent results will enable impact evaluation for a program spanning multiple workgroups with different KPIs and targets.

Table 3-3. Differences of Objectives

Level	Ineffective	Mediocre	Powerful
Level 0. Input	N/A	Everyone in the target audience (supervisors) should complete the program.	Conducted with at least 100 supervisors per month 100% target group completion within two months
Level 1. Reaction	N/A	Supervisors will see value in what they learned.	Upon program completion, supervisors will rate the program value at least a 4 out of 5 on a 5-point scale.
Level 2. Learning	Supervisors will learn about effective counseling discussions.	Supervisors will learn five skills necessary for effective counseling discussions.	Without the aid of reference material, supervisors will demonstrate use of the five skills necessary for effective counseling discussions within the context of a counseling conversation.
Level 3. Application	Supervisors will manage absences using counseling conversations.	Upon completion of the program, supervisors will use counseling conversations to manage absences.	Within 30 days, supervisors will ensure counseling conversations are being conducted in at least 90% of unplanned absence occurrences.
Level 4. Impact	Absenteeism will improve.	Absenteeism will improve within 6 months.	Unplanned absenteeism of retail associates should decrease by 20% within 6 months of the program.
Level 5. ROI	N/A	Achieve a positive ROI.	Achieve an ROI of 25% within the first year.

Input Objectives

Input objectives offer numerous benefits to various stakeholders:
- Sponsors understand the program's timeframe.
- Program owners and evaluators establish milestone targets, coordinate data collection efforts, manage logistics, and ensure facility, technology, and delivery readiness.
- Designers and developers gauge audience size and tailor activities accordingly.
- Facilitators monitor attendance against the objectives and proactively escalate any issues that arise.

Despite these benefits, meeting input objectives is not an indicator of program success but rather an indicator of program execution. Just because you execute a program as intended does not mean it yields business results.

Let's look at a few examples of input objectives across a broad range of parameters:
- **Volume, staffing, scope, audience, and coverage** specify project team requirements, pilot status, participant selection criteria, or the extent to which the program will cover the target audience. For example:
    - This program is intended for high-performing midlevel people leaders as defined by their annual performance rating.
    - Each geographic region will nominate two high performers, resulting in program completion by 2 percent of midlevel people leaders.
    - Program topic areas should fall within the scope of the organization's leadership principles.
    - The project team should include cross-functional representation from each workgroup.
- **Timing and duration** establish the program launch date, how long it will run, the time to achieve coverage objective, and the date the program must be completed by.
- **Efficiency and budget** establish the participant to team member ratio, average task completion times (such as content design), participant program completion time, total program cycle time, and financial expectations for program spend. For example:

- Design the program with a ratio of no more than 10 hours per one hour of content.
- Participants complete all components of the program within three months of their start date.
- The project team will complete a needs analysis and design, develop, execute, and evaluate the program within 12 months.
- The program will cost less than $1,000 per participant.

- **Location, delivery methods, technology, and disruption objectives** can prompt additional discussion among sponsors as they quantify time away from regular job activities. A program may sound great, for example, until it involves 48 hours away from regular job activities. In some cases, you'll have trade-off conversations with sponsors and adjust programs accordingly. In other cases, sponsors accept the disruption but want to see a particular ROI objective in exchange. Here are a few other examples:
  - Leverage a blended approach with a combination of self-paced and virtual instructor-led delivery.
  - Use virtual reality.
  - Include hands-on experience with at least three of the five new products.
  - Combine the training environment and the live production environment.
  - Minimize disruption to no more than two hours per participant.

Reaction Objectives

Reaction is the earliest predictor of success along the chain of impact. Reaction objectives encompass participant perception of program relevance, importance, usefulness, appropriateness, and the experience itself—things like the facilitation, timing, pace, materials, and facility. Reaction also includes participants' intent to use what they learned and motivation to take action. Setting standard reaction objectives for similar initiatives, comparing attainment across different programs, and leveraging open-ended feedback are great ways to identify opportunities early enough to address them. For example, relevance scores below the objective indicate you may need to include additional in-context examples for the content. When defining reaction objectives, focus on actionable insights or those that predict the likelihood of success at the next level, considering the project team as the primary beneficiary. While project sponsors may appreciate a brief overview, prioritize impact and ROI for their interests.

Here is an example of an objective that can be used and compared across multiple programs:

- The average participant rating for the following statement will be at least 4 out of 5 on a five-point agreement scale: "I intend to apply what I learned to improve my performance."

These are examples of powerful reaction objectives:

- Responses to the following question should include no more than 5 percent of respondents expressing the same concern: "What, if anything, do you anticipate may keep you from achieving the program objectives?" The project team will create and execute a support plan to address any roadblock identified by more than 5 percent of respondents.
- The average participant rating for the following statement will be at least 4 out of 5 on a five-point agreement scale: "My instructor provided contextual examples of how to put the training into practice."

Here's an example of an objective that's not actionable:

- The average participant rating for the following statement will be at least 4 out of 5 on a five-point agreement scale: "The program activities contributed to my understanding of the material."

The issue here is that the question does not allow participants to indicate which program activity needed improvement. Thus, if this objective is missed, you can't adjust the program until you determine which activities are not supporting the learning experience.

Learning Objectives

As the next link in the chain of impact, learning objectives define the level of proficiency necessary to enable success at the application level. Skills, learning, knowledge, capacity, competencies, confidence, and contacts are all defined here. "The best learning objectives are those that capture in specific terms what participants must know to be successful" (Phillips and Phillips 2008). Learning objectives guide designers and facilitators in teaching, inform participants of what they'll learn, and align stakeholders on proficiency criteria. Communicated beforehand, they can prepare, excite, and inspire.

CHAPTER 3

Powerful learning objectives outline how learners *demonstrate* knowledge, which aids in measurement plan efficiency and informs designers. Use behaviors or actions that are observable and objectively worded, inclusive of applicable conditions and criteria. Avoid subjective words like *understand, comprehend, know,* and *appreciate* (Phillips and Phillips 2008). Learning objectives can't fulfill their primary purpose of facilitating alignment if they're open for interpretation by different stakeholders. Although inherently subjective, the term "confidence" can serve as a valuable objective and measure, holding particular significance in programs like new-hire training because gaining confidence is an intended outcome of the program experience.

Here are some examples of powerful learning objectives:

- Without the use of resources, identify the five elements of the new strategy.
- Complete each software routine in the standard time.
- Demonstrate all five customer-interaction skills with a success rating of 4 out of 5, as determined by the criteria provided in class.
- Contrast the differences between consumer and commercial loans and type key differences within the standard response time. (Note that this objective includes a mental process, observable component, and criteria).

The following action verbs create powerful learning objectives:

Name	Explain	Complete
Write	Search	State
Prepare	Sort	Build
Describe	Locate	Start
Recite	Stop	List
Reboot	Solve	Compare
Differentiate	Calculate	Recall
Identify	Eliminate	Contrast
Load	Construct	

Practitioner's Tip

Don't get so caught up in writing a powerful learning objective that you forget why you're writing it in the first place. There should be a clear connection between what the objective requires and the proficiency essential for successful application. Concentrate on describing what is *most* important to enable application with as much precision and detail as possible.

Application Objectives

Application objectives describe how the program will achieve its impact objectives. Similar to learning objectives, powerful application objectives include an observable behavior or outcome and criteria, although conditions become less important at this level (Phillips and Phillips 2008).

As discussed in chapter 1, the initial needs analysis includes a step to uncover what participants are or are not doing on the job that is influencing the business impact measure. This information becomes an input for the application objective by providing the observable behavior component. You then establish criteria to define success and combine them to form an application objective.

Application objectives empower designers and facilitators to intentionally shape and deliver content, emphasizing practical use while identifying barriers and offering strategies to minimize or overcome them. Acknowledgment of real-life circumstances contributes to program credibility. When learners grasp the utility of knowledge or skills in their everyday situations, it heightens their motivation to engage. Application objectives can also ensure leaders are aligned with intended outcomes and have criteria for feedback and reinforcement.

Here are some examples of powerful application objectives (Phillips and Phillips 2008):

- At least 99.1 percent of software users will be following the correct sequences after three weeks of use.
- Within one year, 10 percent of employees will submit documented suggestions for saving costs.
- By November, pharmaceutical sales reps will communicate the adverse effects of a specific prescription drug to all physicians in their territories.
- 80 percent of employees will use one or more of the three cost-containment features of the healthcare plan in the next six months.
- 50 percent of conference attendees will follow up with at least one contact from the conference within 60 days.
- Leaders will use all five feedback skills with at least half their direct reports within the next month.

CHAPTER 3

Impact Objectives

Impact objectives should reflect the desired business outcomes you hope to achieve by designing the program and having people experience it. As such, you should write them in business terms, using tangible metrics like output, quality, cost, and time, as well as intangibles like agility, grit, stress, and brand awareness.

While you can keep reaction and learning objectives behind the scenes in the creation and delivery of a training program, you should communicate impact objectives to stakeholders along the way. Program sponsors, participant leaders, and designers and facilitators should have this information prior to program launch; participants should receive it as part of the program, whether it is an advance communication or included as part of the program delivery.

I've seen enthusiastic program managers boasting about performance improvement resulting from their program only to find out program sponsors and executive stakeholders had a different definition of success and impact—either they were expecting a larger improvement than what occurred, or they wanted entirely different KPIs. Defining impact objectives and ensuring stakeholder alignment can prevent this sort of thing from happening—"improve KPI x" is not sufficient to prevent misalignment. It's also not the sort of thing that will rally and focus people because it's completely open-ended. How do you know when you've achieved this objective? How do you even know where to aim?

Here are some powerful impact objectives with clearly defined success criteria:
- After nine months, grievances should be reduced from 12 per month to no more than two per month at the VA center.
- Turnover of high-potential employees should be reduced to 10 percent in nine months.
- The average number of new accounts should increase from 300 per month to 350 per month in six months.
- Unplanned absenteeism of call center associates should decrease by 20 percent within the next calendar year.
- A 20 percent reduction in overtime should be realized for field staff in the third quarter of this year.
- By the end of the year, the average number of product defects should decrease by 30 percent.
- Operating expenses should decrease by 10 percent in the fourth quarter.
- Product returns per month should decline by 15 percent in six months.

ROI Objectives

ROI is the epitome of program success, and ROI objectives set the acceptable threshold for evaluating the program's monetary benefits in relation to its costs. You can formulate them as an ROI percentage, a benefit-cost ratio, or a time period for payback (ROI Institute 2023). Here are examples of each.

After comparing the benefits to the costs, the project should:
- Achieve at least a 20 percent ROI within the first year.
- Achieve a 2:1 benefit-cost ratio.
- Realize an investment payback within six months.

When choosing the method to calculate ROI and establishing an objective, you should consider the program sponsor's preferred ROI method. No matter your choice, share the formula employed and any underlying assumptions that led you to select this formula. This context is necessary to ensure there is a common understanding because the term "ROI" is not always used correctly.

Program sponsors and other senior-level leadership typically show the greatest interest in ROI objectives and consider them to be a key measure of program success. However, ROI objectives also hold value for a broad range of stakeholders, including evaluation practitioners, program managers, and designers and developers. Anyone influencing the program's costs must be familiar with the ROI objective and, equally important, the methodology behind its calculation. This enables stakeholders to make informed decisions, especially if they understand that program costs must be outweighed by anticipated benefits for a positive ROI objective to be met. For instance, program designers can better align program design choices with ROI objectives if they consider how factors such as program duration, time investment, and facilitator requirements influence the cost per participant. This could help optimize the achievement of positive ROI regardless of what may or may not have been established with the input objectives.

Pitfalls When Creating Program Objectives

Two of the most prevalent mistakes made when creating program objectives are the use of subjective language and failure to communicate objectives at the appropriate levels to each stakeholder group. They both pose risks that may manifest into many different issues and result in missing out on the benefits of powerful objectives.

Subjective Language

Practitioners are even more likely to overlook subjective language if they think it has already been defined or is commonly understood. Even if you believe participants are already aligned on something like "great customer experience," avoid including that language in your program objectives.

Rather than phrasing an outcome as "Provide a great customer experience," strive to unpack what "great" means and how you can measure it with observable behaviors. Here's one way to eliminate subjectivity: "During every customer interaction, greet the customer, provide empathy in response to their excitement or concerns, acknowledge customer tenure, and express appreciation."

Or, instead of trying to influence the outcomes of an employee resource group (ERG) initiative using the objective "Increase employee engagement in ERGs," use objectives like, "70 percent of participants will elect to join an ERG within 30 days of program completion" (application) or "ERG members will engage in a minimum of one ERG event per quarter" (application).

Writing powerful objectives requires you to identify the opportunity for improvement and use probing questions to get the necessary input. Let's review some examples of subjective outcomes uncovered during the needs analysis and the probing questions you could ask in response:

- If your starting place for a program objective is "Complete the task as efficiently as possible," you should look deeper into what "as efficiently as possible" might mean. You could ask, "What would that look like?" Your answer would help strengthen the program objective.
- If your initial program objective is "Develop inclusive leaders and teams," you could identify observable behaviors by asking, "What do inclusive leaders do?" or "What are the observable or measurable benefits of inclusivity?"

Failure to Communicate

Failure to communicate objectives at all levels appropriate for each audience may happen if you didn't formalize the objectives in the first place. Or, you might have failed to anticipate the value each level could provide to different types of stakeholders.

Learning objectives and the "what's in it for me?" seem ever-present. However, it's much less common for participants to be told (or guided to define) how to apply what they've learned in the context of their environment. Even less frequent is communication around impact objectives that set clear expectations on the business impact expected to occur as a result of participant application.

In addition to participants lacking a clear, cohesive direction on how and where to channel their energy coming out of the program experience, failure to communicate application and impact objectives may inflate reaction data if participants are only reacting to their knowledge of learning objectives. As a learner, your reaction to a program can change dramatically depending on your expectations for what comes next. The program may be enjoyable until the application and impact objectives are revealed.

The failure to communicate impact is not contained to participants. All too often, leaders facilitate an employee's learning journey from intention to application. If they don't know the learning, application, and impact objectives, that lack of alignment will result in inconsistent or nonexistent program reinforcement. That's how programs become a "one and done" event instead of creating lasting cultural change and sustained performance improvement.

Communicating learning, application, and impact objectives to program participants and their leaders will significantly increase the likelihood of achieving program success at each level.

Summary

Powerful objectives remain an untapped superpower for many practitioners, and negative ROIs persist due to planning and alignment deficiencies that powerful objectives could easily prevent. It is not enough to craft powerful objectives; they must be shared, discussed, and integrated into the fabric of program design and execution. Let this be both a recap and a call to action: Create powerful objectives, communicate them, and reap the benefits of unparalleled alignment.

Knowledge Check

Choose a program you've recently participated in either as an attendee or a leader or member of the project team. What were the objectives for each level? Did they meet the criteria discussed in this chapter? Identify opportunities and correct or create the program objectives.

CHAPTER 3

Now, consider this book. Imagine you are one of the authors. What input, reaction, learning, application, impact, and ROI objectives would you establish? Be sure your objectives include an observable outcome or behavior with applicable conditions and criteria. See appendix B for the answer key.

CHAPTER 4

Planning Your Evaluation Project

KAYCEE BUCKLEY

IN THIS CHAPTER

This chapter explores the techniques to plan a comprehensive evaluation, including planning data collection, data analysis, and project management. After reading it, you will be able to:

- Describe the importance of planning an effective evaluation.
- Develop an evaluation plan using evaluation planning tools.
- Identify data collection and analysis techniques.
- Determine the communication strategy based on your audience.
- Gain management support and resources.

Importance of Planning for an Effective Evaluation

Like any project, planning is essential to the success of your evaluation effort. The evaluation plan establishes what you will measure from the program objectives, what sources you need, how and when throughout the program you will collect and analyze measures, and, finally, how you will communicate them and to whom. Without planning, you might miss important data, fall behind on evaluation activities, and skip steps in the evaluation process, all of which risk the integrity of the data and the credibility of the overall evaluation. Therefore, it goes without saying the evaluation plan drives the entire evaluation process and sets you up for success.

Today, stakeholders expect to see a return on their investment in learning and development programs, proof they achieved the objectives, and their demonstrated value to the organization. The evaluation plan serves as a way to communicate the evaluation methodology to stakeholders and gain alignment and commitment in measuring the program's intent and effectiveness. Showing stakeholders there is a plan to evaluate the program's effectiveness and a clear, proven evaluation methodology gives them the confidence to invest in and support the program.

Evaluation planning begins with defining the scope and what level you should evaluate your program, then moves to preparing evaluation planning documents, and ends with using the evaluation plan to align your team and gain stakeholder support. Use the Evaluation Planning Workbook in appendix A to develop your evaluation plan. The workbook provides examples of the essential tools and templates for you to use for your own planning.

Defining the Scope

After you have established the business and performance needs for your program and developed clear and specific program objectives, you can define the scope of your evaluation. Clarifying the scope and purpose of the evaluation determines the level to which you will evaluate the program. While all learning programs should show the value they bring to the organization, they don't all need to be evaluated at the same level. Programs that require a large investment or are expected to achieve a significant change in the organization require a comprehensive evaluation; other programs may only require follow-up to determine if participants acquired new skills or knowledge relevant to their job or role. Let's look at the reasons for selecting programs at the different evaluation levels:

- **Level 1: Reaction and Planned Action**
    - Demonstrate the program is relevant to the participants' job or role, a worthwhile investment of their time, and applicable to the job or role.
    - Provide insight to participants' intent to use and apply the skills and knowledge learned.
    - Recognize the program as an effective resource in supporting a larger key initiative.
- **Level 2: Learning**
    - Provide proof participants were able to learn a new skill.
    - Prove effectiveness in individuals' ability to obtain new knowledge.

- **Level 3: Application**
  - Demonstrate improvement in significant performance gaps.
  - Transfer learning to organizational strategic initiatives.
  - Pilot program effectiveness.
- **Level 4: Impact**
  - Link program to operational goals and issues.
  - Demonstrate program importance to organizational initiatives.
  - Assess impact to performance and business metrics.
  - Calculate program costs.
  - Assess programs with a large target audience or considerable investment of time.
- **Level 5: ROI**
  - Make the case for a large investment in the program.
  - Engage stakeholders and senior leaders.
  - Forecast and gain support for future programs.
  - Secure L&D as a business partner.

Stakeholder needs often drive the level of evaluation, and these needs may vary depending on the different perspectives of all stakeholders involved and in which the program affects. Understanding why stakeholders need specific program results and what decisions they want to make aids in defining not only at what level to measure the program but also the types of data you will need to collect, what sources you will need to collect the data, and the timing for collecting it. By understanding how you will use the evaluation results and who needs the results for what purpose, you are better equipped to develop your evaluation plan and manage stakeholder expectations.

Practitioner's Tip

When getting support from the top, consider measuring what is important to them to achieve their strategic goals. In planning your evaluation framework, if you are relatively new to this and do not know where to start, my advice is to *just start*. You will feel more comfortable with the process the more you do it and solicit feedback from others.

—Gary Burrus, PhD, SHRM-SCP, THRP, Executive Officer Human Resources, Choctaw Nation of Oklahoma

CHAPTER 4

Appendix A includes a sample selection worksheet that illustrates the criteria for determining at which level to evaluate your programs. Score each criterion from one to five; the total score will help you identify which programs are candidates for impact and ROI evaluation.

Developing an Evaluation Plan

Now that you know at what level you will measure your program, you can identify what data to collect, how to analyze it, and the actions needed to execute the plan. In the end, your evaluation plan will consist of three planning documents: a data collection plan, ROI analysis plan, and project plan.

Data Collection Plan

The data collection plan provides a complete look at the data that you need to collect based on the program objectives and measures for each level of evaluation. This plan answers what measures should be collected, how the data should be collected for each measure, what sources should be used, when the data should be collected, and who is collecting it.

Table 4-1 illustrates a sample data collection plan. Refer to the Evaluation Planning Workbook in appendix A to begin recording your data collection plan.

Let's review each component of the data collection plan.

Program Objectives

In the previous chapter, you learned how to develop program objectives, which provide the specific measures for each level of your evaluation project. These objectives answer your "what to ask" question and establish targets that address expected business needs or outcomes, identified performance gaps, and the intended participant's experience. This in turn leads you toward the data collection method, data sources, and timing at which you will collect the data. Broad objectives are appropriate for evaluation planning, but specific measures of success defined during evaluation planning allow for a more efficient data collection and analysis experience.

The Measures

Measures are the intended goals or targets you plan to achieve as a result of the program and should be identified for each level of evaluation. These measures should align with the

PLANNING YOUR EVALUATION PROJECT

Table 4-1. Data Collection Plan

Level	Broad Program Objectives	Measures	Data Collection Method or Instruments	Data Sources	Timing	Responsibilities
1	Reaction and Planned Action • Participants rate the program as relevant to their job • Participants rate the program effective for their learning • Participants rate the program as a worthwhile investment for career development • Participants agree program aligns with business priorities and goals	• Program receives 4 out of 5 for business results and job impact • Program receives 4 out of 5 for learning effectiveness • Program receives 4 out of 5 for pre-ROI • Program receives 4 out of 5 for alignment	Survey	Participants	Last day of training	Facilitator
2	Learning and Confidence • Discover personal coaching strengths and weaknesses • Identify an individual's skill and motivation for greatest potential • Enhance leadership skills and coach effectively to deliver targeted results • Establish a coaching cadence • Collaborate with colleagues to continue progressing new skills	• Managers assess themselves with a score of at least 3.5 post training • Manager's team assesses their manager with a score of at least 3.5 post training	180 assessment	Participants Participants' teams	Last day of training	Global L&D
3	Application and Implementation • Conduct coaching conversations • Apply coaching skills • Complete activities in the Coaching Playbook	• Conduct at least 1 coaching conversation using the coaching model for each direct report • Achieve an average 4.0 or above on coaching assessment for the participant and the participant's direct reports • 100% completion of the playbook	Survey Coaching assessment Playbook	Sales managers Sales managers, direct reports	3 months after training	Program manager
4	Business Impact • Increase revenue • Improve velocity of opportunity • Improve overall sales performance	• Monthly sales and pipeline advancement	Performance records	Sales dashboards	3 months after training	Program manager
5	ROI 20%					

53

CHAPTER 4

program objectives and be agreed upon as achievable by your stakeholders. Table 4-2 illustrates the chain of impact, including the measurement focus and measures for the different evaluation levels.

Table 4-2. Chain of Impact

Level	Measurement Focus	Typical Measures	Examples
0 – Input and indicators	Input into the program including indicators representing scope, volumes, costs, and efficiencies	• Types of topics or content • Number of programs • Number of people • Hours of involvement • Costs	• 16 hours of training • 250 participants • $750 per participant
1 – Reaction and planned action	Reaction to the program including its perceived value	• Relevance • Importance • Usefulness • Appropriateness • Intent to use • Motivation	• Receive 4 out of 5 in relevance to their job. • Receive 4 out of 5 in alignment to business priorities.
2 – Learning	Learning how to use the content and materials, including the confidence to use what was learned	• Skills • Knowledge • Capacity • Competencies • Confidences • Contacts	• Achieve 80% or above on final assessment.
3 – Application	Use of content and materials, including the confidence to use what was learned	• Extent to use • Task completion • Frequency of use • Actions completed • Success with use • Barriers to use • Enablers to use	• Complete 1 workflow analysis for each customer. • Receive overall self-assessment of 8 out of 10.
4 – Business Impact	The consequences of using the content and materials expressed as business impact measures	• Productivity • Revenue • Quality • Time • Efficiency • Customer satisfaction • Employee engagement	• Increase revenue by 10% by December 31. • Reduce absenteeism by 20% each month. • Improve time to production by 2 weeks.
5 – ROI	Comparison of monetary benefits of the program to program costs	• Benefit-cost ratio (BCR) • ROI (%) • Payback period	• 20% ROI

Source: Phillips and Phillips (2016)

Data Collection Method and Instrument

As you identify your measures, you may already be determining how to collect data for that particular measure. The different levels of evaluation, as well as the type of program you are measuring, can indicate the collection method to use. For example, surveys and questionnaires—which use ratings, scales, and open-ended questions—are a popular choice for determining participant reaction. (Refer to chapters 5 and 6 to learn how to develop effective surveys and questionnaires.)

Data collection will also depend on factors such as validity and reliability, time and cost, and utility (Phillips, Phillips, and Robinson 2013). When selecting the appropriate data collection method and instrument, make sure it will give the most valid and reliable results. Consider the time required for participants to provide the data, as well as how long it will take to gather and analyze it. (Remember, time spent collecting data is a cost to the program.) Finally, when selecting and designing a data collection instrument, consider how useful the data will be and how accurately it can be collected and analyzed.

Table 4-3 describes the common data collection methods, their purpose, and at what level of evaluation they are most useful.

Table 4-3. Data Collection Methods

Method or Instrument	Purpose	Levels Used 1	2	3	4
Surveys and questionnaires	Allows evaluators to quickly and easily collect data from a large audience. Results can be summarized and analyzed.	✓	✓	✓	✓
Tests and assessments	Provides evaluators with immediate knowledge of whether content was learned and can be applied. Tests and assessments can include traditional question-and-answer tests, role playing, or performance assessments.		✓		
Interviews	Evaluators can use interviews when additional details or a deeper look into the data is needed.	✓	✓	✓	
Focus groups	Captures variety of data including reaction, learning, and application. Focus groups can also be used to isolate program effects.		✓	✓	
Action plans	Guides participants on what and how to apply new knowledge and skills, while also providing evaluators with an outlook on the intent to apply. Action plans are then followed up to measure rate of application.			✓	✓
Performance Records	Supplies evaluators with business, performance, and operational data targeted for improvement as a result of the program.			✓	✓

CHAPTER 4

The Data Source

According to Guiding Principle 3 of the ROI Methodology, you should always use the most credible source when collecting and analyzing data. Depending on the program, objectives, measures, and the data you're collecting, sources could include participants, supervisors, peer groups, external sources, and organizational records. The most credible source is the group, individual, or system closest to the measure. If you want to determine how individuals are applying what they've learned, the most credible source would be to ask the participants how and to what extent they are doing so. However, a more objective (and credible) response may be determined by asking their manager to observe how the participant applied the lessons learned. Again, aligning with your stakeholders on what you want to measure and the source from which you will gather your data can establish the credibility you need for the overall program.

> **Practitioner's Tip**
>
> A data collection plan form can be invaluable for planning your evaluation. This document helps you differentiate between the different levels of evaluation and ensures you have established all the necessary details (such as measures, data sources, timing, responsible parties, and stakeholders). Putting the details into the plan helps guide your evaluation conversations with project stakeholders regarding the different evaluation levels and gives everyone a single point of reference for all evaluation-related details for the project. I use this document whenever I work on anything related to evaluations, even if it is just collecting data to Level 2.
>
> —Jil Radtke, Senior Learning System Specialist, Global Commercial Talent Core Diagnostics at Abbott

Timing

Timing is another evaluation element that can be determined with strong, broad program objectives. Data should be collected at the time you want to see the measures improve. For example, if you want to determine participant reaction or whether they have demonstrated the required knowledge or skills, the most optimal time to capture these measures is immediately after the program. However, when capturing application data, it's best to allow participants time to apply the learning—consider waiting 60 to 90 days, for example. For impact data, consider the time it takes for business measures to improve once

PLANNING YOUR EVALUATION PROJECT

participants have had time to apply the skills or knowledge learned. The other things to consider are when the most convenient time is for individuals to respond or provide the data and when you need to communicate it to stakeholders.

Responsibility

Finally, determine who will be responsible for collecting the data. Reaction or assessment data can be collected by the facilitator. The program development or evaluation team can collect other data.

ROI Analysis Plan

Planning how to analyze the data is just as important as how you collect it, especially when evaluating programs to Levels 3, 4, and 5. Table 4-4 illustrates an ROI analysis plan. The Evaluation Planning Workbook in appendix A includes a blank template for you to use.

Table 4-4. ROI Analysis Plan

Data Items	Methods for Isolating the Effects of the Program or Process	Methods of Converting Data to Monetary Values	Cost Categories	Intangible Benefits	Communication Targets for Final Report
• Velocity of opportunity • Revenue • Overall performance	Expert estimation	Sales velocity calculation	• Content development (development costs, SME time, training leads time, vendor travel, and other costs) • Needs assessment • Translations • Facilitator, vendor, project team, and participant travel costs • Material production • Sales manager salary • L&D team salary	• Employee satisfaction • Customer satisfaction	• Global commercial excellence VP • Global L&D team • Area training • Area commercial directors • Area VPs

57

CHAPTER 4

Let's review the different components of an ROI analysis plan.

Data Items
Data items are the measures you listed for either Levels 3 or 4 from your data collection plan. If you are only measuring to Level 3, you would only need to use the first two columns. When measuring to Levels 4 or 5, do not skip this step in the planning process! The information in the ROI analysis plan, isolation methods, data conversation to monetary values, and costs are needed to calculate your program's impact on the business measures and ROI.

Methods for Isolating the Effects of the Program
Isolating the effects of your program demonstrates the direct influence your program had on the measures and establishes credibility. There are several types of isolation methods, including control groups, trend line analysis, forecasting, and expert estimation. The isolation method you use depends on the measure, how the program is designed, working conditions, and other considerations. (Refer to chapter 13 for more information on the types of isolation methods.)

Methods for Converting Data to Monetary Value
Converting data to monetary value is required to demonstrate a return on investment. First, consider the unit of measure and how it can be represented in monetary terms, such as sales revenue, cost of turnover rates, profit linked to customer satisfaction, and cost savings in reduced absenteeism. Methods for data conversion include standard values, historical costs, internal or external experts, databases, other measures, and expert estimations. (Refer to chapter 14 to learn more about the different methods and the steps for converting data to monetary value.)

Cost Categories
According to Guiding Principle 10 of the ROI Methodology, the costs of the solution should be fully loaded for ROI analysis. *Fully loaded* refers to identifying all cost categories associated with developing, delivering, and evaluating your program, including the salaries and benefits of developers, facilitators, and participants, as well as expenses for hosting and conducting your program. Cost categories include analysis costs,

operational costs, maintenance costs, development costs, evaluation costs, and delivery costs. (Refer to chapter 15 for tabulating and prorating costs to calculate the program's fully loaded cost.)

Intangible Benefits

Not all measures can be converted to tangible monetary values, but they are equally as important in demonstrating the program's value. Identifying intangible benefits as a result of your program can show the overall value it brings to the organization. In addition, if some measures require complex steps for converting to monetary value that could risk its credibility, you can mark those as intangible benefits, as stated in Guiding Principle 11.

Communication Targets for Final Report

Evaluation without communication is pointless. Whether good or bad, communicating the results of your program to those involved—such as the participants, project team, stakeholders, and clients—demonstrates a commitment to the program's success, leads to change in the organization, and secures investment in future programs. Consider when you should communicate your results, to whom, what specific information they want to know or you need to provide, and how you will do it. For an ROI analysis plan, select the target audience based on what you want to communicate and what actions you need them to take based on the results of the evaluation. You should share with leadership, management, program participants, and the program team, including external resources that supported the design and development of the program. (Chapter 19 provides more information on communication targets and strategies.)

The Evaluation Planning Workbook in appendix A provides a communication plan worksheet for identifying your target audience, what information you want to communicate to them, the best method for delivering the information, and by when.

Other Influences of Issues During Application

While participants are applying the lessons learned from your program, other influences out of your control may affect your measures. By identifying these influences during the planning phase, you can keep them in mind when isolating the effects of your program and analyzing the data. This can also help you consider which type of isolation method to use or if you should use a combination of isolation methods.

Comments

Capture thoughts, key issues, observations, and important information you need to remember as you execute your evaluation.

Project Plan

While Levels 1 and 2 may be simple enough that project planning is not necessary, other levels typically require extensive and time-sensitive actions, resources, and responsibilities. Planning these detailed actions will ensure all tasks have been identified, timing has been considered, and you are able to secure team members and other resources to execute your evaluation. A project plan helps keep your data collection and analysis on track, because timing is critical for maintaining the integrity of your data.

Different approaches and project planning tools can be used when planning out the details of your evaluation. A template project plan is also available in the Evaluation Planning Workbook in appendix A. No matter the approach you use, your project plan should include activities, associated costs, timing, and responsibility for these key components:

- Project initiation and scope definition
- Evaluation planning
- Communication plan (such as survey notifications and stakeholder presentations)
- Data collection
- Data analysis
- Reporting
- Project close

Your project plan should consider the resources needed, as well as when you need them, to ensure they are available (such as individuals to assist in collecting data from external business systems or supervisors to provide observation data). Table 4-5 provides an example project plan.

Summary

Review your evaluation with the stakeholders and program team to gain support. The evaluation, ROI analysis, and project plans are excellent resources to educate stakeholders on how you will demonstrate the value of the program and gain buy-in to secure resources and funds. Using these plans will also help you acquire any technology or access to systems

PLANNING YOUR EVALUATION PROJECT

Table 4-5. Sample Project Plan

Project Title: _____   **Target Completion Date:** _____

Project Scope: _____

Deliverables	Time to Complete	Est. Cost to Complete	Timeline J F M A M J J A S O N D	Responsibility
Deliverable 1				
Task 1.1	____ hrs	$ ____		____
Task 1.2	____ hrs	$ ____		____
Task 1.3	____ hrs	$ ____		____
Task 1.4	____ hrs	$ ____		____
Estimated Cost of Deliverable 1		$ ____		
Deliverable 2				
Task 2.1	____ hrs	$ ____		____
Task 2.2	____ hrs	$ ____		____
Task 2.3	____ hrs	$ ____		____
Task 2.4	____ hrs	$ ____		____
Estimated Cost of Deliverable 2		$ ____		
Deliverable 3				
Task 3.1	____ hrs	$ ____		____
Task 3.2	____ hrs	$ ____		____
Task 3.3	____ hrs	$ ____		____
Estimated Cost of Deliverable 3		$ ____		
Estimated Cost of Time on Project		$ ____		

Other Resource Requirements (such as printing or technology): _____

CHAPTER 4

you plan to use for data collection methods. The planning documents are also helpful for aligning the evaluation team, including system owners, external sources, and others that you need to help you collect data.

Knowledge Check

Answer each of the questions listed here to check your knowledge. Then, review your answers in appendix B.

1. Why is evaluation planning important, and how can you use your evaluation plan to gain stakeholder alignment?
2. Why is it important to plan the timing of when you want to collect data? When should you collect impact data?
3. Why should your ROI analysis include a fully loaded cost?
4. What are some considerations when selecting your communication target audience?

PART 2
Data Collection

Data collection is the process of asking questions to gather insights about problems and opportunities and evaluate the success with objectives. Just what those questions are, how we should ask them, whom we should ask, and when we should ask depends on the objectives set during the planning phase (See part 1).

ROI Institute's *2020 Benchmarking Study* surveyed a small sample of measurement and evaluation practitioners. These individuals have had experience evaluating programs up to Level 5, ROI. One question asked was the frequency with which they used various data collection techniques. Not surprisingly, surveys and questionnaires are at the top in terms of frequency of use. These self-administered instruments are often used by default. It is important to consider other methods because surveys and questionnaires are often overused and, when used, poorly used. Performance records and the databases that house business measures are the second most frequently used. The easiest and least expensive approach to collecting impact data, this approach is not always feasible for those who are collecting data. For that reason, evaluators may use questionnaires, action plans, and other techniques, asking respondents to access the records and report their findings.

There is no one best way to collect evaluation data. Choosing the most appropriate approach to collect data depends on:
- Type of data
- Time requirements
- Resource constraints
- Cultural constraints

- Convenience
- Usability of the data

Part 2 focuses on some of the frequently used data collection methods. By reading it, you will learn how to:

- Design surveys to collect participant reaction.
- Design questionnaires and surveys for follow-up evaluation.
- Design and deliver tests.
- Conduct interviews.
- Conduct focus groups.
- Use action planning.

CHAPTER 5

Designing Learner Surveys
WILL THALHEIMER

IN THIS CHAPTER

This chapter explores learner surveys, an important tool in evaluating learning programs. After reading it, you will be able to:

- Capture data that provides information relevant to learning effectiveness.
- Use learner-survey questions that send stealth messages to motivate action.
- Avoid common mistakes and the weakest forms of learner-survey questions.

The Importance of Learner Surveys

Learner surveys are important because they can be easily deployed to get leverageable results. Indeed, because they are the most common method for evaluating learning—aside from measuring attendance and completion rates—we might consider them to be the most important method to get right.

Measuring attendance and completion rates can produce misleading results—employees might complete a course successfully but still not learn, or they can learn the wrong information or lose their motivation to apply what they've learned.

Well-designed learner surveys can gather data that is meaningful. And we can leverage them to make learning-design decisions—but only when they are rigorously designed.

CHAPTER 5

The Purpose of Evaluation

To see how learner surveys can be helpful, it's useful to consider the purpose of evaluation. Ultimately, we should be evaluating learning for the following reasons:

1. To make better decisions
2. To take better actions
3. To earn credibility (and in turn gain resources, autonomy, more learners, or more customers)

The first two reasons are paramount because if we make better decisions and take better actions, we'll build more effective learning; therefore, we'll gain credibility (the third reason) so we can continue to improve our effectiveness.

Can learner surveys help us make better decisions and take better actions? Absolutely! But only if they are well-designed. Are they perfect for making better decisions and taking better actions? Of course not. There are no perfect evaluation methods. Even with brilliantly designed learner surveys, we should also be measuring other learning outcomes.

Using LTEM to Discern the Value of Learner Surveys

LTEM (pronounced "L-tem") stands for the Learning-Transfer Evaluation Model and represents a full spectrum of key learning outcomes (Thalheimer 2018). It was designed to measure important results related to learning transfer, but it is not intended to measure other solutions (like performance support, management, or applications solely based on performance sciences). LTEM imbues learning evaluation practice with learning wisdom by including three separate learning outcomes: knowledge, decision competence, and task competence.

LTEM has eight tiers:
- Tier 1. Attendance and Completion (including completion rates and learner progress).
- Tier 2. Learner Activity (including participation, attention, and interest)
- Tier 3. Learner Perceptions (including learner surveys); You are here!
- Tier 4. Knowledge (including knowledge comprehended and remembered)
- Tier 5. Decision Making (including decision ability that is also remembered)
- Tier 6. Task Performance (including task competence that is also remembered)

- Tier 7. Transfer to Work Performance (demonstrated work performance)
- Tier 8. Effects of Transfer (with a nudge to consider multiple stakeholders, including beneficiaries, learners, the organization, customers, sponsors, co-workers, families, friends, investors, community, society, and the environs)

Notice that learner surveys are situated in LTEM Tier 3. This intentional placement is meant to convey that while learner surveys can be valuable, they should be augmented with objective evaluation methods—most notably at LTEM Tiers 4, 5, and 6 (to ascertain how well a learning program produced critical learning outcomes) and LTEM Tiers 7 and 8 (to determine how well it transferred to work performance and results).

Traditional Learner Surveys

Traditional learner surveys, which use Likert-like scales and numeric scales, have also been referred to as *reaction forms, smile sheets, post-course evaluations, student response forms, training reaction surveys,* and *Level 1 evaluations.* Unfortunately, one of these labels—evaluations—is particularly damaging and it's used too often. Using the term "evaluation" conveys the message that surveys are all we need when performing a learning evaluation. Such a notion is abhorrent to good evaluation practice.

Here are some commonly used (but poorly conceived) smile-sheet questions. We'll discuss their flaws later in this chapter:
- I was able to relate each of the learning objectives to the knowledge I gained.
    - *Answer options: strongly agree, agree, neutral, disagree, or strongly disagree*
- The scope of the material was appropriate to meet my needs.
    - *Answer options: 1 (strongly disagree), 2, 3, 4, 5, 6, or 7 (strongly agree)*
- What percentage of new knowledge and skills learned from this training do you estimate you will directly apply to your job?
    - *Answer options: 0%, 10%, 20%, 30%, 40%, 50%, 60%, 70%, 80%, 90%, or 100%*

Problems With Traditional Learner Surveys

There is wide skepticism about traditional learner surveys. A few years ago, I asked learning professionals how useful learner survey data was for helping them improve their learning practices. Most said "only somewhat" or "not very useful." Only 15 percent said their survey data was "very useful."

CHAPTER 5

Our skepticism is backed up by science. Two meta-analyses, which together looked at more than 150 scientific studies, found that smile sheets were correlated with learning results at r = 0.09, where anything below .30 was considered a weak correlation (Alliger et al. 1997; Sitzmann et al. 2008; Uttl, White, and Gonzalez 2008). From a practical standpoint, this means that high marks on our smile sheets could reflect a very effective course but are almost equally likely to reflect an ineffective one. If we get low marks, it's just as likely that our course is poorly designed or well-designed. With traditional smile sheets, we just can't tell.

Problems With Likert-Like Scales and Numeric Scales

One of the problems with smile sheets is that they typically use Likert-like scales (Shrock and Coscarelli 2007). These give learners a statement and ask them to choose between answer choices such as, "strongly disagree, disagree, neutral, agree, or strongly agree." Then, we turn these into numbers, where strongly agree = 5, agree = 4, and so forth.

Likert-like scales have many deficiencies:
- If data is clumped from 3.8 to 4.5, it's hard to determine whether the result is good or bad. It's possible to end up stuck and unsure about what to do.
- The average might seem good, like 4.1, but it's not clear how widely dispersed the data is or whether it's skewed to the right or left.
- The response words, like "strongly agree," are fuzzy and somewhat arbitrary, which makes it hard for learners to respond and hard for us to interpret the meaning of the data.
- Because the options aren't clear, bias is more likely to creep in.
- Data experts recommend avoiding transforming *nominal data* (data made of words, like "strongly agree") into *ordinal* or *interval data* (data made of numbers).
- Learners are not supported in their decision making when faced with these words.
- Learners may not be motivated to answer a wall of Likert-like questions.
- Likert-like scales do not inspire nudging thoughts and actions—so they are generally ineffective in sending stealth messages.

Numeric scales have similar issues and are likely to be even less clear than Likert-like scales.

Problems Resulting From Learners' Poor Intuitions About Learning

The Likert-scale problem is compounded by the fact that humans—when we think about learning—have many poor intuitions. One of the most important things for learning professionals to know—to be good learning designers—is that learners typically have inaccurate ideas about what makes learning effective. In practical terms, we can't just ask our learners what learning designs they prefer. We must also be very careful when we ask about the quality of a learning program they've experienced.

Here are a few examples:

- Researchers Eugene Zechmeister and John Shaughnessy (1980) found that learners are overly optimistic about their ability to remember what they've learned, so they tend to fail to give themselves enough repetition and practice.
- Psychologists Jeffrey Karpicke, Andrew Butler, and Henry Roediger (2009) found that learners fail to use retrieval practice to support long-term remembering, even though retrieval practice is one of the most powerful learning methods.
- Psychologists Panayiota Kendeou and Paul van den Broek (2005) found that learners don't always overcome their incorrect prior knowledge.
- Educational scientists Anja Prinz, Stefanie Golke, and Jorg Wittwer (2018) found that learners with prior misconceptions learned more poorly and made "more overconfident predictions of their [learning] than students who had fewer misconceptions."

The title of Zechmeister and Shaughnessy's famous research article says it all: "When You Know That You Know and When You Think That You Know But You Don't."

As if these examples weren't evidence enough, three recent scientific reviews—conducted by some of the most renowned learning researchers, including Henry L. Roediger, Mark A. McDaniel, and Peter C. Brown (2014); Paul Kirschner and Jeroen van Merriënboer (2013); and Matthew Rhodes (2016)—found that learners often have poor intuitions about what effective learning looks like.

What Do Good Survey Questions Look Like?

Should we ignore what our learners tell us? Should we avoid surveying them at all? No! But we must be thoughtful about how we're asking questions.

We've been surveying learners for decades. It's a tradition and habit that's unlikely to end. Also, it's respectful to ask our learners what they think. So, instead of avoiding surveying, we must improve the way we do it. For example:
- We must ask questions that learners can answer. That is, we must ask questions for which our learners are likely to have accurate intuitions and visibility into the issue being asked about.
- We must avoid biasing question stems and answer choices.
- We must give learners answer choices they can clearly parse and understand.
- We must ask questions that nudge our learners to think correctly about learning.
- We must ask questions about critical factors related to learning and performance.

Practitioner's Tip

For each question you want to include in your learner survey, ask what you are going to do with the data you get back. If you can narrow it down to a limited number of questions, it will be easier for participants to complete, and you'll ensure you don't have an overwhelming number of actions to take at a time. You can swap questions in and out of your survey over time depending on your priorities.

—Rosalyn Sword, Learning Consultant, Department for Business and Trade, United Kingdom.

Performance-Focused Learner Surveys

In 2016, I published the first book on performance-focused learner surveys. After further experience with hundreds of clients, I significantly upgraded the content, and in 2022 I published *Performance-Focused Learner Surveys: Using Distinctive Questioning to Get Actionable Data and Guide Learning Effectiveness.*

Performance-focused learner surveys leverage several innovations in survey methodology. First, they use the distinctive questioning approach—having answer choices that are more concrete and provide more inherent meaning than words like "strongly agree" and "agree." In the question shown in Table 5-1, you see these distinctive answer choices.

DESIGNING LEARNER SURVEYS

Table 5-1. A Distinctive Answer Sample Question

	HOW ABLE ARE YOU to put what you've learned into practice in your work? CHOOSE THE ONE OPTION that best describes your current readiness.
A	My CURRENT ROLE DOES NOT ENABLE me to use what I've learned.
B	I AM STILL UNCLEAR about what to do, and/or why to do it.
C	I NEED MORE GUIDANCE before I know how to use what I've learned.
D	I NEED MORE EXPERIENCE to be good at using what I've learned.
E	I CAN BE SUCCESSFUL NOW in using what I've learned (even without more guidance or experience).
F	I CAN PERFORM NOW AT AN EXPERT LEVEL in using what I've learned.

A second innovation in performance-focused learner surveys is their focus on learning effectiveness. Whereas traditional smile sheets tend to focus on learner satisfaction and course reputation, performance-focused learner surveys focus on factors aligned with learning effectiveness. One point of emphasis is to focus on the four pillars of training effectiveness:

- Motivation to apply the learning
- Understanding and comprehension of key concepts
- Remembering of key concepts and skills
- After-training support

Although other factors are also important for creating effective learning programs, if you do well on these four, you will certainly have a highly effective course.

Table 5-2 shows a question that focuses on understanding and comprehension.

Table 5-2. An Understanding and Comprehension Sample Question

	Now that you've completed the learning experience, how well do you understand the concepts taught? CHOOSE ONE.
A	I am still at least SOMEWHAT CONFUSED about the concepts.
B	I am now SOMEWHAT FAMILIAR WITH the concepts.
C	I have a SOLID UNDERSTANDING of the concepts.
D	I AM FULLY READY TO USE the concepts in my work.
E	I have an EXPERT-LEVEL ABILITY to use the concepts.

CHAPTER 5

Table 5-3 shows a question that focuses on after-training support.

Table 5-3. An After-Training Support Sample Question

	After the course, when you begin to apply this new knowledge at your worksite, which of the following supports are likely to be in place for you? **SELECT AS MANY ITEMS** as are likely to be true.
A	MY MANAGER WILL ACTIVELY SUPPORT ME with key supports like time, resources, advice, and encouragement.
B	I will use a COACH OR MENTOR to guide me in applying what I've learned to my work.
C	I will regularly receive support from a COURSE INSTRUCTOR to help me apply what I've learned to my work.
D	I will be given JOB AIDS like checklists, search tools, or reference materials to guide me in applying what I've learned to my work.
E	Through a LEARNING APP or other means, I will be PERIODICALLY REMINDED of key concepts and skills that were taught.
F	I will NOT get much direct support, but will rely on my own initiative.

Note how the answer choices in Tables 5-2 and 5-3 are distinctive. Learners can wrap their heads around each choice. In this way, we are supporting them in their decision making. By supporting their decisions, we get more meaningful data. Additionally, these questions educate learners about what matters in learning design. The question in Table 5-2 signals that a goal of learning is comprehension, which prompts learners to ask themselves, "Do I clearly understand the content?" The question in Table 5-3 makes a clear point: After-training supports are critical to learning transfer.

Hence, the third innovation in performance-focused learner surveys is that our questions can be used to send stealth messages—to nudge thinking and action. Note how Table 5-3 might get people thinking thoughts like:

- "Hmm, this course is important; maybe we ought to let participants' managers know what was taught and how they can support their direct reports in applying what they've learned."
- "Maybe for this course—because it's so complex—we should provide coaches back on the job."
- "Let's design some job aids to support people when they get back to work."

Think about that! Learner survey questions can help improve our learning practices beyond any data that gets collected. Our questions and answer choices can nudge the thinking

DESIGNING LEARNER SURVEYS

of a variety of stakeholders, including instructional designers, trainers, learners, senior leaders, and anyone else who looks at them.

The fourth innovation represented in performance-focused learner surveys is the standards that are assigned to each answer choice to clarify what the data means and limit interpretation bias. Without standards we tend to look at the data before determining what result is or isn't acceptable. This leads to bias.

An example of these standards is shown in the shaded column of Table 5-4. (Note that this column, along with the question rationale field, is not visible to anyone taking the survey.)

Table 5-4. Adding Answer-Choice Standards to Aid Data Interpretation

Question Rationale: Used to determine how prepared learners feel in being able to take what they've learned and use it in their work.		
HOW ABLE ARE YOU to put what you've learned into practice in your work? CHOOSE THE ONE OPTION that best describes your current readiness.		Proposed Standards *Not shown to learners.*
A	My CURRENT ROLE DOES NOT ENABLE me to use what I've learned.	Alarming
B	I AM STILL UNCLEAR about what to do, and/or why to do it.	Alarming
C	I NEED MORE GUIDANCE before I know how to use what I've learned.	Unacceptable
D	I NEED MORE EXPERIENCE to be good at using what I've learned.	Acceptable
E	I CAN BE SUCCESSFUL NOW in using what I've learned (even without more guidance or experience).	Superior
F	I CAN PERFORM NOW AT AN EXPERT LEVEL in using what I've learned.	Superior or overconfident

I recommend using simple standards, such as alarming, unacceptable, acceptable, superior, and superior or overconfident. (I provided roughly 50 candidate questions in *Performance-Focused Learner Surveys*—which you can use in your own learner survey—and listed standards for each answer choice.) But these standards are just a starting point. It's important to have a discussion within your learning team and negotiate with your key stakeholders to finalize what standards to use.

Note choice F's recommended standard in Table 5-4: "superior or overconfident." This standard is used with over-the-top answer choices and represents the fifth innovation in performance-focused learner surveys. Too often, learners hurry through the questions

CHAPTER 5

without thinking deeply about what we are asking. To slow them down, we can insert over-the-top, "too-good-to-be-true" answer choices. They should be written in such a way that most learners won't select them. If they do, we give them the benefit of the doubt that their response is "superior," but also note the "overconfident" caveat.

One additional innovation represented in performance-focused learner surveys is the data. Instead of looking at averages, which tend to hide information, we can look directly at the percentage of people who choose each answer choice.

In Figure 5-1, 42 percent of learners chose an acceptable response, 22 percent chose a superior option, and so on. (Note that although it's grayscale in this book, this image would normally be shown in color.) With this type of graphic, we are not losing information by transforming the data into numbers or averages. The less data is transformed, the less information is lost.

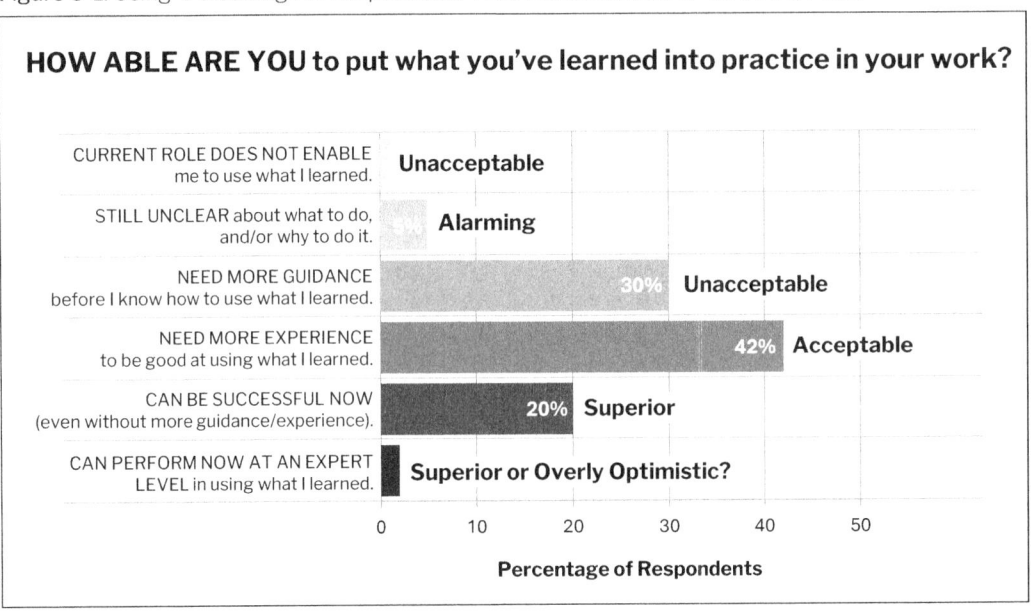

Figure 5-1. Using "Percentage of Respondents Who Selected Answer" as a Data Point

HOW ABLE ARE YOU to put what you've learned into practice in your work?

Response	Percentage	Rating
CURRENT ROLE DOES NOT ENABLE me to use what I learned.		Unacceptable
STILL UNCLEAR about what to do, and/or why to do it.		Alarming
NEED MORE GUIDANCE before I know how to use what I learned.	30%	Unacceptable
NEED MORE EXPERIENCE to be good at using what I learned.	42%	Acceptable
CAN BE SUCCESSFUL NOW (even without more guidance/experience).	20%	Superior
CAN PERFORM NOW AT AN EXPERT LEVEL in using what I learned.		Superior or Overly Optimistic?

Percentage of Respondents

Learners Like These New Questions

I expect your experience with learner surveys mirrors mine: Learners rarely like answering traditional Likert-like questions. They often circle the same number down a paper-based survey or rush through them. Likely, they assume that because we aren't asking very good questions, it isn't worth their time to thoughtfully complete the surveys.

Table 5-5 offers a question you can use to get a sense of how your own learners feel about these new learner survey questions.

Table 5-5. Evaluating Learner Sentiment for New Type of Survey Question

Question Rationale: Used to assess whether learners accept a survey based on this new type of learner-survey question.		
We're using a new type of question to get your feedback. Instead of using a scale from 1 to 5 or choices from strongly disagree to strongly agree, we're presenting questions with more specific answer choices. This question is an example. What do you think about these new questions?		Proposed Standards Not shown to learners
A	They HAVE ABOUT THE SAME LEVEL OF EFFECTIVENESS as the 1 to 5 questions or the strongly disagree to strongly agree questions.	Acceptable
B	They are BETTER because they GIVE ME MORE CLARITY about the choices I'm making.	Superior
C	They are WORSE because they TAKE MORE TIME to think through the answer choices.	Unacceptable
D	Their BENEFITS (BRINGING MORE CLARITY) OUTWEIGH their DOWNSIDES (TAKING MORE TIME).	Acceptable
E	Their BENEFITS (MORE CLARITY) ARE NOT WORTH the extra time required.	Unacceptable
Note: Learners are not shown the text in the gray cells of this table.		
Note: This question is useful if you have skeptical stakeholders. Use this question in your pilot program and first few deployments; then, remove it once you have enough data showing learners prefer these new questions.		

I once did some research using this question. I found two global organizations—the kind with lots of different types of courses. One was a for-profit organization and the second was a nonprofit. We looked at 20 different courses—including technical training, leadership training, other soft-skills courses, and compliance training—and used a performance-focused learner survey with the question in Table 5-5 placed at the end.

The results were stunning: 80 percent of learners liked the new questions better than traditional smile-sheet questions, and 90 percent liked the new questions better than or equal to the old-style questions.

I recommend using this question when you are first rolling out performance-focused learner surveys. You'll be able to see that learners like the new question style better and it reassures any stakeholders in your organization who are resistant to change.

Comment Questions

Comment questions that require open-ended responses are critical as well. Here are three excellent questions you could add to the end of your survey:

- What aspects of the training made it MOST EFFECTIVE FOR YOU? What should WE DEFINITELY KEEP as part of the training?
- What aspects of the training COULD BE IMPROVED? Remember, your feedback is critical, especially in providing constructive ideas for improvement.
- Is there anything else we should have asked? Is there anything you want to tell us?

Note how these questions use personal language. We don't want them to feel like they've come down from some cold, steely entity in corporate. We want to build a partnership with our learners so we get their best ideas for what's working and what's not.

Increasing Response Rates

One complaint some organizations have is that only a small percentage of learners complete learner surveys. This problem is so pervasive that I added a whole chapter in the second edition of my book to address it. I'll share the gist of that here.

There are many things you can do to improve your response rates but two are paramount. First, you need to ask better questions—questions that learners see as well-designed and meaningful. Second, you need to give learners time during the course to complete their surveys. Even waiting to send the survey link until five seconds after the program ends will seriously depress responses.

Other things you can do to increase your response rates include:

- Highlighting the importance and use of the surveys
- Making a personal appeal for the learner's thoughtful perspective
- Sharing with learners how you've used the data in the past
- Sharing with learners that you plan to make changes based on the data they and their fellow learners provide
- Highlighting the organization's values, especially in working together to make things better.

DESIGNING LEARNER SURVEYS

Note that it is counterproductive in the long term to provide incentives, conduct raffles, or pay people to complete learner surveys. These extrinsic incentives can work in the short term, but tend to undermine your learners' sense of autonomy and wreck any chance you have in encouraging them to think of their survey effort as an indication of who they are as a contributor and team player.

Summary

Performance-focused learner surveys offer significant improvements over traditional smile sheets. They are more motivating, produce more meaningful data, can send stealth messages to nudge thoughts and actions, and are an excellent way to build momentum for further learning evaluation improvements. Use the insights offered in this chapter into what good survey questions look like to adopt the performance-focused learner survey approach and get better data to evaluate your training programs.

Knowledge Check

Answer each of the questions listed here to check your knowledge. Then, review your answers in appendix B

Question 1

Sandra is an experienced learning designer and was recently charged with redesigning her organization's technical training program. She decided to use each course's previous evaluation results to improve the learning design. As she looked through the Likert-like question results, she noticed that learners rated the course on laboratory safety at an average of 3.2 on a 5-point scale compared with most other courses that averaged about 4.4. She decided to focus more attention on this lab safety class to dramatically improve it. If you were coaching Sandra, what would you say about this plan?

    A. Sandra, great job! It's good to focus attention where it is most clearly needed.

    B. Sandra, good job! But be careful because that data might be misleading.

    C. Sandra, watch out! Some learner surveys can provide poor information.

77

Question 2

Manny leads his company's learning analytics team and is excited about their current project developing a dashboard to highlight key data for the learning team. Although his team recommends piloting the dashboard using past data—which was gathered using 4-point scales from strongly disagree to strongly agree—Manny persuades the team to use questions with more distinctive answer choices. If you were coaching Manny, what would you tell him?

    A. Manny, it's good to use better question designs, but your dashboard is still incomplete.

    B. Manny, you made a great call in improving your learner survey question designs.

    C. Manny, using a sophisticated dashboard makes the question design less important.

CHAPTER 6

Designing Questionnaires and Surveys for Follow-Up Evaluation

CAROLINE HUBBLE

IN THIS CHAPTER

This chapter describes the questionnaire, which is one of the most common data collection instruments for gathering evaluation data. It is particularly useful when following up about the extent participants used the knowledge and skills learned and the resulting impact to the organization. After reading this chapter, you will be able to:

♦ Create the content for your questionnaire.
♦ Optimize the effectiveness of your questionnaire.
♦ Prepare your questionnaire for distribution.

Steps in Developing Questionnaires

Once evaluation planning is complete, the plans are put into motion thereby initiating data collection. Collecting the data is a critical activity in the evaluation process, and using effective and efficient data collection methods is essential. Because the questionnaire is one of the most valuable tools, it is important to complete these five steps:

1. Secure a plan.
2. Create the content.
3. Optimize the effectiveness.

4. Prepare for distribution.
5. Execute the tool.

By completing these steps and maintaining the scope of the data collection instrument, the foundation is set to gather the necessary data.

Securing a Plan for the Questionnaire

By definition, a *questionnaire* is an instrument designed to ask questions to capture a wide range of data, including attitudes and specific improvement data. A *survey*, which is a type of questionnaire, is more limited and focuses on capturing the respondents' attitudes, beliefs, and opinions (Phillips, Phillips, and Aaron 2013). Because of their ability to be customized to meet specific evaluation needs, questionnaires are frequently used for data collection. Don't assume, however, that they require minimal effort to implement. As with all projects, successfully using questionnaires requires a carefully thought-out plan.

A Clearly Defined Purpose Is Critical to Success

Successful questionnaires are built on sound design that is linked directly to the evaluation study's research questions. To be successful, consider the following:
- Why is the questionnaire needed?
- Based on the organization's needs, culture, and data sources, will a questionnaire work for gathering the data?
- Is a questionnaire the right instrument to collect the data?
- What research questions will the data answer?

Your answers will help you define the feasibility and purpose of the questionnaire. Referencing the data collection plan is also critical. The objectives, specific measures, and data sources provided in the plan help formulate the questionnaire's purpose and ensure the needed data, especially related to application and impact results, is captured.

Maintaining the Scope Keeps the Data Collection Focused

Once you decide the questionnaire is feasible and define its purpose, the next step is documenting its scope. While the questionnaire is a flexible tool that can collect a wide variety of data, this also presents a challenge if it evolves beyond its intended purpose. For

DESIGNING QUESTIONNAIRES AND SURVEYS FOR FOLLOW-UP EVALUATION

example, if you unintentionally or by request incorporate questions that aren't related to the study, the tool will lose focus.

To ensure this doesn't occur, it is essential to adhere to the questionnaire's scope, which is defined by its purpose and goals. Once you've documented the scope, you should maintain it throughout the questionnaire's life cycle.

Detailed Plans Ensure Critical Activities Are Completed

Once you identify the purpose and scope, create a detailed plan for the questionnaire's design, development, and implementation. In addition to the data collection plan, develop a portion of the evaluation project plan to identify the design, testing, and implementation steps (Table 6-1, on the next page). Once identified, incorporate the timeline and resources to complete the work (Table 6-2).

Table 6-2. Sample Evaluation Project Plan—Data Collection

ID	Task	Start	Finish	Resources	Done
2.1	Data collection				
2.1.1	Identify data utility	05.01.24	06.01.24	CH	X
2.1.2	Develop data collection instruments				
2.1.2.1	Create draft follow-up questionnaire	06.01.24	06.12.24	CH	X
2.1.2.2	Review	06.12.24	06.30.24	CH, team	X
2.1.2.2.1	Review with evaluation team	06.13.24	06.20.24	CH	X
2.1.2.2.2	Review with stakeholder team	06.21.24	06.22.24	Team	X
2.1.2.3	Update based on results	06.23.24	06.28.24	CH	X
2.1.2.4	Finalize and test follow-up questionnaire	06.29.24	07.06.24	CH, team	X
2.1.2.6	Develop high response strategy	06.01.24	07.06.24	CH, team	X
2.1.2.6	Finalize follow-up questionnaire communication	06.15.24	07.06.24	CH, team	X
2.1.3	Collect data during program				
2.1.3.1	Level 1 and Level 2 data using standard end-of-program survey and pre- and post-test	05.17.24	05.17.24	SH	X
2.1.4	Collect postprogram data				
2.1.4.1	Level 3 (Application) and Level 4 (Impact) data	07.15.24	07.29.24	CH, team	X
2.1.4.1.1	Implement follow-up questionnaire communications plan	07.10.24	07.31.24	CH, team	X
2.1.4.1.2	Implement follow-up questionnaire	07.15.24	07.15.24	CH, team	
2.1.4.1.3	Close follow-up questionnaire	07.29.24	07.29.24	CH	X

CHAPTER 6

Table 6-1. Sample Data Collection Plan

Level	Broad Program Objectives	Measures	Data Collection Method or Instruments	Data Sources	Timing	Responsibilities
1	**Reaction and Planned Action** • Relevance to job • Recommend to others • Overall satisfied with course • Learned new information • Intent to use material	• At the end of program, 90% of participants will rate the applicable questions a 4 out of 5	End of course evaluation	Participants	End of course	Participants Data in LMS Facilitator (introduce and remind)
2	**Learning and Confidence** • Increase in knowledge, skills, and attitudes regarding selling	• 100% of participants can demonstrate use of the five selling steps • 100% of participants achieve a passing score (85%) in one attempt on the end of program assessment	Role play End of program assessment	Participants	End of course	Facilitator Data in LMS
3	**Application and Implementation** • Ability to use selling steps (including extent able to use) • Frequency of using selling steps • Enablers and barriers to applying selling steps	• 100% of participants can successfully use the selling steps (4 out of 5 on the success scale) • 100% of participants achieve a passing score (85%) in one attempt on the end of program assessment	Questionnaire	Participants	60 days post course	Evaluation team and lead
4	**Business Impact** • Increase in sales of product ABC	• At least 5% increase quarterly in sales of product ABC	Business records	Finance	End of quarter (need to wait until the quarterly report is published to ensure time for improvement)	Program owner
5	**ROI** • N/A	**Comments:** Evaluating program to Level 4: Impact				

Keep in mind the importance of factoring in sufficient time for development and testing. Although they're time consuming, these activities are important because it's extremely challenging to change an implemented questionnaire without compromising the study's credibility.

> **Practitioner's Tip**
>
> Consider how you will use a questionnaire throughout the overall program's timeline. For example, if a program occurs over months, you may need to collect participants' feedback, actions taken, and so on, at different intervals (after the third, sixth, and last session, as well as two months after it ends). Within the plans, be sure to document when you will administer a questionnaire with the appropriate questions.

Creating the Questionnaire's Content

After you document the purpose and outline of the plan, the next task is to develop the questionnaire's content. This process is probably the most labor-intensive part and involves two primary activities: determining the structure and developing the actual questions. These steps ensure the questionnaire has the elements necessary for gathering the data to answer the study's research questions.

The Structure of the Questionnaire Identifies Where to Put the Content

Outlining what and where the content should be placed within the questionnaire is the first step in successfully creating the content. Providing all the relevant information, instructions, and questions in the appropriate place and in an organized manner ensures the respondents can provide accurate and valuable data. A questionnaire has three main areas: the introduction, body, and conclusion.

The Introduction Sets the Tone

The introduction is the first section of the questionnaire the respondent reads, and it sets the tone for the remainder of the instrument. Because of this, include all relevant information to engage the reader. The primary content includes informing the respondents of the purpose of the questionnaire and evaluation study, why they were chosen to participate,

CHAPTER 6

what will be done with the data they provide, the completion date, and a point of contact if assistance is needed. When collecting follow-up data (such as application or impact results), it can be helpful to include a sentence or two to refresh their memory about the program. Finally, incorporate any other specific details, such as whether their responses will remain anonymous and the estimated time it will take to complete.

The Body Drives Successful Data Collection

The body is where the questions are incorporated. Use different sections to keep the questions organized and the respondent focused. A best practice is to divide the questions into sections based on the levels of evaluation, which provides a flow for success.

The Conclusion Thanks the Respondent

Finalizing the questionnaire with a short conclusion section acknowledges the end of the questions and provides an opportunity to thank the respondent for their time and contributions. This section can also include any final instructions and reminders. If using a paper-based questionnaire, provide critical information such as reminding the respondent what to do with the completed document. Finally, repeat the point of contact information in case the respondent would like to follow up.

Developing the Perfect Question Involves a Few Critical Steps

Of all the activities involved in developing a questionnaire, creating the actual questions is the most important and time-consuming task. Asking the right question the right way supports the data collection goals and efficient data analysis. By following three key steps, you increase your opportunity to collect the data you require: identify the question's intent, determine the type of question, and finalize the question.

Identify the Question's Intent

A question's intent is based on the specific objectives identified on the data collection plan. For each evaluation level where data is needed, the specific measure defines the exact data to collect to determine whether the program's objective was achieved. This information forms the intent of the questions.

Determine the Type of Question

Question types range from close-ended to open-ended and from rank order to rating scale; selecting the right one ensures you're asking the question the right way (Figure 6-1).

Figure 6-1. Sample Question Types

Close-Ended Questions

Multiple Choice
While applying the skills and knowledge acquired from the leadership development program, I was supported or enabled by the following (select all that apply):
- ☐ Management
- ☐ Colleagues and peers
- ☐ Confidence to apply
- ☐ Networking
- ☐ Other (please specify)

Single Answer
Of the measures provided here, which one is most directly influenced by your application of the collaborative problem-solving process?
- ☐ Personal productivity
- ☐ Cost savings M Sales/revenue M Quality
- ☐ Time savings
- ☐ Other (please specify)

Open-Ended Questions

Free Text
In addition to the above, what other benefits have been realized by the leadership development program? Use this text box to provide your answer.

[   ]

Numeric
Approximately how many new sales leads did you identify as a result of your participation in the sales marketing retreat?

Rank or Order Question

For there to be successful virtual networking within the virtual learning community, rank the following items in order of importance, with 1 being the most important and 5 the least important:
- Discussion groups
- Professional place to meet with program peers and faculty (e.g., chat rooms)
- Student, alumni, and professor contact information
- Student expertise captured, shared, and valued
- Student personal and professional profiles (e.g., interests and success stories)

Figure 6-1. (continued)

Rating Scale Questions				
Likert Since attending the leadership development program, you have confidence in your ability to meet with individuals to discuss performance concerns.				
Strongly Agree	Agree	Neither Agree nor Disagree	Disagree	Strongly Disagree
Semantic Differential Based on your participation in the brand awareness seminar, please indicate the extent to which your attitude has improved regarding the company's brand message.				
No Improvement	1	2	3	4	5	Significant Improvement

When selecting the question type, consider the consequences of the question format. For example, open-ended questions enable the respondent to freely provide information but may require extensive analysis. For rating-type questions, the choice of an odd- or even-number scale depends on the questionnaire's goal, but there is no conclusive right or wrong option (Fink 2003).

Finalize the Question

Well-written content further guarantees that the right question is being asked the right way and you'll collect the necessary data. As you formulate each question, keep a consistent point of view (first or second person), tone, and tense. It should not contain unfamiliar words, acronyms, or make assumptions about what the respondent knows.

When working with rating-type questions, confirm that the question's statements align with the actual options available. If rating scales involve terminology (for example, very successful to not successful), provide definitions for each choice. This will not only help the respondent select the most accurate choice for their situation but ensure the question's intent is understood by all respondents. Last, review (or have someone else review) the questions to validate that they do not contain leading or loaded statements that could influence the respondent to answer a certain way.

Optimizing the Effectiveness of the Questionnaire

Two final steps are needed before launching a questionnaire. First, draft and review the completed questionnaire to ensure you incorporated the necessary information. Second, test the instrument. Completing these steps ensures optimal questionnaire effectiveness and, thus, success with data collection.

Draft Questionnaires Validate That the Elements Are Incorporated

Drafting the questionnaire ties the content together to develop the completed data collection instrument. This is your opportunity to review the questionnaire's introduction, body, and conclusion to confirm you've included the necessary information. A thorough review also verifies that the questionnaire has an appropriate flow and reading level, and that its overall appearance is professional and appealing. While reviewing the draft, consider how you will administer the questionnaire. Does the survey tool support the type of questions and functionality (for instance, skip logic) needed to administer the questionnaire?

Review the specific content to validate that you have integrated questions that give you the necessary data to complete the analysis. Finally, review the entire document for typos and other editing elements. Remember, the final draft should be an accurate, complete representation of the questionnaire so you can test it to confirm it is ready for distribution.

Questionnaire Tests Confirm Content and Functionality

Completing a thorough test of the tool is one consistent activity that occurs with successful questionnaires. The four main areas to focus on during testing are accuracy, functionality, experience, and alignment. The feedback regarding these areas either confirms the soundness of the tool or provides insight into improvements that need to occur before you administer it. Ask a sample of the actual respondent population (or individuals who are similar to the respondent group) to complete a test run. Developing a document or specific process to capture the required feedback from the test group is a best practice.

Functionality

Whether you administer the questionnaire electronically or by paper, you need to test the functionality of the tool. With an electronic questionnaire, make sure links work, all features are functioning correctly (for example, drop-down boxes, rankings, and so on), and other specific elements are performing as desired (for instance, moving between pages, skip-logic, and so on). For a paper-based questionnaire, review the layout to ensure there is adequate space for responses and the respondent can see the questions.

Experience

Another valuable area to enlist feedback involves the actual experience of completing the questionnaire. Ask the test group to provide feedback about the questionnaire's appearance, flow, layout, and ease of completion. This information, along with identifying how long it took to complete it, further supports a successful launch.

Accuracy

Accuracy of the questionnaire involves confirming that it includes the necessary content, asks the right questions the right way, and provides the appropriate instructions. Also review the validity and reliability of the instrument during the test. To be an effective data collection instrument, the questionnaire needs to provide consistent results over time (reliability) and measure what it is intended to measure (validity; Phillips et al. 2019).

Results

One area that is frequently overlooked during the questionnaire's development involves how you will use and analyze the collected data. After you have the results of the test, review them to confirm their utility. Can you analyze the results to answer the research questions? Can you compare the results with the baseline data? Addressing these types of questions prior to the launch allows you to make adjustments, which ultimately supports efficient data analysis.

Preparing for the Questionnaire's Distribution

With the questionnaire completed, there are few final steps to successfully collecting the data: finalizing the respondent population and performing administrative tasks to prepare for the questionnaire's distribution.

The Right Respondent Group Reinforces Credibility

Determining the respondent population is a key step that you must complete before launching the questionnaire and its information that should be captured in the data collection plan. The sources represent individuals who can provide relevant and accurate information based on their experiences in the program. When using the questionnaire to capture feedback or program follow-up data, you may also have to validate whether the respondent population is still accurate. Because follow-up questionnaires are administered somewhere between 60 and 90 days after participation, there may be changes to the respondents' details (such as having an updated email address or no longer being part of the organization). Completing this quick validation step will help ensure you have the right individuals and contact information.

Once you verify the population as a credible source, the next step is to determine the sample size, which includes how many people will receive the questionnaire, the confidence interval and level, the degree of variability, and the organization's normal response rate (Watson 2001). Table 6-3 outlines the steps for determining the sample size. These factors, and using a sample size table, determine the sample size.

Table 6-3. How to Determine the Sample Size

Step	Example
1. Determine the population size.	350
2. Determine the confidence interval (e.g., margin of error or result's accuracy).	±5
3. Determine the confidence level (i.e., risk you are willing to accept that the sample is within the average).	95% confidence
4. Determine the degree of variability (i.e., the degree to which concepts measured are distributed within the population).	• Estimate divided more or less 50%–50% on the concepts • Using a sample size table, the base sample size needed is 187
5. Estimate the response rate to determine final sample size needed.	Based on the organization's normal 85% response rate, the final sample size needed is 220 (187/0.85)

Source: Watson (2001)

The final consideration is determining whether the responses will be anonymous. Maintaining respondent confidentiality encourages open, candid responses; there is a link associated between respondents remaining anonymous and their honesty (Phillips and Stawarski 2008). If it is challenging to collect anonymous responses, one option is to have a third party resource collect the results.

Administrative Tasks Clear the Path for a Seamless Launch

Obtaining a 100 percent response rate is the ultimate goal. Although this is not always feasible, there are strategies that support achieving high response rates. Guiding Principle 6 of the ROI Methodology states that if no improvement data is available for a population or from a specific source, you can assume that little or no improvement has occurred (Phillips and Phillips 2019). Following this principle, if individuals do not provide data via the questionnaire, you should not make any assumptions about their improvements. Therefore, it is critical to obtain as many responses as possible to ensure you have the data needed to answer the research questions. Here are some strategies for improving your chances of reaching the desired response rate (Phillips, Phillips, and Aaron 2013):

- Have a top executive, administrator, or stakeholder sign the introduction letter.
- Indicate who will see the results of the questionnaire.
- Inform the participants what action will be taken with the data.
- Keep the questionnaire simple and as brief as possible.
- Make it easy to respond—include an addressed, stamped envelope or email address.
- If appropriate, tell the target audience they're part of a carefully selected sample.
- Send a summary of results to the target audience.
- Review the questionnaire at the end of the formal session.
- Add an emotional appeal.
- Allow for completion of the survey during work hours.
- Design the questionnaire with a professional format that attracts attention.
- Use the local point of contact to distribute the questionnaire.
- Identify champions to show support and encourage responses.
- Provide an incentive (or chance for incentive) for a quick response.
- Consider paying for the time it takes to complete the questionnaire.

Additionally, you should develop and follow a comprehensive communication strategy that outlines the content, the delivery method, and the timeline.

Content

The content provides information respondents need to be fully aware about the questionnaire and its purpose. The details include a reminder about the program's objectives, along with the action needed, the process for successfully providing the information, and the expected use of their response. Other information to incorporate includes the point of contact for questions, completion due date, and approximate time it will take to complete the questionnaire. Last, identify relevant information about reminders and thank you communications.

Delivery Method

Although written communication is the most common method, using other delivery methods (for example, reminder phone calls, in-person dialogue, and text reminders) can positively influence the response rate. Having executives or managers communicate the information about the questionnaire increases the awareness and potential response rate.

Timeline

The timeline is the last piece of the communication strategy. As needed, adjust the timeline to prevent distraction with other initiatives. To further support achieving the desired response rate, build in extra time in the event that you need to extend the questionnaire's response time.

Executing the Questionnaire to Collect the Data

With all the elements in place, it is finally time to launch the questionnaire (Figure 6-2). On implementation day, prepare the communication and, if applicable, verify that the electronic questionnaire is ready to accept responses. A best practice is to check for responses shortly after launching the questionnaire. If you receive responses, you have confirmation that the process is working. However, if you don't receive responses, you can double-check that the questionnaire request was received and that it is functioning properly. Provide a response rate when sending out reminders to further encourage individuals to complete the questionnaire. Finally, once you've collected the responses, officially close the questionnaire and begin analyzing the data.

Practitioner's Tip

Make sure to build time into your plan to introduce the follow-up questionnaire activity with the response population. Introduce them to the questionnaire's purpose and why their input is important. If the questionnaire asks for specific data, such as the estimated monetary value of a business measure's improvement, take time to discuss that and share examples. Last, emphasizing the importance of providing responses, even if it is an estimate, will help ensure you have usable data for analysis and reporting.

—Elizabeth A. Bishop, EdD, Senior Talent Development Advisor, St. Jude Children's Research Hospital

CHAPTER 6

Figure 6-2. Sample Follow-Up Questionnaire

Our records indicate that you participated in the leadership program. Your participation in this follow-up questionnaire is important to the program's continuous improvement and the effect the program is having on the organization. Completing this questionnaire will take approximately 30 minutes, and we request your responses by January 31, 2025. Should you have any questions, please contact caroline@roiinstitute.net. Thank you in advance for your contributions!

Application

1. I used at least one technique from the leadership program to improve my leadership capabilities.

    Strongly disagree   Disagree   Neutral   Agree   Strongly agree

2. I completed at least one step in my action plan for becoming a better leader.

    Strongly disagree   Disagree   Neutral   Agree   Strongly agree

3. I applied the leadership framework I learned during my participation in the leadership program (select the applicable answer).
    - ☐ Completely successful (completed independently, with no assistance)
    - ☐ Generally successful (can complete without assistance more than 50% of the time)
    - ☐ Somewhat successful (can complete without assistance less than 50% of the time)
    - ☐ No success (not able to complete, even with assistance)
    - ☐ No opportunity to use

4. I spend the following percent of my total work time on tasks that require the knowledge and skills covered in the leadership program (select the applicable answer).

    0%   10%   20%   30%   40%   50%   60%   70%   80%   90%   100%

5. While applying the knowledge and skills from the leadership program, I was supported by the following (check all that apply).
    - ☐ Tools and templates provided
    - ☐ My management
    - ☐ Colleagues and peers
    - ☐ Confidence to apply the materials
    - ☐ Networking
    - ☐ Other, please describe: _____

6. The following deterred or prevented me from applying the leadership program's knowledge and skills (check all that apply).
    - ☐ No opportunity to use the material
    - ☐ Lack of support from management
    - ☐ Not enough time
    - ☐ Lack of confidence to do it
    - ☐ Lack of resources
    - ☐ Other, please describe: _____

Impact

7. As a result of applying the skills I attained from the leadership program, the listed measures have improved as follows. (Note: When answering these questions please reference the following scale.)
    - No improvement = The measure has improved by 0% in the past three months.
    - Limited improvement = The measure has improved by at least 25% in the past three months.
    - Some improvement = The measure has improved by at least 50% in the past three months.

- Strong improvement = The measure has improved by at least 75% in the past three months.
- Significant improvement = The measure has improved by at least 90% in the past three months.
- N/A = This measure is not applicable to my work.

	No Improvement	Limited Improvement	Some Improvement	Strong Improvement	Significant Improvement	N/A
Productivity	☐	☐	☐	☐	☐	☐
Sales and revenue	☐	☐	☐	☐	☐	☐
Quality of work	☐	☐	☐	☐	☐	☐
Cost savings	☐	☐	☐	☐	☐	☐
Efficiency	☐	☐	☐	☐	☐	☐
Time savings	☐	☐	☐	☐	☐	☐
Teamwork	☐	☐	☐	☐	☐	☐
Innovation	☐	☐	☐	☐	☐	☐
My job satisfaction	☐	☐	☐	☐	☐	☐
My employees' job satisfaction	☐	☐	☐	☐	☐	☐
Customer satisfaction	☐	☐	☐	☐	☐	☐
Other	☐	☐	☐	☐	☐	☐

If other is selected, please describe the other measures that were positively influenced by the program. _____

8. Recognizing that the other factors could have influenced these improvements, I estimate the percent of improvement that is attributable (i.e., isolated) to the leadership program to be (express as a percentage where 100% represents fully attributable): _____%

9. My confidence in the estimation provided in the previous question is (0% = no confidence; 100% = certainty): _____%

10. I have the following suggestions for improving the leadership program: _____
_____
_____
_____

Thank you again for your time and valuable contributions!

CHAPTER 6

Summary

The data you collect is only as good as the instrument you use to collect it. Use the step-by-step process for implementing questionnaires provided in this chapter as part of your measurement and evaluation process—from proper planning before you create the questionnaire and constructing effective questions to preparing to distribute and eventually executing it. By following these steps, you can ensure you receive valid and reliable data that's ready to analyze.

Knowledge Check

For each question, select the best formatted and written option. After you've finished, check your answers in appendix B.

Question 1

Option A:

Did you experience barriers to applying what you learned in the program?
- ❑ Yes
- ❑ No
- ❑ Other (please specify)

Option B:

While applying the knowledge and skills acquired from your ICT procurement for practitioners program participation, what barriers deterred or prevented you from successfully applying what you learned? (Check all that apply.)
- ❑ Lack of adequate resources available
- ❑ Lack of confidence to apply knowledge and skills
- ❑ Lack of knowledge and skills required to improve performance
- ❑ Lack of peer support
- ❑ Lack of supervisor or manager support
- ❑ Lack of sufficient time to apply
- ❑ No opportunity to use
- ❑ Other barriers to application (please specify)

Question 2

Option A:

Using the new call tracking database has increased my productivity by _____%.

Option B:

Using the new, top-of-the line call tracking database has helped me be more productive.
- ❏ Strongly agree
- ❏ Agree
- ❏ Disagree
- ❏ Strongly disagree

Question 3

Option A:

Since your participation in the program, have you frequently used the five processing steps?
- ❏ Yes
- ❏ No
- ❏ Other (please specify)

Option B:

Since your participation in the program, how frequently have you used the five processing steps?
- ❏ Complete daily
- ❏ Complete at least once a week
- ❏ Complete every two weeks
- ❏ Complete at least once a month
- ❏ Complete at least once in past six months
- ❏ N/A (no opportunity to use)

Question 4

Option A:

As a result of participating in the process X program, to what extent were you able to use the five processing steps?
- ❏ Completely successful (guidance not needed)
- ❏ Somewhat successful (some guidance needed)
- ❏ Limited success (guidance needed)
- ❏ No success (not able to do even with guidance)
- ❏ N/A (no opportunity to use)

Option B:

Where you able to successfully use the five process steps?
- ❏ Yes
- ❏ No

Question 5

Option A:

As a result of the team building conference, there has been a reduction in silo-thinking in the departments.
- ❏ Strongly agree
- ❏ Agree
- ❏ Disagree
- ❏ Strongly disagree

Option B:

As a result of the team building conference, the sharing of best practices across departments has occurred.
- ❏ Strongly agree
- ❏ Agree
- ❏ Disagree
- ❏ Strongly disagree

CHAPTER 7

Designing and Delivering Tests

CINDY L. HILL AND ERIC T. VINCENT

IN THIS CHAPTER

This chapter describes the process of creating valid and defensible criterion-referenced tests for measuring an individual's performance against a standard of competency. After reading it, you will be able to:

- Plan a test that measures what it claims to measure.
- Create test items.
- Determine a cut-off score.
- Evaluate the items to ensure proper functioning.

Foundations of Test Design

Tests should measure what they claim to measure consistently and reliably while also being fair to all examinees. The test content should be relevant to the job, and the test results should help stakeholders make effective decisions. The degree to which a test has these qualities is indicated by two technical properties (reliability and validity) and one learner-centered property (fairness).

A test score is reliable if it is dependable, repeatable, and produces consistent information. A reliable test consistently yields similar scores for examinees with comparable levels of knowledge and skills. Scores are reliable when they are free from measurement error—unaffected by inconsistencies irrelevant to the purpose of the test. A test score is valid when it measures the specific knowledge and skills that the test intended to measure.

CHAPTER 7

Reliability and validity should not be viewed as absolutes but on continuums. So, how reliable and valid does a test have to be? The answer depends on the consequences of testing error. If the decisions based on the results are critical to protecting the health and safety of clients or employees, or are essential to the organization's survival, then the test should have very little error. This means the test needs evidence of high reliability and validity.

Fairness refers to the equitable treatment of all examinees throughout the testing process and a lack of bias in the test itself. Equitable treatment in the testing process includes appropriate and standardized testing conditions, as well as appropriate testing conditions for examinees with disabilities. Bias occurs when one group has an unfair advantage over another in answering test items correctly. The language of test items should promote the test's primary purpose, which is to accurately measure the relevant characteristics of the examinees. Bias can introduce errors that influence an examinee's performance. While absolute fairness in testing may not be possible, it should always be the goal.

Validity, reliability, and fairness are the foundation of test design and must be kept at the forefront of the designer's mind as they plan the test, create the test items, set the passing standard, and evaluate the performance of the test items and the test itself. Figure 7-1 depicts how validity, reliability, and fairness are closely connected and depend on one another, contributing individually and collectively to the quality and effectiveness of a test.

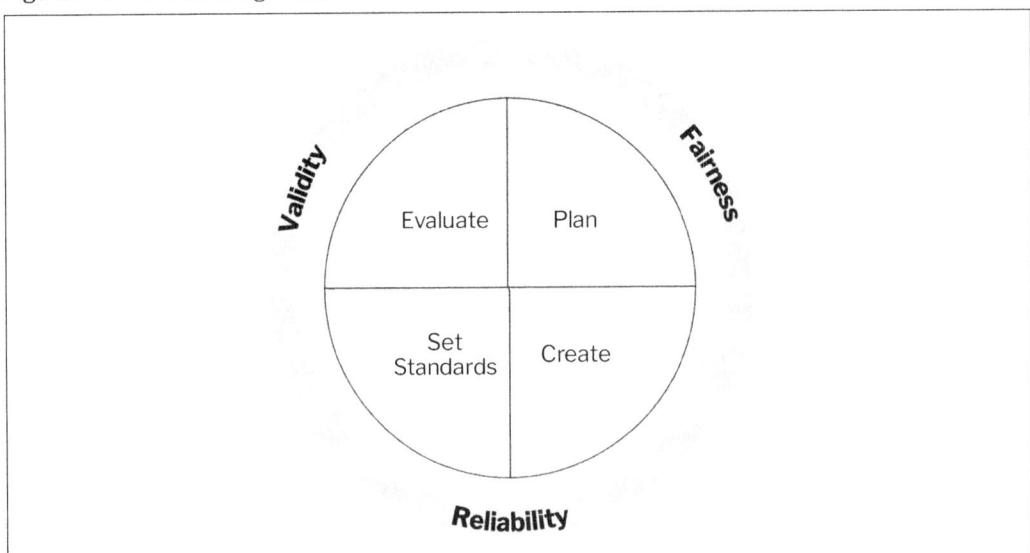

Figure 7-1. The Test Design Process

Plan the Test

A test plan defines the scope of the test—delineating its objectives and limitations—and guides the test's development and use. The key to developing a reliable, valid, and fair test is to make a test plan and follow it throughout the test's development and delivery process. The amount of detail in a test plan depends on its purpose. However, all test plans should be documented in writing and provide specific answers to these basic questions:

- What are the purpose, goals, and desired outcomes?
- Who will you test? (For example, what is their age, gender, race, language proficiency, and reading level?)
- What item formats will you use?
- How many test items will you need?
- How much time will you need or allocate for the test?
- How will you deliver the test?
- What is the timeline for development?
- What resources (including labor) will you require?
- Who will receive the results, and how will you deliver and explain them?

The purpose of the test determines whether it should be criterion- or norm-referenced. A criterion-referenced test compares an examinee's performance to a predetermined, specific, and measurable objective standard. Criterion-referenced tests are typically used to check whether trainees have mastered the training content and to evaluate the training program's effectiveness. A norm-referenced test compares the score to a norming group and reports where the examinee falls in relation to other examinees as a percentile. For example, a percentile of 75 indicates that the examinee's test performance equals or exceeds 75 out of 100 examinees on the test.

Number of Items

A test reflects a sample of an examinee's knowledge, skills, or abilities (KSAs) as they relate to performing a task. A typical driving test is an example. If the driving test occurs in a small rural area, we can't be confident that the person can drive in a large city; or, if the test occurs on a sunny day, we can't be confident the person can drive in poor weather conditions. The best we can do is take an adequate sample so we're confident saying the examinee has the KSAs to perform the task. A longer test generally allows for a more accurate and reliable assessment than a shorter test, but they are more expensive to create and administer (Shrock and Coscarelli 2007).

When deciding how many items to include for each content area, consider the following:
- **Criticality.** Can the outcomes affect the safety of employees, the public, or clients? Can they affect the company's success (for example, the bottom line)? If yes, assign more items for the test overall or to that area.
- **Consequences.** What are the consequences of misclassifying someone based on the results of the test? For example, would a low score mean they simply have to retake a 30-minute online class or would it make them ineligible for a promotion? Severe consequences require more items.
- **Size.** How large is the sample of KSAs being covered by the test? Larger numbers of KSAs require more items.
- **Homogeneity.** The greater the similarity of the material, the fewer test items are needed. For example, a test covering addition and multiplication doesn't require as many items as one covering addition, multiplication, subtraction, and division.
- **Resources.** This is where practicalities come in. Administering a three-hour test with 150 items might be desired, but is it worth the resources required to develop such a test, and can employees be spared for three hours to take it?

By forming and using a test plan throughout the development and delivery process, stakeholders will be much more confident that the test is measuring what it is supposed to measure. More importantly, you'll be able to determine whether employees gained the competencies required and critical decisions can be made based on the results.

Create the Test Items

Test items in an exam can take different forms. For example, a test item may present a question with a set of response options, provide instructions for a written response, offer a statement for individuals to express their agreement level, or provide task-based instruction to create a product or follow a procedure. In a training context, test items should be chosen to match and evaluate the achievement of learning outcomes.

Learning Outcomes and Cognitive Levels

Learning outcomes are statements about what learners should achieve. Some outcomes are simple while others are more complex, requiring time for learners to develop specific KSAs. Ensuring alignment between outcomes and test items is crucial to validate if learners have achieved these outcomes.

Learning outcomes typically adhere to Bloom's cognitive levels, but a summative test can be successfully designed using only three cognitive levels—recall, interpretation, and problem solving—each blending two of Bloom's levels:

- **Recall** (remember and understand). These test items show whether the examinee remembers the facts, details, concepts, principles, and procedures relevant to the subject area. Examples include:
  - Describe the steps of the process . . .
  - Define the meaning of . . .
  - Identify the missing step . . .
- **Interpretation** (apply and analyze). These test items use information to summarize, compare, translate, and make judgments about the meaning of a phenomenon or situation. Examples include:
  - What is the most (least) effective method for . . .
  - Explain the cause of . . .
  - Make a table that summarizes . . .
- **Problem solving** (evaluate and create). These test items use acquired knowledge and understanding to find solutions to new or unfamiliar situations. Examples include:
  - Identify the next step to solve this problem . . .
  - Devise a procedure to accomplish . . .
  - Create a new procedure to . . .

Item Writing Best Practices

Test items should be well written so the examinee can concentrate on answering the question, rather than trying to understand what it means. Items should measure important content, avoid complication, and follow these best practices:

- **Significance**. Include content that is both useful and relevant for demonstrating competence, and avoid including trivia or concepts learned before the training course.
- **Clarity and readability**. Clear items are straightforward, understandable, and unambiguous. Readability refers to using a sentence structure and vocabulary that is suitable for the intended audience.
- **Style consistency**. Provide item writers with guidelines on grammar, terminology, graphic quality, font style and size, abbreviations, acronyms, and best practices to ensure consistent and parallel construction.
- **Plausibility**. Plausible items help test takers engage meaningfully, preventing confusion or frustration. Incorrect options should seem reasonable to those who aren't familiar with the training material.
- **Additional resources**. Calculators, dictionaries, work documents, computer systems, and other equipment may be needed to answer items assessing certain learning outcomes.

Multiple Choice

A multiple-choice item comprises a *stem* (either a question or a statement) and its *options*—the choices provided, including the *key* (the correct answer) and *distractors* (the incorrect answers). While research supports the use of three options instead of four, all options should be of consistent quality and plausibility (Haladyna and Rodriguez 2013).

Best practices for writing item stems include:

- **Level**. Is the topic at the appropriate cognitive level?
- **Positive framing**. Item stems should guide examinees to identify correct answers rather than incorrect ones. Avoid negative framing (such as the terms *not*, *except*, and *least*) unless necessary. If used, capitalize and bold or underline the negative word in the stem, refraining from additional negatives in the options.
- **Clueing**. Avoid providing unfair advantages to test wise but unprepared examinees by eliminating clues. Refrain from repeating stem words exclusively in the key and avoid additional grammar clues, such as ensuring singular or plural agreement or using "a or an" to indicate the key's starting letter.
- **Window dressing**. Provide essential information without introducing unnecessary details that could complicate understanding the question. Stems

should only present sufficient background information to clarify the situation or context.
- **Focus**. Examinees should be able to make a reasonable guess about the answer before reviewing the answer options. The stem should be focused enough to guide examinees' thoughts in the correct direction.
- **One question**. Each item should test only one concept. A two-part question doesn't enable the test developer to determine if the examinee understands both parts, or if they simply guessed on one part.

Best practices for writing item options include:
- **One correct answer**. Mark only one option as correct; the others should be incorrect but plausible for guessers. If there's no universally agreed-upon correct answer, consider the "best" answer the one that experts would deem to be the best among the options.
- **Homogeneity**. All options should have similar content, grammatical structure, and length for consistency.
- **No overlap**. Options should be mutually exclusive and distinctive. They should not overlap, be equivalent to, or be contained within any other option.
- **Logical order**. Whenever possible, present options in chronological, ascending, descending, or alphabetical order.

Set Standards

Standard setting ensures that test scores accurately reflect the KSAs being assessed and establishes clear benchmarks for classifying test takers into different levels of achievement or proficiency. This helps maintain the validity and fairness of the assessment process, providing reliable results that can be used for decision-making purposes.

The standard is essentially the *threshold score* (or *cut score*), which separates test takers into different levels: Those scoring below the score are classified into one level, while those scoring at or above it are placed into the next, higher level. The most common standard-setting method involves establishing a single cut score to categorize test takers into a "pass" or "fail" group. Setting the cut score too low can result in inadequate skill development and reduced work quality; setting it too high can result in wasted resources and the exclusion of competent trainees. Overall, it is essential to strike the right balance to ensure that the cut score accurately reflects the desired level of effective training and skill development without being overly prohibitive.

CHAPTER 7

Criterion-Referenced Cut Score Methods

Criterion-referenced tests need a reliable method to avoid arbitrary or inconsistent classification of examinees. Common methods for setting these standards include:

- **The Angoff method** is the most widely researched method (Cizek and Earnest 2016). Table 7-1 outlines the steps for completing a modified Angoff method to set a cut score.

Table 7-1. Modified Angoff Steps

Step	Directions
1	Select an expert panel • Experts represent diverse factors like race, gender, age, and location. • Experts understand the traits of minimally competent practitioners.
2	Define minimal competence • Experts review the test content outline, course objectives, and job analysis data. • Document specific examples of expected performance, such as "What errors are unacceptable?" and "What knowledge is essential?" • "Imagine a line of 100 trainees ranked from most to least knowledgeable. Decide when to stop and identify the point where someone has the minimum knowledge required to pass the test."
3	Administer the test to experts • Experts take the test to enhance their understanding of the test items. • The average expert score can be used to ensure the passing score isn't set too high.
4	Initial item ratings • Provide a copy of the test, answer key, item difficulties (if available), and rating form. • Remind experts to rate no higher than 95% due to test anxiety and measurement error and no lower than the probability of guessing. Base ratings on likely outcomes rather than ideal outcomes. • Ask experts to estimate the percentage of minimally competent trainees out of 100 who they believe will answer each item correctly and assign this percentage to each item on the test.

5	Review item ratings
	• Calculate the group averages and standard deviations.
	• Address items with significant variations in ratings through group discussion.
	   ◦ Reconsider ratings after discussion.
	   ◦ There's no need for consensus but rather consistency in rating approach.

6	Secondary item ratings • Ask experts to independently rate the items a second time.
7	Establish passing score • Calculate group averages and standard deviations. • Have the experts collaborate to determine the passing score based on the data and document the decision rationale.

- **The Bookmark method** provides subject matter experts with the items in a test ordered from most to least difficult. The SMEs are asked to set a bookmark between the test items that separate different levels of proficiency.
- **The Borderline Group method** involves selecting judges, defining skill levels, identifying borderline test takers, collecting their scores, and setting the passing score at the median of the borderline group.
- **The Contrasting Group method** requires selecting judges, defining skill levels, and gathering test scores and judgments from selected takers. The test takers are then separated into "qualified" and "unqualified" groups, and the cut score is determined by the percentage of qualified takers at each score level.

These methods all rely on expert judgment. For tests that are not connected with employment decisions (such as hiring, promotion, or licensure), a less rigorous method may be appropriate.

Preset Cut Scores

Cut scores may be preset by organizations, professions, unions, and lawmakers before tests are developed to uphold standards of competence, protect public safety, and ensure accountability within regulated industries. This can streamline test development because it allows developers to focus on creating items that meet established standards from the start.

Practitioner's Tip

It may be tempting to simply adopt a familiar passing standard, such as 70 or 80 percent, without considering the test item difficulty. However, it is vital to conduct a passing score study to establish the threshold for candidate success or failure.

—Stephanie Wagner Wilson, Stephanie Wilson Consulting, LLC

Evaluate Test Results

This chapter has presented a systematic approach to test development that, when followed, should produce reliable, valid, and fair scores. Now, you need to examine the data to determine if the individual items are functioning properly. Item-level data analysis provides a quantitative method for measuring item quality. Even if the test is only administered once, evaluating its results will provide feedback for your item writers and identify areas for improvement.

Using Item-Level Data to Improve Item Quality

When conducting an item analysis, having as much data as possible is optimal (such as 100 examinees). Nonetheless, data from just one examinee can confirm the correctness of the keyed answers. An incorrect key jeopardizes the validity, reliability, and fairness of a test score. Specifically, results from an item analysis can identify:

- **Miskey**. An incorrect option was recorded as the correct answer.
- **Double key**. There was more than one correct answer.
- **Guessing**. There was no clear best response—all four options in an item were selected somewhat equally by otherwise well-performing examinees.

You can use the following statistics to evaluate item performance and compute them using a simple spreadsheet program:

- **Difficulty index or P-value** reflects the percentage of examinees who answered an item correctly and is expressed as a decimal. If an item has a difficulty index of 1.00, then 100 percent of the examinees answered it correctly. This could mean that the item is too easy, the examinees just completed the training program, or the item itself is flawed (for instance, if the options or the stem are clueing the correct answer). If an item has a difficulty index of 0.33, then only 33 percent of the examinees answered the item correctly. This could mean that the item was a miskey or a double key; however, a low difficulty index may be understandable if the examinees were both experts and nonexperts.
- **Point-biserial correlation** shows how effectively an item distinguishes between those who did well on the exam and those who didn't. Each item's key has a point-biserial coefficient ranging from +1.00 to -1.00. If all examinees answer an item correctly or incorrectly, its coefficient is 0.00. A positive coefficient means those who answered correctly usually performed well overall, while those who answered incorrectly usually performed poorly. A negative coefficient means those who did well overall missed the item, while those who did poorly got it right. Items with negative coefficients aren't useful for good tests. The closer the

coefficient is to 1.00, the better the discrimination, with an acceptable range of 0.10 and above.
- **Distractor patterns.** The P-value and point-biserial correlation can both be used to evaluate the performance of each distractor (the wrong answers). While the difficulty index is the P value of the key, the P values of distractors can also be used to determine the percentage of examinees who chose each of the incorrect options. The point-biserial correlation can also be used to evaluate how a particular distractor is performing. While the correct answer should have a positive point-biserial correlation above 0.10, the distractors should have either a low point-biserial or a negative one.

Let's look at an example. Table 7-2 shows the distractor patterns for an item with a difficulty index of 0.69, indicating that 69 percent of examinees answered the item correctly. The point-biserial correlation is 0.34, indicating that the examinees who answered the item correctly also performed well on the entire test. The P values for the distractors indicate that 3 percent of examinees chose distractor 1, 23 percent chose distractor 2, and 5 percent chose distractor 4. The test developer may want to review distractors 1 and 4 to determine how they could be improved.

Table 7-2. Distractor Pattern

	Distractor 1	Distractor 2	Key 3	Distractor 4
P value	0.03	0.23	0.69	0.05
Point-biserial correlation	-0.05	-0.26	0.34	-0.19

Case Example: Test Items for a Food Handler Training Course

A basic food handler course includes the following outcome: "The trainee will accurately check food temperatures and distinguish between properly cooked and undercooked items, ensuring adherence to safety standards."

The associated learning objectives consist of identifying the acceptable range of safe cooked food temperatures, understanding the risks associated with undercooked food, and acquiring techniques for the proper use of a food thermometer.

CHAPTER 7

To measure the achievement of this outcome, the comprehensive nature of the content and the applicable cognitive levels must be considered. The learning outcome goes beyond knowing the correct food temperature—the trainee must know how to use that temperature to maintain safety standards.

Example items at varying cognitive levels that are related to the content in the example learning outcome include:

1. What is the recommended holding temperature for chicken curry to prevent bacterial growth and ensure food safety?
   A. 135°F (57°C)
   B. 140°F (60°C)
   C. 150°F (66°C)
   D. 165°F (74°C)
2. You are working in a restaurant kitchen, and the chef has just prepared a batch of chicken curry. The chef asks you to monitor the holding temperature of the curry until it is served. What action should you take to ensure the food safety of the chicken curry?
   A. Place the curry in a cool area to prevent overcooking.
   B. Check the internal temperature of the curry using a food thermometer.
   C. Visually inspect the curry to maintain its color and texture before serving.
   D. Reheat the curry to a higher temperature just before serving.
3. You are tasked with reheating a batch of chicken curry and rice. The cafeteria is experiencing a high volume of orders, and you need to efficiently ensure that the reheated meals meet safety standards. Describe the steps you would take to safely reheat the chicken curry and rice, confirming that both have reached the recommended internal temperatures. Additionally, address any potential challenges you might encounter during the reheating process and how you would overcome them to maintain food safety.

Because the learning outcome requires *applying* what examinees have learned, most of the associated test items should be written at the interpretation level. Items at this level would include distinguishing between properly cooked food, summarizing ideas, interpreting data and charts, and creating examples to demonstrate comprehension. Items written *only* at the recall level will not adequately measure achievement of the learning outcome because they are limited to recognizing and retrieving facts, details, or concepts without much analysis.

DESIGNING AND DELIVERING TESTS

Concentrating on the cognitive level specified by the learning outcomes ensures you create items that are accurate and aligned with the test's intended purpose.

Summary

This chapter described the process of creating valid and defensible criterion-referenced tests. Test designers should be guided by professional documents such as the Standards for Educational and Psychological Testing produced by the American Educational Research Association, American Psychological Association, and National Council on Measurement in Education (2014); the Principles for the Validation and Use of Personnel Selection Procedures produced by the Society for Industrial and Organizational Psychology (2018); and the Uniform Guidelines on Employee Selection Procedures, which have been adopted by the Equal Employment Opportunity Commission (EEOC) and various other federal agencies.

Knowledge Check

Answer these questions to check your knowledge. Then, review your answers in appendix B.

1. Identify the cognitive levels of the sample items in the case study.
2. Read and evaluate the last sample item in the case study. Is it aligned to the learning outcome for the food handler course?
3. What can be done with items that are not written in alignment with learning outcomes?
4. What is the item writing error in this sample item?

    Which of the following is *not* a correct way to handle raw chicken?

    A. Thawing it on the counter at room temperature
    B. Washing it thoroughly before cooking
    C. Using separate cutting boards for raw meat and other foods
    D. Cooking it to an internal temperature of 165°F

CHAPTER 8

Conducting Interviews

HENRI VAN DEN IDSERT

IN THIS CHAPTER

This chapter focuses primarily on semistructured key-informant interviews but draws on information from different disciplines and areas of practice. It unpacks some of the major challenges associated with authorship, confirmability, and bias. After reading it, you will be able to:

- Develop an analytical framework.
- Develop an interview protocol.
- Undertake interviews systematically.
- Manage and analyze your data.

Preparing for an Interview

When preparing to conduct an interview, you should map out what you plan to ask and how you will ask it beforehand.

Developing the Analytical Framework (the What)

Good research, regardless of discipline, hinges on objectivity and systematic data collection and analysis. To achieve this, you need to develop a robust analytical framework or model that guides your interview process and ensures you explore key conceptual and thematic areas. You likely picked up this book to learn more about capacity strengthening, program initiatives, innovation, and monitoring and evaluation. Within these areas of work, you are probably dealing with *theories of change* and *logical frameworks* that underpin causal pathways and assumptions about how an initiative, program, process, or service is meant to improve the lives and work of people or the functioning of an institution, unit, team or product. In this case, you'll likely be testing various assumptions or hypotheses, and engaging in a research approach that is both normative (Were objectives achieved?) and formative (What needs to be improved?) and employs some degree of deductive and inductive analysis. Deductive reasoning uses theory to reach conclusions, while inductive reasoning starts with observations to gradually reach conclusions.

You can draw on a range of tools derived from evaluation practice to aid in the development of analytical frameworks. *Better Evaluation* (2014) developed a useful tool called the Rainbow Framework, which allows you to organize your research plans into a series of tasks, in turn prompting you to select the appropriate method and process associated with each one. The Rainbow Framework's tasks are clustered in seven groups:

1. Managing the evaluation
2. Defining the scope
3. Framing the questions and parameters to be evaluated
4. Describing how data collection methods are linked to questions and context
5. Understanding and analyzing causal pathways
6. Synthesizing and summarizing evidence across data sources
7. Reporting and using the evidence for decision making

Development and evaluation practitioners also commonly use a Theory of Change (ToC) approach to conduct program analysis and demonstrate how and why an initiative works (Table 8-1). ToC approaches first emerged in the 1990s in the United States and grew out of the more traditional logical framework approach developed in the 1970s (Stein and Valters 2012). At their core they are meant to:

- Analyze the broader trends and factors that influence change in relation to a thematic area.
- Outline pathways between activities and outcomes for organizations or programs.
- Develop a comprehensive framework to assess the influence of chosen pathways and underlying assumptions about how change occurs.

In program and project evaluation, an evaluation matrix is another valuable tool that systematically links key components including research questions, evaluation criteria, data sources, data collection, and analytical methods, as well as the means of verification (CDC n.d.; USAID 2015). This tool sets out the details for how you will evaluate a topic or theme, program, or training course (Table 8-2). The matrix links each question and subquestion (the rows) to the means for answering that question (columns), which allows you to determine the thematic areas of interest and questions most relevant for the stakeholders you plan to interview.

Table 8-1. Example Simplified Theory of Change Dimensions

\multicolumn{6}{c}{Overall Vision or Goal Statement}
Input	Processes and Activities	Outputs	Outcomes	Impact	Assumptions
Resources needed to complete the task (e.g., people, places, materials, and funding)	Key activities carried out to produce outputs and expected results	Measurable indicators and results derived directly from the activities (e.g. number of people trained and number of training sessions)	Immediate or intermediate measurable changes in behavior, knowledge, attitude, or practices of people, or meaningful changes in how systems or processes function	Measurable longer-term transformative changes in people's lives or how a system functions	Internal and external factors, events, and conditions needed for the initiative to work
Initiative's areas of work	\multicolumn{5}{c}{Initiative's intended results}

Table 8-2. Example Evaluation Matrix Dimensions

Evaluation Criteria	Evaluation Questions	Sub Questions	Data Sources	Data Collection Methods or Tools	Means of Verification (Indicators)	Methods for Data Analysis
Effectiveness, efficiency, relevance, sustainability, or impact	(Add one row for each question)	(Add one row for each subquestion)	Stakeholder type or secondary literature	Key informant interview, focus group discussion, or survey	Success, standard, key performance indicator, objective, or goal	Kirkpatrick model, value for money, ROI, contribution analysis, or randomized control trial

Developing Your Interview Protocol (the How)

This chapter primarily focuses on the conduct of semistructured key informant interviews (KIIs). Educational psychologist Steiner Kvale (1996) described interviews as "conversations where the outcome is a coproduction of the interviewer and subject." His emphasis was on situating the interview within the philosophy of research methods, where the purpose is to unfold the subject's life world—"an interchange of views" that, if done well, can give access, insight, and information.

Considering that KIIs are typically no longer than an hour, good preparation requires a thorough understanding and testing of your analytical framework. You cannot realistically cover all the concepts or thematic areas within an interview, so you need to be aware of the areas most relevant to the interviewee, or where their opinion matters the most. Thus, you need to profile your interviewee to identify their specific interests, influence, and levels of power in relation to the thematic areas of your analytical framework and ultimately your research objectives. In my experience, evaluative research design and interview tools often prioritize the perspectives of powerful stakeholders like managers, executives, and gatekeepers. This approach overlooks the experiences of those who benefit from programs but lack decision-making authority. This creates evidence and knowledge gaps regarding the experience of program beneficiaries. To address this imbalance, we need to develop tools that ensure the voices and experiences of program beneficiaries are adequately captured in evaluations.

Developing the interview protocol is perhaps the most important and time-consuming phase of the interview process. It is critical at this stage to have a good grasp of the subject matter and how questions (that is, thematic areas) are related to one another. I highly recommend you review existing literature and consult experts in the field and experienced qualitative researchers, which will enhance your ability to ask good questions and follow-up probes. You may also wish to pilot the interview protocol prior to conducting your interview to help improve your instrumentation. Pilot programs allow you to practice your questions in a way that maximizes your time and ensures important thematic areas are not overlooked.

Practitioner's Tip

When developing your interview protocol, remember to:
- **Conduct a stakeholder analysis.** Identify areas in your analytical framework where different stakeholder perspectives would be the most insightful. Consider their role and level of influence within your framework and research objectives.
- **Develop inclusive and tailored interview questions.** Craft questions that capture the experiences of both decision makers and program beneficiaries, and make sure stakeholder perspectives are represented in your analysis and reporting.

Conducting the Interview

There's an art and science to conducting effective interviews. It begins with establishing a connection with your interviewee. Then, once the ice is broken, you can probe for deeper insights into the thematic areas. But you must be careful about how you word your questions to avoid leading the interviewee. Let's explore each aspect in turn.

Building Rapport (the Introduction)

Semistructured interview questionnaires consist of thematically organized open-ended questions. They are designed to stimulate a conversation about perceptions and opinions and rely heavily on the interviewer's probing skill. These thematic or process-oriented questions are always linked to the main research questions but are broken down into targeted subquestions relevant to the interviewee. The structure of the questionnaire always begins with an introduction of the interviewee, the objectives and purpose of the study or interview, a guarantee of anonymity or confidentiality, the option to withdraw at any time, and a request for consent to conduct the interview. It is critical you manage expectations during the introduction so the interviewee understands the outcomes of the study or interview and how the objectives could benefit or influence them personally or professionally. During the introduction, you should provide an overview of the thematic areas that will be covered, the anticipated time it will take, and information about how the interviewee's opinions and perception matter in relation to the study's purpose and objectives.

The introduction's tone will likely determine the flow and level of engagement for the remainder of the interview. At this point, the interviewee is determining whether they like you as a person and what the consequences are of speaking to you. How you appear, your gender, race, culture, attire, demeanor, and the physical location of the interview could all influence their responses. Pick a private location where you won't be interrupted. In addition, because most KIIs take place in a location chosen by the interviewee, if you notice the space is not ideal when you arrive, it is better to request a different location before starting.

Breaking the ice is a social skill, and while there are no written rules, it generally helps to find a point of interest, to show appreciation for any cultural differences you might have, or to point out something amusing or funny you experienced on your way there. It also helps to do some background research into the interviewee's profession or area of work. Sharing some of your knowledge prior to the formal introduction, and how it matters in relation to

CHAPTER 8

the study, might spark a chain of thought and ideas for the interviewee that will be valuable to the KII. It is important to be humble and thankful and to acknowledge how much you value the interviewees' time and opinions. You also need to reflect on whether the questions are perceived by the interviewee as being respectful and culturally sensitive—if not, you should change the questions or alter the order in which you approach them thematically.

Conducting the Interview (the Art of Probing)

At this point, the ice is broken and the formal introduction is out of the way. You now have a good indication of the thematic areas you want to cover and some indication of how you should frame the questions (based on the sociocultural aspects and interpersonal dynamics you picked up during the introduction). The first question is important because it sets the scene for the next and so on. In general, opening questions are a good opportunity to raise those thematic areas or topics you think the interviewee is most passionate about.

Many interviewers (including myself) choose to ask the respondent to introduce themselves and speak about their work. This provides another opportunity to pick up on which thematic areas to probe further and gives you time to structure your thoughts and notes after the introduction (where you were doing all the talking). Other interviewers like to immediately start with a thought-provoking question—often related to an issue with differing opinions or known tensions. This approach allows you to quickly assess the interviewee's position on a spectrum of opposing views, but only if you frame the question in such a way that it clearly presents the opposing views and welcomes any new perspectives on the matter.

Whichever approach you choose for the opening question, remain general and broad for now because being too technical may jam up the flow of the conversation. Asking about strategic choices (if you are interviewing managers) or the quality of a service or product provides a good opening question.

Probing questions seek to understand why the interviewee feels a certain way about a topic or view. These underlying reasons need to be clear to you because you'll be expected to explain these opinions and views in your final report. However, these conversations are not always straightforward; you may be dealing with a short-answered or short-tempered person, for example. While it is generally difficult to circumvent the mood of an interviewee, a good tactic is to gently remind them of the importance of their opinion in relation to the study's objective, as well as how their answers could benefit their work and personal circumstance.

Another good tactic is sharing how you interpreted their answer and asking whether that is how they want you to convey the message to a broader audience. This should get their attention and will often force them to reflect on their response, which will prompt them to either confirm or give you supporting arguments. It also helps limit your own confirmation bias as a researcher and practice what philosopher Edmund Husserl and psychologist Clark Moustakas have termed as *epoché*—namely, the ability to set aside your own assumptions about a phenomenon and let the interviewee describe it in their own words (Cairns-Lee, Lawley, and Tosey 2022a).

Dealing With Confirmability (the Authorship Phenomenon)

The way you phrase your questions will influence the response you get. Leadership professor and researcher Heather Cairns-Lee and colleagues (2022a) point out that little guidance exists about researcher reflexivity and the influence of *leading questions* beyond emphasizing "the need to avoid leading questions," which ultimately affect the trustworthiness of findings and have implications for knowledge claims made by researchers. They term this the *authorship* phenomenon, in which the potential for the constructs and meanings presented in research findings are derived more from the interviewer's questions and confirmability than the interviewees' responses.

While there are many forms of researcher reflexivity, the focus of their research is on the interviewer's awareness of the wording of questions and the potential effect that wording has on interviewee responses. They identify three distinct features of questions that have the potential to lead: introduced content, presuppositions, and evaluation.

Introduced content refers to a situation in which the interviewer introduces a concept or term that is new to the interviewee, often resulting in the interviewee adopting that terminology or concept. Consider the following example question: "We've been discussing the team's performance since the leadership training. One of the objectives was to enhance 'synergy' among team members, where everyone works together to achieve more than they could individually. Would you say the training helped your team develop a stronger sense of synergy?"

Here the interviewer introduces the concept of synergy and frames it as a desirable outcome of the training. Once this term is mentioned in relation to the team's performance, the interviewee might feel compelled to view the training through this lens.

Presuppositions can take two forms:

- The structure of the question presupposes a situation that the interviewee has not previously stated exists.
- The question presupposes a logical relationship or causal effect between two or more items not specified by the interviewee.

In both instances, unless the interviewee rejects the presupposition, they are likely to adopt the assumptions made by the interviewer. For example, the interviewer might ask: "The leadership training focused heavily on developing a more empathetic leadership style. Did you find this approach to be effective in motivating your team?"

This question assumes the training promoted an empathetic leadership style and that team motivation was direct result. It also suggests a binary answer (effective or not), which might nudge the interviewee toward a positive response that aligns with the assumption.

Evaluation occurs when the interviewer expresses an opinion or evaluation (judgment) about something the interviewee says. This may serve to undermine the interviewee's opinions or confidence in their own experience and make them more susceptible to leading questions and statements. Consider this exchange:

- Interviewee: "The role-playing exercises in the leadership training felt a bit artificial. They didn't really capture the complexities of real-world situations we face with the team."
- Interviewer: "Hmm, that's surprising. Those exercises were designed by leadership development experts and have been shown to be very effective in other organizations. Perhaps you didn't connect with them personally, but I wouldn't dismiss their overall value."

Here the interviewer downplays the interviewee's opinion. They also make the interviewee question their own judgment by referencing "leadership development experts" and adopting an overall dismissive tone. A more constructive alternative would be for the interviewer to say something like, "Thanks for sharing that perspective. Can you elaborate on what aspects of the role-playing exercises felt artificial? Perhaps we can identify areas for improvement in future training sessions."

It is important to note that authorship often occurs unwillingly or subconsciously, and that researchers are most susceptible to this when they are probing spontaneously without examining their own questions beforehand. Cairns-Lee and colleagues (2022b) propose a typology method called the *cleanness rating*, which helps identify leading questions and offers ways to address and mitigate this problem. Their rating method is derived from Clean Language

Interviewing (CLI) principles, which offer insights into dealing with the issue of authorship after the fact, but more importantly, during the design-phase of the interview protocol.

> **Practitioner's Tip**
>
> When conducting the interview, remember to:
> - **Identify potential leading elements.** Review your interview questions for instances where you might be introducing new concepts (such as "synergy"), making assumptions (such as saying "focused on empathy"), or expressing judgments (such as "surprising").
> - **Employ the cleanness rating method to assess your questions for potential bias.** This approach encourages you to rephrase questions to be more neutral and open-ended.
> - **Pilot test your interview questions,** even with just one person, to identify any areas where the wording might be leading or confusing.

Transcription and Analysis

Transcription and data analysis is a complex aspect to the interviewing process. You'll need to make decisions about how to manage all the data you gather through your interviews, whether to transcribe after or during the interview, and how to properly code the data to aid analysis.

Developing a Systematic Framework for Data Management

Much has been written on managing qualitative data in a systematic way, including using interpretive phenomenological analysis, thematic content analysis, semiotic analysis, and iterative categorization. These methods are all preoccupied with the systematic organization of unstructured qualitative data so that it can be compared across units of observations (or interviewees) and analyzed meaningfully. Transcribing, organizing, coding, and analyzing data is a time-consuming and challenging process, so it's important to ensure that it's done systematically. In addition, this part is rarely discussed openly, and the stages between coding and publication are often vague or poorly explained (Neale 2016). Because most research iteratively collects and analyzes data, there is often no rigid distinction between them. This makes qualitative data analysis less standardized than statistical analysis.

Whether you choose to take written notes during the interview or to record the conversation, you will need to transcribe your notes and recordings. In some fields of study, *naturalized transcription*—or capturing every utterance (including time-gaps, emphasis, and syllables)—is required; for example, this is common in psychology or in studies dealing with addiction. More common fields of study adopt *denaturalized transcription*, where the focus is only on extracting informational content, often not even verbatim.

You can use a range of analytical methods once the transcribed data is available, including deploying software programs like NVivo, MAXqda, and Atlas.ti. Analytical methods may involve thematic analysis, framework approaches, constant comparison, analytical induction, content analysis, conversational analysis, discourse analysis, interpretative phenomenological analysis, or narrative analysis. What they all have in common are key processes in coding, identifying or isolating emergent themes or phrases and patterns, and finding commonalities and differences in opinion and underlying explanations.

Systematic Reflexive Interviewing and Reporting

Another layer of complexity is that research or fieldwork typically involves more than one researcher. This means that you may need to analyze data, not only across interviewees, but also across interviewers. In many cases, interviewers engage in what researcher Nicholas Loubere (2017) terms "reflexive dialogue," or a process in which researchers jointly analyze their interview notes and reach a consensus on key findings and conclusions for report writing. The reflexive dialogue approach argues that it is better to begin coding and analysis in real-time during fieldwork rather than afterward, and thus facilitate critical engagement with emergent themes.

Systematic reflexive interviewing and reporting (SRIR) is a good alternative to the process of recording interviews and transcribing them into text through verbatim transcription prior to coding and analysis. This method is only possible if two or more researchers are undertaking interviews, and it has implications in terms of time management and general levels of exhaustion of the researchers—who are expected to compare notes and emerging themes shortly after the interview has been conducted and derive their preliminary analysis and interview reports from this process.

Challenges With Verbatim Transcription

Verbatim transcripts are generally the preferred method if the researcher is less experienced or not as familiar with the design elements of the conceptual framework or thematic areas of interest. However, there are challenges associated with verbatim transcription, such as maintaining the anonymity of data and dealing with sensitive subjects. Transcribing a recorded interview is challenging, especially when considering all the incomplete sentences, incoherent thoughts, self-corrections, partial utterances, and dialects inherent to human speech.

While advancement in technology, particularly artificial intelligence and machine learning, makes it possible to easily transcribe recordings, verbatim transcriptions can lead to rigidity issues if the researcher struggles to abandon theoretically laden methodological choices or change analytical focus when new information (themes) are introduced. This can often perpetuate the authorship problem.

There is also the added difficulty that people often do not want to be recorded—the act of recording may influence the interviewee's openness and change the nature of the interview. If friends, family, or other curious onlookers enter the interview, asking for their consent to record can be disruptive and as equally challenging as asking them to leave.

Nicholas Loubere (2017) argues that important information is often presented when the recorder is off, and relying on verbatim transcription to transform interviews into data implicitly limits the type of information collected. Also, consider the potential time-lag between conducting the interview, transcribing the interview notes, and analyzing the data. In many cases, analysis doesn't happen until long after the interviewers complete their fieldwork. This can lead to what Loubere calls the "decontextualization" of data, in which information and contextual knowledge is lost in the process of transcribing and analyzing long after the interview. As he describes:

> Ultimately, the attempt to pin down the interview through its transformation into text leads to an epistemology that sees "truth" and the resultant "knowledge" as emanating from words that have been textualized—a process that necessarily strips away some of the context. This proves problematic for open-ended and flexible research that seeks to interrogate the continuously unfolding dynamics between researcher and research participant, and sees the research project as a co-production, which is replete with different types of meanings and understandings that need to be interpreted critically, reflexively, and iteratively.

A Combined Approach

The advantage of SRIR is that it forces you to co-review and validate pre-analyzed data outputs during the fieldwork stage by asking interviewers to collaborate and create flexible interview protocols that are tailored to different stakeholders. It's also easier to use qualitative data analysis (QDA) software packages if you use preliminary analysis reports. These protocols are used to structure the interview and guide notetaking. Importantly, SRIR involves reviewing the interview data and tools immediately after conducting the interview to engage in a process of *reflexive dialogue* to identify important themes and information, as well as reflect on ways in which the interview protocol can be improved and adapted while in the field.

The two methods for transcribing data need not be mutually exclusive, and proponents of the SRIR method argue for a combined approach so you can use and identify verbatim quotations more easily and triangulate between transcripts. The value of SRIR is in developing a systematic framework for collecting, organizing, and analyzing data during the fieldwork process, in real-time and in conjunction with other researchers.

Coding

Coding (also known as *indexing*) is a core element of the interviewing process and is undertaken increasingly using QDA software. Coding involves reviewing all data line-by-line and organizing the interview text into key issues or themes (codes). New codes are added as additional themes or issues emerge, often creating a hierarchical tree of codes, organized by broader issues and more focused ones. Researcher and qualitative social scientist Joanne Neale (2016) explains that data analysis is underpinned by three concurrent activities (Miles and Huberman 1994):

- Data reduction (simplifying, abstracting, and transforming raw data)
- Data display (organizing the information by assembling it into matrices, graphs, networks or charts)
- Conclusion drawing and verification (interpreting data and testing provisional conclusions for their plausibility)

She goes on to argue that it is helpful to simplify qualitative data analysis, and that this should involve just two core stages: description and interpretation. Simplifying (or reducing) the raw data and then displaying it in matrices or charts (not dissimilar to a spreadsheet) facilitates both description and interpretation by allowing the researcher to systematically and comprehensively compare the data across and within codes. It allows you to explore similarities and differences between topics and themes and between interviewees or units of observation—a process described as *iterative categorization* in Neale's work. You can thus thematically organize codes at a higher level of analysis but also at a lower or more focused level of analysis within those overarching themes; for example, according to issues you are exploring or issues that come up in your data (challenges, contradicting opinions, operational enablers, institutional bottlenecks, and so on).

You can code data *deductively* (based on pre-existing theories or hunches about key issues or thematic areas) or *inductively* (based on issues emerging as important from the data itself during the analysis process). Similar to what has been proposed in this chapter regarding having a good analytical framework, Neale (2016) explains the importance of having a clear progression from the study's aims or objectives to the study's conclusions. Coding should therefore begin with your deductive codes (that is, the themes and questions your interview protocol design is based on). You can then supplement deductive codes with more inductive codes derived from emergent topics in the data. The two types of codes can be useful in complementing, expanding, qualifying, or even contradicting your initial hypotheses or assumptions. Codes should mirror the topics and prompts used in any data collection instrument, and they're often numbered to ensure they remain consistent with the questions in the data collection instrument.

Practitioner's Tip

When transcribing and analyzing the data, remember to:
- **Enhance reflexivity and data validity.** Reflect on the interview data and tools immediately after the interview so you can identify important themes and areas for improvement in the protocol, leading to more valid data.
- **Prioritize context over rigidity.** Focus on capturing the essence of the interview and contextual information, rather than getting bogged down in verbatim details that might hinder analysis.
- **Embrace emergent themes.** Don't be limited by pre-determined codes. Use iterative categorization to incorporate new themes that arise during data analysis, creating a more nuanced understanding of your research question.
- **Maintain a systematic coding process.** While incorporating new themes, ensure a systematic approach to coding. Organize codes hierarchically, with broader themes encompassing more focused ones derived from your data.

Summary

Conducting successful key informant interviews depends on thorough planning, good questioning, and robust data analysis. This chapter showed you how to use an analytical

CHAPTER 8

framework to guide the interview and create a focused question guide. Through effective questioning techniques, you can build rapport and use follow-up questions to gain deeper insights. And you can mitigate challenges like data analysis time with alternative interviewing methods like SRIR for real-time analysis.

Knowledge Check

Answer these questions to check your knowledge. Then, review your answers in appendix B

1. What are the three distinct types of leading questions?
2. What is the difference between deductive and inductive coding?
3. How can deductive and inductive coding be used together in interview analysis?
4. What are the advantages and disadvantages of verbatim transcription in qualitative research?
5. What is systematic reflexive interviewing and reporting (SRIR)?
6. How can SRIR improve the quality of your data analysis?

CHAPTER 9

Conducting Focus Groups

KATINKA KOKE

IN THIS CHAPTER

This chapter explores focus groups, how to tailor them to your specific context in training evaluation, and how to implement them. After reading it, you will be able to:

- Define what a focus group discussion is about.
- Tailor a focus group to the specific context or need in training evaluation.
- Conduct a focus group discussion.

What Is a Focus Group Discussion?

A focus group is a qualitative data collection method you can use to collect insights from participants and deepen a specific theme related to the evaluation. It can serve as an alternative or addition to key informant interviews and questionnaires. Thus, a focus group can be standalone (the principal source of data), supplementary (enhancing another primary method of data collection), or complementary (used along with other data collection tools).

Focus groups are different from key informant interviews (see chapter 8) insofar as they are conducted with small groups rather than in one-on-one interviews. They can be structured or semistructured and usually mix predefined interview questions with free-flowing discussion. In contrast to interviews, focus groups also allow for discussion and engagement between participants. The contributions from participants should stimulate and influence the

---

Disclaimer: The views expressed herein are those of the author and do not necessarily reflect the views of the United Nations.

thinking and sharing of others. While interviews require an interviewer, focus groups usually have a facilitator who encourages participants to express their thoughts, intervenes to ask follow-up questions, probes for deeper insights, and manages group dynamics.

There are three types of focus group questions:
- **Engagement questions** engage people with simple questions to foster conversation and introduce the subject.
- **Exploration questions** get to the heart of the discussion.
- **Exit questions** check to see if anything was missing in the discussion.

When used as a supplementary tool, focus groups may ask follow-up questions to questionnaire responses to dive deeper into new insights and clarify questions. Focus groups can complement questionnaires, key informant interviews, knowledge tests, and document review.

The recommended number of focus group participants is somewhere between four and 12, but there is no consensus in the research literature. There is also flexibility to its duration, with an ideal time anywhere between 60 and 90 minutes.

Focus group participants may be selected following a stakeholder analysis and based on different sampling strategies; for example:
- **Voluntary response sampling** occurs when an announcement is made and participants are allowed to sign up.
- **Convenience sampling** involves those who are easily available or present in a location.
- **Stratified sampling** selects participants based on age, gender, work function or level, or other characteristics of interest.
- **Judgment sampling** is based on responses to a previously administered questionnaire.

Focus groups are particularly relevant when quality judgments are subjective, when several individual judgments can reduce the degree of subjectivity, and when it is important for the group to hear from others (Phillips and Phillips 2016). Focus group techniques can be more efficient than individual interviews because they require less time. Nevertheless, don't underestimate the time required for preparation or the risks of power dynamics, sensitive opinions, and participants' discomfort in group settings. To decide if a focus group is the most appropriate method, reflect whether you prefer obtaining detailed personal accounts about the unique training experience of particular people or sacrificing details about individuals in favor of engaging participants in active comparisons of their training experience (Morgan 1998).

Tailor a Focus Group Discussion to a Specific Context or Needs

As with all data collection instruments, to maximize focus group effectiveness, you need to tailor them to the individual or organizational context. Figure 9-1 depicts the factors you should consider to ensure an effective focus group: objective, method, format, timing, and target audience.

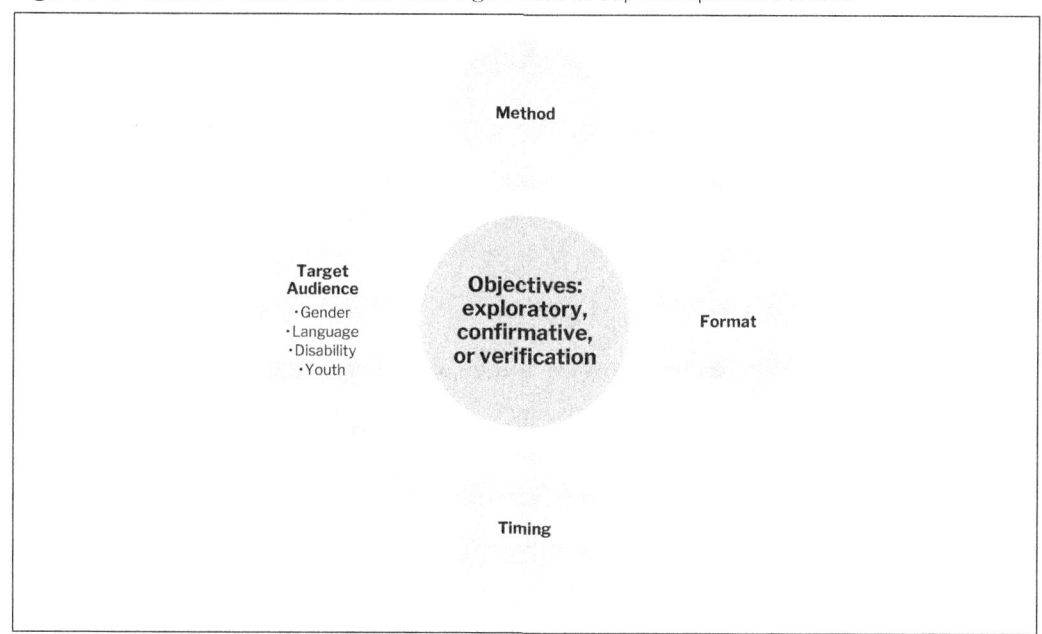

Figure 9-1. Factors to Consider When Tailoring a Focus Group to a Specific Context

Objective

You may pursue different objectives with a focus group, but you need to define the objective in the very beginning. An overarching question to consider is: "What do you hope to learn or achieve through the discussion?" The objective may be exploratory (such as establishing a certain theory), confirmative (such as finding evidence for

127

or against a hypothesis), or consist of verifying information collected through other means, such as questionnaires.

Method

Select the focus group method based on the defined objective and the target group's characteristics. The most common method involves using semistructured discussion questions that may or may not follow up on participants' responses to questionnaires.

Depending on the objective, other methods or a combination of several methods may be used, such as brainstorming to generate solutions to a specific problem (for example, the future target for certificate of completion rates). Alternatively, it's possible to use ranking and rating style questions to rank the order of factors that have influenced successful application of knowledge and skills or prevented it.

> **Practitioner's Tip**
>
> Creative exercises using visuals, videos, or scenarios can help participants connect to the discussion questions. You may use this technique for the icebreaker or during the discussion. Other activities can include asking participants to write out ideas on a topic and organizing ideas with the group.

Format

A focus group can be held in a face-to-face, online, or hybrid setting. Since 2020 and the COVID-19 pandemic, online focus groups have become much more accessible, and meeting software allows for such use. The main advantage is the ability to organize focus groups that include participants based in different locations. Face-to-face discussions often help participants fully concentrate and avoid getting sidetracked by incoming emails or calls.

Hybrid discussions can be used if participants are grouped in different locations, with some remote and others face to face. In this case, it's recommended to have an online moderator in addition to the in-room facilitator to ensure full attention is given to both groups of participants.

Timing

Focus groups can be *formative* and take place during the training implementation or *summative* and be organized after the training has taken place. When you use focus groups to establish indicators or targets, they can also take place before the training program is implemented (for example, to help define or refine learning objectives and ensure that the training design responds best to their needs).

Target Audience

Determine the demographic characteristics of the participants who will be invited before deciding on a sampling strategy and ensure the target group is fully represented. Consider factors such as age, gender, work function or level, or other characteristics of interest. Also consider whether you want to invite participants with similar or contrasting views. In most cases, homogenous groups are preferred, but heterogenous groups can be useful if the objective is to collect feedback from different and contradictory perspectives. You may need to adjust your focus group techniques and style to the target audience (for example, senior leaders may need a different approach than youth). In the area of training, target audiences could be arranged by type of group and include training participants, training managers, instructional designers, supervisors of participants, trainers and online moderators, and implementing partners.

Let's look closer at a few specific factors to consider:

- **Cultural context**. When working in multicultural environments, be sensitive to the cultural context for those involved and consider aspects of equity, inclusion, and social justice.
- **Gender**. You may want to consider whether your groups should be mixed gender or single gender, depending on the evaluation. The gender of the facilitator also requires consideration if the discussion topics are sensitive, such as gender asymmetries.
- **Language**. In multilingual and multicultural contexts, consider upfront if everyone is comfortable using the chosen language. If not, hold focus groups in different languages and translate the results afterward. (Online translation tools are helpful for accomplishing this.)
- **Disability**. Consider providing support for the people in your focus group (hearing or seeing or special accessibility requirements). For example, show images and text.
- **Youth**. Depending on the context, young people may be part of your target training audience. Obtain parental consent for any participants under the

CHAPTER 9

age of 18. In addition, it may be beneficial to consider using a focus group facilitator who is a similar age or has a background in the interest to avoid power asymmetries (CohenMiller et al. 2022).

Case Example

Larger capacity development projects, such as peacekeeping and geospatial analysis for climate resilience and following natural disasters, are typically male dominated. When evaluating these projects, evaluators made the decision to conduct women-only focus groups, with the intention of allowing this underrepresented population to freely express themselves away from their male counterparts. This also allowed the facilitator to delve deeper into questions related to inclusion, gender-sensitivity of the training program, and gender-based violence, among others.

Practitioner's Tip

As part of the evaluation of a joint master's degree program, focus groups were used to collect insights from training managers and participants. Depending on the location of training managers, some focus groups were organized online and others face-to-face. Focus group discussions with participants were organized in English, French, and Spanish to allow participants to express themselves in the language most comfortable for them, when possible.

Focus Group Discussion Questions in the Training Context

Typically, in a post-training context, focus groups are used to collect insights from participants about application and impact of a training program.

Example application questions include:
- How have you applied the knowledge and skills from the training program?
- How much of your working time do you spend on tasks that require the knowledge and skills you obtained through the learning event?
- What factors enabled you to apply the knowledge and skills to your work? Why? What barriers prevented you from being more successful?
- How confident are you in applying the knowledge and skills you learned? Could

you explain what led you to your reply? To what extent is the gained confidence due to the training event? Express your answer in percentage.
- Are you still using the knowledge and skills? If so, could you give a specific example of a situation you experienced that illustrates the success or improvements (or failure) of the application of the knowledge and skills you acquired through training?
- Looking back, please compare your current behavior at work with your behavior prior to the learning event. Has your behavior changed due to acquiring the new knowledge and skills or strengthened your existing knowledge and skills? Additionally, could you describe what exactly has changed in your job performance (such as tasks, actions, procedures, or steps)?

Example impact questions include:
- How has your organization or employer benefited from your participation in the training event?
- What has changed about you or your work because of your participation in this training event? How have you performed better on the job since completing the training?
- What impact measures have improved due to this change? By how much?
- What other factors contributed to your changed behavior at work, if any?
- Recognizing that other factors could have influenced your improvement, please estimate the percentage of your improvement that is attributable to the training event. Express this number as a percentage out of 100. How confident are you with your response (from 0 to 100 percent)?

Sometimes focus groups are used to convert measures to monetary value. For example, as described in chapter 16, when a standard value for a measure is not available and there are no other techniques deemed useful, participants in a focus group might estimate the monetary value based on their experience with the issue causing the measure to underperform. Focus groups can also be useful for isolating the effects of the program if other techniques are not feasible. For example, when measures improve, those individuals who are closest to it may have a sound perspective why that happened. Participating in a focus group setting allows them to describe the basis for their estimate while hearing what others have to say. Then, focus group participants can estimate what they believe the contribution is and adjust for error in that estimate.

In a pretraining context, you can use focus groups to define a target or indicator of success for a training program. For example, consider this scenario: As part of an evaluation to understand the decreasing trend of certification rates for training programs, you organize focus groups with training managers, participants, and other certification-issuing training organizations. You're hoping to leverage their insights to set realistic targets for certification rates going forward.

You start the focus group process with the aim of collecting answers to these two questions:

1. As a key performance indicator, what percentage target should the organization aim to achieve for training completion and certification or other relevant measures linked to job or organizational performance? Please explain your response.
2. What would be an appropriate indicator to measure the outcomes of the planned training?

Then, you adjust the questions to each target audience and compose different ones for each group:

- **Training managers.** You may ask about reasons for decreasing trends, best practices, and areas for improvement. Good practices are collected, mainly related to learner engagement strategies. You may also ask about the use of artificial intelligence (AI) and behavioral science to influence certification rates.
- **Other actors in the learning industry.** You may ask about the effects of the COVID-19 pandemic on their organization, what indicators they use to measure the increase in learning after a training program, what types of certifications they issue, how they track learner completion and what targets they set, and how they differentiate certification targets by training event characteristics. Similarly as with training managers, you may also explore the effects from the use of AI and behavioral science on certification rates.
- **Training participants.** You may ask about deterrents of completion and value of the certification. In addition, you may ask unsuccessful training participants about changes they experienced following event participation.

Conduct a Focus Group Discussion

Before conducting a focus group, it is crucial to be aware of the preparations required. You can break up your preparation into tasks to do prior to the focus group, during the focus group, and after the focus group.

CONDUCTING FOCUS GROUPS

Before the Focus Group

Figure 9-2 represents the flow of activities that occur before the focus group.

Figure 9-2. Flow of Activities Prior to Organizing a Focus Group

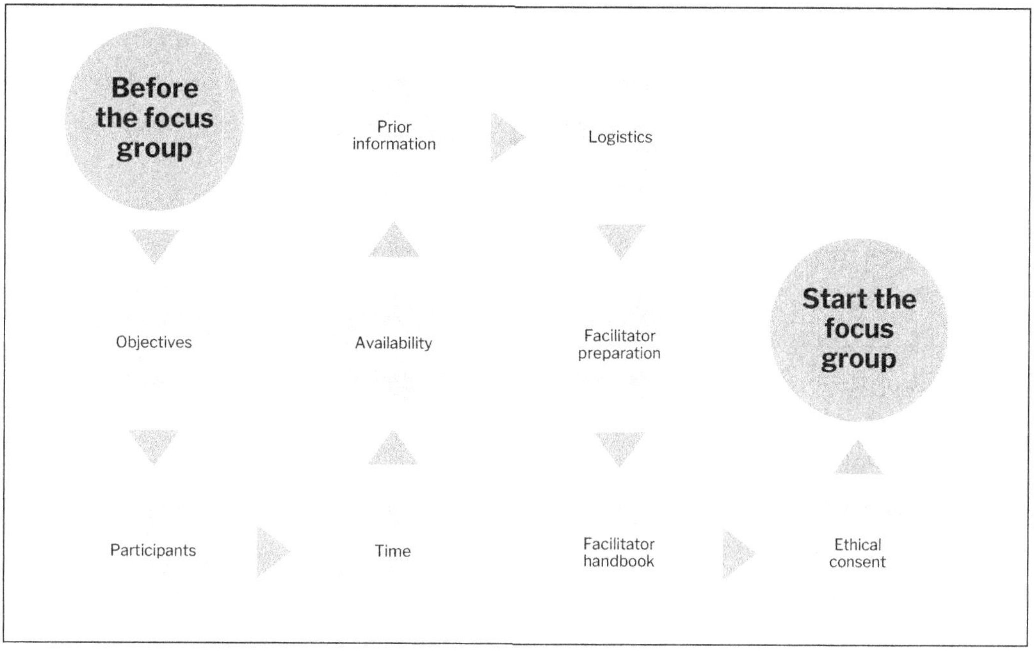

Before the focus group → Prior information → Logistics

Objectives ← Availability ← Facilitator preparation → Start the focus group

Participants → Time → Facilitator handbook → Ethical consent

Let's look at each step in more detail:

1. **Objectives**. Define the objectives of the focus group and develop questions that align with them.
2. **Participants**. Select the participants according to your chosen sampling strategy. Ensure that they are able to provide informed answers to your questions.
3. **Set the time**. Think about time zones and provide time slot options for participants to choose from. AI tools can help you schedule focus groups and automatically send out calendar invitations.
4. **Availability**. Monitor participants' availability to ensure you can reach the targeted number of participants or invite additional participants as needed.
5. **Prior information**. Share key information regarding the purpose, duration, and setting with participants to ensure clear expectations and that they can all make an informed decision.

6. **Logistics**. Reserve a room or generate a link to the online platform. Consider the room setup and seating arrangements—ideally participants can make eye-contact with one another and sit in a circle. Consider accessibility aspects and test equipment including recording devices. Determine whether you're going to offer refreshments.
7. **Facilitator preparation**. If you are not the facilitator, make sure they are well prepared. This includes understanding the objective and the context, reading questionnaire responses, preparing supporting documents, and being aware of participants' profiles.
8. **Facilitator handbook**. Create a handbook with discussion questions, time foreseen for each question, useful follow-up questions, and behaviors to adopt to make participants feel at ease. Limit the number of total questions and structure them by theme and in a logical order. Test the focus group discussion questions by sharing them with a peer or supervisor and asking for feedback.
9. **Ethical consent**. Prepare an ethical consent form. Depending on the audience and organizational policy, you may also need to prepare ethical consent forms for the facilitators to ensure they're practicing ethically appropriate behavior.

During the Focus Group

Figure 9-3 shows the flow of activities that occur during the focus group.

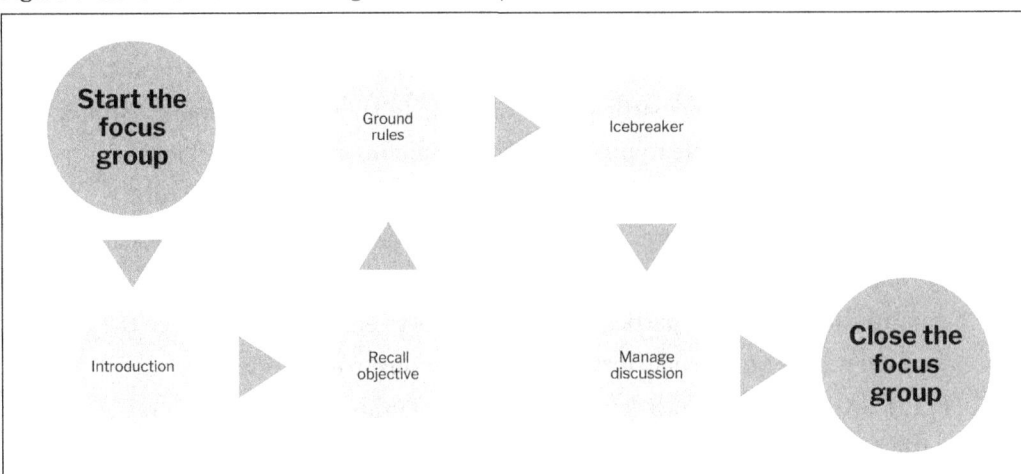

Figure 9-3. Flow of Activities During a Focus Group

Start the focus group → Ground rules → Icebreaker → Introduction → Recall objective → Manage discussion → Close the focus group

Let's review each step:
1. **Introduction**. Welcome and thank participants for their time. If you are not the facilitator, introduce them.
2. **Objective**. Explain the focus group's purpose; be transparent about objectives.
3. **Ground rules**. Present the ground rules for the discussion, including the importance of listening to others and respecting other participants' opinions. Explain that there are no wrong answers and highlight the confidential or anonymous nature of the focus group. If conducted online, obtain consent from participants before starting the recording and give assurances that the recording will only be used in conjunction with the evaluation and will not be disseminated. Establish a safe atmosphere.
4. **Icebreaker**. Ask participants to briefly introduce themselves and their background. This may be combined with a short icebreaker exercise, such as check-in questions.
5. **Manage discussion**. Use PowerPoint or a flipchart to present the questions so participants can reference them during the session. Ask one question at a time and listen carefully to responses. Encourage quieter participants by inviting comments and using probing questions. If anyone is dominating the conversation or speaking for too long, manage the time and redirect off-topic discussions. If participants disagree about a statement or question, take note and ask others what they think. Demonstrate active listening by paraphrasing and summarizing long, complex, or ambiguous comments. Note them in the PowerPoint slide or on the flipchart to clarify the comment for everyone in the group. It is crucial to avoid bias and remain neutral. Refrain from using body language (such as nodding or raising eyebrows), agreeing or disagreeing, or praising or denigrating any comment made.
6. **Closure**. Thank all participants for their participation and ask if they have any other questions about the evaluation process.

Practitioner's Tip

Useful probing questions include:
- That's an interesting insight, could you talk about that a bit more, or does anyone else have similar or different experiences that they would like to share?
- Help me understand what you mean.
- Could you give an example?

—Brook Boyer, Director, Division for Strategic Planning and Performance, UNITAR

CHAPTER 9

After the Focus Group

Figure 9-4 shows the flow of activities that occur after the focus group has ended.

Figure 9-4. Flow of Activities After Conducting the Focus Group

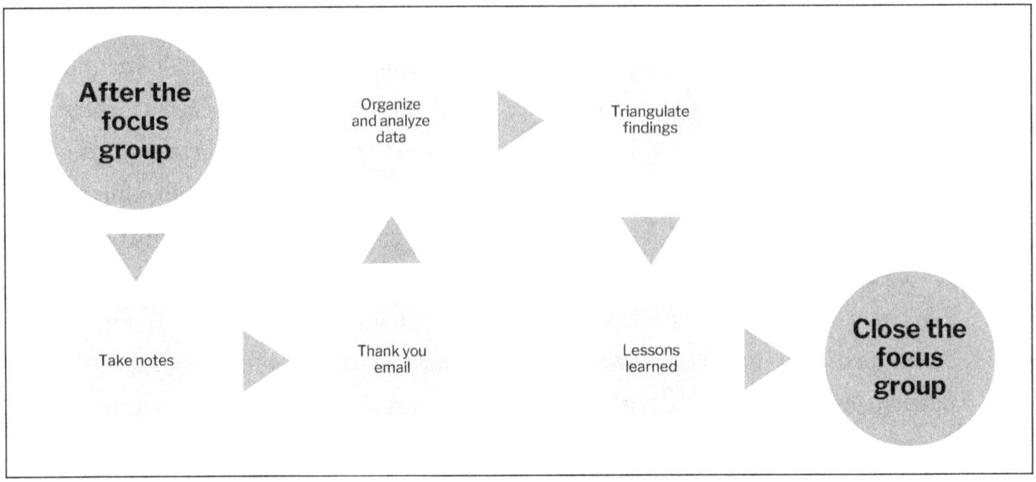

Let's review each step:

1. **Notes**. Immediately after all participants leave, take note of any key points made while they're still fresh in your mind. For online focus groups, you might be able to use AI transcription tools for note-taking purposes or to transcribe audio or video files.
2. **Email**. Send an email to thank participants and remind them that you'll share the results of the overall evaluation at a later stage. Follow up on any individual requests if needed.
3. **Organize and analyze data**. Review key notes and pair them with notes from listening to the recording. Organize the data using qualitative analysis and categorize responses by pattern or theme.
4. **Triangulate**. Triangulate findings with other data sources from questionnaires, interviews, or document review. Consider using more than one data source to validate your findings.
5. **Lessons learned**. Write down lessons learned to inform the next focus group and refine the approach. A good practice is to return to participants and ask them to

confirm the evaluators have captured their voices appropriately (CohenMiller et al. 2022).
6. **Report**. Report on findings and develop recommendations. AI tools can help summarize notes.

After the focus group's end, you should analyze the qualitative data collected. (You can read more about qualitative data analysis in chapter 12.) However, because data collected through interviews and focus groups is considered subjective, it is crucial to determine the data's substantive significance instead of its statistical significance (Quinn Patton 2002). To do so, consider how solid, coherent, and consistent the evidence from the focus groups is in support of the findings and in comparison with data collected from other sources.

Practitioner's Tip

Ensuring good participation cannot be emphasized enough. Communicate to the focus group how important their participation is (and what benefit they could take away from it, such as learning from the experiences of others). If you think a participant has a particular experience to share, let them know in advance. To maximize the chances of good participation, personalize invitations by addressing participants with their name instead of sending mass emails. Moreover, highlight the importance of the exercise and explain how the focus group contributes to the purpose. In addition, respect participants' availability and agendas—be realistic when estimating time requirements and avoid starting or finishing late. Everyone is short on time, so reflect on what is critical to share and what can be left out. Finally, keep promises and do not forget to share the final copy of the report with participants when ready. This can influence willingness to participate in future focus groups.

—Brook Boyer, Director, Division for Strategic Planning and Performance, UNITAR

Summary

Focus groups are qualitative data collection instruments. Conducted with small groups in contrast to one-on-one interviews, they can be standalone, supplementary, or complementary. In contrast to interviews, focus groups also allow for discussion and engagement between participants. To maximize the benefits of a focus group, you should tailor it to the training evaluation's specific context and needs and to the participants' characteristics and cultural background. To conduct a focus group, remember the tasks you should prepare for prior, during, and after it.

CHAPTER 9

Knowledge Check

Use these questions to check your knowledge. Find the answers in appendix B.

1. True or false: In a focus group discussion, participants need to always have homogenous profiles.
2. Reflect on if a woman-only focus group could allow participants to speak more freely and express different concerns in a specific context.
3. True or false: A focus group in a post-training context can include questions from different levels of the evaluation framework.
4. When can focus groups occur in relation to a training program?
    A. After training has taken place
    B. During or after training has taken place
    C. Before, during, or after training has taken place

CHAPTER 10

Using Action Planning as a Measurement and Transfer Strategy

EMMA WEBER

IN THIS CHAPTER

This chapter discusses the power of using action plans for data capture and learning transfer. After reading it, you will be able to:

- Define action planning and its purpose.
- Understand why action planning often fails.
- Know what to include in an action plan.
- Implement practical ways to follow up on action plans.

What Is Action Planning?

Action planning is when learners make a commitment to what they will implement back in their role, either after attending a learning program or as part of a program. An *action plan* is the link between what an employee learns and what knowledge they will apply in their role. Therefore, action planning is an instrumental tool for creating learning transfer. In *The Six Disciplines of Breakthrough Learning*, Roy Pollock, Andy Jefferson, and Calhoun Wick (2015) define *learning transfer* as "the ability of a learner to successfully apply the behavior, knowledge, and skills acquired through learning, to the job, with a resulting improvement in job performance."

Only when employees apply what they've learned back in the workplace and in their day-to-day role do learning programs create impact for your organization. Knowing the information isn't enough; being able to demonstrate the new skill or simply doing it in a one-off skills test or evaluation isn't enough. Applying that knowledge consistently day to day—often among pressures of a work environment—is when the learning is truly valuable. Consider it another way: TD professionals often consider the end of a learning program to be when someone has finished attending that program or consuming the content; instead, the true end occurs when the knowledge makes an impact and is fully used in the workplace.

An action plan can capture key data points, which makes it easy to measure and evaluate the learning program. We will look at examples of this later in the chapter.

It's important to clarify that skills practice between learning modules differs from action planning. TD professionals typically give learners activities to complete between learning modules so they can practice what they've learned on the job. All too frequently, however, the assumption of the facilitator or the learning professional is that once a learner has successfully tried or practiced a skill on the job, it will become a day-to-day behavior. A 2004 study by Robert Brinkerhoff, professor at Western Michigan University, found that less than 20 percent of learners never apply what they learned in training and 65 percent of learners try to apply what they learned but revert back to their old ways (Phillips 2016).

Considering three different factors helps to identify if an activity is designed to transfer the learning into on-the-job sustained behavior change or to practice the skill in a real work environment:

1. Has the individual reached a level of competence (through a skills practice or similar) that they can use the skill in a real-life scenario?
2. Does the individual choose the activity themselves or is it a prescribed activity they have been given?
3. Is the activity the same for everyone in the program regardless of context or experience?

If any of these apply, then the activity is probably part of a skills practice. While this remains an important part of the learning journey, it isn't part of the transfer phase. The learner is still developing the skills to a point where they can be transferred.

What Action Plans Look Like

Table 10-1 shows an example action plan for a GROW Coaching program.

USING ACTION PLANNING AS A MEASUREMENT AND TRANSFER STRATEGY

Table 10-1. Example Action Plan for a GROW Coaching Program

Date: _____ Program name: GROWing Your Conversations
Participant name: _____ Participant email: _____
Session 1: Date: ____ Time: ____ Session 2: Date: ____ Time: ____ Session 3: Date: ____ Time: ____
TLA coach name: _____ TLA coach phone number: _____

What Are You Trying to Achieve? *What specifically will you implement from the program? By when?*	Why Is It Important to You? *What does it mean to you personally? Why is that important to you?*	Measures and Success Indicators *How will you know you have been successful? Describe seeing, feeling, and hearing success.*	What Is Your Current Status? *Where are you now on a scale of 1 (low) to 10 (high)?*	Next Steps *What actions can you take within the next 48 hours? What are the future steps?*
Have biweekly coaching conversations with my direct reports. Ideally I will adopt this straight away, and tailor my conversations to GROW moving forward.	When I think of GROW being used in and out of the workplace, it provides a structured and consistent approach to framing goals. I want to give my staff the same opportunity and make sure I'm coaching them to achieve goals that will benefit the team and individuals.	• The feedback I have received from my team is positive. • Staff are clear about their role and position expectations. • There is an overall positive culture in the team. • Employees are thinking and leading the conversation about their own goals, ideas, and development.	5	• Discuss the GROW concept with my team so they are comfortable with the change in approach. • Have a GROW conversation with one of my direct reports. This doesn't need to be a performance review discussion; it can be centered on a problem or issue they're facing.
Give effective feedback to my staff.	Often the situations that come through can be tough to respond to and provide feedback in a consistent way.	• Issues that were arising are no longer occurring. • Employees understand why they received feedback and use GROW conversation to come up with their own ways to resolve or address things.	5	• I received feedback from a customer regarding a conversation they had with a member of my team. I'll have a GROW conversation with the employee.
Be more of an active listener in meetings	Getting a better understanding of what is going on will make my life easier. I will also be more efficient.	• I won't miss information and I will better understand what is going on.	6.5	• Listen to the recommended podcast on active listening.

CHAPTER 10

The data collection method in this example uses a simple, self-rated score, which provides a baseline as the individual progresses with their goal or commitments when the action is created and then later in the learning journey with a report-out graph. Importantly, it allows you to use the action plan for advanced data collection, which links organizational KPIs to the specific actions an individual is taking as part of a learning program. This will fast-track your ability to link data to program outcomes and assist at the evaluation stage.

Example questions to add include:

- Given the commitment or goal you have set, what current business KPI will this goal influence?
- What is your current KPI that relates to this goal or commitment?
- Where is the KPI collected, by whom, and how often?

Giving the learners additional guidance on identifying a KPI can be helpful, particularly for soft skills such as leadership or coaching behaviors.

In a program for managers to improve their coaching skills, it is likely that the impact measurement will be based on the items they are coaching their direct reports on, rather than the increased efficiency or effectiveness of the coaching itself.

Practitioner's Tip

Here are some questions to include in your action plan:
- What skills would you like to commit to implementing from the program? Set a goal.
- What will success look like?
- Why is this goal important to you?
- What level were you at with this goal before attending the program? (Use a scale of 1 to 10)
- What specific actions will you take to progress toward this goal? In what situation can you take these actions?

You can find an action plan template in appendix A. To get more detailed information and guidance visit TurningLearningIntoAction.com.

Another popular format for action plans is "stop, start, continue," which asks learners, "What will you stop doing, start doing, or continue doing because of the learning program?" One of the challenges is that it's very easy for actions to fall into the continue category or be punitive for the individual if they fall into the stopping category. Replacing something that is being stopped with a more productive behavior will get better outcomes.

Why Does Action Planning Fail?

Action planning is such a simple concept, yet simple isn't always easy. All too often, the action planning step in the measurement and evaluation process fails in practice.

Successful action planning relies on having the right people in the program and learning content that is relevant to their role now. It relies on getting people to the point where they have acquired the skills, at least to a basic level, and can start applying them in their role. For the purposes of this chapter, we are making the assumption that these basics are already in place. If not, refer to your learning design and chapter 1 in this book. However, even with these assumptions, action planning can still fail.

Let's examine nine reasons why action planning fails and what you can do to prevent it.

Insufficient Time Is Invested in Action Planning

Facilitators often underestimate the importance of including time for action planning in training programs, sacrificing it for covering more content during group discussions. However, this overlooks action planning's critical role as a bridge between learning and the workplace, cementing behavioral changes. This is where learners make decisions about implementation and where the brain begins to forge new paths for these behaviors. Action planning is essential, not an afterthought.

Practitioner's Tip

It can be more challenging to create effective action plans in the virtual classroom than in a face-to-face classroom environment. For a thorough review of the specific steps and techniques you can take to make virtual learning more effective and engaging, and thus ensure successful action plans, read *Designing Virtual Learning for Application and Impact: 50 Techniques to Ensure Results* by Cindy Huggett, Jack J. Phillips, Patricia Pulliam Phillips, and Emma Weber (2023).

Action Planning Is Conducted at the End of Training

It sounds so logical to put action planning at the end of the training program, but this is not the time to begin the process. It requires a tradeoff between the quality of action plans and the completion of content. You may argue, how can people create action plans when they haven't covered all content or exercises? It is better to get quality reflection and action planning from 75 percent of the content (which can then be amended or added to later), than to learn 100 percent of the content and generate a low-level action plan both in numbers and quality. Learners can also confuse the action plan with a Level 1 feedback form if they're asked to do them both at the end of the program. Separate the documents. Action planning is about the future (what will you do), while Level 1 feedback is focused on sharing what has happened so far.

Insufficient Time Is Given for Reflection During the Program

Action planning should provide the opportunity for learners to review the knowledge gained and new insights from the program. If you haven't given learners time to reflect during the program, action planning is harder to do because they won't be able to consolidate their thoughts as easily.

People Want to Complete Their Action Plan After They Leave the Program

People are reflective by nature and typically want to go away and think about their action plan before committing to what they want to apply. However, my experience has shown that if someone leaves the learning environment before action planning, it takes between five and seven follow-ups for them to create their action plan. This means the individual has to be asked repeatedly to create an action plan, despite giving assurances they would do it on the flight home or by the end of the week. One option is to capture a base action plan during the program (virtual or face-to-face) and then amend it when (and if) they choose to reflect after leaving the learning environment.

Facilitators Tell Learners What to Put on the Action Plan

The desire to take the pressure and stress off learners and reduce their cognitive load can drive facilitators to become prescriptive about what learners put on their action plans. Self-determination theory, however, shows us that learners want agency over their learning. Couple this with what we know from adult learning principles, and everyone will gain better results if learners choose what goes on their action plans—they are the experts in their own roles and contexts.

Facilitators Think Action Planning Is Not Part of Their Role

"I can't make people create an action plan." It's not uncommon for trainers and facilitators to feel powerless about what will happen when someone leaves the learning environment. They can also feel powerless to help people with the action planning step. Action planning should be like any other training activity. It's not the facilitator's role to make people participate in a discussion or a role plan, for example, but setting up the conditions for success helps overcome any reluctance. Make action planning engaging, meaningful, and a standard part of your programs.

Commitment to Action Plan Falters From Design to Execution

It's not uncommon to include robust action planning in a learning program's design documents. The instructional design team and the key stakeholders who have signed off on the program have signed off on a design with robust action planning. However, by the time the program design is implemented (whether virtual or face-to-face), the action planning phase may be reduced in importance or dropped completely. Typically, lack of action planning is not a design issue—it's an execution issue.

Prescribing SMART Goal Setting Hampers Enthusiasm

Setting SMART goals (specific, measurable, achievable, realistic, and timely) is a common, well-known goal-setting strategy. If someone wants to use the SMART goal format, that is great, but forcing a learner to follow that format can kill their excitement and passion for a goal. Any goal that shows that a learner knows where they are and where they want to get to is a good goal. For example, they could use a scale of one to 10 (which helps the brain identify the knowledge gap), and then outline descriptors between their current state and desired state to identify the specifics of what needs to change.

There Is No Follow Up With the Action Plan

An action plan's value plummets if no one else sees it or follows up with it after it's been created. When learners write an action plan but don't see any results, it can lead to despair and a reluctance to write an action plan just for the sake of it. Ensuring that an effective follow-up strategy is in place and communicating it clearly will help reduce this problem. We'll discuss this more later in the chapter.

CHAPTER 10

What Can Be Done?

What can learning professionals do to ensure successful action planning? First, successful action planning comes from successful learning programs. Regardless of the learning environment, face-to-face or virtual, you can apply these solutions to set yourself up for success (Table 10-2 outlines the solutions that are best suited for different problems):

- Switch your mindset to thinking of the action plan as essential.
- Allow sufficient time and don't compromise on this—action planning may be the most important part of your learning initiative.
- At this stage, don't think of a group of learners (for example, the October cohort). Instead, think of 15 individual learners. Getting action plans from the group isn't important; getting 15 individual action plans is the key. Encourage each learner to choose actions that are meaningful to them individually and that they believe will make an impact in their role.
- Allow time for reflection and application discussion throughout the program so the action planning phase allows learners to consolidate their insights and decide which are the most important actions to take back in the workplace to create value from the program.
- Never action plan at the end of a training program or module—use the 75 percent rule. While waiting till the end of the session seems logical, this seriously compromises the quality of the action plans. Instead, start working on action plans when you're 75 percent of the way through the content for the session. Learners can always add to them later. (For more information, refer to the Action Planning Masterclass in appendix A.)
- Always have a follow-up process in place for the action plans.

A final note here about whether to capture action plans with pen and paper or via technology: There are theories about the brain and hand connection when handwriting, yet we all know that as we handwrite less and less in today's technological climate, the act of using a pen and paper can actually cause anxiety for some people. Technology provides a more accessible format. In addition, if you are using the action plans to collect key metrics and as a baseline for some of your analysis, having the action plans in an accessible technology format is essential. Technology also makes action plans easier to review, read, and distribute, which will be beneficial not only in the follow-up stage but also in checking their quality. When using technology within an organizational environment, however, you will need to be mindful of data privacy protocols and cyber security.

USING ACTION PLANNING AS A MEASUREMENT AND TRANSFER STRATEGY

Table 10-2. Reasons Action Planning Fails and Actions to Mitigate These Risks

Problems \ Solutions	Know action planning is essential	Allow time	Focus on the individual not the group—let them take ownership	Reflect throughout the program and consider application	Never action plan at the end of a program—use the three-quarter rule	Always have a follow-up strategy for action plans
Insufficient time is invested in action planning		x		x		
Action planning is conducted at the end of the training session					x	
Insufficient time is given for reflection during the program				x		
People want to create action plans after they leave the program		x		x	x	
Facilitators tell learners what to put on the action plan			x			
Facilitators think action planning isn't part of their role	x	x				
Commitment to action plan falters from design to execution	x					
Prescribing SMART goal setting hampers enthusiasm			x			
There is no follow up of the action plan						x

CHAPTER 10

Following Up on Action Plans

Once learners create action plans, what happens next is the key to driving results in the organization. Think about your current situation—what do learners do with their action plans right now? Do you ask them to share their plans with their managers? Is that the extent of it? Do you have any insight as to what else happens to the learners' action plans once the training program ends?

If your answer is no, it means that the learning team isn't connected with the results from a measurement and evaluation standpoint. And, it also means that your visibility is reduced at this crucial stage in the training process.

For best results and the highest level of impact, use a methodology that focuses on behavior change to follow up on your action plans, such as the Turning Learning Into Action (TLA) process (Figure 10-1). When it comes to applying learning back in the workplace, it can be easy to imagine that the biggest barrier to change is getting learners to remember to do it. While this may be true for technical programs, most training today deals with soft skills or human skills, which are not so mechanistic to apply.

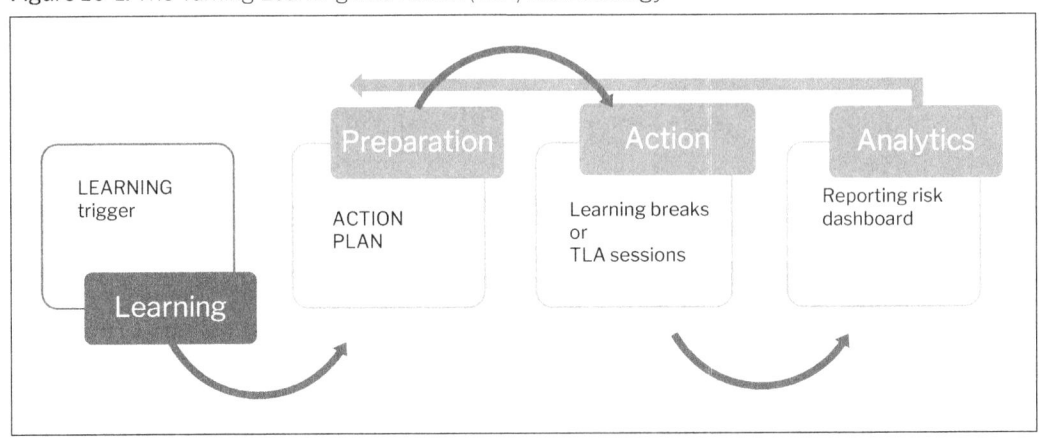

Figure 10-1. The Turning Learning Into Action (TLA) Methodology

Preparation	Action	Analytics
LEARNING trigger	Learning breaks or TLA sessions	Reporting risk dashboard
ACTION PLAN		
Learning		

Application of learning is far more complicated than sending people a quick reminder of what they said they would do. In fact, this can often be damaging because learners perceive the training department to be nagging them to change, which is never an effective way to get an outcome. As humans, our behaviors are governed by our thoughts, feelings, values, beliefs, fears, needs, and identity. Getting into this complex web of human drivers can be simplified by asking powerful questions to help the learners identify what will support them in moving forward and drive sustained ownership for the behavior change.

Broadly speaking, you can follow up on action plans in three different ways:

- **With a human.** This could be through the learner's manager, an internal or external specialist, or a buddy, depending on your available resources (including budget, skills, and time).
- **With technology.** Chatbot technology is readily available to create these follow-up conversations through self-reflective processes that drive both accountability and change. Coach M, which I have developed, is one example (Figure 10-2).
- **With a combination of humans and technology.** Often called "augmented follow up," this process involves augmenting human conversations with technology to make them more scalable.

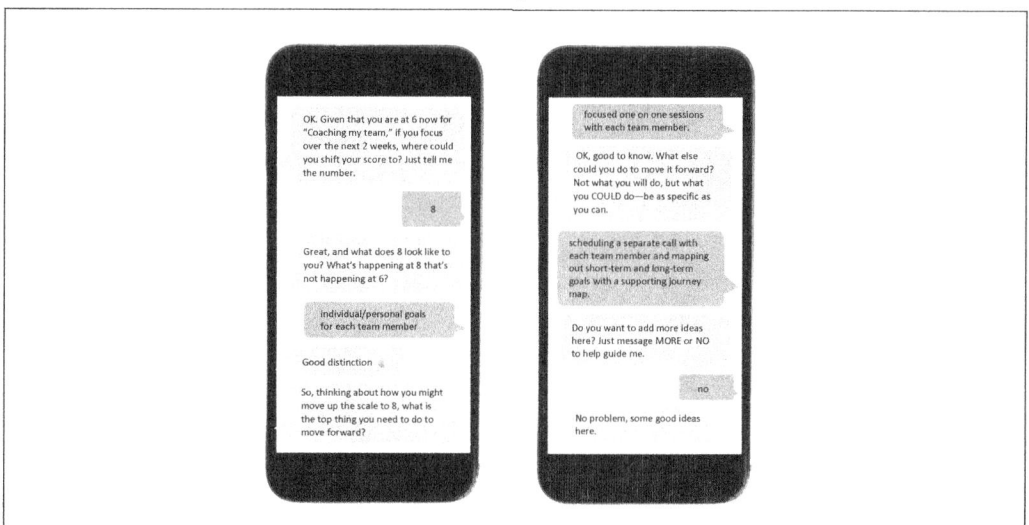

Figure 10-2. Coach M Conversational Extract Examples

Technology is by far the most scalable option. Imagine the level of data you can collect to contribute to the evaluation of your programs. Using a chatbot to drive an entire conversation will increase the depth of data that can be gathered to evaluate impact and results. (Figures

CHAPTER 10

10-3 and 10-4, for example, show two dashboards created using chatbot data.) To ensure a well-designed, reflective-based chatbot experience, learners need to discuss their action plans in a prebooked conversation with the chatbot coach for between 20 and 30 minutes on multiple occasions. (The case study example at the end of this chapter shows how my company used the chatbot Coach M to support the follow-up of action plans for an equity, diversity, and inclusion program.)

While manager follow-up has been the standard process for many years, studies have shown that even when primed and given tools for transfer, less than 50 percent of managers actually sit down and follow up with learners and discuss what they're applying from the program. Even in the best cases, this is typically only a single conversation and likely won't be sufficient to create the program's desired outcomes. As a result, many learning teams are implementing other processes to support their learners, including adding short transfer conversations into the learning design. This is an effort to ensure the action plans drive results that generate the impact the organization is looking to achieve.

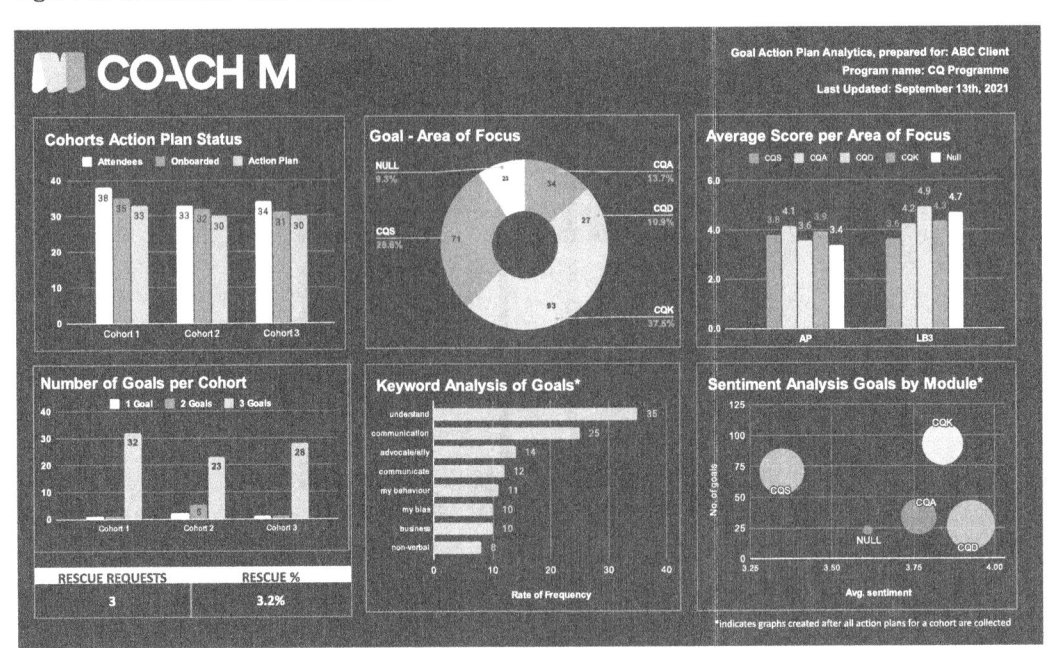

Figure 10-3. Coach M Action Plan Dashboard

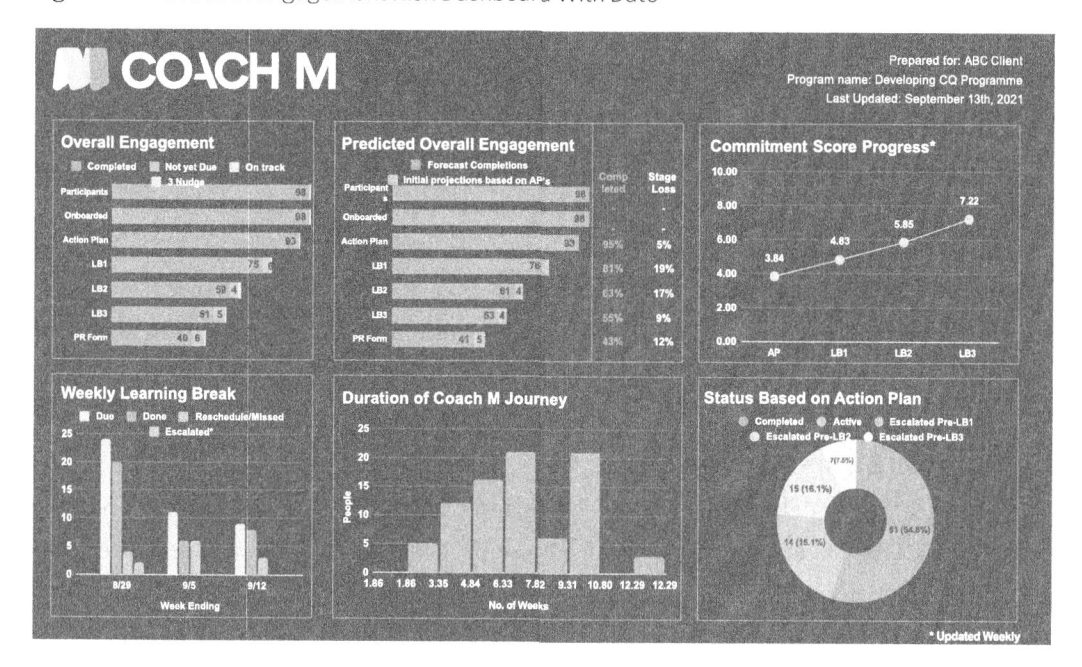

USING ACTION PLANNING AS A MEASUREMENT AND TRANSFER STRATEGY

Figure 10-4. Coach M Engagement Risk Dashboard With Date

Case Study: Delivering Behavioral Change in Diversity and Inclusion

Diversity and inclusion programs often fail. When a global membership organization representing 50,000 members set out to deliver a new diversity and inclusion strategy, they recognized that to genuinely embed cultural sensitivity and awareness and deliver behavioral change, they would need to facilitate learning transfer. A key element of the initiative was having each learner involved create an action plan.

George Floyd's death on May 25, 2020, sparked a global conversation about systemic racial inequality. For the organization, it triggered a period of self-reflection—the organization realized it had not given adequate attention or resources to tackling injustice, systemic racism, and discrimination.

Not only did the organization need and want to change, but as the custodians of their industry, they recognized it was their responsibility to address the industry's lack of diversity caused by inaccessibility and discrimination.

CHAPTER 10

A Rigorous Approach to Behavioral Change

The organization was acutely aware that without a robust approach to learning, the diversity and inclusion initiatives would fail. Embedding cultural sensitivity and awareness and creating actual behavioral change can't be achieved through learning alone.

The nature of DEI (diversity, equity, and inclusion) learning programs makes achieving behavioral change that much more difficult—to change our behaviors, we have to acknowledge that we're inherently biased and discriminatory, participate in some uncomfortable introspection, and identify what about us needs to change. This is much harder to achieve than a behavioral change in other contexts. Thus, the cultural intelligence (CQ) learning program needed to be practical, insightful, and scalable.

A Scalable Learning Model

The organization and Lever-Transfer of Learning developed a CQ learning program for executives, managers, and more than 300 staff. Together, they developed three targeted learning programs involving a combination of assessments, virtual workshops, and e-learning, combined with TLA conversations and the chatbot Coach M, to deliver the transfer of learning and create behavioral change at scale.

Learning Transfer—The Crucial Step in Embedding Learning

Often, programs bombard learners with information only for them to quickly forget what they've learned or fail to apply it. The necessary change in behavior never occurs. Achieving truly lasting change requires the most robust of training reinforcement approaches to create measured learning transfer.

To facilitate the leap to effective learning transfer, the CQ methodology was combined with the TLA methodology. Action plans were created as part of the training program, and these were followed up using TLA, which was delivered through one-on-one conversations with the participant using coaches or Coach M conversational technology at various intervals after the training course. Proven and practical, TLA puts reflection that is specific, structured, and accountable at the heart of the learning transfer process, increasing the training program's ROI. Coach M supports learners in a structured way to slow down and reflect on their specific learning commitments.

The Results

During the CQ learning program, each participant created up to three specific goals for how they would apply what they learned. Throughout the TLA process, the individual was asked to score and rescore their progress against these goals and outline the actions they'd taken to illustrate that score. To date, the goal was 64 percent for the executives, 106 percent for managers, and 54 percent for staff.

Alongside this data is the recorded feedback, which demonstrates what that progress looks like in action. Participants were asked about changes they made and the program's benefits or results. The stories behind the metrics were incredibly insightful for the organization, which was able to track behavioral change in real-time. These insights also demonstrated that the program had not only successfully shared the information, but that it was actually being applied in the workplace.

Case Study: Building Leadership Capability

When a global eye care device company set out to build leadership capability among their frontline sales managers, they knew that achieving sustainable behavior change would require a deeper approach. Marie Daniels, learning and development associate director, worked in collaboration with Lever-Transfer of Learning to develop an extension to their learning program grounded in a robust focus on learning application.

From the outset, it was understood that the most important outcome would be achieving sustainable behavior change. The application of the content was especially important in this context, because transforming leadership behaviors is a complex process. As such, learning transfer—the application of the learning as part of day-to-day behaviors—was front of mind early in the implementation process. It was not treated as an add-on or afterthought.

The program format was a blend of self-directed learning content, a three-day face-to-face program, self-directed application exercises, and conversations with Coach M. The program's topics included a coaching model, behavioral preferences, emotional intelligence, and time management. At the end of the face-to-face program, managers were prompted by Coach M to create an action plan with up to three specific goals for how they would apply what they'd learned. For example, goals included "Identifying my emotional triggers" and "How I can manage them more effectively?" as well as managing difficult conversations with associates and practicing courageous conversations.

Part of the appeal of this approach was the ability to demonstrate and measure individual action plan goal progression using the Coach M dashboard. Learners were given prompts to participate in three learning breaks with Coach M at different intervals following the program. During these breaks, learners could pause from business as usual to focus on their goals and chat with Coach M about their action plans. Learners were asked to score and rescore their progress against their goals and outline the actions they'd taken that illustrated their score.

Summary

This chapter explored why action planning is an important part of creating the impact from your learning initiatives and the measurement and evaluation of those initiatives. Exploring what can go wrong helps you plan for the steps that you can take to ensure success at this stage, as well as the ultimate success of your program. Take time to reflect to ensure that you turn your learning from this chapter into action.

Knowledge Check

Reflecting on your insights from this chapter, consider:

- How often have you been using action planning as a tool to drive impact and evaluation?
- What do you need to consider now for future action planning?
- What three actions can you take to improve the quality of your action plans?
- What follow-up processes will you put in place to support the application of action plans back on the job?

PART 3
Data Analysis

While the evaluation model shows data analysis following data collection, the focus of data analysis begins in the planning phase. Appropriate data analysis is imperative if stakeholders are to make good decisions based on the information evolving through the evaluation process. But what is appropriate data analysis? Well, it depends on:

- Type of data
- Population size
- Acceptable error
- Type of measures
- Time requirements
- Resource constraints
- Cultural constraints
- Convenience

Good analysis balances the experimental context with the organizational context. Program participants, their supervisors, peers, and direct reports do not function in a lab. They work in dynamic organizations where decisions are swiftly made in some cases with minimal information. So, providing the best data possible, given the constraints on the analysis opportunities, is a must. To be successful, evaluators must know how to analyze data and be able to balance accuracy with costs, ensuring the results are reported in the right context. This includes knowing enough about statistics to recognize what statistics does and does not do. It requires knowing how to analyze qualitative data enough to make meaning out of words. It also requires knowing why and how to isolate program effects so practitioners can answer the simple question, "How do you know it was your program that delivered results?" and how to convert measures to money so the magnitude of the problem or the value of program benefits are clear.

Part 3 covers these fundamental issues and more. By reading it, you will learn basic analysis techniques, including how to:

- Use basic statistics in evaluation.
- Analyze qualitative data.
- Isolate the effects of training on improvement in business measures.
- Convert measures to monetary value.
- Capture program costs.
- Calculate ROI.
- Measure intangible benefits.
- Forecast ROI.

CHAPTER 11

Using Statistics in Evaluation
TIMOTHY R. BROCK

IN THIS CHAPTER

This chapter explores the use of *basic* statistics to achieve two outcomes: Improve the usefulness of your evaluation data by identifying trends and hidden patterns, and improve your credibility as a talent development professional by properly using statistics so leadership can make data-driven decisions. After reading this chapter, you will be able to:

♦ Apply a logical approach to using statistical methods to analyze your evaluation data.
♦ Select the appropriate statistical methods to generate credible findings.
♦ Interpret the statistical findings to provide pattern and trend insights from your evaluation data.
♦ Report your evaluation results using the correct statistical terminology.

You Have Collected Your Evaluation Data—Now What?

Talent development professionals are expected to evaluate their programs to determine how well they met their objectives. After collecting the data, you want to analyze it to answer program objective questions using different perspectives offered by statistical methods. Statistics provide tools and techniques to help you organize, describe, and interpret the meaning of your measured data. It is essential to start with this perspective because you want your statistics to show how your training programs drive the organization to improve its operational efficiencies and organizational effectiveness. In other words, you want to show the value of what you do (Phillips and Phillips 2022).

Your statistics won't have any value if they are not done with a purpose. They could also undermine your credibility and the credibility of your evaluation effort. Incorrectly using measurement and statistics terms can also undermine your credibility. This chapter will help you proceed with statistical assessments with confidence.

> This chapter will not cover the statistical equations you must learn or solve because many software programs (such as JASP, SPSS, and Microsoft Excel) will do them for you. You can find more information about these equations by reviewing a few statistics books.

Types of Measurement Data and Statistics

Here's the good news: Most talent development professionals already use the common and established categories of measurement data. However, many do not give themselves credit for doing this because they are not using the correct terms to communicate.

There are four levels of measurement data (not to be confused with the levels of evaluation): nominal, ordinal, interval, and ratio. These four levels are divided into two types of measures—discrete and continuous. *Discrete measures* (also known as *categorical*) are limited to countable names and labels (or qualitative data). *Continuous measures* (also known as *numerical*) contain an infinite range of numbers (or quantitative data). Examples of the types and levels of measurement are summarized in Table 11-1.

You are likely already gathering each level of measurement data when you evaluate your training programs. Consider an end-of-course evaluation. Attendees complete a survey about their perceptions, typically using a Likert scale. What do you do with their responses? Count how many of each response was selected (nominal), and then order them from the most selected to the least (ordinal). Then, you assign a numerical value to each response to indicate where it falls on an interval scale to compare these responses to other data sets. A ratio scale is not included because no true zero value exists for perceptions. When reporting your evaluation data, describe it using these levels of measurement data to communicate your logical analysis and interpretation.

Table 11-1. Measurement Data Schema

Measurement Level	Count Labels	Order Matters	Equal Intervals	Interval Values Start From 0	Example
Nominal	X				The course content is useful for my job success. • Strongly agree • Agree • Neither agree nor disagree • Disagree • Strongly disagree
Ordinal	X	X No intervals			Arrange nominal selections from: • Most preferred to least preferred • Most important to least important • Most selected to least selected • Level of agreement
Interval	X	X	X Can go below zero		Used to measure test scores, dates, and attitude or perception. On a scale from -5 to +5, with -5 being not useful and +5 being useful, how useful was this course for your job success? -5 -4 -3 -2 -1 0 1 2 3 4 5
Ratio	X	X	X	X Can not go below absolute zero	Used to measure age, money, weight, distance, and behaviors. How many days this week did you use the training program job aid? 0 1 2 3 4 5 6 7

You are now ready to move from the levels of measurement data to using statistics to see and show the value of what you do. There are two types of statistics: descriptive and inferential. *Descriptive statistics* describe or summarize raw data. When evaluating a training program, you can use a small sample data set of a larger population (for example, one or two training cohorts) to describe the data by using statistics to look at it from different perspectives. You are looking for data set trends or patterns to offer insights hidden in the collected data. You'll use descriptive statistics as the baseline for *inferential statistics*, which allows you to make estimated generalizations (or inferences) about a larger population. The following section explains how to use descriptive statistics to see and show the value of your training programs.

CHAPTER 11

Descriptive Statistics

When you hear the terms *distribution*, the *measures of central tendency*, and *standard deviation*, think descriptive statistics. This type of analysis uses actual, not inferred, data collected through surveys or questionnaires, tests, interviews, focus groups, and observations to describe the data from different perspectives.

Including statistics with your evaluation analysis equips you to do three things:

1. Summarize a significant amount of information.
2. Determine the relationship between items.
3. Compare the differences in performance between two groups.

Statistics begin by describing the distribution of data sets to analyze them.

Distribution

Descriptive statistics determine the distribution of a data set to analyze it from three perspectives. The first perspective uses three measures of central tendency (mean, median, and mode). The second and third measures (dispersion and variance) use the central tendency values to calculate the spread of all the data points from the central tendency values and each other using variability measures. The distribution is typically visualized using tables or graphs. A simple case study provides context to understand these perspectives and statistical tests because "data can and should be read like a story" (Nelson 2021).

Suppose you were tasked with creating a training program to improve the productivity rate of an underperforming department. Before management commits to training all 100 people in the department (the population), they want you to train one class of 15 as a pilot group (your sample) to statistically analyze the effectiveness of the course using unit-hour productivity rates. Department supervisors monitor that performance data daily. After the training program, they share the preprogram baseline and the postprogram unit-hour data (Table 11-2). This data indicates that the program improved the unit-hour productivity rate for the sample group.

Table 11-2. Unordered Distribution of Pilot Preprogram and Postprogram Unit Hours by Employee

Employee #	1	2	3	4	5	6	7	8	9	10	11	12	13	14	15	Total
Preprogram	43	45	61	59	56	54	49	52	55	60	50	55	58	56	63	826
Postprogram	47	59	79	69	63	55	51	58	72	63	61	60	65	63	67	932

Measures of Central Tendency (Mean, Median, and Mode)

You now want to determine the center or middle of the distribution data set to establish the anchor value for all distribution analyses. This central tendency analysis provides the first statistical insight from the data set.

Three commonly used measures to do this are the sample mean ($\bar{x}$), median (Mdn), and mode (Mo), which determine the center from three different perspectives:

- **The mean** (or average) is calculated by adding each numerical score and dividing it by the number of participants. It is the mathematical center of the data set. Therefore, interval and ratio data are required to measure its central tendency.
- **The median** is the middle score when you reorder the data sequentially (for example, 2 is the median of the data set 1, 2, and 3). Think of the median line that divides a two-lane highway to ensure vehicles stay on their side of the road. The median requires ordinal data, such as ordered numbers (interval or ratio) or alphabetical category labels.
- **The mode** is the most common (or popular score). Think of apple pie á la mode being more popular than plain apple pie. You can have one or more modes in a data set. You can use this central tendency measure for nominal, ordinal, interval, and ratio data.

Practitioner's Tip

Don't confuse a mean with a median or a mode. For example, LeBron James has averaged 27 points, 7 assists, and 7 rebounds per game over his career of 1,760 games. Yet, he has never had a 27-7-7 statistic in a game (O'Connell 2024). Average is not the same as middle or most common.

In Table 11-3, the preprogram and postprogram data sets are reordered so that they're numbered from lowest to highest. Using an ordinal approach makes identifying the median and modes easier.

Table 11-3. Ordinal Preprogram and Postprogram Data Sets

	1	2	3	4	5	6	7	8	9	10	11	12	13	14	15	Mean	Median	Mode
Pre-	43	45	49	50	52	54	55	55	56	58	59	60	61	63	66	55	55	55
Post-	47	51	55	58	59	60	61	63	63	63	65	67	69	72	79	62	63	63

CHAPTER 11

This central tendency analysis allows you to see and show the value of your training program in greater detail than simply adding the total scores of both data sets. All three measures indicate that unit-hour productivity improved. In addition, these central tendency values establish the three values necessary to take your descriptive statistics analysis to the next level.

Measures of Dispersion (Range and Interquartile Range)

Once you define the center of the data set, you'll want to determine how far the numbers are spread apart from one another and from the center you just defined. The closer they are to the center of the data set and one another, the less variability between the numbers. A lower variability gives greater confidence in the generalizations you can infer from this pilot course toward the larger population in the department waiting to get trained. Typical measures of spread (or dispersion) are range, interquartile range, standard deviation, and variance. This chapter also includes the coefficient of variation as a descriptive statistic option.

Range (R)

The *range* defines how far apart the high and low numbers are in a data set. Note that in Table 11-3, the high and low numbers for the preprogram data set are 43 and 66, and they are 47 and 79 for the postprogram data set. The range for the preprogram data set is 23 (or 66 minus 43), and it is 32 (or 79 minus 47) for the postprogram data set. We do not know yet whether the range accurately reflects all the numbers or if high or low outliers influence it. Determining the interquartile range will answer that question.

Interquartile Range (IQR)

You can divide your data set into four ranges of numbers (called *quartiles*), which allows you to see the internal range or spread found around the center of your data sets (mean, median, and mode) and eliminate outliers.

The following steps demonstrate how to determine the first and third quartile (Q1 and Q3) values for the data set of 15 numbers (N):

1. Use this formula to determine Q1: (N+1)/4. This gives you a Q1 of 4: (15+1)/4.
2. Multiply the Q1 score by 3 to determine Q3: 3 × ([N+1]/4). Q3 is 12: 3 × ([15+1]/4).
3. Determine the 4th and 12th values in this ordered set of 15 numbers (using Table 11-3).

USING STATISTICS IN EVALUATION

4. Subtract the 4th value from the 12th for the pre- and postprogram data sets to determine the interquartile range: 60 minus 50 = 10 (preprogram data) and 67 minus 58 = 9 (postprogram data).

These interquartile ranges of 9 and 10 indicate that the intervals between the internal numbers are closer to the central tendency mode are less dispersed than the high-low 23 and 32 ranges because they do not include the skewed outlier values. This can give you greater confidence that the training program will have similar improvement results for the rest of the department.

Histograms provide a visual depiction of the data set distribution and the measures of central tendency. The histograms in Figure 11-1 show the spread from the central tendency measures of the preprogram and postprogram unit hours.

Figure 11-1. Preprogram and Postprogram Histograms Showing Data Distribution From Mean, Median, and Mode

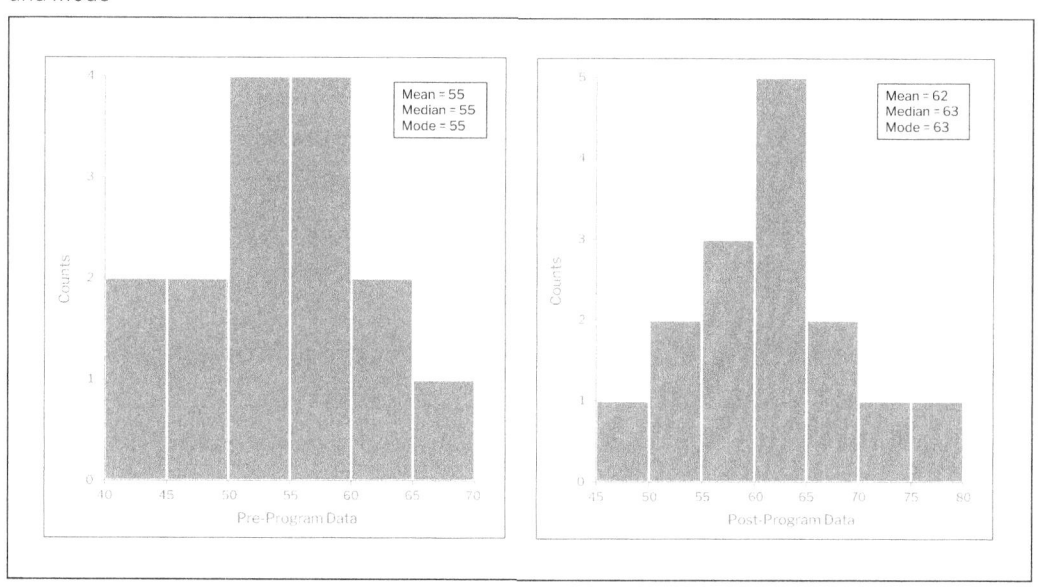

The three central tendency measures indicate slight variation, making them credible for comparative and inferential analysis. The spread of the data units higher and lower than the central tendency measures indicates a credible normal distribution.

If the data were skewed, the histogram distribution in Figure 11-1 would look different because values would not be evenly distributed higher and lower from the mean. For example,

163

CHAPTER 11

the center histogram in Figure 11-2 indicates that the three central tendency measures are at the center of the data set. The histograms to the right and left suggest that the central tendency mean and mode measures are skewed higher or lower.

Figure 11-2. Normal and Skewed Central Tendency Examples

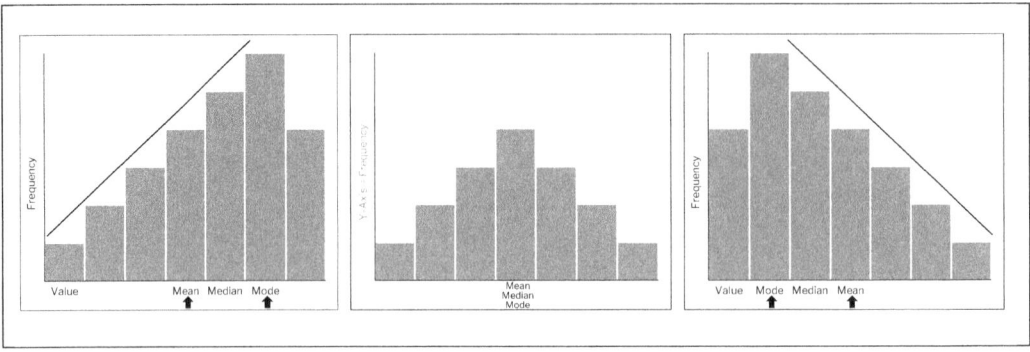

The histogram on the left has a negative skew because the mean reflects a lower average value than the mode. The right histogram has a positive skew because the mean reflects a higher average value than the mode. In a skewed central tendency situation, you want to use the median as your central tendency measure because outliers are least likely to skew the measure from the center of the data set.

Measures of Variance (Standard Deviation, Variance, and Coefficient of Variance)

For the measures of dispersion, you were looking at the spread between two data points. For the range, you looked at the range between the highest and lowest numbers. You narrowed the spread to the range between the first and third quartile for the interquartile range (IQR) to compensate for outlier values. Now, it's time to shift from the range within the data set to the variability between the data intervals.

Standard Deviation (SD or s)

What makes the standard deviation different from the measures of dispersion is that you determine how far each measure in the data set is, on average, from the central tendency

USING STATISTICS IN EVALUATION

mean. Like the high–low and interquartile range, you want a low standard deviation because that indicates less variability between your measures.

The standard deviation formula looks intimidating, but is not difficult to calculate once you understand the formula:

$$S = \sqrt{\frac{\Sigma(x_i - \bar{x})^2}{n - 1}}$$

The xi represents an individual data set measure. The $\bar{x}$ represents your central tendency mean value, which is 62. The Σ means *the sum of*. The seven steps in Table 11-4 show how to apply this formula to the first (47) and last (79) values in the postprogram data set, rather than all 15 numbers (the n in the formula). A software program can calculate the standard deviation after you enter the data set and mean values. The standard deviation is 8.018 for the postprogram data; preprogram standard deviation is 6.475 (note that the preprogram calculation is not shown in Table 11-4).

Table 11-4. Standard Deviation Calculation Steps Example

Step 1 x_i	Step 2 $x^i - \bar{x}$	Step 3 $(x_i - \bar{x})^2$	Step 4 $\Sigma(x_i - \bar{x})^2$	Step 5 n − 1	Step 6: $\Sigma(x_i - \bar{x})^2 / n - 1$	Step 7 $S = \sqrt{\frac{\Sigma(x_i - \bar{x})^2}{n-1}}$
47	47 − 62 = -15	-15² = 225				
79	79 − 62 = 17	8² = 64				
			900	15 − 1 = 14	900 / 14 = 64.3	√64.3 = 8.018

Note: Steps 1, 2, and 3 show the first and last numbers of the 15 postprogram data set in Table 11-3. If the data set numbers 2 through 14 were included, the sum of Step 3 would equal the total at Step 4.

The standard deviation allows you to determine if the productivity unit hour measures fall within a normal distribution, which expects 95 percent of the data set values to fall within two standard deviations of the mean. This distribution is visualized in a histogram that uses only the mean central tendency number (Figure 11-3) unlike Figures 11-1 and 11-2, which used the mean, median, and mode).

These histograms indicate that 95 percent of the preprogram and postprogram unit hour measures fall within two standard deviations of their mean. You can report that the standard deviation analysis suggests a normal distribution of the preprogram and postprogram productivity unit hours. This measure of spread technique strengthens the argument that the pilot training program results indicate you can expect a similar unit hour improvement distribution success for the rest of the department when trained.

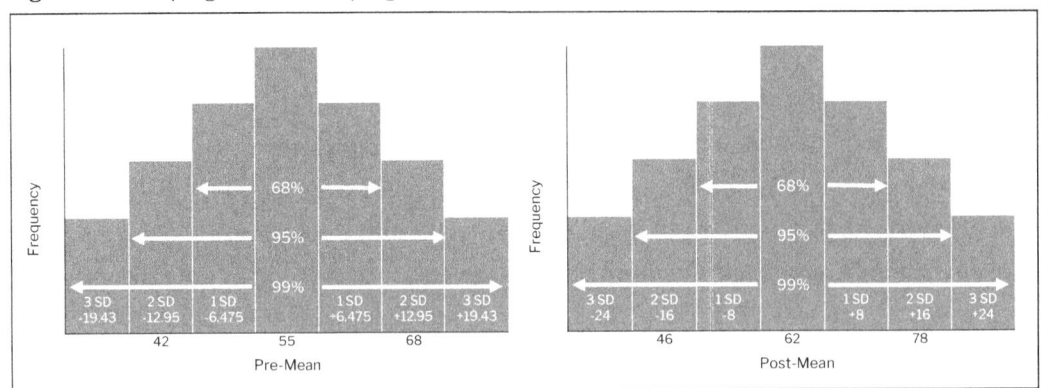

Figure 11-3. Preprogram and Postprogram Unit Hour Standard Deviation Distribution

Variance (s²)

It is challenging to interpret the variance on its own. You use this measure of spread with other statistical tests like analysis of variance (ANOVA) to compare data sets. Variance is calculated using the standard deviation formula, but skipping the last square root step. You can also square the square root (your standard deviation) to determine the variance.

Coefficient of Variation (CV)

The coefficient of variation (CV) uses the standard deviation and the central tendency mean to calculate a ratio for unlike data sets to compare them. You must use ratio data for this variation test. For our example, let's say you want to determine the correlation between training program test scores and participants' years of experience in their jobs. To calculate the CV, you'll divide the standard deviation by the mean times 100 (CV + [SD/M] × 100).

The test scores variable has a CV of 9.28 percent (standard deviation is 7.7 and the mean is 83 or [7.7 / 83] × 100). For the years of service variable, the standard deviation is 4 and the mean is 15, so the CV is 26.67 percent (or [4 / 15] × 100). This normalizes the standard deviations to allow a comparison. The two values show greater variability in years of service than test scores, indicating that the test scores are more consistent and had a greater influence on improved performance than experience.

USING STATISTICS IN EVALUATION

> **Practitioner's Tip**
>
> A z-score test calculates how many standard deviation units a single score is above or below the mean. This score provides additional insights into the variance between data measures. For example, the individual with 58 unit-hours is in the bottom third of these measures. However, the z-score provides a unique perspective. If you subtract this 58 score by the mean (62) and divide it by the standard deviation (8), you get a z-score of -0.5. This means the 58 value is less than one standard deviation below the mean value. A positive or negative z-score indicates that the value is greater or less than the mean. A z-score of 0 means the z-score is the same as the mean. The larger the z-score, the further it is from the mean.

Inferential Statistics

Inferential statistics make inferences about a general population using descriptive statistics sample data analysis results. You use the sample data from your descriptive statistics to infer or generalize about the larger population. Inferential statistics use comparisons expressed as generalizations to define a range of potential numbers about a population and a degree of confidence in those numbers. Two types of inferential statistics are correlation tests and regression tests. This section will briefly cover a correlation test.

Correlation Coefficient

Suppose you want to know the strength and direction (positive or negative) of the correlation between the two variables related to your training program evaluation data. A common correlation test is Pearson's correlation coefficient (r). The calculation is not easy (nor is the formula). You will want to use a software program for this calculation.

In the coefficient of variation, you compared test scores to job experience and learned that test scores affected productivity more. Now, you want to compare test scores with postprogram unit-hours productivity to understand the strength of the correlation between these two variables and whether the correlation is positive or negative. Using a software program, enter each of the 15 test scores and postprogram unit hour values for each ID number. The calculated r value is 0.9489. To determine the strength and direction of the correlation, compare the calculated value to a general description of the different values that occur between -1.0 and +1.0. A value of 0.9489 indicates a very high degree of positive correlation between the test

CHAPTER 11

scores and the performance measures. Figure 11-4 is a scatter plot that shows where each test score (X-axis) and unit hour (Y-axis) by individual intersect.

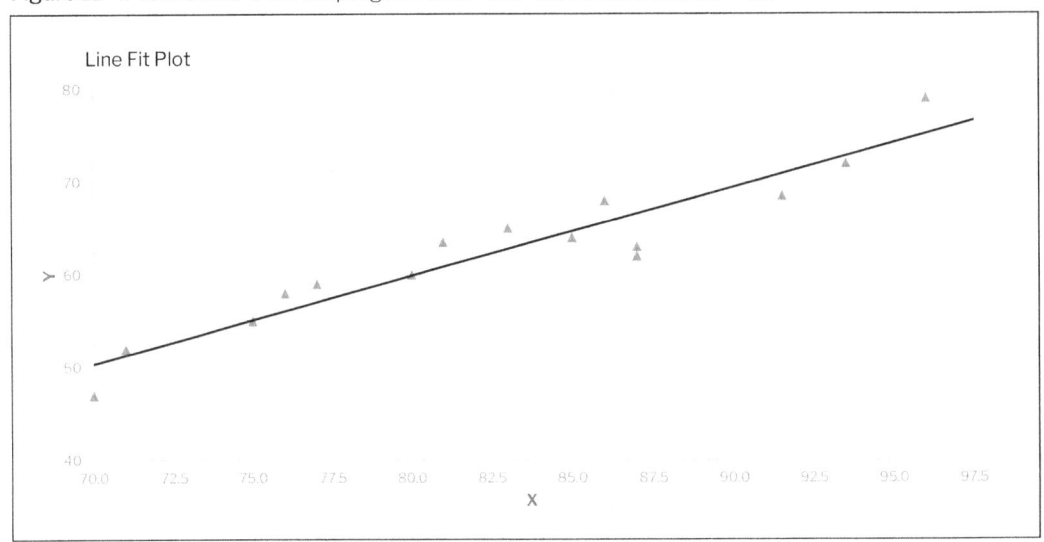

Figure 11-4. Test Score and Postprogram Unit-Hour Correlation Scatter Plot

This scatter plot visualizes a positive correlation between test scores and postprogram unit-hours productivity. A negative correlation line would appear higher to lower from left to right, indicating that the higher their job performance, the worse they did on their test scores. Including this statistic in your evaluation statistical analysis strengthens your assertion that the program was effective with the pilot group, and the low dispersion indicated by your other statistical tests strongly indicates that equivalent results can occur with the larger population.

Practitioner's Tip

Be careful with your confidence level when using inferential statistical data for making decisions because they are inferred estimates.

Summary

Statistics is a vital tool for seeing and showing the value of what you do. By measuring data required to answer the talent development program's objectives' effect on its workforce's perceptions, knowledge and skills, and job performance, the organization can judge whether its impact and ROI are worthwhile. This demonstrates the quality and effectiveness of the training and equips the organization to decide whether to continue the program, improve it, or put their money elsewhere to achieve organizational goals and objectives. You can refer to Table 11-5 to determine which statistics options are appropriate for each type of measurement data.

Table 11-5. Types of Measurement Data and Statistics Options

If you have:	You can do this:
Nominal data	• Mode • Frequency counts • Bar charts
Ordinal data	• Median and mode • Percentiles • Frequency distribution table • Bar graph
Interval data	• Mean, median, and mode • Standard deviation • Histograms • Pearson's correlation coefficient
Ratio data	• Mean, median, and mode • Range • Coefficient of variation • Pearson's correlation coefficient

Knowledge Check

Your organization of 50 sales representatives has decided to delay approving a training program company-wide pending the results of a pilot course limited to 10 sales representatives. This training program must improve the number of sales they close in a quarter. The data in Table 11-6 provides the test scores from the training program, the preprogram and postprogram quarterly sales data, and the level of experience (LoE) in months provided by the sales managers for the 10 training program participants.

CHAPTER 11

Use Table 11-6 to answer these questions. Then, review your answers in appendix B.

1. Determine the measures of central tendency (mean, median, and mode), dispersion (range and IQR), and standard deviation of all four data sets.
2. Calculate the coefficient variation for the test scores and LoE.

Table 11-6. Test Scores

Rep ID	1	2	3	4	5	6	7	8	9	10
Pre	53	61	43	52	71	38	36	84	61	56
Test	95	85	94	90	87	94	92	98	87	92
Post	94	86	92	83	96	84	90	92	89	81
LoE	7	8	6	6	5	3	4	9	8	5

CHAPTER 12

Analyzing Qualitative Data

DAMIEN M. SANCHEZ

IN THIS CHAPTER

This chapter explores the value of qualitative data for L&D professionals who are trying to make the business case for their projects. After reading it, you will be able to:

♦ Define qualitative data.
♦ Describe qualitative data collection and analysis methods.
♦ Analyze quantitative data using R code.

Defining Qualitative Data

Qualitative data can provide valuable insights for understanding just about any person or situation. This understanding is hard earned because of the work and time required to perform qualitative data analysis. This chapter will highlight the basic definitions of qualitative data and assert its value in identifying the intangible benefits of training. It will also review several qualitative data analysis methods, including content analysis and grounded theory. Finally, it will demonstrate how to analyze qualitative data using analytic enabled techniques that reduce the time required.

To remember what type of data *qualitative data analysis* is based on, think of the "l," which stands for language. Qualitative data is all about word-oriented data. It is data that is rich in context and can provide great depth to any evaluation or research project. This term is not to be confused with *quantitative data analysis* (where the "n" stands for numbers).

CHAPTER 12

The Value of Qualitative Data

Qualitative data is valuable because it provides context—the "why" behind the metrics organizations use to measure their success. For L&D solutions, it illuminates how organizations can maximize their efforts by clearly understanding the reason for changes in metrics. Take for example a fictitious organization called Quan Corp, which only looks at its sales numbers; its fictitious competitor, Qual LLC, looks at sales numbers but also gathers qualitative data from sales associates. Both organizations understand their sales numbers, which enables them to measure their performance. However, Qual LLC will also know why its sales numbers are changing and can use its qualitative data to make data-driven decisions that influence its bottom line and ultimately set it apart in the competitive marketplace.

Qualitative data can also help make the business case because of its ability to accurately describe the intangible benefits of any solution. An *intangible benefit*—a data item not directly associated with monetary value—is worth collecting because it can reveal additional value and the factors that drive the success of any initiative.

Although it's not as easy to assign monetary values to intangible benefits compared to quantitative data, they can still be quantified beyond testimonials and meaningful quotes. We'll discuss analytics-enabled methods for quantifying qualitative data in this chapter. Before performing analytics, however, you must have qualitative data to analyze. Therefore, it is essential to describe traditional instruments that you can use to collect qualitative data.

Qualitative Data Collection Instruments

The most common instruments for collecting qualitative data are interviews, focus groups, and open answer fields on surveys and questionnaires.

Interviews

Interviews are best for developing in-depth understanding. They allow two people to talk to one another and dig deep into the details of a subject. They're best done when following a predefined, specific protocol of questions. One drawback to interviews is that they tend to take a long time to conduct and analyze because of the amount of data that they produce. (See chapter 8 for more details on using interviews to collect qualitative data.)

Focus Groups

Focus groups are excellent for building group consensus. They require less time to conduct than interviews because many people participate in a single event. Focus groups tend to work best when there are about 10 people in them. The focus group facilitator is critical for keeping the group centered on the topic at hand. Establishing ground rules and procedures should always be done before the focus group starts to ensure everything goes as planned.

Facilitators must also pay attention to who they include in a focus group. For example, it's generally not a good idea to put direct reports and their manager in the same focus group because the direct reports will likely defer to what their manager thinks. Facilitators should make sure the people in the room have equal levels of influence to ensure everyone has a voice. (See chapter 9 for more details on using focus groups to collect qualitative data.)

Open-Ended Questions on Surveys and Questionnaires

Open-ended questions in surveys and questionnaires can generate qualitative data that is as simple or complex as you want. Simple data is generated by answer choices labeled "other," while complex data includes multi-paragraph responses to in-depth questions with large text fields.

The general benefit to using open-ended questions is that the answers are typically being input directly into a computer, which facilitates analysis. In contrast, interviews and focus groups typically require time consuming collection and transcription. Although you can facilitate many transcription tasks using built-in video conferencing software functions or by playing recorded audio to a voice recognition program, open-ended question types comparatively require a lower level of effort to analyze. (See chapters 5 and 6 for more details on using surveys and questionnaires to collect qualitative data.)

Improving the Quality of Qualitative Data

Regardless of the type of instrument you select to perform qualitative data collection, performing a traditional analysis can be daunting. Applying analytic methods can relieve a great amount of that burden because much of the analysis is automated; however, any quality issues with the data will be magnified. The adage "garbage in, garbage out" certainly applies here. You can improve the quality of qualitative data by focusing on the questions asked regardless of the delivery method, because that's what drives the answers. (Note, however, that some questions are best suited for online or face-to-face instruments.)

Let's review some tips to help generate the highest quality qualitative data possible.

Don't Use Yes-or-No Questions In Live Settings

Yes-or-no questions won't generate any rich responses, so they're a waste of valuable time in a live setting. Instead, always ask open-ended questions so participants can develop depth and detail in their answers. Open-ended questions produce detailed data that helps facilitate data-driven decision making about any subject of inquiry.

Focus on Facilitation of Face-to-Face Techniques

Facilitation skills are key to collecting good qualitative data from interviews and focus groups. Ensure that anyone who is conducting an interview or focus group is well-trained because any inconsistencies in how they ask questions will influence the responses provided.

People who facilitate focus groups have a particularly challenging job because they need to keep the discussion on track. Establishing and enforcing ground rules for the focus group is vital. The facilitator's approach is also important because they need to know when to stop asking questions and pursue additional details. Facilitators of both data collection methods need to be aware of how to appropriately interpret any nonverbal responses as well. These considerations should be attended to long before a facilitator is sitting in front of the people who answer their questions.

Engage Stakeholders in Developing Questions

Working with people to collect qualitative data is a responsibility. Avoid causing anyone any undo discomfort or psychological harm—what you ask and how you ask it can absolutely risk doing just that. Questions matter. Context matters. Use a participatory approach to develop the interview and focus group questions or online surveys and questionnaires by engaging local stakeholders and representatives from your target population. Develop the questions together and test the instrument prior to starting any formal data collection. Doing so will ensure you collect qualitative data in a way that acknowledges experience and humanity.

Qualitative Data Analysis Methods

Once you have qualitative data in hand, it is time to consider how to analyze it. There are several qualitative analysis methods. This chapter discusses two foundational methods—content analysis and grounded theory—which can be used to analyze qualitative data sets of any size. Both offer distinct advantages, including how accessible they are to L&D professionals of diverse professional backgrounds.

Content Analysis

Content analysis is a foundational qualitative data analysis method because of its simplicity. In a nutshell, content analysis requires the analyst to read all of the qualitative data. The method was introduced by Klaus Krippendorff in the 1980 book *Content Analysis: An Introduction to Its Methodology*. Immersing yourself in data is the whole point of a content analysis. Read all the transcripts and posts, listen to all the interviews, and watch all the videos. Anyone can perform a basic content analysis because it is effectively a document review. Becoming familiar with all the collected qualitative data allows for a complete understanding of the context of any learning solution.

Grounded Theory

In 1967 in *The Discovery of Grounded Theory: Strategies for Qualitative Research* (1967) Barney Glaser and Anselm Strauss introduced *grounded theory*, which allows researchers to use the qualitative data content to develop themes. It lets the data speak for itself rather than imposing a preconceived notion or research construct to interpret it. This reduces bias by removing the researcher's opinion. Conducting grounded theory research requires creating labels for language trends. While reading through transcripts, an analyst should note any labels and statements related to those labels. Upon completion of the first labeling cycle, the analyst should review the labels and statements and make any necessary modifications to consolidate similar items. The end result is a completely labeled data set. These labels are quantifications of qualitative data.

CHAPTER 12

> **Practitioner's Tip**
>
> When analyzing qualitative data, approach the task with an open mind because the inquiry is exploratory in nature. Keep the questions you are trying to answer simple and focus them on what you want to improve with the organization. Keep your audience in mind and make sure you can communicate your results with useful visualizations to help them understand the findings.
>
> —Nick V. Flor, PhD, Associate Professor, Information Systems, Anderson School of Management

Drawback of Traditional Qualitative Analysis Methods

While qualitative data is rich with detail and can identify intangible benefits for any learning initiative, it does come with baggage. Collecting and analyzing qualitative data using content analysis and grounded theory can take inordinate amounts of time because it requires hours spent transcribing audio recordings of interviews or reading through transcripts of focus groups. Most talent development professionals do not have time to analyze qualitative data—in fact, they are often being asked to do more with much less. Thus, when collecting qualitative data is not feasible as part of an evaluation, many opt to use satisfaction surveys with Likert scales and pre- and postlearning assessments with multiple-choice questions. However, the latest advances in technology and data science now provide attractive options for L&D professionals who want to examine the context of their programs and also gather intangible benefits. The rest of this chapter is dedicated to introducing modern data analytics methods that can drastically reduce the amount of time needed to analyze qualitative data.

Sentiment Analysis

Sentiment analysis is the most accessible modern data analytic technique talent development professionals can use to understand their qualitative data. By identifying sentiment words in the data and assigning scores to them, you can quickly determine whether qualitative data is positive, negative, or neutral. For example, a small sample of positive and negative sentiment words could look like Table 12-1.

Table 12-1. Sentiment Word Table

Word	Category
Great	Positive
Nice	Positive
Fantastic	Positive
Useful	Positive
Bad	Negative
Naughty	Negative
Horrible	Negative
Wretched	Negative

The positive words are worth 1 point, while the negative words are worth -1 point. *Sentiment analysis* involves identifying all the positive and negative words in the data and then adding up the scores. If the end result is 0, the sentiment is neutral. The score produced by a sentiment analysis is known as a sentiment score.

Sentiment scores can quickly show whether people responded positively or negatively to a question. For example, "What changes, if any, should we make to this course?" is a common end of course evaluation question. Two potential responses are:

- Great course! It was valuable and I learned useful information.
- Wretched course content was not relevant to my job.

It's clear that the first comment is positive and the second is negative. A sentiment analysis would score the first response with a 2 (a point each for "great" and "useful"). The second response would receive a -1 score (a point deducted for "wretched"). The overall sentiment score for these two statements is 1 (the difference between 2 and -1 is 1).

Calculating a sentiment score is fairly straightforward, but the task becomes more complicated as the number and length of responses increases. This is where using analytic software like R to perform the sentiment analysis comes in.

Practitioner's Tip

R is a free, open-source data analysis program that is popular in data science circles. From the outside looking in, it might seem impossible to learn how to use a program like R because it works based on text commands—users essentially need to write simple computer programs to analyze data. However, the code needed to run an analysis is provided in the exercise later in this chapter.

CHAPTER 12

Beyond Sentiment Analysis

Sentiment analysis depends on finding positive and negative words in qualitative data. However, it's possible to find and analyze any word or phrase. First, identify a phenomenon of interest and organize the words and phrases that represent the phenomenon into discreet categories. It is often easiest to use phenomena that are well established, like the social construction of knowledge, sales skills, or emotional intelligence. Within the categories, add words and phrases for R to identify—this is known as a *lexicon*. Table 12-2 shows a sample lexicon for a custom analysis.

Table 12-2. Custom Analysis Lexicon

Word	Category
I feel	Self-awareness
My actions	Self-awareness
My intent	Self-awareness
I understand	Empathy
Feelings	Empathy
Help	Empathy
Let's go	Motivation
Drive	Motivation
Persevere	Motivation

The more words and phrases you include, the more accurate your custom analysis will be. Also note that phrases typically produce more accurate results during analysis because they carry important context that can differentiate noise from the phenomenon of interest.

In contrast to a sentiment score, a custom analysis generates counts of the lexicon's words and phrases. This effectively quantifies the qualitative data, which allows for the quick summarization of large amounts of data without having to read a single post. Categorized qualitative data is easy to report in tables and graphs and is credible even to people who think quantitative data is the ultimate measure of truth. Performing a custom sentiment analysis allows talent development professionals the flexibility to fit the results of qualitative data analysis to their needs and make a business case for their programs.

ANALYZING QUALITATIVE DATA

> **Practitioner's Tip**
>
> You can apply what you learned about sentiment analysis in this chapter to conduct a small research project in your organization. Look at an online discussion among a group of people or a Zoom transcript and ask yourself about the trends you are observing. Apply custom sentiment analysis techniques to figure out how many people responded using given terms.
>
> —Charlotte Nirmalani (Lani) Gunawardena, PhD, Distinguished Professor Emerita, Organization, Information, and Learning Sciences Program

Summary

This chapter described qualitative data and various data analysis approaches. The power of applying analytic techniques is to analyze enormous data sets and produce almost real-time findings. However, the techniques might tempt some to think there is no need to verify the findings or be familiar with the data being analyzed. Quite the opposite is true. The analytic techniques presented in this chapter are not intended to replace the talent development professional. Instead, these analytic techniques are tools you can use to quickly understand data and the general trends within. They're intended to make analysis more efficient and avoid the painstaking work it would otherwise take to develop similar findings using content analysis or grounded theory. Always verify findings by reviewing the data being analyzed and avoiding assumptions.

True power is realized when you can use analytic techniques to develop just in time findings that are responsive to the needs of decision makers. Then, you can help your organization better understand the impact of your learning programs and ultimately facilitate the success of your programs and your organization. For additional analysis techniques related to those described in this chapter, see the forthcoming book *Knowledge Co-Construction in Online Learning: Applying Social Learning Analytic Methods and Artificial Intelligence* by Charlotte Nirmalani (Lani) Gunawardena, Nick V. Flor, and myself.

CHAPTER 12

Exercise: Conducting Sentiment Analysis Using R

You can perform a sentiment analysis without reading a single response thanks to data science advances and a program called R. The following exercises provide the R code needed to perform both a traditional and custom sentiment analysis.

Installing R

To install R on a PC, download the program from the official R website (r-project.org). Select the download mirror (called a Comprehensive R Archive Network) that is closest to your physical location to speed up the download. Then, run the installer. It will provide various prompts to facilitate the installation process. The default program configuration is adequate for most L&D professionals.

Formatting Data for Analysis

Once the program is installed, you'll need to prepare your data for analysis. R requires files to be saved in a specific format with a specific structure. The first step is to download your qualitative data (typically from an LMS, survey, or questionnaire administered online).

CSV Format

Format your data in a comma separated value (CSV) file. This file type is very common and can be exported easily from a spreadsheet program like Excel if your LMS or online survey tool does not export to CSV. If the qualitative data originates in a word processor like Word, simply copy that data into a spreadsheet program.

Save the CSV file to your computer's Documents folder—R works out of that location by default.

Table Structure

R requires data to be formatted as directed in this chapter. You will need to name the data columns so you can refer to them during the analysis (R works by identifying the column names). Table 12-3 shows the ideal structure for your CSV file.

ANALYZING QUALITATIVE DATA

Table 12-3. Sample Data

ID	Text
Josh	I didn't feel prepared to apply the techniques learned in real-life sales situations.
Frank	Some of the content felt outdated and not applicable to modern sales practices.
Marcos	The training felt too basic, and I was hoping for more advanced techniques.
Alexa	I appreciated the practical exercises that helped reinforce learning.
Chance	The pacing of the training sessions was inconsistent, leading to confusion at times.
Mohammed	The training provided valuable insights into effective sales techniques.
Nick	The training didn't adequately address the challenges specific to our industry.
Ramon	The course materials were well-organized and easy to follow.
Lillian	The real-life examples shared during the sessions were incredibly helpful.
Wes	I found it challenging to stay engaged during certain parts of the training.
Brad	The training materials were poorly organized and difficult to follow.
Quentin	There was not enough focus on overcoming objections, which is crucial in sales.
Raj	I would recommend this program to anyone looking to improve their sales skills.
Bob	I liked the emphasis on building strong customer relationships.
Samantha	The interactive nature of the training kept me engaged and focused.

The "ID" column should list pseudonyms or some sort of identifier; the "Text" column should list the qualitative data. For the code provided in the upcoming exercises to work, your data needs to have at least two columns and use the same column headers as Table 12-3. Note that additional columns can be included in the analysis, but those two columns are required. If you want to try using R but do not have data of your own, input Table 12-3 into a spreadsheet program and save it as a CSV.

Input the Sentiment Analysis Code Into R

The code provided is meant to be copied and pasted directly into R. Note that it will be necessary to replace the name of the files being imported unless the qualitative data has the same name indicated in the code.

The code provided also includes some plain explanations, which are denoted using a # at the beginning of the line. The explanations apply to the commands that follow. These can also be copied and pasted into the program because it doesn't interpret anything that comes on a given line that starts with a #.

CHAPTER 12

To perform a sentiment analysis, use the following R code and a CSV of your data:

```r
# installs and loads the tidytext package which provides the framework
needed to perform the sentiment analysis
install.packages("tidytext")
library(tidytext)
install.packages("dplyr")
library(dplyr)

# Stores the CSV data within R in groups according to the columns in the
CSV and displays a summary of what is loaded. Change 'your_data.csv' to
match the file name of your CSV
grouped_data <- read.csv("your_data.csv") %>%
group_by(id) %>%
mutate(line = row_number()) %>%
ungroup ()
grouped_data

# Takes the 'grouped_data' variable and creates tokens which are
discreet words out of the data
tokens <- grouped_data %>%
unnest_tokens(word, text)

# Load the Bing sentiment lexicon included in tidytext
get_sentiments("bing")

# Joins the sentiment lexicon with the tokenized data
sentiment <- tokens %>%
inner_join(get_sentiments("bing"), by = "word", relationship =
"many-to-many")

# Calculate the sentiment scores
sentiment_summary <- sentiment %>%
 group_by(sentiment) %>%
 summarize(count = n())

# Display the sentiment scores
sentiment_summary

# Plot sentiment scores in a graph
install.packages("ggplot2")
library(ggplot2)
ggplot(sentiment_summary, aes(x = sentiment, y = count)) +
 geom_bar(stat = "identity", fill = "skyblue") +
 labs(title = "Sentiment Analysis", x = "Sentiment", y = "Count")
```

Input the Custom Sentiment Analysis Code Into R

Performing a custom sentiment analysis using R requires the following files:
- CSV with qualitative data structured like Table 12-3.
- CSV with a custom lexicon formatted like Table 12-2. Label the first column "Word" and include words and phrases that need to be found. Label the second column "Category" and add the category labels associated with each corresponding word or phrase. If you do not have a custom lexicon, input Table 12-2 into a spreadsheet and save it as a CSV.

Use these CSVs to perform a custom qualitative data analysis. The difference between this process and the sentiment analysis is that you're loading the custom lexicon instead of the lexicon referenced in the sentiment analysis code. To perform a custom phenomenon analysis, use the following R code:

```
# installs and loads the tidytext package which provides the framework
needed to perform the analysis
install.packages("tidytext")
library(tidytext)
install.packages("dplyr")
library(dplyr)

# Stores the CSV data within R in groups according to the columns in the
CSV and displays a summary of what is loaded. Change 'your_data.csv' to
match the file name of your CSV
grouped_data <- read.csv("your_data.csv") %>%
group_by(id) %>%
mutate(line = row_number()) %>%
ungroup ()
grouped_data

# Assuming 'grouped_data' is your text data stored in a data frame with
a 'text' column. If there is not a column named 'text', change this
value to match where your data is stored
tokens <- grouped_data %>%
 unnest_tokens(word, text)

# Read the customized lexicon
custom_lexicon <- read.csv("custom_lexicon.csv")

# Join the custom lexicon with the tokenized data
phenomenon <- tokens %>%
 inner_join(custom_lexicon, by = "word", relationship = "many-to-many")
```

```
# Summarize scores
analysis_summary <- phenomenon %>%
 group_by(category) %>%
 summarize(count = n())

analysis_summary

# Visualize sentiment scores (optional)
install.packages("ggplot2")
library(ggplot2)
ggplot(analysis_summary, aes(x = category, y = count)) +
 geom_bar(stat = "identity", fill = "skyblue") +
 labs(title = "Custom Analysis", x = "Categories", y = "Count")
```

Knowledge Check

Answer these questions to check your knowledge. Then, review your answers in appendix B.

1. Qualitative data is mainly focused on words instead of numbers.
   - ❏ True
   - ❏ False

2. What are the features of a grounded theory analysis? (Check all that apply.)
   - ❏ Running R code to analyze the data
   - ❏ Reading transcripts
   - ❏ Consolidating labels into larger categories
   - ❏ Creating labels for language trends

3. The sentiment analysis framework can be applied to just about any phenomena.
   - ❏ True
   - ❏ False

CHAPTER 13

Isolating the Effects of the Program

JACK J. PHILLIPS AND DAVID MADDOCK

IN THIS CHAPTER

This chapter explores techniques for isolating the effects of programs from the effects of other factors when evaluating impact measures. After reading it, you will be able to:

♦ Explain the importance of isolating the unique contribution of a program to impact outcomes.

♦ Identify techniques available to isolate the effects of a program.

♦ Select the appropriate isolation technique for any program.

The Importance of Isolating the Effects of a Program

With impact data collected, the next important issue is to isolate the effects of the program from other influences. This critical component of measurement and evaluation can help build and ensure your credibility by acknowledging that factors other than the program can influence the business results.

In organizations, programs are implemented within complex systems of people, processes, and events. The only way to determine the connection between a particular program or project and the measured business impact is to deliberately isolate the effects of the program on the specific business outcomes of interest. This ensures that the data analysis allocates only that part of the performance improvement that is connected to the program. Without this important step, the study's conclusions will lack credibility because other organizational

CHAPTER 13

efforts—such as job redesign, incentives, rewards, compensation, technology, operational systems, and other internal processes—might also affect the program's results. Factors external to the department or function area, or to the organization, can also influence performance. Thus, it's unwise to give full credit for performance results to a single program without accounting for other factors that clearly have a similar potential to influence results. Credible evaluation requires an effort to ensure that only results directly attributable to the program are reported to stakeholders.

> **The Risk of Not Isolating the Effect**
>
> Erica was excited. She was presenting to the CEO, who had begun several talent initiatives, including the Leadership Institute, which Erica had designed and developed. Now she was giving her first report on the impact of the Leadership Institute, including data showing significant increases in important metrics, such as employee engagement, safety performance, employee retention, and productivity. She ended with a summary indicating how successful the Leadership Institute had been to date.
>
> When she was finished, the CEO reminded Erica about several other new initiatives, including the organization's new performance management system, the improved employee benefits package, the "Do No Harm" program, and a recent organizational realignment.
>
> "How do you know what effect the Leadership Institute had on the results you're showing when considering the impact of these other initiatives?" the CEO asked. Erica's stomach churned as she began to respond. She didn't have a credible answer, and the CEO was about to realize the same thing.
>
> "I'm sure the other programs had some impact," Erica responded. "You cannot isolate the effects of a soft program like leadership development."

Techniques for Isolating the Effects of a Program

Fortunately, a variety of techniques can be used to isolate the effects of a program from other influences. Each technique has different advantages and drawbacks, and the choice of which to apply depends on the situation. These techniques include:

- Experimental versus control group arrangement
- Trend line analysis of performance data
- Forecasting performance data with modeling
- Participant's estimate of impact

- Management's estimate of impact
- Estimates based on expert opinion or previous studies
- Calculation or estimation of the impact of factors other than the program
- Customer estimate of impact

These techniques can reasonably be condensed into a smaller number of manageable categories, including control groups, trend and forecast analysis, and estimates. We'll explore these techniques in the rest of this chapter, but note that other books provide greater technical detail and more statistical sophistication, which is beyond the scope of this chapter and book. *Value for Money* is one such resource (Phillips et al. 2019).

Practitioner's Tip

Identify the isolation technique during evaluation planning. This allows you to select the best technique for the specific context and to review this part of the evaluation plan with key stakeholders. It is easier to collect additional data early in the process than to try to gather data after an evaluation process is conducted.

Chain of Impact: The Initial Evidence

Before presenting the techniques, examine the chain of impact implied in the different levels of evaluation, which must be in place for the program to drive business results (Figure 13-1). The chain of impact models the results and process by which we intend to achieve those results. Isolation of program effects, although not itself a link in this chain, should also be applied to the business results data to determine the change that can be attributed uniquely to the program.

The chain of impact assumes that measurable business impact achieved from an L&D program is derived by applying skills and knowledge on the job over a specified time after a learner completes the program (training programs serve as a common example). Thus, successfully applying program material on the job should stem from new knowledge, skills, or attitudes learned in the program, which are measured at Level 2. For business results to improve (Level 4), this chain of impact implies that measurable on-the-job applications are realized (Level 3) when new knowledge and skills are learned (Level 2).

CHAPTER 13

Figure 13-1. The Chain of Impact

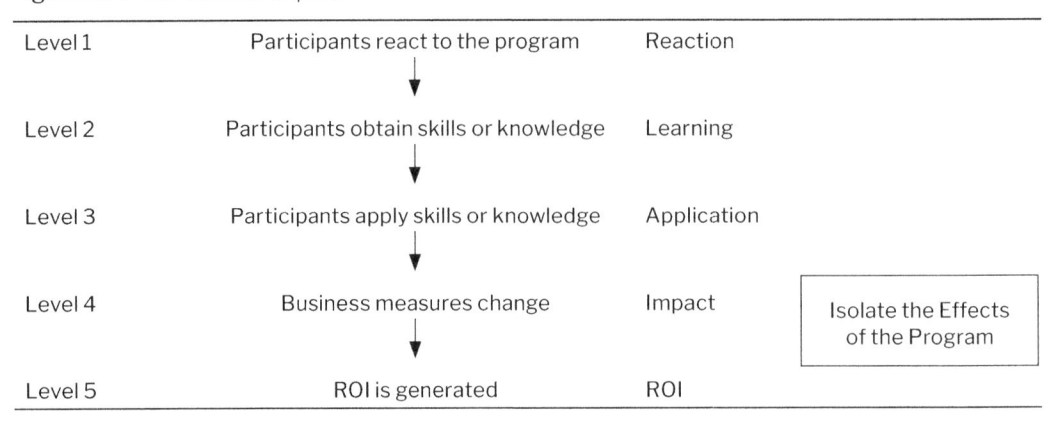

Level 1	Participants react to the program	Reaction	
Level 2	Participants obtain skills or knowledge	Learning	
Level 3	Participants apply skills or knowledge	Application	
Level 4	Business measures change	Impact	Isolate the Effects of the Program
Level 5	ROI is generated	ROI	

Attributing business impact to the program is difficult without evidence of the chain of impact. Concluding that the program caused any performance improvements is illogical if there is no learning or application of the material on the job. Literature and practice support this approach (Alliger and Janak 1989). A practical requirement, therefore, is to collect data across all levels of evaluation when conducting an ROI evaluation. You can also use lower-level evaluation data to help isolate and explain the effects of the program in higher-level evaluations.

Despite its importance, the chain of impact does not prove a direct connection between the program and business impact. Isolation is necessary to make this direct connection and determine the amount of improvement attributable to the program.

Using Control Groups

The classic approach to isolate the impact of a program is using control groups in an experimental research design (Wang, Dou, and Lee 2002). This involves observing an experimental group that participates in the training program and a control group that does not. When the training program is the only the difference between the two groups, you can attribute any differences in outcomes to the program, because it was the only driver of performance changes. We'll present the basic control group design here, but different situations require variations of the design. (These topics are addressed in more detail in *Isolation of Results: Defining the Impact of the Program*; Phillips and Aaron 2008).

The basic control group design has an experimental group and a control group, as illustrated in Figure 13-2. The experimental group participates in the program, whereas the control group

ISOLATING THE EFFECTS OF THE PROGRAM

does not. You collect data on both groups before and after the program. The results for the experimental group, when compared with the control group, reveal the impact of the program.

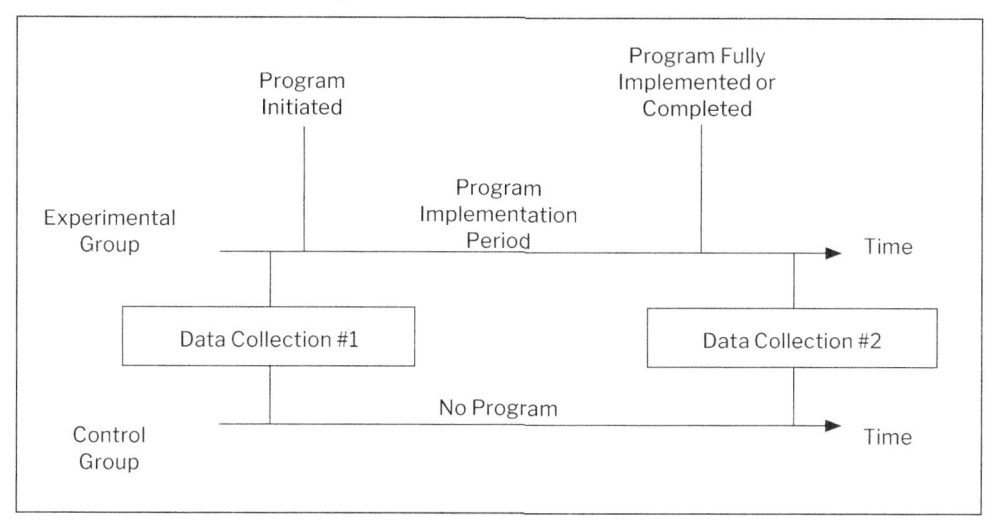

Figure 13-2. Control Group Design

There should be no significant differences between groups in characteristics that can influence the final outcome data, independent of the program's outcome. The participants in each group should be randomly selected and at approximately the same job level, experience, ability, working conditions, and possibly even location.

Practically speaking, control group designs aren't always feasible, so TD professionals must explore other approaches of isolating the effects of the program on performance. Organizations face tradeoffs between research principles and feasibility: Higher costs are often associated with measurement and evaluation, and the very nature of a control group assumes that some will receive the potential benefits and others will not. A control group evaluation design also implies a longer evaluation timeline. Consider the following questions to help determine if a control group is the best isolation technique for your program:

- Is the population large enough to divide into groups?
- Is the population homogeneous—representing similar jobs and environments?
- What measure is influenced by the program?
- What variables may be influencing the measure? (These variables will be used to select the comparison groups for the control group arrangement.)

- Using the Pareto principle (that roughly 80 percent of outcomes come from 20 percent of causes), which variables most strongly influence the output measures?
- Can the program be withheld from a particular group? This may occur naturally if it takes a long time to roll out a program. It's possible that a group of employees could take the program as many as three to six months after the first group of participants. In this case, you could compare the last group with the first group. Other times, there may be ethical or financial implications to withholding a program from a particular group.
- Is a pilot offering planned? Could the pilot group be matched with other groups for comparison?

Here are several tips for using a control group arrangement:
- Keep the groups separated by different variables affecting the measure, such as different locations, different shifts, or different staffing.
- Minimize communication between the groups.
- If possible, do not tell the control or experimental group that they are part of an experiment and being compared with others.
- Monitor data on a short-term basis to check for improvements in both groups.
- Look for the Hawthorne effect (a change in behavior caused by the special attention of the study itself rather than the program) from the experimental group.
- Interact with the group as required by the program design but try to minimize other interactions.
- Do not create expectations beyond the norm that may influence the results (for example, do not tell people that they are a special group and top performance is expected).

Control groups are a powerful and credible method for isolating the impact of an initiative. If you can't establish a control group, but have access to a data set that includes participants who were involved in a program and participants who were not, you can use a method called a *propensity score match* to mimic the structure of a control group from randomized data. It is beyond the scope of this chapter to explain propensity scoring, but there are statistical analysis texts on the subject if you are interested (Guo and Fraser 2014). This technique also pairs well with the more advanced statistical techniques discussed in the models and forecasting section of this chapter.

Using Trend Lines and Forecasts

When a control group analysis is not feasible for isolating the impact of a program, the next logical choices are trend line analysis and modeling. A *trend line analysis* is a simple process of forecasting the measure in question using preprogram data. The second method, a *modeling* technique, is more general and can be used when other influences have entered the process because you develop a mathematical relationship or model to forecast the data.

Trend Line Analysis

This approach uses previous performance on the outcome measure as a baseline to draw a trend line that extends into the future. Once the program ends, you compare actual performance with the projected value shown by the trend line. Any improvement in performance over that predicted by the trend line can be attributed to the program, as long as two conditions are met:

1. **The trend established prior to the program was expected to continue without the program.** The process owners should provide input to reach this conclusion. If the answer is no (indicating other factors would affect the outcome trend), you should not use the trend line analysis. If the answer is yes, ensure the second condition is also met.
2. **No other new variables (or influences) entered the process following the program to influence the measure beyond the program's influence.** If the answer is yes, you must use another method. If the answer is no, the trend line analysis will develop a reasonable and credible estimate of the program's impact.

Figure 13-3 shows an example of a trend line analysis for employee turnover in a government contact center. The vertical axis reflects the level of turnover (annualized). The data is from before and after first-level managers participated in a training program focused on how to create an improved employee experience. As shown in the figure, there was an upward trend in the data prior to implementing the training program, which then had a dramatic effect on turnover.

The temptation is to measure the improvement by comparing the average turnover rates six months prior to the program (45 percent) to those from six months after the program (35 percent), which yields a 10 percent difference. However, a more accurate comparison is reviewing the six-month trend value after the program (55 percent) compared with the actual

CHAPTER 13

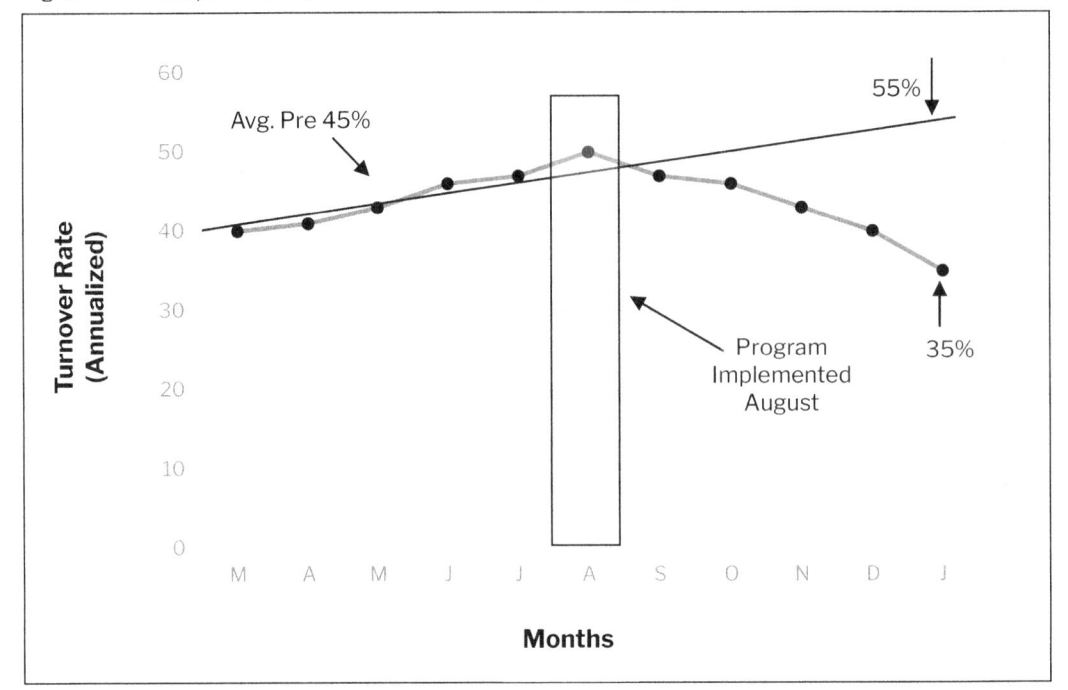

Figure 13-3. Sample Trend Line of a Turnover Reduction Program

value after six months (35 percent), which yields a difference of 20 percent. Using this more conservative measure increases the accuracy and credibility of the isolation process. In this case, the two conditions outlined for an effective trend line analysis were met.

Preprogram data must be available and it should have a reasonable degree of stability. If the data's variability is high, the trend line's stability becomes an issue. If you cannot assess the stability of the data from a direct plot, use a more detailed statistical analyses to determine whether the data is stable enough to make the projection (Salkind 2000). You can project a trend line with a simple analytical function available in many calculators and software packages, such as Microsoft Excel. The primary advantage of this approach is that it is simple and inexpensive. If historical data is available, it's used to draw a trend line and estimate the differences. Although not exact, it provides a quick assessment of a program's potential impact.

Using trend line analysis can be straightforward and credible, as long as you can successfully answer yes to these four questions:
- Is historical data available for the measure at hand?
- Are at least six data points available?
- Does the historical data appear to be stable when plotted over time?
- Is it anticipated that there will be no other influences, factors, or processes implemented at the same time of the program?

Forecasts From Modeling

A more analytical approach to trend line analysis uses forecasting methods to predict a change in performance variables, usually through a regression calculation. Regressions are used to predict outcomes, such as changes in stock prices or probable SAT scores. This approach presents a mathematical variation of trend line analysis and accounts for other variables present while the program is implemented. You then compare the actual performance of the outcome measure with a forecasted value of that measure. A mathematical model can include multiple data points you collected to explain a trend, which allows you to examine what *proportion* of the change was due to your program.

The forecasted value takes this additional influence into account. A linear model, in the form of $y = ax + b$, is only appropriate when one other variable influences the output performance and that relationship is characterized by a straight line. In a linear equation model, the line represents the value of the historical relationship between your two variables (such as profits and months). If time (months) is on the axis, the portion of the line that extends past historical data and into the future is your forecast of anticipated performance improvement. If multiple variables are influencing the performance, the relationship will be characterized by a trend line within a scatter distribution. While linear models allow you to compare the difference between actual performance and forecasted performance, the multiple model allows you to look at data you already have and determine how much of the difference was explained by your program.

A challenge with this predictive approach, especially if you need to account for additional influences, is that it requires more sophisticated statistical techniques and software for multiple variable analyses. Even then, it may not be possible to fit the data to the model.

CHAPTER 13

Application of Forecasting Methods

A large retail store chain with a strong sales culture implemented a sales training program for sales associates. Applying the new skills should increase the sales volume for each associate. An important measure of the program's success was the sales per employee, collected six months after the program and compared with the same measure prior to the program. The average daily sales per employee prior to training, using a one-month average, was $1,100 (rounded to the nearest $100). Six months after the program, the average daily sales per employee was $1,500.

After reviewing potential influencing factors with several store executives, only one factor—the level of advertising—appeared to change significantly during the observation period. The advertising staff developed a mathematical relationship between advertising and sales using the historical values. Their simple linear model yielded the following relationship: $y = 140 + 40x$, where y is the daily sales per employee and x is the level of advertising expenditures per week (divided by 1,000). The least squares function used to derive this equation is a routine option on some calculators and included in many software packages.

The level of weekly average advertising expenditures in the month preceding the program was $24,000, and the level of expenditures during the six months following the program was $30,000. Assuming that any other factors influencing sales were insignificant, store executives determined the impact of the advertising by plugging in the new advertising expenditure amount (30) for x and calculating the average daily sales, which yielded $1,340. Therefore, the new sales level caused by the increase in advertising was $1,340. The new actual sales value was $1,500; so $160 ($1,500–$1,340) could be attributed to the program.

The primary advantage of this approach is that it can predict business performance measures without implementing the program, as long as appropriate data and models are available. It can be especially useful to have a statistical forecast about how a product, stock, or program will perform under given conditions. A sufficiently advanced model can even allow the user to examine how the forecast will change if an input variable changes. This is actually the basis for how many machine learning models predict changes in the stock market or global economic forces. Using more complex models can be a helpful option for practitioners familiar with the assumptions and requirements of general linear model techniques. (Note that while presenting more complex specific methods is beyond the scope of this chapter, you can find more information in other publications, such as *Principles of Forecasting*; Armstrong 2001). However, you do not need complex approaches to unearth the value when using the straightforward methods described in this chapter.

Using Estimates

If the previously discussed techniques are not feasible, consider using estimates to isolate program effects. Estimates are subjective and should be considered only after all other approaches have been exhausted. However, they can provide a powerful and credible approach to connecting the program to business results. Organizations with dynamic environments and time constraints will make decisions with the best available data. The key is to follow the credibility rules outlined in the ROI Methodology's Guiding Principles.

When using estimates to isolate program effects, make sure they're coming from the most credible source—typically program participants or their managers or customers. Take a conservative approach and make sure to account for the error or reliability of the estimates.

Participant and Manager Estimates

The effectiveness of this approach assumes that you can use the data sources to determine or estimate how much performance improvement can be attributed to the program. When using this technique, you need to identify one or more business measures prior to program implementation, and then you must see improvement following the program; additionally, you'll need to link the program to the specific amount of performance improvement to determine its monetary impact. You can collect this information using focus groups, interviews, or questionnaires. (Detailed guidelines for collecting estimate data using each of these approaches can be found in other sources, such as *Survey Basics* by Phillips and Aaron [2008]).

This process may raise some concerns. Estimates lack the objective accuracy desired by some researchers. The input data may also be unreliable if participants are incapable of providing this type of estimate, either because they aren't aware of which factors contributed to the results or are reluctant to provide data. If the questions come as a surprise, the data may be scarce.

Several advantages make this technique attractive. It is a simple process, easily understood by most participants and others who review evaluation data. It is inexpensive and takes little time for analysis, which makes the results an efficient addition to the evaluation process. Participant estimates originate from a credible source—the individuals who produced the improvement or their immediate manager—and the process to develop the estimates is easy. Estimates taken from a group of people are usually accurate—the "wisdom of crowds" claims that findings collected from many people will result in better decisions than findings collected from a few (Surowiecki 2004).

The relative ease with which you can collect this data, however, should not entice evaluators into an overreliance on this approach. Always consider more rigorous approaches first. If time and resources permit, estimates can provide a corroborating and enlightening data source even when other methods are also feasible. It can also be useful to collect multiple methods of data to ensure the estimates confirm what you see in other methods of analysis.

As with the very act of measurement, isolating the effects of a program may never be completely precise and error free. Estimates can be sufficient for clients and senior leaders who tend to readily accept the approach. Living in an ambiguous world, they understand that estimates have to be made and may be the only way to approach an issue. They understand the challenge and appreciate the conservative approach to estimation (with error adjustment), often commenting that the actual value is probably greater than the value presented. This process is particularly appropriate when the participants are managers, supervisors, team leaders, technical staff, and other professional and technical employees.

The steps to estimating the contribution of a program include:

1. Obtaining the actual change in impact measure after the program is implemented
2. Identifying the factors that contribute to the improvement in the impact measure
3. Estimating the contribution of the improvement specifically due to the program under evaluation given the variety of factors (typically reported as a percentage)
4. Describing the basis for the estimate
5. Adjusting for error in the estimate by identifying the level of confidence associated with the estimated contribution (typically reported as a percentage)

The Estimation Process

A large financial institution had implemented various initiatives to increase opportunities for branch staff to cross-sell several products. The initiatives included sales training, incentive systems, goal setting and management emphasis, and marketing.

Six months after the sales training, one measure being tracked showed improvement—credit card accounts had increased by 175 per month on average. The training team wanted to know how much of the increase was due to the sales training. To find out, they sent branch managers a questionnaire that included a series of questions focused specifically on the contribution of the sales training.

The branch managers assembled their teams to determine the causes of the increase in credit card accounts. Together they identified the contribution of each factor and adjusted for

ISOLATING THE EFFECTS OF THE PROGRAM

error in their estimates by reporting their confidence in the estimation. Adjusting for error provides the lowest possible estimate. Their findings are shown in Table 13-1.

Table 13-1. The Estimation Results

Monthly Increase in Credit Card Accounts: 175

Contributing Factors	Percent of Average Impact on Results	Percent of Average Confidence Level
Sales training program	32%	83%
Incentive systems	41%	87%
Goal setting and management emphasis	14%	62%
Marketing	11%	75%
Other	2%	91%
Total	100%	

The contribution of the sales training program for the branches was calculated by multiplying the number of credit card accounts (175) by the contribution factor (32 percent) by the confidence estimate (83 percent). Based on this calculation, the training team estimated that the sales training program could be attributed to 46.48 new credit card accounts per month.

Customer Estimates of Program Impact

One helpful approach in some narrowly focused situations is to solicit input directly from the customers. In these situations, you would ask customers to share how much of their decision to purchase a product or service was based on a project, program, advertising, or promotion. This technique focuses directly on what the program has delivered at the impact level (sales).

One common measure of customer reaction is the net promoter score, which is a measure from -100 to 100 that consolidates the likelihood of a customer to recommend your business or service. Many online survey platforms now include tools to collect and calculate this score. A net promoter score can be taken at any point in the value chain of outcomes. If customer estimates are taken after the impact, the questions about estimates could be taken before or after the net promoter question.

Of course, you can only use customer estimates in situations where you can obtain their input. Even then, customers may not be able to provide accurate data. They must be able to see the influencing factors to isolate them. However, because customer input is usually credible, the approach is helpful for the situations in which it can be used.

CHAPTER 13

Summary

This chapter explored isolating the effects of a program, a critical step when making the connection between results and the program. Various techniques are available, including control groups, trend lines, forecasting, and estimates, which may come from a variety of sources. You should always follow this step when evaluating programs at the impact and ROI levels.

Knowledge Check

As part of a quality improvement program, an electronics components manufacturer conducted a series of training programs. One measure of quality is reject rate, which is the percent of items returned for rework. The business conducted a continuous process improvement program (CPI) in July to improve the reject rate in one work unit. After the program was completed, the training staff measured the impact of the program on the reduction of rejects. Figure 13-4 shows the reject rate six months before and after the program was implemented. The trend lines show the relative trends and midpoint values both before and after the program. Use the figure to determine the improvement in reject rates due to the program. Then check your answers in appendix B.

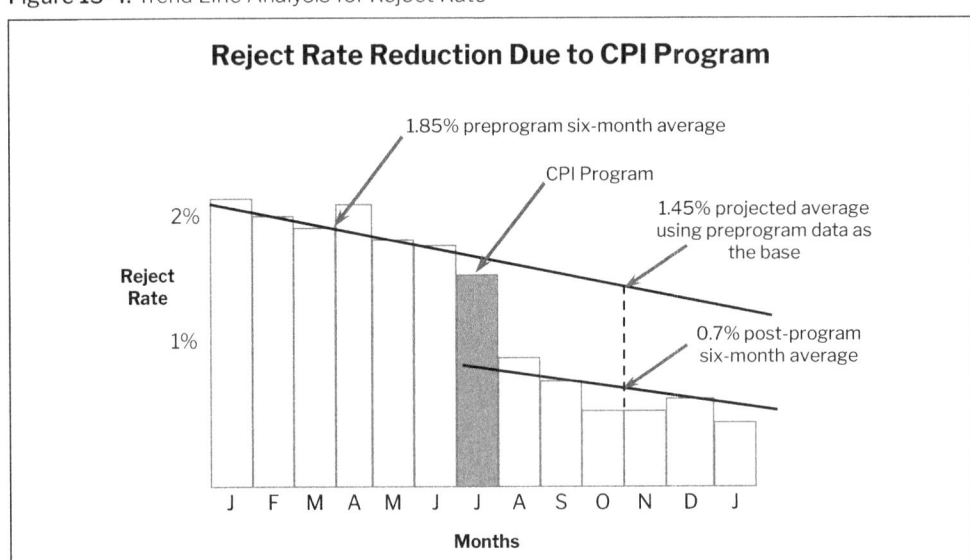

Figure 13-4. Trend Line Analysis for Reject Rate

Reject Rate Reduction Due to CPI Program

- 1.85% preprogram six-month average
- CPI Program
- 1.45% projected average using preprogram data as the base
- 0.7% post-program six-month average

Months: J F M A M J J A S O N D J

CHAPTER 14

Converting Measures to Monetary Value

PATTI P. PHILLIPS

IN THIS CHAPTER

This chapter explores techniques to convert measures to monetary value and calculate the monetary benefits of your program. After reading it, you will be able to:

- Explain the importance of converting a measure to money.
- Identify techniques to convert a measure to money.
- Apply five steps to calculate the annual monetary value of improvement in a measure.

Why Converting Measures to Money Matters

Money talks. It describes the magnitude of a problem or opportunity, the benefits of improving a situation, and, of course, the cost of programs and processes. While a program can be shown to be a success by providing business impact data, this information isn't always sufficient. For example, a program may reduce the number of complaints from disgruntled employees by 10 percent, which translates to an average reduction of seven complaints per month or 84 complaints per year. That may not seem like much of an improvement at first, but think about it in monetary terms. For example, let's say addressing one complaint costs $6,500 in team member time and resources. If the program reduces complaints by 84 per year, that is a cumulative cost savings of $546,000 (84 × $6,500). Now, the benefit of reducing complaints is much more evident.

Let's look at a few other reasons to convert measures to money.

CHAPTER 14

Showing the Payoff
Money demonstrates the potential payoff for addressing a problem or opportunity. It defines why an organization should invest in a program and indicates the extent to which a problem or opportunity is worth pursuing. For example, if a company is incurring fines due to compliance violations or an excessive number of accidents, the value of investing in new programs is apparent when the results are converted to monetary value. The best way to get the attention of a potential program sponsor is to place the problem or opportunity in the context of money.

Value Equals Money
For some stakeholders, the most important value of any program is its monetary contribution. Because executives, sponsors, clients, administrators, and other leaders are concerned with the allocation of financial resources, they want to see evidence of a program's contribution in financial terms. Often, for these key stakeholders, stating outcomes in any other terms doesn't provide enough information to determine where to allocate resources.

Money Normalizes Program Benefits
Investing in talent development leads to many benefits. In fact, a single program might contribute to improvement in multiple measures. Converting these measures to a monetary value allows the program evaluator to compare different measures in similar terms.

For example, an increase in productivity of 70 percent sounds good. So does a 30 percent improvement in quality, especially if these improvements exceed the target. But what if you need to compare the two outcomes? On the surface, one might think increasing productivity by 70 percent is of greater value than improving quality by 30 percent. However, a 70 percent increase in productivity may be worth $200,000, compared to $400,000 for the improvement in quality. Converting the values to money shows that the high-value improvement in this case is quality.

Converting Data to Money Is Similar to Budgeting
Professionals and administrators work with budgets and are expected to develop them with an acceptable degree of accuracy; thus, they are comfortable tabulating costs. When it comes to benefits, however, they may not have the same comfort level, even though

both processes use similar techniques. Defining the benefits of a program in terms of cost savings or cost avoidance may make it easier to identify the value of the program. The monetary benefit resulting from a program becomes a natural extension of the budget.

Monetary Value Is Vital to Organizational Operations

With global competitiveness and the drive to improve operational efficiency, awareness of the costs related to processes and activities is essential. In the 1990s, this emphasis gave rise to activity-based costing (ABC) and activity-based management. ABC is not a replacement for traditional general ledger accounting. Rather, it is a translator or medium between cost accumulations—that is, the specific expenditure account balances in the general ledger—and the end users who must apply cost data in decision making. In typical cost statements, the actual cost of a process or problem is not readily discernible. ABC converts inert cost data to relevant, actionable information. This has become increasingly useful for identifying improvement opportunities and measuring the benefits realized from performance initiatives (Cokins 1996). Understanding the cost of a problem and the payoff of the corresponding solution is essential for proper business management.

Monetary Benefits Are Necessary for Calculating ROI

Return on investment (ROI) is a fundamental accounting metric that compares the annual monetary benefits of a program or project to its costs. However, the benefits of a program must be converted to money before they can be compared to the program costs. It is only by converting benefits to the same type of measure as program costs (which is money) that the two can be mathematically compared and ROI calculated. While there is mention of the concept of ROI and its importance in evaluating training throughout this book, it is discussed in more focused detail in chapter 16.

Techniques to Convert a Measure to Money

Converting measures to money is not new. Monetary values are placed on a variety of measures including the benefits of public parks, the value of human life, improvements in productivity and quality, and the lifetime value of customers. Let's review some techniques for converting measures to money.

CHAPTER 14

Standard Values

Most of the data around measures that matter in an organization has already been converted to money. If it is important enough to drive a program or project, then someone has calculated its monetary value. These standard values are used to convert output data, quality measures, and employee time to money.

Converting Output Data to Monetary Values

When a program has produced a change in output, you can determine the value of the increased output using the organization's accounting or operating records. Output measures include revenue and productivity measures. So, if a program leads to an increase in sales, then you can convert the sales revenue from the unit sold to profit using the standard gross profit margin. Using the profit margin accounts for the cost of goods sold.

For example, if average weekly store sales per salesperson increase by $1,700 per week as the result of a program and profit margin is 2 percent, the monetary value of the increase in sales is $1,700 × 0.02 = $34 per week per person. That does not sound like a lot. But, let's assume that 75 people participated in the program. If you multiply $34 by the number of participants who generated that profit, then the added value to the organization is more impressive: 75 × $34 = $2,550 profit per week. Still not impressed? If those 75 people work 48 weeks per year, you'll see a yearly profit increase of $122,400 ($2,550 × 48) due to that program. (Chapter 13 describes how to isolate the effects of the program.)

While $122,400 in profit for one year from a group of 75 people may still not be impressive, if the program cost $50,000 to implement and it generated $122,400 in profit, the ROI would be 145 percent.

$$\text{ROI} = \frac{\$122{,}400 - \$50{,}000}{\$50{,}000} \times 100 = 145\%$$

Whether that is a good return or not depends on the target. But if you consider the typical return on investment in capital investments ranges from 10 to 15 percent, it's pretty good. (Chapter 16 explains the ROI formula in more detail.)

If you're considering a measure of productivity, you can reflect the value of the increased output in the accumulated savings if additional output is realized without increasing input. Most organizations have already calculated the standard costs associated with these outputs.

For example, if you are an insurance company, one measure of productivity would be claims processed. The standard value of a claim processed might be $10.00 per claim. If an agent increased the number of claims processed by one per day for 220 days, that would be an added value of $2,200 per agent (220 × $10) over one year due to improving productivity.

Converting Quality to Monetary Value

Quality is a critical issue in most organizations, so managers typically track the cost incurred to improve quality outcomes. And because many TD programs are designed to improve quality, the program owners must place a value on improvement in relevant quality measures. For some quality measures, the task of assigning a monetary value is easy.

For example, if quality is measured by a defect rate, the value of improvement is the cost of repairing or replacing a defective product. This standard value might have originally been calculated as:

$$\frac{\text{Number of people} \times \text{Number of days} \times \text{Cost per person per day}}{\text{Number of defects repaired}} = \text{Average cost of repairing a deficit}$$

Converting Employee Time to Monetary Value

Reducing the use of employee time is another common objective. A program might enable teams to perform tasks in a shorter timeframe or with fewer people. While there are a variety of benefits to saving time, the most obvious is reducing the labor costs of performing the work or engaging in an activity. You can calculate the monetary value by multiplying the hours saved by the labor cost per hour (including the benefits factor). For example, after attending a time management program, participants estimated that they saved an average of 74 minutes per day, which is worth $31.25 a day or $7,500 a year. (The $31.25 per day was calculated using the participants' average salary plus the benefits factor.)

Practitioner's Tip

When converting time to money, it is important to account for how the saved time is used. If it's not used productively, then the value of time saved to the organization is nil.

Historical Costs

Historical records may contain the value of a measure or reveal the cost (or value) of a unit of improvement. This technique involves identifying the appropriate records and calculating the cost components of the measure in question. For example, a large construction firm implemented a program to improve several safety-related performance measures, ranging from OSHA fines to total workers' compensation costs. Using a year of data from the company's records, the team was able to calculate the average value of improvements in each safety measure.

Internal and External Experts

When historical costs aren't available, another technique is using internal or external experts. A resident expert in an area may be able to provide the monetary value for a measure. For example, labor relations experts may know the value of labor union member grievances at different levels. External experts might also provide valuable insight into the value of a measure. Whether working with internal or external experts, be cognizant of their time spent helping you. This is particularly important when targeting a positive ROI, because you will need to include that cost in your denominator calculation and thus might affect the result.

Databases

The internet and local or university libraries are other places practitioners can look to when converting measures to money, especially when there are no standard values, historical costs, or experts. Look in journals and other references that reflect the industry in which the measure resides. For example, if you run a program that affects turnover of restaurant wait staff, you should review turnover research from the hospitality industry. When my team did this for a client, we found a study conducted by Cornell University's School of Hospitality Management that provided the information (Hinkin et al. 2000). If searching databases is not a good use of your time, ask a librarian.

Linking With Other Measures

Statistics can be used to link more subjective measures with those more easily converted to monetary value. This is frequently done by gathering survey data along with operational measures and conducting analysis to determine correlations between measures. This classic approach is relatively simple if the data is readily available; otherwise, it is more efficient to use another technique. The cost of converting a measure using statistical analysis can sometimes outweigh the cost of the evaluation and even the cost of the program. One frequently replicated approach, developed by Sears, involves connecting employee attitude to customer impression to revenue. Sears was able to use this strategy to predict the amount that revenue in a given store would increase if the employees' attitudes about their jobs and the company improved (Rucci, Kim, and Quinn 1998).

Practitioner's Tip

All organizations use estimates. When necessary, use industry standard estimates and monetary values for similar business problems. If your organization is large enough to have a finance department, partner with them to develop the estimates and convert measures to monetary values. The key is to develop conservative estimates and to be transparent with the organization.

—Gary Burrus, PhD, SHRM-SCP, CRP, Executive Officer of Human Resources, Choctaw Nation of Oklahoma

Estimates

Much of the data used in any type of research is based on some form of estimate. Nevertheless, the use of estimates from participants, managers, and supervisors to convert a measure to money is somewhat less credible than the techniques described so far in this chapter. When using estimates, the key is to obtain input from the most credible source—the person or people who know best about the measure under review. These sources of data are asked to provide three pieces of information:

- Their estimated value for the measure
- The basis for their estimated value
- Their confidence in their estimated value

Consider this example. Unexpected absences were causing problems in a local plant, so the performance team instituted a new program to reduce these absences. Due to its cost, they wanted to conduct an ROI study to show the value of the program.

To calculate the ROI, they had to develop the monetary value of improvement in unexpected absences. They had no record of standard values, historical costs, or databases with an acceptable value, so they decided that the best source to provide an estimate would be the supervisors who were dealing with the absences.

The evaluator held a focus group for five supervisors in the plant, asking each supervisor three questions:
- What happens when an unexpected absence occurs in your work unit?
- Given what happens, how much do you think one absence per day costs?
- How confident are you that your estimate is correct?

As shown in Table 14-1, each estimate was adjusted for confidence. The adjusted per absence costs were then totaled and averaged. The average cost of a single absence was calculated to be $177.55.

Table 14-1. Example of Using Estimates

Supervisor	Est. Per Day Cost	% Confidence	Adjusted Per Absence
1	$200	90%	$180.00
2	$210	80%	$168.00
3	$300	75%	$225.00
4	$175	95%	$166.25
5	$150	99%	$148.50
			$887.75
Average adjusted per day cost of one absence			**$177.55**

Let's review the data conversion techniques we've discussed in this chapter, along with examples of how to apply each one:

- **Standard values** include output to contribution, cost of quality, and employee time. Examples include:
  - Sales (profit margin)
  - Donations (overhead margin)
  - Unproductive work hours (hourly wage, adjusted for benefits factor)
  - Repackaging (standard value based on time savings or hourly wage)
  - OSHA fines (fines associated with incident)
  - Unit per person hour (profit of one additional product produced per person per hour at the same cost)
- **Historical costs.** Examples include:
  - Sexual harassment grievances (litigation costs)

- Food spoilage (cost to replenish food inventory)
  - Turnover of marine engineers (average replacement costs plus separation costs)
- **Internal and external experts.** Examples include:
  - Electric utility rate (internal economist)
  - Grievances (labor relations expert)
  - Human life (internal risk manager; note that economists have developed two methods to value a human life. The first is to estimate the individual's lost earnings for their remaining life. The second is to consider a person's acceptance of high-risk jobs and their related higher salaries as payment for a higher probability of death.)
- **External databases.** Examples include:
  - Turnover midlevel manager (ERIC database)
  - Turnover of restaurant wait staff (Google search)
- **Linking with other measures.** Examples include:
  - Employee satisfaction (linked to customer satisfaction which is linked to profit)
  - Customer complaints regarding baggage mishandling (percent of complaints linked to percent who will not repurchase a seat on an airline linked to lost revenue)
- **Estimates** can be made by participants, supervisors, managers, the TD team, or customers. Examples include:
  - Unexpected absence (supervisor estimate [basis provided] × confidence adjustment)
  - Unwanted network intrusions (participant estimate [basis provided] × confidence adjustment)

Five Steps to Convert a Measure to Monetary Benefits

Once you know the value, you can follow a five-step process to convert a measure to annual monetary benefits:

1. Identify the unit of measure.
2. Determine the value of the measure (V).
3. Determine the change in performance in the measure (ΔP). Note this is after you isolate the effects of the program.

4. Annualize the change in performance of the measure (AΔP).
5. Calculate the annual monetary benefit (AΔP × V).

A manufacturing company initiated a new program to reduce unexpected absences in one of its larger plants. Based on supervisor estimates, one absence cost the organization $177.55. Prior to the program, the company had a 7 percent absenteeism rate. Six months after the program, the absenteeism rate had dropped to 4 percent. Using a combination of trendline analysis and manager estimates, it was determined that the program could account for 40 percent of that reduction.

A total of 120 employees worked in the plant for 240 days per year. Here's the calculation the TD team used to determine the annual savings from the reduction in absenteeism attributed to the program.

1. **Unit of measure:** 1 unexpected absence
2. **V:** $177.55
3. **ΔP:** (0.07 − 0.04) × 0.40 = 0.012 or 1.2 percent
4. **AΔP:** 0.012 × 120 × 240 = 345.6 absences
5. **AΔP x V:** 345.6 × $177.55 = $61,361.28

Thus, the program's annual monetary benefits were $61,361.28. This number is also necessary for calculating the program's ROI. If the program cost $50,000, then the ROI would be 23 percent:

$$\text{ROI} = \frac{\$61,3661.28 - \$50,000}{\$50,000} \times 100 = 22.72\% \text{ or } 23\%$$

A Word About Intangible Measures

For some measures, converting to money is not necessary or even feasible. These measures are the program's intangible benefits. The decision to convert a measure to money isn't always a matter of whether it *can* be done, but rather if it *should* be done. You can use the following four-part test when deciding whether to convert a measure to money:

1. **Is there a standard value?**
    A. If yes, convert the measure to money.
    B. If no, move to question 2.
2. **Is there a technique to convert the measure?**
    A. If no, report the measure as an intangible benefit.

B. If one or more techniques will work, move to question 3.
3. **Can you implement the chosen techniques using minimal resources?**
   A. If it will cost too much money or consume too many resources, report the measure as intangible. Do not spend more on data conversion than the evaluation itself.
   B. If yes, move to question 4.
4. **Can you convince an executive in two minutes or less that the value reported is credible?**
   A. If yes, convert the value to money.
   B. If no, report the measure as an intangible benefit. Note that while the goal is to report a high monetary benefit for a program, maintaining the credibility of the results is more important. It is better to report a low monetary benefit along with important intangible benefits than to convert all measures to money and lose credibility of the data.

Heeding the advice in these four steps will enhance the credibility of your results as well as your approach; it will also support the integrity of your ROI calculation. (Chapter 17 addresses the issues of intangibles in more detail.)

Summary

Converting measures to money is an important step in the measurement and evaluation process when you want to:
- Determine a program's financial benefits.
- Normalize benefits to make comparisons between different measures.
- Give quantitative meaning to a benefit.
- Calculate the ROI in a training investment.

This chapter offered several techniques for converting a measure to money. By using those techniques and the following guidelines, you should feel confident in your pursuit of calculating monetary values for business measures.

1. Plan ahead. If you want to report monetary value for improvement in your program, obtain early approval for your approach to obtain the value of each measure.
2. If you have standard values for measures, use them.

CHAPTER 14

3. Use the most credible source for data.
4. If there is no improvement data, assume the program led to little or no results. This conservative approach will enhance the credibility of your results.
5. When using estimates, adjust for error by asking your sources to state their level of confidence in the estimated values.
6. You should throw out extreme measures and unsupported claims. If someone provides an estimated monetary value well beyond the norm, throw it out so it doesn't skew your data. In addition, throw out any data that doesn't include a basis for the estimate; don't guess at how they reached that number.
7. For short-term programs, assume only first year benefits.
8. When in doubt, leave it out. The key is to follow conservative standards. If you are unsure of the credibility of a value or if it costs too much to convert a measure to money, report the improvement as an intangible benefit.

Knowledge Check

Try your hand at converting the benefits of a program to monetary value.

Background

You have been asked to calculate the ROI from action plans used in a leadership program with 30 participants. You are analyzing the results four months after the training is completed. You have already received, analyzed, isolated, and annualized the plans from 18 participants. Ten participants did not provide data.

Now, you must analyze the data from the two remaining plans—Medicine Gelatin Manager and Bill Burgess—to determine the benefits. Then, you'll be able to use the results of all 30 participants to calculate the program's ROI.

Here's what you know so far:

- 30 participants completed the program.
- 18 participants submitted plans. Their data has been analyzed, isolated, and annualized, and the total monetary benefit influenced by the training is $54,109.
- 10 participants did not provide data.
- 2 additional action plans remain to be analyzed: Medicine Gelatin Manager (Figure 14-1) and Bill Burgess (Figure 14-2).

Figure 14-1. Medicine Gelatin Manager Action Plan

Part II. Action Plan for the __Leadership 101__ Program

Name: Medicine Gelatin Manager   **Objective:** Elimination of Gel Waste

Improvement
Measure: Quality

Current
Performance: 8,000 kgs' waste monthly

Target
Performance: Reduce waste by 80%

Analysis

A. What is the unit of measure? __Waste reduction__ Does this measure reflect your performance alone?   Yes ☐   No ☒
If not, how many employees are represented in the measure? __32__

B. What is the value (cost) of one unit? __$3.60 per kilogram of gelatin mass__

C. How did you arrive at this value? __This is the cost of raw materials and is the value we use for waste.__

D. How much did this measure change during the last month of the evaluation period compared to the average before the training program? (Monthly value). __Currently 2,000 kgs' monthly waste__

Please explain the basis of this change and what you or your team did to cause it.
6,000 kilograms of waste eliminated. Reduction in machines from 19 to 12 created additional savings but did not calculate. Gains in machine hours (efficiency) in the Encapsulation Department. More awareness of gel mass waste and its costs. Key contributing factors were problem-solving skills, communicating with my supervisors and technicians and their willing response, and my ability to manage the results.

E. What percentage of this change was caused by the application of methods from __Leadership 101__ (0% to 100%)   __20 %__

F. What level of confidence do you place on the above information? (100% = Certainty and 0% = No confidence)   __70 %__

G. If your measure is time savings, what percentage of the time saved was applied toward productive tasks? (0% to 100%)   __N/A %__

Actual Intangible Benefits

Gelatin mass waste has been a problem for our company since start-up. With low efficiency in the Encapsulation Department and the mistakes made in the Gel Department, the waste was out of control. In the past few months, efficiency has increased and the Gel Department has stabilized, and as a result, waste is down considerably.

CHAPTER 14

Figure 14-2. Bill Burgess Action Plan

Part II. Action Plan for the Leadership 101 Program

Name: Bill Burgess, Senior Engineer   **Objective:** Enable my team to sustain continuous improvement by end of next quarter

Improvement **Current** **Target**
Measure: Time savings **Performance:** 32 hrs unproductive time per month   **Performance:** Zero unproductive hours

A. What is the unit of measure? Team hours saved per month   Does this measure reflect your performance alone? Yes ☐ No ☑
If not, how many employees are represented in the measure? 8

B. What is the value (cost) of one unit? $52.00 for each hour saved

C. How did you arrive at this value? Team member salary is $40.00 per hour. I added 30% for benefits.
30% of $40 = $12 $40 + 12 = $52 per hour.

D. How much did this measure change during the last month of the evaluation period compared to the average before the training program?
(Monthly value). Improved from 32 hours of unproductive time per month to only 8 hours for entire team.

Please explain the basis of this change and what you or your team did to cause it.
Improvement in unproductive time. Got my team involved in identifying key result areas and improvement needs and they came through. My ability to listen and not be judgmental played a key part in the results they achieved. Each hour saved due to increased productivity (resulting in less unproductive time) is credited to the program. 100% of the hours saved has been used in productive ways to benefit the company, and most of what was applied to achieve these results was because of what I have learned from the training program...

E. What percentage of this change was caused by the application of methods from Leadership 101   (0% to 100%)   75%

F. What level of confidence do you place on the above information? (100% = Certainty and 0% = No confidence)   95%

G. If your measure is time savings, what percentage of the time saved was applied toward productive tasks? (0% to 100%)   90%

Actual Intangible Benefits

Because of my new approach with my team, they respond better by taking the initiative and working together to achieve results. As I continue to practice what I learned from training, my confidence increases, and I will be able to accomplish more and feel better about myself.

CONVERTING MEASURES TO MONETARY VALUE

Instructions

Analyze the action plans for Medicine Gelatin Manager and Bill Burgess using these five steps:

1. Identify the unit of measure.
2. Determine the value of the measure (V).
3. Determine the change in performance in the measure (ΔP).
4. Determine the annual change in performance (AΔP).
5. Calculate the annual monetary benefit (AΔP x V).

Record your results in Table 14-2, which already includes the data from the other action plans. Check your answers in apppendix B.

Table 14-2. Benefits of the Leadership Program

	Your Answer Goes Here
Medicine Gelatin Manager	$
Bill Burgess	$
18 other participants	$54,109
10 other participants	0
Total benefits	$
Cost of the program is	$60,000
What is the ROI?	

213

CHAPTER 15

Identifying Program Costs
JUDITH CARDENAS

IN THIS CHAPTER

This chapter explores the most relevant techniques for identifying program costs. After reading it, you will be able to:

- ♦ Articulate the importance of developing and monitoring costs.
- ♦ Identify types of values associated with programs and initiatives.
- ♦ Identify the challenges of capturing costs.
- ♦ Identify sources of program costs.

The Importance of Identifying Program Costs

In today's fast-paced business landscape, managers are facing increasing demands for accurate and timely financial information. Gone are the days when a simple total program cost was sufficient. Savvy managers are now seeking a deeper understanding of how and why money is being spent, driving the need for a more comprehensive cost profile.

Developing a cost profile, which includes both direct and indirect costs, is a crucial decision-making tool for effectively monitoring and managing resources. Tabulating program costs is also an essential step in measuring and evaluating training initiatives. This data serves as the foundation for calculating the ROI of a training program.

The talent development function calculates the costs of training programs for a variety of reasons, including to:

- Determine overall training expenditures.
- Determine relative cost of each program.
- Predict future program costs.

- Calculate a program's ROI.
- Evaluate alternatives to a proposed program.
- Plan and budget for next year's operation.
- Develop a cost pricing system.
- Integrate data into other systems.

In the past, training costs were associated with training budgets. Today, training is often touted as an investment, which allows organizations to look beyond the budget when determining program costs. When looking at the cost of training, it's important to consider the fully loaded (direct and indirect) costs related to assessing, designing, developing, implementing, and evaluating a training program, especially when calculating the ROI. For example, the cost associated with the time participants are involved in a program includes the salary plus the benefits earned during the timeframe of the given program. (Note that you should always include a cost in the calculation, even if the organization's cost guidelines do not require it.)

Practitioner's Tip

Reporting costs without reporting the benefits puts funding at risk. Senior executives recognize training costs are quite high, and only communicating that information highlights the expense. When most executives see training costs, they ask a logical question: What benefits are we receiving by spending this money? By balancing the costs with the benefits, the team can mitigate the risk that senior leaders will react negatively.

Cost-Monitoring Issues

The most important task is to define which costs to include in a training cost profile, and whether they should be prorated or expensed.

Sources of Program Costs

You can capture and categorize program costs into three major sources:

- **Training team expenses** often represent the greatest portion of training costs and are transferred directly to the client or program sponsor.
- **Participant expenses** include direct and indirect costs.

- **External resources** include payments to external training venues (such as hotels and conference centers), equipment, suppliers, and providers of services prescribed in the program.

These costs are often understated, but financial and accounting systems should be able to track and report them.

Prorated Versus Direct Costs

Once you develop and implement a program, you should capture the related costs and expense them to the specific program. Three cost categories—needs assessment, design and development, and acquisition—should be prorated over the life of a program. (Note that if the manager evaluating the program uses a conservative approach, the calculated lifetime will be short). The prorating timeframe differs among organizations. Some prorate program costs over a year of operation, while others prorate costs over two or three years (Phillips and Zúñga 2008).

Let's consider an example of how to use prorated development costs in an ROI calculation. A large pharmaceutical company developed a program that cost $150,000. This program's anticipated lifetime was three years (after which it would need to be updated) and about 900 people would participate in the program during that time. To be conservative, the training department decided to prorate the cost over the first three years of the program. Thus, the prorated program development cost was calculated to $167 per participant ($150,000 development cost divided by 900 participants in a three-year span). Later, when the training team evaluated the program based on a sample of 50 participants, it used this value when calculating the development cost for the ROI ($167 × 50 = $8,350).

Major Cost Categories

The most important task in tabulating program costs is to define which ones to include. Table 15-1 shows the recommended cost categories for a fully loaded, conservative approach to estimating costs. Each category is briefly described in this section.

Needs Assessment and Analysis

It is important to capture the costs associated with conducting a needs assessment. These costs include the time of team members who conduct the assessment, direct fees, expenses of external consultants who conduct the assessment, and internal services and supplies.

Table 15-1. Training Program Cost Categories

Cost Item	Prorated	Expensed
Needs assessment	✓	
Design and development	✓	
Acquisition	✓	
Delivery		
· Facilitator's salary and benefits		✓
· Coordinator's salary and benefits		✓
· Program materials and fees		✓
· Travel, lodging, and meals		✓
· Facilities		✓
· Participants' salaries and benefits		✓
· Contact time		✓
· Travel time		✓
· Preparation time		✓
Evaluation and reporting		✓
Overhead for training and development	✓	

Source: Phillips and Phillips (2016)

Design and Development

One of the most significant cost categories is the cost associated with designing and developing a program. These costs may include internal staff time for design and development, and the cost of supplies, videos, software, and other materials directly related to the program. They may also include external fees for consultation and support.

Acquisition

If an organization lacks the team or expertise to internally develop programs, it may instead purchase programs to use directly or in a modified format. The associated acquisition costs include the purchase price for facilitator materials, train-the-trainer sessions, licensing agreements, webinars, assessment tools, and other costs for rights to deliver the program.

Technological Support

Some programs require technological support. For example, participants may need to take an online assessment prior to program participation. Additionally, if the program is

IDENTIFYING PROGRAM COSTS

offered in a hybrid format, the training content may be delivered using a variety of technology platforms.

Delivery and Implementation

The program's delivery and implementation often represents the largest segment of program cost and is composed of five major subcategories:

- **Salaries and benefits for the facilitator and coordinator.** This includes proportionally allocated salaries based on the amount of time spent on the program. Calculate these costs for internal facilitators and coordinators, as well as any external facilitators and consultants. Include the benefits factor when calculating labor costs for internal staff; in the US, this factor usually ranges from 30 to 50 percent.
- **Salaries and benefits of the participants.** This represents the cost of taking employees off the job to attend a training program and is calculated based on the time spent in the program. Include the benefits factor in this calculation too.
- **Travel, lodging, and meals.** The direct travel costs for participants, facilitators, and coordinators represents all expenses related to lodging and meals during travel, as well as throughout the program. If refreshments are offered throughout the training session, capture and record those costs as well.
- **Facilities.** Capture the cost of the facilities used, regardless of whether the session was offered at an external facility or inside the organization. For meetings or sessions held at external facilities, this cost is simply the direct charge from the conference center or hotel. If the program is conducted in-house, estimate how much it costs to use that space by asking the building's facilities manager or reviewing rental rates for similar spaces in a local hotel. (Note that the use of a conference room represents a cost for the organization, and thus should be noted in your estimate, even if in-house facilities costs aren't typically recorded.)
- **Program materials and fees.** Calculate the delivery costs of specific program materials, such as notebooks, textbooks, how-to manuals, instruction guides, software, technology, case studies, exercises, electronic download materials, and participant workbooks. In addition, note any license fees, user fees, and royalty payments, along with the cost of pens, paper, certificates, calculators, and personal copies of software.

Evaluation and Reporting

Program evaluations and reporting their results should be part of the program cost calculation. Evaluation costs include the cost associated with developing the evaluation strategy, designing instruments, collecting data, performing data analysis, and preparing and distributing reports. Cost categories include time, materials, hardware or software used to collect or analyze data, and any purchased instruments or surveys.

Overhead

The final cost category is overhead, which represents any additional costs within the training department not directly related to a particular program. Typical overhead items include the cost of administrative support, departmental office expenses, salaries of managers, and other fixed costs. Remember that you can prorate overhead costs by dividing them by the number of people trained during a year, the number of programs offered during a year, or the number of training hours a year.

For example, here's how one organization prorated overhead costs across the number of training days. After tabulating all the expenditures in the budget not allocated directly to a particular program, the organization's total overhead was $548,061. Next, it determined that the total number of participant days during that year was approximately 7,400. (Note that a five-day program offered 10 times a year is equivalent to 50 participant days.) Finally, it divided the total unallocated overhead by the total number of participant days, calculating that $74 overhead should be allocated to each day of training ($548,061 / 7,400 = $74). Later, the organization used this calculation to allocate $222 in overhead when calculating the ROI of a three-day leadership program ($74 × 3).

The key to this process is using a simple approach that allocates any costs in the department not already allocated to a specific program. It is also important to remember that it's OK to use estimates because you shouldn't spend too much time on this issue. In fact, some organizations use logical rationale to estimate overhead, spending no more than 10 or 15 minutes on the issue.

Cost Estimation

Many organizations develop cost estimations to help track training costs. Appendix A includes a Cost Estimation Worksheet that summarizes analysis, development, delivery, operations and maintenance, and evaluation costs. It also contains a few formulas that make it easier to estimate the costs.

In addition to cost-estimating worksheets, organizations provide the current rates for services, supplies, and salaries. (Note that this data usually needs to be updated because it becomes outdated quickly.) The most appropriate way to predict costs is by tracking the actual costs incurred in all phases—from analysis to evaluation—of all programs. This allows you to see how much is spent on programs, as well as in the different categories. Until adequate cost data is available, however, you'll need to provide a detailed analysis of the worksheets for cost estimation.

Table 15-2 presents a fully loaded cost profile for a four-week leadership development program that included personal and learning coaches assigned to participants. Costs shown include those for the first group of 22 participants. A fully loaded cost profile makes the total value of investing in training more transparent than simply accounting for the training supplier and materials alone.

Table 15-2. Leadership Development Cost Profile Example

Program Costs	
Analysis, Design, and Development	
External consultants	$525,330
Training department	28,785
Management committee	26,542
Delivery	
Conference facilities (hotel)	142,554
Consultants and external costs	812,110
Training department salaries and benefits (for direct work with the program)	15,283
Training department travel expenses	37,500
Management committee (time)	75,470
Project costs ($25,000 x 4)	100,000
Participant Salaries and Benefits (Class Sessions)	
(Average daily salary x benefits factor x number of program days)	84,564
Participant salaries and benefits (project work)	117,353
Travel and lodging for participants	100,938
Cost of materials (handouts and purchased materials)	6,872
Research and Evaluation	
Research	110,750
Evaluation	125,875
Total Costs	**$2,309,926**

Source: Phillips et al. (2024)

CHAPTER 15

Summary

Capturing and reporting costs is a critical part of measuring and evaluating training. This is particularly true when an ROI calculation is planned. Historically, capturing costs provided a synopsis of expenses related to a particular program or event. Today, managers use cost data to compare programs internally and externally, track resources, and monitor efficiencies. Tracking costs helps program staff manage resources carefully, consistently, and efficiently. This chapter focused on the different cost categories and methods for extrapolating cost data, which provides a stronger evaluation framework.

> **Knowledge Check**
>
> Now that you have read this chapter, try your hand at prorating development costs.
>
> A large financial institution wants to prorate the cost of developing a major leadership development program over the life of the program. The leadership program will last approximately 18 months, and the intent is for 200 supervisors and team leaders to participate. The development costs were $250,000. Due to the program's high-profile nature, senior leaders want to see an ROI calculation for at least one group of 25 participants.
>
> Here's a summary of the data:
>
> - Development costs = $250,000
> - Program life = 18 months
> - Number of participants = 200
> - Number of participants included in the ROI study = 25
>
> Based on the information provided, answer the following questions:
>
> 1. What is the per person cost of developing the leadership development program?
> 2. How much of the development costs will be included in the ROI study?

CHAPTER 16

Calculating the Return on Investment

BERYL OLDHAM

IN THIS CHAPTER

This chapter provides insights into the importance of calculating ROI for training programs and outlines the steps involved in the process. After reading it, you will be able to:

- Calculate ROI based on a program's monetary gains and associated costs.
- Present ROI alongside other performance metrics for a comprehensive assessment.
- Identify programs suitable for ROI evaluation.

The Importance of ROI

The phrase "show me the money" represents the universal desire among organizational leaders to understand the financial returns on their investments across various programs. This request is shared by organizations both large and small—from huge global corporations to small community care trusts—and yet it remains an important but somewhat elusive metric for many.

Many organizations are still trapped in an activity-based reporting mindset. This is especially true for measuring the effectiveness of training programs, which are often placed in the "too-hard" basket when it comes to metrics. However, given the finite nature of monetary

CHAPTER 16

resources, careful budget allocation is important and organizations want investments that yield optimal returns.

L&D professionals need to be able to show the value of what they do using real numbers—even for soft or intangible topics such as leadership development or coaching. We need to move away from activity-based measures of value and instead embrace proving value by measuring a program's impact on business performance.

Before we dive into ROI calculations, however, the first step is to clear up any confusion around the definition of ROI.

ROI Defined

ROI is a financial metric that compares a program's monetary benefits against its costs. It is the ultimate measure of program success for many reasons, including that it defines program benefits and costs in monetary terms, which allows for an equal comparison of the two.

ROI is the metric necessary to show the economic contribution of a program in response to the phrase "show me the money."

Organizations use ROI projections for a range of projects from implementing new systems using forecasting techniques to measuring all types of project initiatives, including learning programs. However, ROI isn't restricted to programs that drive revenue and ultimately profit. It is also applied to programs focused on cost savings and cost avoidance because ROI indicates efficient use of resources. Efficiency can be gained through profit generation, cost savings, and cost avoidance. Regardless of the organization (for profit, nonprofit, government, or charitable trust) or the program (sales, leadership, technology implementation, or humanitarian), ROI is applicable.

While there are many measures that indicate economic value, typical ROI metrics for comparing monetary benefits to costs include benefit-cost ratio (BCR), ROI, payback period (PP), and net present value (NPV; Phillips and Phillips 2019).

Benefit-Cost Ratio (BCR)

BCR, one of the oldest economic metrics, is an output of cost-benefit analysis (CBA). CBA is a decision-aiding tool used to quantify in monetary terms the value of all consequences associated with a government policy or an investment project for all members of society.

It compares the monetary benefits of an investment to the investment itself, and it results in a ratio.

The BCR equation is:

$$BCR = \frac{Benefits}{Costs}$$

To calculate the BCR:
- Identify the annual benefits or gains from implementing a program.
- Convert the benefits to monetary value using either profit, cost savings, or cost avoidance associated with the investment (see chapter 14 for more details).
- Determine the cost (or investment) of the programs (see chapter 15).
- Identify the intangible benefits of program implementation.
- Compare the monetary benefits to program costs.
- Compare the result to another program or a standard for acceptance.

Consider this example: A program returned $300,000 in monetary benefits from profit, cost savings, and cost avoidance. It cost the organization $150,000. The BCR would be calculated as:

$$BCR = \frac{\$300,000}{\$150,000} = 2:1$$

The 2:1 BCR ratio shows that there is a $2 return for every $1 invested in the program. A BCR above 1:1, which indicates break-even, is sometimes considered to be acceptable, depending on the potential for benefits, the cost of the solution, and the perspective of key stakeholders.

Return on Investment (ROI)

ROI is the ultimate measure of profitability derived from investments and remains a fundamental tool for evaluating such returns. Despite its historical roots in finance, its widespread adoption for assessing operational effectiveness gained momentum in the 1960s (Horngren 1982). Today, ROI is a standard metric in business circles and has gained prominence for evaluating the economic impact of various investments, such as training programs.

Historically, BCR was a tool for assessing feasibility, while ROI relied on historical data. Presently, BCR is used to gauge actual outcomes, while ROI is projected prior to committing to a program or project. ROI compares a program's annual earnings (or net program benefits) against the investment (or program costs) and is represented as a percentage.

The equation for calculating ROI is:

$$ROI = \frac{\text{Net benefits}}{\text{Costs}} \times 100$$

For example, a program that cost $150,000 and achieved $300,000 in total benefits would generate an ROI of 100 percent:

$$ROI = \frac{\$300,000 - \$150,000}{\$150,000} \times 100 = 100$$

A 100 percent ROI shows that for every $1 invested in the program, that dollar is returned along with a gain of $1. This additional $1 signifies the return on the investment.

Similar to BCR, reasonable return rates for ROI hinge on many organizational factors, such as the ROI of alternative investments and the benchmark against which ROI is evaluated. For some projects, an ROI of 0 percent is acceptable—like the BCR of 1:1, it indicates break-even.

Practitioner's Tip

Net program benefits are calculated by subtracting the program's costs from its monetary benefits. A shortcut for calculating ROI is to subtract 1 from the BCR and then multiply by 100 (Phillips, Phillips, Paone, and Gaudet 2019). Thus, a BCR of 2 is equivalent to an ROI of 100 percent.

Payback Period

You may need to estimate the timeframe within which an investment will recoup its costs. This duration, known as the payback period (PP), is determined by comparing the initial investment with the annual cash flows or monetary benefits generated by the program. The calculation for the payback period essentially involves reversing the BCR formula:

$$PP = \frac{\text{Costs}}{\text{Benefits}}$$

The payback period is typically reported in terms of months or years. For instance, using the example of a program that yields $300,000 in monetary benefits while costing the organization $150,000, the payback period can be calculated as:

$$PP = \frac{\$150,000}{\$300,000} = 0.5$$

By multiplying 0.5 by 12 months, you would determine that the program's payback period amounts to six months. In other words, decision makers can anticipate recovering their investment in less than a year. Payback period can then be compared with other potential investments or a predefined standard.

ROI, BCR, and PP are all suitable metrics for evaluating the financial benefits of investing in people development. Despite being assets to an organization, people are not treated on the accounting books in the same manner as other assets such as equipment, land, and buildings. Additionally, most training programs are short-term, often taking only a few months, weeks, or days to fully implement. In light of this, achieving a payoff within the first year of such an investment is preferable, if not essential (Phillips and Phillips 2008, 2009).

Table 16-1. Comparison of PP, BCR, and ROI

		PP	BCR	ROI
Benefits	$300,000	6 months	2:1	100%
Costs	$150,000			

Net Present Value (NPV)

Net present value (NPV) stands out as a frequently employed technique in capital budgeting decisions, a topic often central to discussions on ROI. NPV is a discounted cash flow (DCF) method that considers the time value of money and is typically applied in long-term decision-making situations.

NPV uses a predetermined rate to discount anticipated cash inflows (program benefits) and outflows (program costs) to their present value at a specific point in time. These anticipated benefits are then aggregated, with the initial investment removed. This process effectively converts future benefits and costs into a single present dollar value. If the benefit's present value exceeds the investment, the program is deemed a favorable investment (Friedlob and Plewa 1996; Nas 1996).

CHAPTER 16

Consider a simple application of this technique: Let's say there's a plan to purchase a software as a service (SaaS) cloud-based learning management system (LMS). The subscription and maintenance cost of a three-year license for 3,000 learners is $120,000. The initial outlay in year 0 is $50,000. The remaining balance will be paid over the next two years at $35,000 per year. No benefits are expected until year 1. The anticipated future net benefit is a labor savings of $100,000 in year 1 and year 2 (Table 16-2).

Table 16-2. LMS Benefits and Costs

	Year 0	Year 1	Year 2
Benefits (Labor Savings)		$100,000	$100,000
Costs	$50,000	$35,000	$35,000
Net Benefits		$65,000	$65,000

To calculate the NPV, the value of the benefits must be reduced by a discount rate. (Note that this discount rate is usually higher than the interest rates the company would have received had they invested the funds in the bank or another investment.) Let's assume a discount rate of 7.5 percent for this example.

To calculate the NPV, begin with what you know:
- **Initial outlay (I_0)** = $50,000
- **Future net benefits (NB_n)** = $65,000 per year for two years
- **Discount rate** = 7.5 percent

In formula form, the NPV is:

$$NPV = -I_0 + \sum_{n=1}^{N}\left[\frac{NB_n}{(1+r)^n}\right]$$

$$NPV = -50{,}000 + \left[\frac{65{,}000}{(1+0.075)} + \frac{65{,}000}{(1+0.075)^2}\right]$$

$$NPV = -50{,}000 + [60{,}465.12 + 56{,}246.62]$$

$$NPV = -50{,}000 + 116{,}711.74$$

$$NPV = \$66{,}711.74$$

So, what does this tell us? The initial investment was $50,000. The present value of the future net benefits (for two years) totals $66,711.74. This indicates that the investment in the LMS, if all goes as planned, will generate a positive return.

This is another way of expressing the return the organization will receive for its investment. Is this a good return? As with the BCR and the ROI, it depends on the target to which the NPV is being compared.

> **Practitioner's Tip**
>
> **Net present value (NPV)** represents the cash flow an investor would receive because of a multiyear investment. It is used to determine the amount of cashflow (benefits) to come. NPV also assumes a steady stream of benefits. **Return on investment (ROI)** as a percentage is more suitable for training investments due to its simplicity and versatility along with the variability in the outcomes resulting from programs that lead to behavior change. It is also more suitable due to the short-term nature of most training programs and the stakeholder's desire to see results sooner rather than later. ROI measures the efficiency of an investment by indicating where that investment stands now in addition to the potential future ROI.

ROI Targets

Just like any metric, the meaning of an ROI hinges on the objective against which it's compared. Establishing an ROI objective lends significance to the metric; otherwise, it becomes merely a comparison of monetary benefits versus costs. Here are some considerations for setting an ROI target:

- **Align the ROI target with that of other investments.** For instance, if your organization typically achieves a 20 percent return on other investments, it may be sensible to set the ROI objective for your training program at a similar level.
- **Consider setting the ROI target slightly higher than that of other investments.** When the right people participate in the right program for the right reasons, training can significantly affect the organization. A target of 25 percent is often suitable for training investments (based on numerous studies).
- **Opt to set the ROI target at break-even.** This equates to an ROI of 0 percent (or a BCR of 1:1). Break-even targets are frequently adopted by government and nonprofit organizations.

- **Involve the client in establishing the ROI target.** While collaborating with your client, assess the economic opportunities for generating revenue, cutting costs, and avoiding expenses. Consider the available solutions to help achieve the business objectives. By examining the financial opportunities, program costs, and the likelihood of program effectiveness, you and your client can set a reasonable ROI target.

Reporting ROI in Performance Contexts

While it's critical to report an ROI against a target, presenting the ROI within the framework of other performance measures is equally essential. ROI shows the economic contribution of a program. However, when reported in isolation, stakeholders lack insight into how you arrived at that figure, which hinders program improvement and obscures intangible benefits. For instance, if an ROI shows a loss, it's impossible to determine the underlying reasons without supplementary information. Similarly, if an ROI calculation shows a 250 percent return, without additional data, the mechanism behind such a significant economic contribution remains unclear. A chain of impact unfolds as individuals engage in programs and projects within the context of the five levels of evaluation (Phillips 1983).

ROI is just one of six data types within the chain of impact (Figure 16-1). While ROI stands as the ultimate measure, it's not the sole indicator of program success because other significant outcomes manifest during program implementation. Reporting ROI alongside other performance measures provides stakeholders with additional significance and actionable information to guide program-related decisions.

Figure 16-1. Chain of Impact

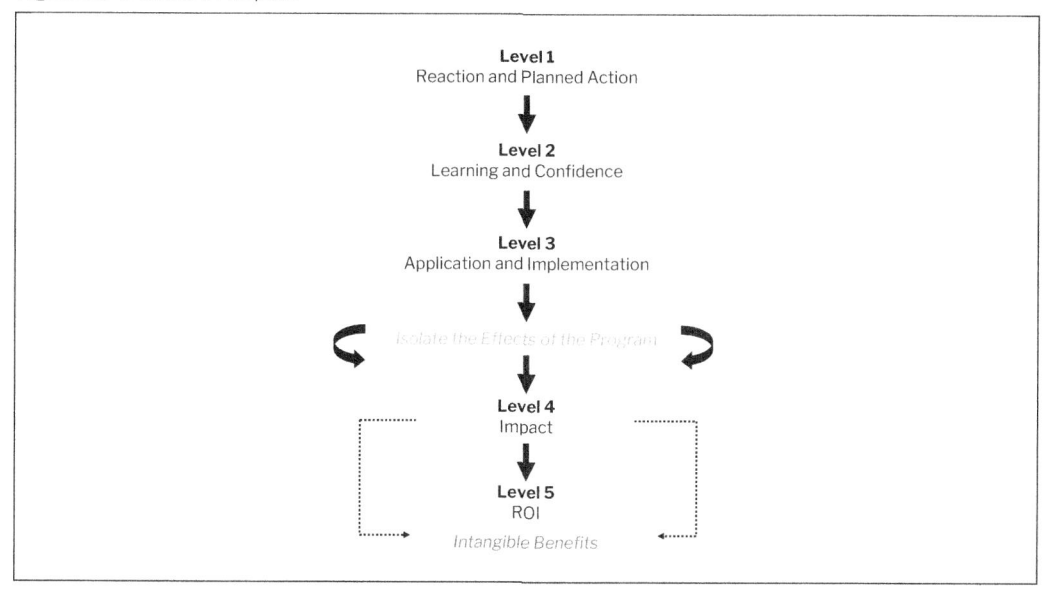

```
                    Level 1
            Reaction and Planned Action
                       ↓
                    Level 2
            Learning and Confidence
                       ↓
                    Level 3
          Application and Implementation
                       ↓
            Isolate the Effects of the Program
                       ↓
                    Level 4
                    Impact
                       ↓
                    Level 5
                     ROI

              Intangible Benefits
```

Selecting Programs for ROI Evaluation

You may choose not to calculate ROI for every program. In fact, while only 5 to 10 percent of all programs are candidates for ROI evaluation, ROI Institute's *2020 Benchmarking Study* found that as many as 18 percent of programs are evaluated to this level (ROI Institute 2020). With this in mind, ROI is suitable for programs that:

- Have a long life cycle (at some point, this level of accountability should be applied)
- Are integral to the organization's operational objectives (ROI can demonstrate whether a program enhances value)
- Are closely aligned with the organization's strategic initiatives (programs of such significance necessitate a high level of accountability)
- Require substantial investment to implement (costly programs consuming significant resources warrant this level of accountability)
- Are highly visible and potentially contentious (such programs often demand accountability to address criticism)
- Target a large audience (programs designed for all employees may warrant ROI analysis)

- Attract the attention of top executives (ROI may be necessary if senior management wants to see a program's financial impact)

After completing this chapter, take some time to evaluate your programs. Assess each one against the outlined criteria to determine whether it's a candidate for ROI analysis. Target selecting between 5 and 10 percent of your programs for ROI evaluation.

Case Study: Calculating the ROI of a Global Sales Coaching Program

Let's review an ROI calculation I did with a large global company based in New Zealand, which is labeled Company NZ for the purposes of this case study.

Company NZ piloted a sales coaching program for 68 participants in four regions: Auckland, Chicago, Dubai, and Mexico. They were surveyed as part of the evaluation and 51 participants (or 75 percent) responded. The fully loaded cost for the entire pilot group was $611,562 NZD. After six months, the earnings before interest and taxes (EBIT) improved across the four regions by $25,531,074 NZD. The program effects were then isolated; the EBIT benefit attributable to the program using actual financial data for the six-month period immediately following the program was $3,244,304 NZD. This figure was then doubled to represent a 12-month period.

We then calculated the BCR, ROI, and PP:

$$\text{BCR} = \frac{\$6,688,608}{\$611,562} = 10.94:1$$

Interpretation: For every dollar invested, there were $10.94 in benefits.

$$\text{ROI} = \frac{\$6,688,608 - 611,562}{\$611,562} \times 100 = 994\%$$

Interpretation: For every dollar invested, $9.94 was returned after the investment is recovered.

$$\text{PP} = \frac{\$611,562}{\$6,688,608} = 0.09 \times 12 = 1.08 \text{ months}$$

Interpretation: The investment will be paid back in 9 percent of one year, which is equivalent to just over a month.

Summary

Calculating ROI for training programs has become standard procedure in numerous organizations. By adhering to specific guidelines, you can establish meaningful and credible ROI metrics for programs within your organization that contribute to business outcomes. Consider these best practices as we wrap up this chapter:

- **Use the ROI calculation that is most familiar to your finance and accounting team.** While some definitions may seem innovative and hold significance within certain functions, it's essential to adhere to widely recognized business standards.
- **Maintain conservative calculations.** Given the inherent assumptions involved in ROI, adopting conservative standards ensures the calculated ROI remains believable.
- **Establish an appropriate target.** When presenting an ROI calculation, contextualize it within an objective. This can align with the guidelines outlined in this chapter or be based on the ROI of an alternative solution.
- **Provide the ROI in conjunction with other performance measures.** By incorporating ROI into the broader context of success metrics, you give stakeholders clarity on the methodology behind the ROI and the necessary steps for continuous improvement. Remember, ROI is just one component of a larger narrative of program success; tell the complete story to enable stakeholders to make informed decisions regarding the training program.

Knowledge Check

Try your hand at calculating BCR, ROI, and PP for an absenteeism reduction program. Check your answers in appendix B.

The program has an annual monetary benefit of $260,750 and cost $125,000.

1. What is the BCR? What does it tell you?
2. What is the ROI? What does it tell you?
3. What is the PP? What does it tell you?

CHAPTER 17

Measuring Intangible Benefits
NADER BECHINI

IN THIS CHAPTER

This chapter explores why intangible benefits are crucial in learning and development. After reading it, you will be able to:
- Measure the intangible benefits of your programs.
- Align intangible measures to the business.
- Discuss the value of intangible benefits in your own L&D initiatives.

The Value of Intangible Benefits

As we navigate deeper into an era when knowledge and technology reign supreme, the valuation of intangible assets becomes increasingly pivotal. The transition from a tangible to an intangible economy underscores the growing importance of intellectual capital, innovation, and brand value. Much of the world is moving from an economy that is all about physical things to one that values ideas and knowledge. What really makes a company successful are the things you can't always see or touch, like how innovative its products are, how involved its employees feel, and how well they share knowledge with one another. Even though we can't always see these things in the usual money-based business reports, they're very important for determining how well a company does.

This change is mostly due to our increased proficiency with using technology and analyzing data. Instead of just focusing on things we can touch, like buildings and machines, we're now investing more in brands, how we work together, our company culture, and our reputation. With the help of advanced data analysis, we're starting to figure out how to put a dollar value on these hard-to-measure assets. This includes using AI to make better decisions, make customers happier with more personalized experiences, and come up with new ideas. This is changing the old ways of doing business into a new style that's all about being quick to adapt, ready for change, and always learning. Take the healthcare industry for example—the amount of money a hospital makes and what changes it should implement are now being linked to measures of how happy its patients are. In the past, patient happiness was seen as too hard to measure.

The way we look at measurement, particularly the ROI, for L&D is changing. As organizations increasingly recognize the importance of human capital development, the metrics used to evaluate L&D initiatives are evolving to encompass a wider range of intangible and hard-to-measure benefits. This evolution reflects a deeper understanding of the multifaceted impact of L&D programs, which extend beyond immediate financial returns to include enhancements in employee engagement, innovation, and organizational culture. The integration of AI and machine learning in L&D measurement practices offers promising avenues for capturing the nuanced effects of these programs and providing richer insights into their true value. By leveraging advanced analytics, organizations can uncover the intricate ways in which L&D initiatives contribute to strategic goals, paving the way for more informed and effective investments in human capital.

Critical intangible benefits—such as improved teamwork, collaboration, and enhanced organizational reputation—are often overlooked components of organizational success. These benefits, while not always quantifiable in monetary terms, significantly contribute to a program's success by fostering a positive and productive work environment. The real value of intangible benefits lies in their transformative potential, creating a workplace where innovation and employee satisfaction flourish, which in turn drives long-term organizational growth and sustainability.

Aligning intangible benefits with business objectives is essential for maximizing their impact. By embedding the evaluation of these benefits within the broader framework of organizational goals, you can ensure a holistic assessment of their contribution to strategic success. Although intangible benefits may not correlate directly with traditional financial metrics, they originate from identified needs for improvement, such as better team dynamics or enhanced customer satisfaction. Systematic measurement and reporting of these benefits, as part of a comprehensive ROI analysis, underline their significance in strategic planning and underscore their role in achieving key business objectives.

This chapter aims to demystify the concept of intangible benefits, providing a clear framework for identifying, measuring, and leveraging them effectively.

> **Practitioner's Tip**
>
> Without identifying and shedding light on intangibles, the true picture of ROI is incomplete, especially in nonprofit organizations where intangible benefits far outweigh the value of their programs and services.
>
> —Leena Merdad, Secretary General, Ektefaa Charity Organization

Exploring Different Types of Intangible Benefits

Let's look at the intangible benefits that significantly influence organizational culture and performance. These benefits, though not always visible, are crucial for shaping the workplace environment and driving success.

- **Increased employee engagement and satisfaction.** Yale's happiness class, "The Science of Well-Being" offered by professor Laurie Santos, serves as an example of fostering intangible benefits through engagement and satisfaction. This initiative underscores the universal desire for well-being in both academic and professional settings, demonstrating that job satisfaction and employee engagement are pivotal for productivity and retention. Similarly, the ambiance of a local bakery, enriched by the staff's genuine enthusiasm, illustrates how employee engagement can transform customer experiences and turn occasional visitors into loyal patrons. These scenarios highlight the intrinsic value of cultivating a positive work environment where employees feel valued and connected to their work and workplace.
- **Improved organizational culture.** A robust organizational culture—defined by shared values, beliefs, and practices—can significantly influence a company's success. Culture affects every aspect of an organization, from decision-making processes to employee behavior and customer service standards. Cultivating a positive culture encourages innovation, collaboration, and a sense of belonging among employees.

- **Enhanced employee morale and motivation.** High employee morale and motivation are directly linked to increased efficiency, better quality of work, and higher employee retention rates. Organizations can boost morale by recognizing achievements, providing opportunities for professional growth, and ensuring a supportive work environment.
- **Stronger knowledge retention and transfer.** In today's knowledge-driven economy, the ability to retain and effectively transfer knowledge within an organization is invaluable. This ensures that critical information and skills are preserved and shared, enhancing innovation and maintaining a competitive edge.
- **Increased innovation and creativity.** An organizational culture that fosters innovation and creativity is vital for long-term success. Encouraging employees to think creatively and pursue innovative solutions leads to the development of new products, services, and processes that can set a company apart from its competitors.
- **Enhanced customer satisfaction and loyalty.** The intangible benefits of high customer satisfaction and loyalty cannot be overstated. Satisfied customers are more likely to return and recommend the company to others, driving revenue growth and enhancing the company's reputation.

These intangible benefits play a pivotal role in an organization's overall success and sustainability. By recognizing, nurturing, and effectively leveraging these benefits, companies can create a competitive advantage and achieve their strategic objectives.

Practitioner's Tip

The true worth of training lies in its ability to cultivate intangible yet transformative outcomes, including improved problem solving, heightened employee engagement, and increased organizational responsiveness. Quantifying these elusive yet invaluable benefits empowers learning leaders to showcase a training program's strategic impact, maximize its return on investment, and position it as a powerful driver of sustainable competitive advantage.

—Arwa Alqarni, L&D Design Senior Specialist, Riyadh Airports Company

Common Challenges in Measuring Intangible Benefits

There are distinct challenges when measuring the impact of intangible benefits due to their qualitative nature and the absence of standardized metrics. To navigate these complexities, organizations must adopt innovative approaches and methodologies.

Let's review some key challenges and actionable strategies for effectively quantifying intangible benefits, thus ensuring a meaningful integration into organizational evaluation frameworks.

- **Navigating subjectivity and qualitative dimensions.** The inherent subjectivity of intangible benefits—such as organizational culture and employee morale—complicates their quantification. These benefits are perceived differently by various stakeholders, which makes uniform measurement challenging. To address this, organizations should employ diverse data collection methods (such as sentiment analysis, employee surveys, and net promoter scores) to capture a broad spectrum of perceptions and experiences. This multipronged approach facilitates a more nuanced understanding of intangible benefits.
- **Establishing standardized metrics.** The lack of universally recognized metrics for intangibles hampers comparative analysis and benchmarking efforts. Organizations should actively participate in industry collaborations and engage with standard-setting bodies to develop and adopt metrics that accurately reflect the unique value of their intangible assets. This collaborative effort can lead to the establishment of industry-wide benchmarks, which in turn enhances the comparability and reliability of intangible benefit measurements.
- **Clarifying cause-and-effect relationships.** Determining the direct impact of specific initiatives on intangible benefits is often obscured by complex interdependencies within organizational processes. Advanced analytical techniques, such as predictive modeling and regression analysis, can help clarify these relationships. Furthermore, control group comparisons and longitudinal studies, including the analysis of trends and factors associated with those trends, can provide empirical evidence of the effectiveness of initiatives, thereby strengthening the case for investment in solutions that drive the more subjective measures.

- **Mitigating bias and perception influences.** Personal biases and subjective perceptions can skew the evaluation of intangible benefits. To counteract this, organizations should implement objective assessment methods, including blind evaluations and diverse assessment panels. Additionally, training evaluators on recognizing and mitigating biases can further ensure the integrity and accuracy of intangible benefit evaluations.

Overcoming the challenges associated with measuring intangible benefits requires a strategic blend of innovative data collection methods, collaborative standardization efforts, sophisticated analytical techniques, and rigorous evaluator training. By embracing these strategies, organizations can effectively quantify the value of intangible assets, thereby enriching their strategic decision making and enhancing their competitive edge.

Finding the Intangibles

Identifying intangible benefits requires a structured approach to uncover the less tangible outcomes of L&D initiatives. This section outlines the initial steps—frame, initiate, navigate, and delve (FIND)—to recognize and plan for evaluating these intangible assets.

Frame Stakeholder Expectations

Clear communication with all stakeholders is paramount from the outset. It's essential to establish a common understanding of the program's goals and the anticipated intangible benefits. This early alignment helps set realistic expectations and ensures that everyone is on the same page regarding the program's objectives and potential outcomes. For instance, in a large-scale change management project, you can facilitate a unified vision of success by involving leaders, participants, and their supervisors in preliminary discussions about expected intangible benefits, such as improved teamwork and communication (Phillips, Phillips, Paone, and Huff Gaudet 2019).

Initiate Evaluation Planning

Effective evaluation of intangible benefits starts with a comprehensive plan that considers both tangible and intangible outcomes. Selecting methods and tools that can accurately capture the nuances of intangible benefits is crucial. An initial assessment may reveal intangible aspects, such as employee morale or organizational culture, which are worth monitoring. Identifying these aspects early on aids in crafting a robust evaluation framework that encompasses all potential benefits of the program.

Navigate Data Collection

Collecting data on intangible benefits often involves a mix of qualitative and quantitative methods. Surveys, interviews, and focus groups can unveil unanticipated intangible gains. (Review chapters 5, 6, 8, and 9 for more on these methods.) For example, participants in a leadership development initiative might report enhanced team dynamics and improved collaborative efforts as key outcomes. Adopting a flexible and comprehensive approach to data collection ensures you have a thorough understanding of the program's intangible benefits.

Delve Into Data Analysis

Analyzing data related to intangible benefits requires tailored analytical techniques that illuminate their impact. While it may not always be feasible to conduct in-depth analyses for every intangible benefit, establishing a clear link between the program and these benefits is vital. In cases where direct measurement is challenging, intangible benefits can be presented as supporting evidence of the program's success, enriching the overall evaluation with qualitative insights.

Strategies for Quantifying Intangibles

To effectively quantify the value of intangible assets, it's essential to use qualitative and quantitative methods that are tailored to capture the nuanced impact of these assets on your organization. IMPACT provides a handy mnemonic for achieving this:

- **Identify clear objectives.** Begin by setting objectives that align with your organization's strategic goals. Define how intangible assets like brand reputation and organizational culture contribute to these goals, ensuring each objective is SMART—specific, measurable, achievable, relevant, and time bound.
- **Measure key performance indicators (KPIs).** Use KPIs to track the performance of intangible assets over time. Choose indicators such as innovation indices or customer satisfaction scores that reflect the impact of these assets and can be measured reliably.

- **Perform surveys and collect feedback.** Surveys are a powerful tool for collecting data on the perceptions and experiences associated with your intangible assets. Whether it's customer feedback on brand perception or employee input on workplace culture, this feedback is crucial for identifying areas of strength and opportunities for improvement.
- **Analyze behavioral metrics.** Look into behavioral metrics that shed light on stakeholder interactions within your organization. This might include tracking customer retention rates to evaluate loyalty or monitoring innovation adoption rates among employees.
- **Conduct benchmarking and comparative analysis.** Comparing the performance of your intangible assets against industry standards or competitors can offer valuable context. This benchmarking can illuminate where your organization stands and where you might be able to enhance your intangible assets.
- **Tap into technology and analytics tools.** In today's digital age, technology and analytics tools can unveil insights that might be missed through traditional methods. Predictive analytics, sentiment analysis, and data visualization can uncover trends and patterns and offer a deeper understanding of the impact of your intangible assets.

By integrating these strategies, you can comprehensively assess the value of your intangible assets, harnessing this information to inform strategic decisions and gain a competitive edge. Each strategy provides a piece of the puzzle, contributing to a holistic view of how an intangible asset drives your organization forward.

Practitioner's Tip

Without measuring the intangible benefits of training through specific metrics, L&D initiatives may fail to maximize their contribution to overall organizational performance and success. It's essential to clearly link and align these initiatives with the organization's strategy and measure their intangible benefits; otherwise, they risk being arbitrary, irrelevant, or perceived as such.

—Mohammed Al Howshan, Director of Talent Development, Saudi Food and Drug Authority

> **Practitioner's Tip**
>
> By quantifying intangible elements, an organization can unlock critical insights into the effectiveness and influence of their training initiatives or projects.
>
> —Ameena Janahi, Senior HR specialist, Bahrain Customs Affairs

Communicating Intangible Benefits to Stakeholders

To effectively communicate the value of intangible benefits to stakeholders, it's essential to adopt a multifaceted approach that blends tangible evidence with compelling narratives, clear data presentation, and robust credibility.

> **Practitioner's Tip**
>
> Measuring the intangible benefits of L&D initiatives will help the organization diagnose performance obstacles and decide what adjustments are necessary to successfully drive growth.
>
> —Mahmoud bin Eid, Training Planning Director, Ministry of Communications and Information Technology

Target Evidence and Isolate Effects

Isolating the effects of a learning solution is a critical step in demonstrating the value of intangible benefits. This process involves identifying specific improvements attributed to the program and quantifying their impact. For example, in a leadership development program at the World Bank Group, participants reported significant enhancements in their work and team relationships as a direct result of the training program (Phillips et al. 2019). These improvements, although intangible, were an important piece of the program's success.

The challenge occurs when trying to convert these intangible measures to monetary values. In instances where credibility of conversion is questionable—such as monetizing death prevention in a malaria reduction program—it's best to report these benefits as intangibles. Linking intangible benefits to a program typically involves a systematic approach, such as using a five-point scale to gauge the program's influence on these benefits. This process shows the significance of intangible benefits as an integral part of program evaluation, which adds a special layer to understanding its overall impact.

Engage With Narratives

Telling stories is a great way to get people interested and to share the importance of intangible benefits. When you tell a good story about what a program has done, it helps people see how much the benefits positively influenced people and the organization as a whole.

Let's illustrate this idea with a quick story about why the Roads and Transport Authority (RTA) built new roads and bridges. The RTA built the roads and bridges to make people happier, reduce traffic jams, and make the roads safer; however, they didn't measure these benefits in a usual ROI way. Instead, RTA's "happiness department" noticed that when people were happier with the transit system, they tended to spend more in the city, which in turn helped the local economy (Phillips et al. 2019).

Lay Out the Data

Effectively presenting data involves more than just showcasing quantitative outcomes; it requires highlighting the qualitative improvements that contribute to a program's success. Through a balanced presentation that includes both statistical data and the narratives behind these numbers, stakeholders can gain a comprehensive understanding of the program's impact. This dual approach ensures that the full spectrum of benefits, both tangible and intangible, is communicated clearly.

Leverage Credibility

Building credibility through evidence-based results is crucial for overcoming skepticism toward intangible benefits. In addition, demonstrating tangible outcomes helps validate the effectiveness of a program and its associated intangible benefits (Phillips et al. 2019). By effectively communicating results and their connection to intangible benefits, you can address any skepticism and reinforce the program's overall value.

Use these strategies to provide stakeholders with a clear, compelling, and credible understanding of the intangible benefits' significance, which will ultimately reinforce their contribution to organizational success.

Case Study: Improving Belonging, an Important Intangible

This case study was adapted from Franklin et al. (2023).

At Vertex, a sense of belonging is essential to employees. In fact, analysis of employee pulse survey data showed that sense of belonging was the top driver of employee satisfaction. However, Vertex also knew that an employee's sense of belonging and engagement dropped the longer their tenure with the company. According to historical data, employees with less than three months' tenure had the highest scores for belonging. But after six months, scores dropped and plateaued at a lower level.

To determine how to sustain that initial high level of belonging and engagement, Vertex invested in a new-hire initiative geared toward increasing overall job satisfaction.

As part of this initiative, new hires watched a video during their first week in which other Vertex employees shared their own challenges as they started roles at Vertex and how they overcame them. They watched the video again after three months and were also invited to write a reflection of their onboarding experience, which served to reinforce the message (an essential aspect of the program).

To isolate the effects of the program, Vertex created two groups—an initiative group and a control group—and randomly assigned new hires to them. The initiative group watched the inspirational video described earlier, while the control group watched a video focused on Vertex's corporate values.

Fifty-four percent of participants chose to reflect on their onboarding experience. In addition, all new hires in the study completed surveys as part of their regular onboarding process and participated in regular pulse engagement surveys. Each survey included two statements for employees to respond to using an agreement scale: "I feel a sense of belonging at Vertex" (to measure belonging) and "I am happy working at Vertex" (to measure employee satisfaction). These scores were tracked over time to measure whether the initiative had a meaningful impact.

The initiative group showed initial high scores, followed by a downward trend; however, scores surged upward again around the six-month and nine-month marks, and remained high through the one-year mark. The differences between the initiative group and the control group were statistically significant (p-value < 0.05), meaning the program's impact was real and not random. Employee engagement scores also increased for program participants at six months posthire and were sustained beyond the nine-month mark. One unexpected benefit of the program was an observed higher impact overall on younger employees (those under the age of 35) as well as those from underrepresented groups.

Investing in this new-hire initiative to drive employee belonging proved to be worthwhile. It demonstrated that efforts to ensure new employees believe they belong at the company during the "job honeymoon" would pay off in longer term sustained job satisfaction.

Case Study: Successful Implementation of Intangible Benefit Measurement

In southeastern Colorado, the St. Mary-Corwin Medical Center embarked on a unique journey—its new farmstand prescription program was aimed at addressing the high levels of morbidity due to obesity and diabetes in Pueblo County. Under the leadership of Linda Stetter, director of mission integration and spiritual care, the program not only provided nutritional support to marginalized communities but also ventured into the realm of intangible benefits. In one notable case, the program allowed a patient and their family to avoid unnecessary medical procedures and drove a staggering 701.5 percent ROI based on this single avoidance (Phillips et al. 2019). However, the true value transcended these numbers. Beyond the physical health improvements, the program fostered trust, engagement, and mental well-being among the participants, while also cultivating a sense of community, trust, and forward-thinking through volunteering efforts.

Case Study: Real-World Applications and Results

Inspired by innovative approaches to colon cancer surgery in the United Kingdom, a physician in the Canadian provincial health system initiated a trial to improve surgery procedures, provide better patient outcomes, and save costs. The trial, which compared a small sample of patients undergoing the new procedures with a control group, demonstrated remarkable improvements in patient care, including no complications, infections, or readmissions, and a reduced length of stay for the experimental group. This led to an impressive 118 percent ROI and convinced the senior team to adopt the new procedures system-wide (Hubbard 2017; Phillips et al. 2019). This real-world case highlights the tangible impact of intangible benefits, such as enhanced patient care and operational efficiencies, showcasing the potential for significant improvements in healthcare delivery.

Summary

This chapter reiterates the importance of measuring intangible benefits resulting from L&D programs; it also describes how challenging it can be to value and measure these intangibles. The difficulties often come from not being able to clearly see the effect of certain actions, the fact that intangible assets are based on opinions and feelings, and that some people might not believe in or agree with putting numbers on things that are usually seen as more about quality than quantity. These issues show how important it is to follow the advice shared in this chapter—to have strong methods, to involve and listen to different people, and to be open to looking at intangibles in many ways to really understand their true impact.

Knowledge Check

Answer these questions to test your knowledge. Then, check your answers in appendix B.

1. What are the intangible benefits of L&D?
   A. Benefits that can be easily measured and quantified
   B. Benefits that are difficult to measure and often not directly related to financial gain
   C. Only the benefits that relate to employee salaries
   D. Tangible assets like computers and software used in L&D programs

2. How can organizations align intangible benefits with their business objectives?
   A. By ignoring intangible benefits because they are not important
   B. By integrating intangible benefits into their financial statements
   C. By incorporating intangible benefits into the program's evaluation framework to reflect broader impacts
   D. By focusing solely on tangible benefits

3. What is a common challenge of measuring intangible benefits?
   A. They are too easy to measure, making the process trivial
   B. Intangible benefits are subjective and qualitative
   C. Intangible benefits do not really influence business outcomes
   D. All stakeholders readily agree on the value of intangible benefits

4. Which method is *not* mentioned as a way to quantify intangible benefits?
   A. Using KPIs relevant to intangible assets
   B. Conducting extensive financial audits
   C. Performing surveys and collecting feedback
   D. Analyzing behavioral metrics

5. What role does storytelling play in communicating the value of intangible benefits?
   A. It is discouraged because it can distort the facts
   B. It is crucial for making intangible benefits relatable for the audience
   C. It has no role in professional business settings
   D. It's only useful in marketing and has no place in L&D

CHAPTER 18

Forecasting ROI
SUZANNE SCHELL

IN THIS CHAPTER

This chapter describes how to forecast ROI using a step-by-step process. After reading it, you will be able to:

♦ Explain why forecasting is important.
♦ Forecast ROI at different times.
♦ Apply 10 steps to forecast ROI for a training program.

Why Forecast ROI?

"We are all forecasters. When we think about changing jobs, getting married, buying a home, making an investment, launching a product, or retiring, we decide based on how we expect the future will unfold," write Phillip Tetlock and Dan Gardner, authors of the bestselling *Superforecasting: The Art and Science of Prediction* (2016). So it should come as no surprise that stakeholders are increasingly requesting an ROI forecast.

The reason behind the request could be:

1. **The program is expensive.** Investing substantial resources into a training program can cause financial uncertainty. Will the high expenditure be offset by the financial benefits? There may be a high level of reluctance to invest the resources unless they are confident there will be a positive ROI. For example, when a large mining company had a very negative score on an employment satisfaction survey, it was determined that the managers' limited leadership skills were resulting in a dissatisfied workforce. The HR team proposed a leadership development program for all managers, but it came with an extremely high price tag. The CEO realized

the solution was necessary, but, due to the investment amount, required an ROI forecast to grant approval.

2. **There is uncertainty in the program.** If executives and sponsors perceive the program as risky, their decision to move forward could be dependent on an ROI forecast. High-risk programs have the potential to deliver a negative effect on the organization. To eliminate the uncertainty, the business case and data required should ultimately include a forecasted ROI. For example, a healthcare organization experienced a high level of sepsis infections in one of the hospitals it was managing. This high level of sepsis led to some deaths. In addition to the high cost of treating sepsis, the image and reputation of the hospital were significantly damaged. Part of the overall solution included a training program for all frontline healthcare professionals on early detection of sepsis. This program was expensive, and if it didn't significantly reduce sepsis rates, the organization would face further reputational damage. The executives requested to see a forecast for how financially successful the program would be, but also how it could improve the hospital's reputation.

3. **Develop a reliable predictor for future ROI forecasts.** Until a forecast is compared to the actual ROI, it is merely a forecast of what could happen with no reliability. However, if the forecasted ROI has a defined relationship with the actual ROI, it could become a credible predictor for future programs. How does that work? If there is a plan to evaluate a program to Level 5 ROI, it's possible to compare the actual results to the forecast. Establishing reliance on the forecast may eliminate the need for calculating the actual ROI, which equates to a cost savings because the forecast is based on inexpensive estimates and assumptions.

4. **It is an organizational or regulatory requirement.** Some organizations require an ROI forecast for any program that exceeds a certain budget level. For example, a health authority in Canada requires comprehensive business cases from healthcare organizations for all funding requests. Any funding request that exceeds $250,000 must include an ROI forecast.

Beyond the reasons why a stakeholder may request an ROI forecast, having one simply enhances the business case for training programs. Best practice is to include an ROI forecast, even if it has not been requested, because that will get the executives' attention. A typical business case includes the costs of the program and the expected learning results. A forecasted ROI using a credible process also includes the anticipated application of the learning, estimated business impact, and potential intangible benefits. Your chances of gaining approval and funding substantially increase when you offer a forecast upfront. If the forecast is negative, you can avoid investing in the wrong solution.

Forecasting ROI at Different Levels

ROI forecasts can be developed at different times throughout the program implementation and evaluation process and using different levels of data. Unfortunately, the ease, convenience, and costs involved in capturing an ROI forecast create trade-offs in accuracy and credibility. There are five distinct time intervals during a solution when you can develop the ROI (Table 18-1).

Table 18-1. ROI at Different Levels

ROI With	Data Collection Timing (Relative to the Initiative)	Credibility	Accuracy	Cost to Develop	Difficulty
		Least credible	Least accurate	Least expensive	Least difficult
Preprogram forecast	Before				
Level 1 data	During				
Level 2 data	During				
Level 3 data	After				
Level 4 data	After	▼	▼	▼	▼
		Most credible	Most accurate	Most expensive	Most difficult

Table 18-1 also shows the relationship between the timing of the ROI and the factors of credibility, accuracy, cost, and difficulty (Phillips and Phillips 2016). Let's review them in more detail:

- **You can develop a preproject forecast using estimates of the impact of the program.** This approach lacks credibility and accuracy but is the least expensive and easiest to calculate.
- **You can use Level 1 Reaction data to develop an anticipated impact, including the ROI.** In this case, participants anticipate the chain of impact as you

CHAPTER 18

implement a program, driving specific business measures. This is done after the project has begun. While accuracy and credibility increase from the preprogram basis, this approach still lacks the credibility and accuracy desired in many situations. However, it is still easily accomplished and a low-cost option.

- **If a program includes a substantial learning component, you can use Level 2 Learning data to forecast the ROI.** This approach is applicable when formal testing shows a relationship between test scores and subsequent business performance. When this correlation is available (it is usually developed to validate the test), you can use test data to forecast subsequent performance. Then you can convert the performance data to monetary impact and develop the ROI.
- **When frequency of skills or knowledge use is critical, you can convert Level 3 Application measures to a value based on the concept of utility analysis.** While this is particularly helpful in situations that involve developing competencies and placing value on improving competencies, it has limited applications in most projects.
- **Finally, you can develop the ROI forecast from Level 4 Business Impact data converted directly to monetary values and compared to the cost of the program.** This is not a forecast; rather, it is postprogram evaluation and serves as the basis for other ROI calculations.

Using postprogram Level 4 Business Impact data is the preferred approach for calculating ROI, but because of the pressures outlined here, examining ROI calculations at other times and with other levels is sometimes necessary.

Preprogram ROI Forecasting in 10 Easy Steps

Let's spend a little more time on preprogram forecasts. Perhaps one of the most useful ways to convince a sponsor of a program's potential benefit to the organization is to forecast the ROI prior to its implementation. The process is similar to the postprogram analysis, except that the business impact and program costs are projected. This projection is based on what you think will happen given the opportunity to improve measures, the objectives and design of the program, the participants involved in the program, and the context in which participants work.

FORECASTING ROI

> **Practitioner's Tip**
>
> As competition for funding becomes more complex, teams seeking funding and system improvement must demonstrate how they can accurately track and confirm that the project delivers the results as stated. ROI forecasting provides such a road map for decision makers.
>
> —Kelly Murphy, Executive Consultant, Medical and Academic Affairs

Figure 18-1 shows the 10-step model for developing a preprogram forecast. (This a modified version of the 12-step ROI Methodology process.) The preprogram forecast process estimates the impact measure improvements versus measuring the actual improvement after program implementation. Data collection follows a minimal resource process using interviews, focus groups, and surveys with subject matter experts. The fully loaded costs of the program are also estimated to determine the denominator in the ROI forecast calculation.

Figure 18-1. ROI Forecast Preprogram Model

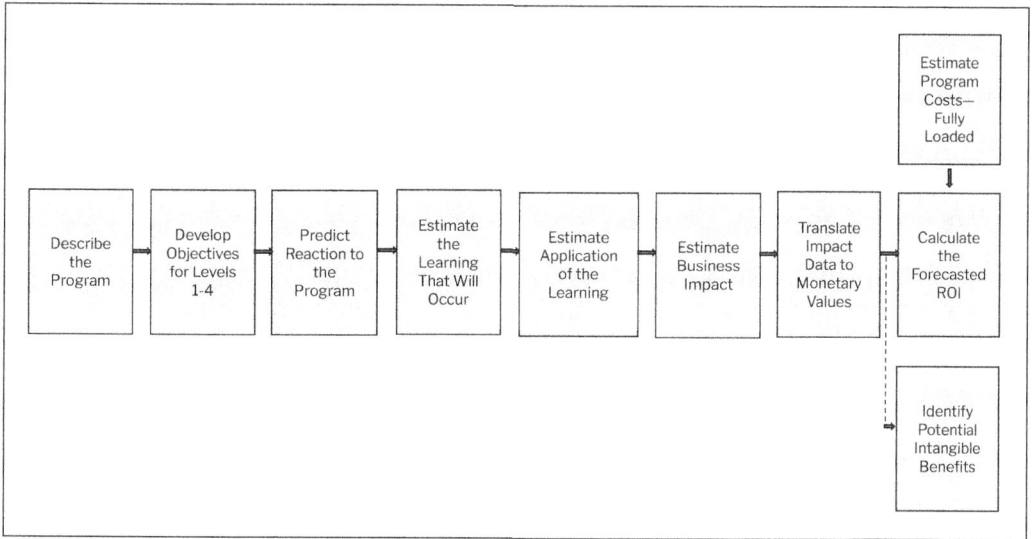

Describe the Program → Develop Objectives for Levels 1-4 → Predict Reaction to the Program → Estimate the Learning That Will Occur → Estimate Application of the Learning → Estimate Business Impact → Translate Impact Data to Monetary Values → Calculate the Forecasted ROI

Estimate Program Costs—Fully Loaded

Identify Potential Intangible Benefits

The forecast process begins with describing the program so everyone involved understands its goals. Define the why, which leads to the business need for the program and the impact objectives it will drive and improve. Data estimated at Levels 1, 2, and 3 strengthen the

CHAPTER 18

quality of the estimated Level 4 Impact data. The selected experts then estimate the improvement in the impact measures.

1. Describe the Program

A clear and all-encompassing description of the program is essential. It's critical that the selected experts understand the program so they're able to provide credible estimates at all levels of data. The description needs to include program content, timing, who is involved, and any other components that will contribute to a complete description.

2. Develop Objectives for Levels 1–4

ROI Institute has conducted or reviewed more than 5,000 evaluation studies, and the number 1 cause of program failure is lack of business alignment. For an ROI forecast to be credible, there needs to be a connection between the program and impact measures. This defines the why for the program.

Chapters 1, 2, and 3 provide the process to align the program to the business, analyze performance gaps, and develop powerful program objectives, which will need to be followed when conducting a preprogram forecast. The reaction, learning, application, and impact objectives set up the measures that the experts will estimate. Level 4 Impact objectives include tangible and intangible measures, which will also assist the experts in their impact estimate.

3. Predict Reaction to the Program

The next step is anticipating the participants' reaction to the program, which provides an indicator of potential buy-in from the participants. Here's an example estimation question you could present to the experts:

> To what extent do you anticipate the participants' response to the following will be on a scale of 1–5 (where 1 is low and 5 is high)?
> - The program is relevant to my job.
> - The program is important to the organization.
> - I intend to use the skills and competencies from this program.

Monitoring the responses you receive is critical because a low score or negative reaction can result in program failure.

4. Estimate the Learning That Will Occur

You must also estimate what participants will learn in the training program. Review the learning objectives to determine whether the program design meets the learning objectives outlined when the program was initially developed.

5. Estimate Application of the Learning

In this step, you need to anticipate how participants will apply what they learn in the program back on the job. Application objectives are helpful for collecting these estimations through a survey, focus group, or interviews. In addition, you can ask experts to estimate the level of application and frequency of application for the objectives, as well as anticipated barriers and enablers to application. Use these anticipated barriers and enablers to improve the program pre-implementation, which in turn will enhance program success.

6. Estimate Business Impact

This is a critical step in the forecasting process. Steps 3, 4, and 5 provide estimated results data on reaction, learning, and application and build toward estimating Level 4 impact. Ask the experts to review the Level 4 impact objectives and estimate the improvement expected in each measure in absolute amounts or percentages. This data is required for calculating the forecasted ROI.

It is important to note that the forecasted financial ROI is calculated using estimates, which are not always accurate, even when collected using a credible process. This means you should apply an error adjustment to your forecast. Ask the experts for their confidence level on the value of improvement they estimated on the impact measures. The confidence level is expressed as a percentage, with 0 percent indicating "no confidence" and 100 percent indicating "certainty." The error confidence level adjusts the expert estimate down, avoiding overstating the estimate. This provides credibility in the estimate, as well as a conservative potential level of success and ROI to the decision makers.

7. Translate Impact Data to Monetary Values

You must then convert the change in impact measures to monetary values. There are standard values for many of these measures, but other techniques are available in lieu of them, such as referencing external databases or obtaining estimates from stakeholders or experts. (Refer to chapter 14 for more information about converting impact measures to monetary values.)

8. Identify Potential Intangible Benefits

Intangible benefits are the valuable Level 4 Impact benefits resulting from the implementation of a program that cannot be converted to a monetary value. You can identify the program's potential intangible benefit improvements in step 2 as part of the objectives at Level 4. Ask the experts to estimate the extent to which the intangible benefits will be improved by the program.

9. Estimate Program Costs

This step requires forecasting the program's fully loaded costs. (Refer to chapter 15 to review the cost categories comprising the total costs.) Note that while some of the costs are fully allocated to the program, some are prorated. You'll need to include all direct and indirect costs in your estimate.

10. Calculate the Forecasted ROI

Using the total estimated annual monetary benefits and the fully loaded estimated costs, you can use the ROI formula to calculate the forecasted ROI:

$$\frac{\text{Estimated benefits} - \text{Estimated costs}}{\text{Estimated costs}} \times 100 = \text{Forecasted ROI (\%)}$$

Following these 10 steps will result in a credible ROI forecast.

Isolating the Impact—Not Required

A postprogram ROI evaluation includes a very important step—to isolate the impact measure improvement to the program. Because other influences contribute to improvement, credibly showing program contribution requires exploring these influences and assigning a level of program impact.

This step is embedded in the process for a preprogram forecast because you're asking experts to estimate the improvement in impact measures that the program will deliver. Those estimates are isolated to the program.

Selecting Experts

The credibility of the ROI forecast depends on the credibility and trust of the experts you select to provide the estimates throughout this 10-step process. Potential experts include sponsors, prospective participants, subject matter experts, external experts, executives, and managers. Consider these attributes when selecting experts for your ROI forecast:
- Experience with similar programs
- Understanding of the program
- Conflict of interest or bias to be eliminated

ROI Forecasting After Program Launch

Earlier in the chapter, I outlined a few basics of forecasting ROI at different intervals aligned with Levels 1–4 evaluation after program launch. Let's now explore what that looks like in more detail.

Level 1 ROI

A simple approach to forecasting ROI for a new program is to add a few questions to the standard Level 1 evaluation questionnaire. As in the case of a preprogram forecast, the data is not as credible as in an actual postprogram evaluation; however, a Level 1 evaluation does rely on data from participants who have actually attended the program.

Table 18-2 presents a series of questions that can be used to develop an ROI forecast. They ask participants to detail how they plan to use what they have learned and the results that they expect to achieve. You can also ask them to convert their anticipated accomplishments into an annual monetary value and show the basis for developing the values. Requesting that they adjust their values with a confidence estimate makes the data more credible while allowing participants to reflect on their uncertainty with the process. You can then calculate the monetary benefits of the program and compare them to the projected program costs and calculate the ROI forecast. While not as reliable as actual data, this process provides some indication of potential program success.

Table 18-2. Questions for Level 1 ROI

As a result of this program, what specific actions will you attempt as you apply what you have learned?
Indicate what specific measures, outcomes, or projects will change as a result of your action.
As a result of these anticipated changes, estimate (in monetary values) the benefits to your organization over a period of one year. $_____   What is the basis of this estimate?
What confidence, expressed as a percentage, can you put in your estimate?   (0% = no confidence, 100% = certainty) _____ %

Level 2 ROI

Other approaches to forecasting include the use of Level 2 test data. You can validate a reliable test, reflecting the program's content against job performance data (impact measures). If there is a statistically significant relationship between test scores and job performance, test scores should relate to improved job performance. You can convert the performance data to monetary value and use the test scores to estimate the monetary impact from the program. When compared to projected costs, you can forecast the ROI.

This technique has slightly more credibility than a Level 1 forecast because it relies on test data and statistical analysis. Unfortunately, many programs do not use validated tests as measures of learning, so this technique is not as feasible as some people would like.

Level 3 ROI

A final approach to forecasting ROI is with Level 3 data, which attracts the attention of many practitioners who can't access business impact data. Originally based on utility analysis, this approach has been modified for more widespread use. While still subjective, it can be useful in forecasting value added by improving competencies. This approach follows six steps:

1. Identify the competencies being developed in the program.
2. Determine the percentage of jobs requiring these skills.

3. Determine the monetary value of the competencies using the salary and benefits of participants.
4. Determine the increase in skill level due to the program.
5. Calculate the monetary benefits of the improvement.
6. Compare the monetary benefits to the cost of the program.

Let's review a basic example of forecasting ROI using Level 3 data. Ten supervisors attend a four-day developmental program that costs $65,000 fully loaded. The average salary (plus benefits factor) of the 10 supervisors is $110,000.

The program team followed these steps to forecast the ROI based on improvement in participants' supervisory skills:

1. **Identify competencies:** Supervisory skills, communication skills, motivation, managing diversity, and planning, controlling, and evaluating work.
2. **Determine percentage of jobs requiring these skills:** 85 percent.
    - This is the group average.
3. **Determine the monetary value of the competencies using salary and benefits of participants:** $93,500 per participant or $935,000 for the group.
    - Multiply the percentage of skills used on the job by the job's value: 85% × $110,000 = $93,500 per person.
    - Multiply the total per person by the number of people in the group: $93,500 × 10 = $935,000.
4. **Determine increase in skill level due to program:** 15% increase.
    - This is an average of the group based on a comparison of on-the-job competency assessments pre- and postprogram.
5. **Calculate the monetary benefits of the improvement:** $140,250.
    - Multiply the dollar value of the competencies by the improvement in skill level: $935,000 × 15% = $140,250.
6. **Compare the monetary benefits to the cost of the program:** ROI of 116%.
    - Determine program net benefits, divide by program costs, and then multiply by 100.

$$\frac{\$140{,}250 - \$65{,}000}{\$65{,}000} \times 100 = 116\%$$

CHAPTER 18

Case Study: Preprogram ROI Forecast: Retention Improvement at a Healthcare Organization

SCS is a healthcare organization with several sites employing approximately 7,500 people. The organization was experiencing very high turnover of nurses and team assistants, putting significant strain on the organization. The head of HR was aware of the high-stress levels, burnout, absenteeism, and poor morale. In addition, she worked with finance to determine the cost of turnover to the organization and found that the 18 percent turnover rate was costing close to $10,000,000 annually.

Using steps 1 and 2 of the ROI Methodology, HR conducted a needs analysis and sourced a leadership skills and competencies training program that focused on retention called Star Solutions. SCS decided to use one hospital site to pilot the program—30 managers would participate three full-day sessions. The turnover rate was 20 percent in this hospital, which had an annual cost of $1,000,000.

Part of the business case to implement the program included a preprogram ROI forecast.

Program Objectives

SCS selected nine experts—three participants with different leadership roles, three SCS supervisors, two SCS HR professionals, and a subject matter expert—to estimate the program's reaction, learning, application, and impact scores. They were all very aware of the turnover problem and had a good understanding of the Star Solutions program.

The vendor delivered a thorough presentation that outlined the program's objectives:

- **Reaction:**
  - The program is relevant to my job.
  - The program is necessary.
  - I intend to use the skills and competencies.
- **Learning:**
  - Learn the day-to-day leadership skills and competencies.
  - Know how to effectively conduct stay interviews.
  - Know how to build an employee relationship strategy with all employees.
- **Application:**
  - Use the leadership skills and competencies daily.
  - Conduct stay interviews with employees within three months.

FORECASTING ROI

- Develop a relationship strategy with all employees within three months.
- **Impact:**
  - Reduce turnover by 2 percent in three months and 5 percent in six months.
  - Reduce absenteeism by 5 percent in six months.
  - Improve employee morale.
  - Reduce employee stress.

Forecasted Results Summary

After reviewing all the information, the experts came to the following predictions:

- Reaction to the program would be very positive (above four on a five-point Likert scale for all three objectives).
- A high amount of learning would occur.
- Application of the learning would be successful. (The timing of application was estimated to be up to six months.)
- The average estimate of turnover reduction was 5 percent in six months (with an average confidence of 82 percent). This credible estimate converted to a monetary value of $250,000.
- Forecasted ROI was 343 percent based on estimated benefits and costs (Table 18-3).

Table 18-3. Estimated Benefits and Costs

Benefits:	
Estimated impact in 6 months (drop of 5%)	$250,000
	To annualize: x 2
Predicted intangibles are lower stress, burn-out, and absenteeism	$500,000
Costs: Stars Solutions	
Direct cost:	
Star Solutions pilot program fee	$55,000
Evaluation	$8,000
Facility	$3,000
Participant time (hourly wage x time)	
Cost for 30 managers: ($65 x 24) x 30	$46,800
Total Estimated Fully Loaded Program Costs	**$112,800**
Forecasted ROI	**343%**

Summary

This chapter demonstrated how to forecast ROI calculations. Most practitioners focus on Level 3 and 4 data for ROI forecasts because ROI estimates at Levels 1 and 2 have low credibility. Forecasting ROI using Level 4 data offers higher credibility and accuracy, although it can be more costly and sometimes difficult to develop.

> **Knowledge Check**
>
> True or false:
>
> 1. An ROI forecast can only be completed using expert-estimated Level 4 data.
> 2. Impact data needs to be isolated when calculating a forecasted ROI.
> 3. Estimated impact data for a training program is best obtained from the vendor delivering the program because they know it best.
> 4. Converting impact data to a monetary value follows the same process for a forecast ROI as for calculating the actual ROI.
> 5. Program monetary benefits divided by program costs = program ROI.
> 6. A Level 3 ROI forecast is credible.

PART 4
Results Optimization

Part 4 of this book describes the last two steps in the measurement and evaluation process: telling the story and optimizing results. These two steps put evaluation to work. We can plan an evaluation to the nth degree; we can collect data using textbook protocols; we can analyze the data until we have nothing left to analyze. But, if no action is taken, the evaluation process becomes just another activity.

The first step is to report results. Quantitative data shows the results obtained through the evaluation; qualitative data tells the story. Together, these two types of data develop a powerful profile of what is and isn't working with training programs. There are multiple reasons to report data—to inform the status of a program, to monitor performance in key measures, to evaluate success in meeting objectives, and to manage training as a business. The key is to present relevant results so the audiences believe and accept them and feel compelled to act. Using an approach that is standard across industries allows talent development leaders and program owners to benchmark against others. But, it's how programs perform against the target set from within that matters most.

In the end, however, the purpose of measurement and evaluation is to improve programs and processes. Data without action is, well, just data. A mindset of curiosity emboldens program owners to learn from what works and what doesn't.

Part 4 offers a specific use case describing how financial analysis was used to make program decisions. Additionally, you'll gain insights on how to:
- Tell your story.
- Visualize data.
- Implement the ISO standards for reporting.
- Use black box thinking.

CHAPTER 19

Telling the Story

KEVIN M. YATES

IN THIS CHAPTER

This chapter explains the importance and challenges of communicating your evaluation results to diverse levels of management in an unbiased and objective manner. After reading it, you will be able to:

♦ Devise a communication plan for your evaluation results.

♦ Choose the appropriate communication method.

♦ Adjust your communication approach to different stakeholders.

Case Study: Insights Discovery at Indeed

Insights is a people development company helping organizations globally improve the effectiveness of individuals and build better teams across organizations. Its Insights Discovery solutions are based on verified psychology, focusing on building awareness for individuals, teams, and leaders to understand themselves and others better and improve relationships in the workplace. The heart of the Insights Discovery process is a personality-based instrument that categorizes personalities into four unique colors (fiery red, sunshine yellow, earthy green, and cool blue). This helps individuals determine why others behave the way they do and how they might be perceived by others.

After Indeed—the world's number 1 job site with more than 300 million unique visitors every month—implemented the Insights Discovery process, it wanted to know the value of that process. Insights engaged an ROI consultant to evaluate the process at the impact and ROI levels and present the results to executives at Indeed and Insights. As the ROI consultant presented, the success of this engagement began to evolve with a carefully selected sample of 1,304 individuals who had recently participated in the process. The consultant team tracked the success of the Insights Discovery program along five outcome levels (reaction, learning, application, impact, and ROI) and the intangibles (the measures not converted to money).

The reaction, tracking eight measures, was impressive and extremely positive. Most importantly, the participants saw the Insights Discovery process as vital to their professional development. It was a good use of their time and something they would recommend to others. The learning metric was also impressive because participants learned about themselves and how to work with others using the Insights Discovery process. The application was even more successful—participants adapted their behavior to work with others more effectively, identified other peoples' preferences by observing their behavior, and openly shared information and knowledge within the team. In all, 13 important behaviors or actions showed a marvelous improvement. The evaluation also revealed how carefully planned the program implementation was and that it was very successful. Immediate managers supported it directly because they were involved in teaching, role modeling, and supporting the process. Insights Discovery had become part of Indeed's culture.

The results connected to the program included talent retention, reduction in days to proficiency, individual time savings, reduction in time to promotion, and increased innovation and agility. When these measures were converted to money and compared with the program cost, the study showed that the program generated an amazing—almost unbelievable—ROI. This was due to the program's successful implementation, impressive data collection, and credible processes and conservative standards with which the ROI was calculated. The intangibles connected to the program that weren't converted to money and thus not in the ROI calculation—such as emotional intelligence, communication, collaboration, and teamwork—were also impressive.

Overall, Indeed was satisfied with the results of this evaluation, confirming the program's success and return on investment. It was also valuable information for Insights because it could use it to show how its work added value and delivered a huge positive ROI for Indeed, suggesting that others could achieve the same value (ROI Institute 2023).

This case study outlines the importance of having a story to tell executives when a major program is conducted and evaluated. Presenting the results to senior executives is an important activity that should be considered for any major project that will attract executive attention.

Why Reporting Results Is Critical

An evaluation project requires planning and great attention to detail to ensure it achieves its desired outcomes. However, this does not always happen because evaluation is multifaceted and somewhat complex. Collecting data and producing a successful outcome is meaningless unless you also communicate the findings effectively to the proper audiences in a timely manner so you or others can leverage the results for improvements. The story must be told.

Principles for Communicating Results

Style can be as important as substance when reporting results. Managing the complexity of the message, audience, or delivery medium can be demanding, but you can achieve exceptional results by following a few general principles outlined here.

Timely Communication

Timing the communication of results can affect how well they are accepted and how effectively and quickly they are acted upon. Communicate results as soon as they are known so decision makers can take immediate action. Realistically, however, it may be best to communicate at a time that is most convenient to the audience to maximize the results of the evaluation.

> **Practitioner's Tip**
>
> Maximize the evaluation study's results by ensuring the greatest number of key stakeholders attend the presentation and that the current work environment is favorable to a robust discussion of the findings.

Targeted Communication

Communication will be more effective if it is crafted early in the planning process and tailored to a particular group's interests, needs, and expectations. The results discussed in this chapter mirror outcomes at all levels, including the six types of data (reaction, learning, application, impact, ROI, and intangibles).

CHAPTER 19

Appropriate Media Selection
Selecting the correct medium for your communication can determine the effectiveness of the message. Whenever appropriate, direct communication is the preferred method; however, there are also a variety of other methods for telling the story of L&D success. (We'll discuss them in more detail later in this chapter.)

Unbiased Communication
Let objective, credible, and accurate results speak for themselves. Sometimes, in the excitement of "wanting to make a splash," overinflated or controversial opinions may leak into a report. Although these statements may get attention, they can detract from the accuracy of the results and turn off the recipients.

Use these pointers to make your communication process credible:
- Give credit to participants and their managers.
- Fully address the evaluation methodology to give credibility to the findings.
- Clarify data sources and explain why they are credible.
- State and support any assumptions made during the analysis and reporting.
- Be pragmatic and only make claims that are supported by the data.

Testimonials From Respected Individuals
Testimonials from individuals with recognized stature, leadership roles, or influence can have a strong bearing on how effectively messages are accepted. Opinions of your audience can be strongly swayed with this level of support.

Communication Plan

You should pay strict attention to detail in your communication plan to ensure that each target audience receives the proper information in a timely fashion and knows the appropriate actions to take.

There are five basic steps to planning the communication of your evaluation project:
1. Analyze the need for communication.
2. Identify the target audience.
3. Develop the communication documents.

TELLING THE STORY

4. Deliver results through appropriate media.
5. Analyze reactions to communication.

Analyze the Need for Communication

The program, setting, and sponsor's unique needs dictate specific reasons for communicating program results. The most frequent reasons are:
- Securing approval for a program and allocating time and money
- Gaining support for a program and its objectives
- Enhancing the credibility of a program or a program team
- Reinforcing the processes used in a program
- Driving action for program improvements
- Preparing participants for a program
- Showing the complete results of a training program
- Underscoring the importance of measuring results
- Explaining techniques used to measure results
- Marketing future projects.

While this list encompasses many reasons, it's important to acknowledge that individual circumstances, context, and audience may introduce additional factors.

Identify the Target Audience

As part of developing the overall communication plan, give significant thought to who should receive program results. The target audience will likely have diverse job levels and responsibilities, so choose communication methods accordingly. Examining the reason for the communication is always a sound basis for determining audience selection.

Try asking the following questions when determining whom you will send your communication to:
- Are they interested in the program?
- Do they want to receive the information?
- Has a commitment been made to communicate with them?
- Is the timing right for communicating with this audience?
- How would they prefer to receive the results?
- Are they likely to find the results threatening?
- Which communication method will be most convincing to this group?

When considering the different members of your target audience, think about these perspectives:
- The project manager should know and understand the target audience.
- The program team should examine specific needs and why they need that information. Each group will have its own level of detail relative to the information desired.
- The program team should try to understand any audience bias or differing views. Although some will immediately support the results, others may be skeptical or impartial.
- The project sponsor is perhaps the most important audience member. This individual (or group) initiates the program, reviews the data, and weighs the final assessment of program effectiveness.
- Senior management is responsible for allocating resources to the program and needs information to help justify expenditures and gauge the effectiveness of efforts.
- Selected groups of managers (or all managers) are important to increase both support and credibility.
- The participants' team leaders or immediate supervisors are essential to involve because they're most likely to be able to encourage participants to put what they've learned into practice and reinforce the objectives of the program.

Develop the Communication Documents

The type of formal evaluation report will correlate with the level of detailed information presented to the different audiences. Brief summaries of results with appropriate charts may be sufficient for some communication efforts. On the other hand, projects that require a high level of approval and considerable funding will necessitate a much more comprehensive write-up, possibly a full-blown impact study. Regardless of what type of report you intend to prepare, give credit for success entirely to the participants and their immediate leaders, avoid boasting about results, and ensure recipients will fully understand the methodology.

The flow of your communication document should address the following issues:
- The reason for evaluating the program
- The rationale for designing the evaluation

TELLING THE STORY

- The evaluation methodology used
- Results and outcomes for the program
- Conclusions and recommendations

An example of a comprehensive impact study is outlined in Figure 19-1.

Figure 19-1. Format of an Impact Study Report

- Executive summary
- General information
  - Background
  - Objectives of study
- Methodology for impact study
  - Levels of evaluation/ROI model
  - Collection methods and issues
  - Data analysis procedures
    - Isolating the effects of training
    - Converting data to monetary values
    - Assumptions

  Builds credibility for the process.

- Program categories
- Results: General information
  - Response profile
  - Success with objectives
- Results: Reaction
  - Data sources
  - Data summary
  - Key issues
- Results: Learning
  - Data sources
  - Data summary
  - Key issues
- Results: Application and Implementation
  - Data sources
  - Data summary
  - Key issues
- Results: Business impact
  - General comments
  - Links with business measures
  - Key issues
  - Barriers and enablers
- Results: ROI and its meaning
- Results: Intangible measures

  The results with six measures: Levels 1, 2, 3, 4, 5, and intangibles.

- What makes this credible
- Findings and actions
  - Conclusions
  - Recommendations
- Exhibits

CHAPTER 19

Deliver Results Through Appropriate Media

Even a program's most favorable outcomes can be undermined if they are not presented in a suitable format or environment. Certain communication methods may be more effective for one group than others; for example:

- **Meetings** are typically held with executives, management, stakeholders, and staff.
- **Detailed reports** are used to communicate impact studies, internal and external case studies, and major articles.
- **Brief reports** convey executive summaries, slide overviews, one-page summaries, and brochures.
- **Digital reporting** is best for websites, email, blogs and social media, and videos.
- **Mass publications** are used for announcements, bulletins, newsletters, brief articles, and press releases.
- **Case studies** represent an effective way to communicate the results of a project, particularly when explaining measurement methodologies in a group setting.

Practitioner's Tip

A case study based on evaluation results provides a great teaching tool for your audience because it allows them to take the conceptual model of gathering data and apply it to authentic business situations. Supporters of the case study method point out that these studies produce a more comprehensive report than one generated using statistical or data analysis alone. Although the case study may be focused on one key business metric, the final study is more robust because it addresses conditions that go beyond the numbers, such as corporate vision, economic environment, or leadership mandates.

Scorecards and dashboards are performance management tools that concentrate on various performance indicators and can include financial outcomes, operations, marketing, process performance, customer perspective, or any other appropriate measure.

Analyze Reactions to Communication

The level of commitment and support managers, executives, and sponsors express will mirror how successfully you have communicated the project's results. Top management may also show a positive perception of results by allocating requested resources and voicing their commitment.

When you communicate major project results, you might consider administering a feedback questionnaire to the audience or a sample of the audience to evaluate their understanding or acceptance of the information presented.

Communication Opportunities

The remainder of this chapter will focus on three important opportunities for telling the impact story:
- Providing routine feedback on project progress
- Telling a story with the results
- Presenting results to senior leadership

Providing Routine Feedback on Project Progress

By routinely collecting reaction and learning data, you can gather feedback promptly and make any necessary adjustments throughout the project. However, it can be complex to provide this feedback to several different audiences using different types of media, so you must be proactively manage the process.

The following steps—some based on the recommendations from Peter Block's 2011 book *Flawless Consulting*—are suggested for providing feedback and managing the overall process:
- Communicate quickly and appropriately.
- Simplify the data.
- Examine the role of the project team and the client in the feedback process.
- Use negative data in a constructive way.
- Use positive data in a cautious way.
- Ask the client for reactions to the data.
- Ask the client for recommendations.
- Use support and confrontation carefully.
- React to and act on the data.
- Secure agreement from all key stakeholders.

These steps will help move the project forward and generate useful feedback, often ensuring that adjustments are supported and can be executed.

CHAPTER 19

Telling a Story With the Results

Numbers cannot tell the whole story, and other means of communication are required to define and articulate results. Stories are uniquely useful in their ability to bring people onto the same page and organize information so it can be presented in an efficient and accessible manner.

Stories foster empathy and connectedness because they prioritize information and objectives and provide a clear beginning, middle, and end. The narrative structure of a story provides a teaching tool that can make complex data or relationships easier for an audience to understand. Because the important ideas are set in a metaphor, storytellers and listeners can both move past arcane details and focus on the problem at hand. The immediacy of the story helps people track the important relationships while empathizing with the subject. This allows for a richer experience and fosters greater insight into the nature of the program, its place in the organization, and how the participants' choices contribute to its success (Mootee 2013).

The simple rationale for telling stories is that they work. Let's look at eight of Paul Smith's 10 most compelling evidence-based reasons to tell stories (2012):

1. Storytelling is simple.
2. Storytelling is timeless.
3. Stories are contagious.
4. Stories are easy to remember.
5. Stories inspire.
6. Stories appeal to all types of audiences.
7. Stories fit in the workplace where most of the work happens.
8. Telling stories shows respect for the audience.

A logical structure is helpful to develop stories. Although the structure can vary, you can use this checklist for most stories:

- **Hook**
    - Why should they listen to this story?
- **Content**
    - Where and when did it happen?
    - Who is the hero? (Are they relatable?)
    - What do they want? (Is that worthy?)
- **Challenge**
    - What is the problem or opportunity? (Relevant?)

- **Conflict**
  - What did the hero do about it? (Honest struggle?)
- **Resolution**
  - How did it turn out in the end?
- **Lesson**
  - What did they learn?
- **Recommended action**
  - What do you want them to do?

Another storytelling expert, Carmine Gallo (2016), offers 10 storytelling secrets:

1. Make stories at least 65 percent of your presentation.
2. Use simple words and analogies to hide complexity.
3. Enrich your story with specific and relevant details.
4. Deliver serious topics with a side of humor.
5. Tell authentic and personal stories tailored to your audience.
6. Be succinct; use a few well-chosen words.
7. Use pictures to illustrate your story.
8. Wrap data in stories to make a personal connection.
9. Take every opportunity to hone your presentation skills.
10. Don't make your story good; make it great.

Presenting Results to Senior Leadership

Perhaps one of the most challenging and stressful types of communication is presenting an impact and ROI study to the senior leadership team. This involves persuading a discerning and analytical group that you attained exceptional results within a reasonable timeframe while addressing key points. It's essential to ensure leadership comprehends the process fully.

Two potential reactions can create challenges. First, if the results are very impressive, leaders may have a hard time accepting the supporting data. Second, if the data is negative, you'll need to ensure that leaders don't overreact to the results and look for someone to blame. Several guidelines can help you proactively plan and execute this process properly:

- **Arrange a face-to-face meeting with senior team members to review the results.** If they aren't familiar with the ROI Methodology or evaluation framework you use, this meeting is necessary to make sure they understand the process. Be careful about the length of this presentation—their time is limited and it's best to keep it under an hour. Following the meeting where you share results, providing an executive summary, rather than the entire report, may be adequate.

- **Do not disseminate results before the initial presentation or during the session; instead, save them until the end.** This will allow you to present the process and collect reactions before the target audience sees the ROI calculation. Present the ROI Methodology step by step, showing how you collected the data, when it was collected, who provided it, how you isolated the effect of the program from other influences, and how you converted data to monetary values. Present any assumptions, adjustments, and conservative approaches, along with the total cost of the program, so the target audience will begin to buy into your process for developing the ROI.
- **Reveal the results one level at a time, starting with Level 1, moving through Level 5, and ending with the intangibles.** This allows the audience to observe the reaction, learning, application and implementation, business impact, and ROI procedures. Allocate time for each level as appropriate for the audience. This helps mitigate possible emotional responses to a highly favorable or unfavorable ROI.
- **Show the consequences of additional accuracy if this is an issue.** Opting for increased accuracy and validity typically entails higher costs. Address this issue when necessary, agreeing to add more data if required. Collect concerns, reactions, and issues involving the process and adjust accordingly for the next presentation.

Collectively, these steps can help you prepare and present of one of the most important meetings in the ROI Methodology—the executive briefing.

The purpose of the executive meeting is to:
- Create awareness and understanding of ROI.
- Build support for the ROI Methodology.
- Communicate the results of the study.
- Drive improvement from the results.
- Cultivate effective use of the ROI Methodology.

When holding an executive briefing, keep these ground rules in mind:
- Do not distribute the impact study until the end of the meeting.
- Be precise and to the point.

TELLING THE STORY

- Avoid jargon and unfamiliar terms.
- Spend less time on the lower levels of evaluation data.
- Present the data with a strategy in mind.

An executive briefing should follow this presentation sequence:

1. Describe the program and explain why it is being evaluated.
2. Present the methodology process.
3. Present the reaction and learning data.
4. Present the application data.
5. List the barriers and enablers to success.
6. Address the business impact.
7. Show the costs.
8. Present the ROI.
9. Show the intangibles.
10. Review the credibility of the data.
11. Summarize the conclusions.
12. Present the recommendations.

Summary

Communicating results and telling the impact story does not always receive the attention it deserves because it is multifaceted and somewhat complex. But if you fail to properly execute your communication plan, you won't realize the full effect of results and measurable outcomes, and therefore the value of the study may be lost. This chapter reviewed this critical step in the overall evaluation process.

Knowledge Check

In the first quarter of last year, you joined a project team to develop marketing plans for increasing the percentage of environmentally green goods sold by the household cleaning business unit. Because the effect on the company's bottom line was potentially dramatic, the team included senior managers, marketing reps, sales training, human resources, and workplace learning and performance staff, along with a few high-performing sales reps. A senior marketer agreed to be the project sponsor.

A major part of the strategy was creating a product training course for the sales team. After three weeks of home study, 500 representatives were brought to corporate headquarters for a week of training on new products, competition, and business planning.

During the initial strategic planning session, a comprehensive study was conducted on the program to gather results from reaction through business impact. Because all representatives were required to undergo training, it wasn't possible to leverage an experimental and control group for measuring impact. Instead, it was determined that results would be measured using the participants' estimate of impact on key business metrics.

A reaction and learning evaluation were completed by all participants at the end of the home study and in-house training. Three months after the in-house training, the evaluation team emailed a comprehensive behavioral change evaluation, which included questions about estimation and confidence. In all, 366 of the 500 participants completed the evaluation.

Finally, after eight months, the project team emailed everyone the report, which contained some results, partial recommendations, and promises of a more comprehensive report later in the fourth quarter.

1. As someone involved in this training and study, would you consider this method of reporting the evaluation results acceptable? If not, why?
2. If you were on the team designing the measurement study, how would you have created the communication plan?

CHAPTER 20

Visualizing Data
PEGGY PARSKEY

IN THIS CHAPTER

This chapter discusses a crucial element of building your data story: how to display and visualize your data and information. Effective data visualization helps transform complex datasets into clear, intuitive visuals, enabling stakeholders to quickly grasp patterns, trends, and outliers. When you follow the basic principles of data visualization, you will enhance understanding of the data and more effectively facilitate informed decision making. After reading this chapter, you will be able to:

♦ Describe the fundamentals of data visualization, including how humans perceive information.

♦ Design effective visualizations based on your objectives and type of data.

♦ Visualize Likert, categorical, and qualitative data used in the L&D function.

Learning organizations generate a significant volume of data and information. Learning management systems (LMSs) contain data on courses, registrations, consumption, tests, and administrator actions. Financial systems track program budgets, L&D salaries, and expenditures for materials, technology, and resources. Evaluation systems house data on assessments, surveys, feedback forms, and performance. And because these systems may not provide everything leaders require, L&D practitioners regularly combine existing data or generate new data for one-off or ongoing analyses.

This data ends up in static reports, interactive dashboards, and PowerPoint decks that practitioners and leaders review, share, and discuss. But these reports don't create themselves.

Between the data collection and release of the reports, there is a critical transformation process that converts raw data into graphic representations that help inform decisions and actions. This multifaceted process is this chapter's focus.

The Fundamentals of Data Visualization

Effective data visualization ensures that the audience can quickly process information, identify key messages from the visual, and determine what, if anything, to do about it. Three actions are essential to creating effective visuals:
- Clarify the objectives of data visualization.
- Address the capabilities and limitations of how humans perceive information.
- Follow guidelines to ensure data accuracy, minimize bias, and select the appropriate visual.

Objectives of Data Visualization

The primary objectives of data visualization are to make data more accessible, understandable, and actionable, as well as to empower users to derive insights, make informed decisions, and communicate effectively with others. Specifically, data visualization:
- **Aims to make complex datasets more accessible and understandable to a wide audience.** Visual presentation allows viewers to quickly grasp key insights, patterns, and relationships that may not be apparent from raw data alone.
- **Helps identify anomalies, outliers, and patterns in the data that may require further investigation.** Visually highlighting discrepancies or deviations from expected patterns enables users to identify potential errors or areas of concern.
- **Serves as a powerful communication tool for sharing information and insights with stakeholders, colleagues, or the public.** Presenting data in visually compelling and engaging ways enables decision makers to identify correlations and relationships, leading to better-informed decisions.

How Humans Perceive Information

Effective data visualization considers human capabilities and limitations in perceiving information based on the Gestalt theory of psychology. This theory identifies six principles

VISUALIZING DATA

that describe how we process information and are important to remember when creating visualizations: enclosure, closure, connection, continuity, proximity, and similarity. Table 20-1 depicts each principle, provides a graphic example, and identifies an application of the principle to data visualization.

Table 20-1. How Humans Perceive Information

Principle	Definition	Graphic Example	Application in Data Visualization
Enclosure	Elements appearing within a common boundary or enclosure are seen as a group or unit.		Use borders and fill colors or shading in tables and graphs to group information and set it apart.
Closure	Incomplete shapes or elements are perceived as complete when the viewer fills in the missing information.		Apply the concept of closure with missing data or incomplete information. Viewers infer the missing data points to perceive a complete picture.
Connection	Objects that are connected are seen as part of the same group.		Use a dumbbell chart to connect and compare demographics (e.g., compare application rates of employees who reported high vs. low levels of manager support).
Continuity	Elements arranged in a line or curve are seen as more related and part of a continuous pattern than elements not on the line or curve.		Arrange data in a sequential or directional manner to demonstrate the data flow or progression over time or project phases. Observers will perceive items not in the flow as being separate.
Proximity	Objects or shapes that are close to one another are seen as a group.		Use white space to separate linked information from surrounding data. Place dashboard widgets close together to convey relationships.
Similarity	Objects that share similar characteristics (e.g., shape, size, color, or texture) are seen as part of a pattern or group.		Assign consistent meaning to colors across charts and graphs (e.g., in each view, circle means "good" and square means "action needed").

281

Guidelines For Visualizing Data

While data visualization is a powerful tool, when not executed with care, visualizations can also distort information. It's imperative that designers and practitioners are aware of potential pitfalls.

Maintaining Accuracy

Data must be accurate, complete, and relevant to the overall purpose of the visualizations. A best practice is to check for anomalies or potential errors in the data prior to displaying it in a chart or graph. Visualizations can also serve as a useful tool for checking data accuracy. For example, a practitioner could use visuals to review:

- Outliers—single data points far outside the average value of other data points—which may point to potential errors that the analyst did not uncover during data cleaning
- Distribution of the data inconsistent with past results
- Missing values that can undermine the data story

Avoiding Bias

It's important to represent large and complex datasets accurately, both in terms of what the practitioner chooses to display as well as how to display it. Avoid these two common sources of bias:

- **Cherry-picking** involves selecting only data points that support the argument or story. Selecting a subset of the data can result in misleading conclusions and give the impression that the findings are stronger than they are.
- **Graph distortion** creates displays that make effects seem larger than they are. For example, when presenting data in bar charts or line graphs, designers may choose to save space by changing the scale. When effects are small, changing the scale can make the differences look larger than they really are. Consider Figure 20-1, which shows two different visual representations of the same datasets. The vertical axis in the chart on the left uses a scale of one to five to show the average Likert score, while the chart on the right condenses the scale to 3.5 to 4.5. This adjustment of the vertical axis scale visually exaggerates the difference between the three datasets.

Figure 20-1. Graph Distortion

Align Visualizations to the Type of Data

The range of visualization choices can be overwhelming. If practitioners have a favorite view, they may choose to use it even if it isn't appropriate for the data, such as using trend lines for discrete data or pie charts for items that are not part of a whole. The next section of this chapter provides guidance on how to select the right chart to display your data.

Designing Effective Data Visualizations

Understanding basic design concepts will shape how your visualizations look. You'll also need to consider what message you want your visuals to convey to your audience. These two elements will guide you in selecting the right graph for your needs.

Design Concepts

Visualizing data may seem simple: Throw data into a line graph or bar chart, pretty it up a bit, and voila! The chart is ready for review. Instead, consider these four design concepts to ensure the clarity and impact of your graphs or charts:
- Maximize "data ink" to convey information efficiently while minimizing unnecessary elements.
- Use color judiciously to enhance understanding and emphasize key points.
- Include clear and concise legends to provide context and interpretation.
- Minimize the amount of information presented to avoid overwhelming the audience and maintain focus on the most relevant insights.

Chapter 20

Data Versus Nondata Ink

In data visualization, *data ink* refers to the ink or graphical elements that directly represent the data, while *nondata ink* encompasses all other visual elements. Data ink is essential for effectively communicating insights, because it directly communicates the dataset's values, trends, and relationships. Nondata ink—such as gridlines, borders, and decorative elements—can distract from the core message.

Figure 20-2 includes two bar charts displaying the same dataset. Note how the chart on the left focuses on the data ink (the bar charts and the values) and minimizes nondata ink, while the chart on the right accentuates the nondata ink (heavy gridlines and bold labels) and distracts from the data.

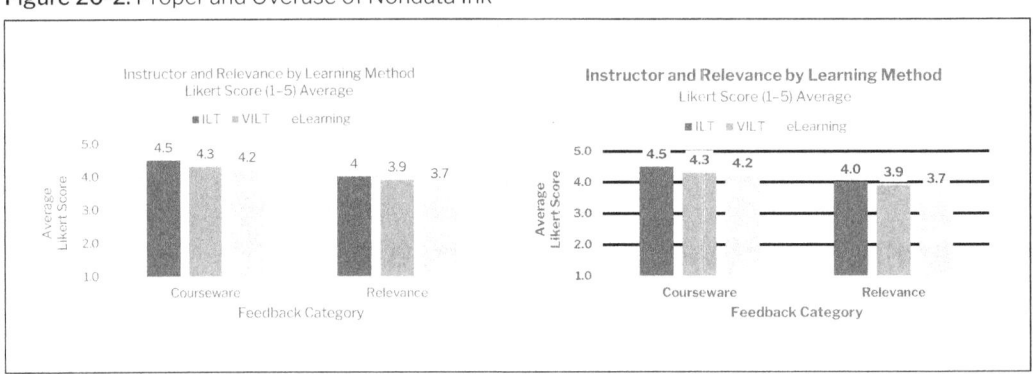

Figure 20-2. Proper and Overuse of Nondata Ink

Use of Color

Use color judiciously in data visualizations because it directly influences how the viewer interprets and understands the data. Color can highlight key insights, differentiate between data categories, and add visual appeal to the visualization. However, excessive or inappropriate use of color can lead to confusion, distraction, and misinterpretation of the data. Here are a few tips:

- **Use muted colors** for most data and reserve bright colors for highlighting important insights.
- **Gray is an effective background color** that allows other colors to stand out more vividly, which makes it an ideal backdrop for highlighting trends, patterns, and outliers in the data.

VISUALIZING DATA

- **Always consider color blindness** when designing or using a color palette. Refer to websites that provide guidance on how to transform an existing color palette into the colors and hues a color-blind individual would see to determine whether you need to adjust your color choices (Nichols n.d.).

Legends

A legend for a chart or graph maps the data series or categories (for example, the type of learning, regions, or business units) to distinct visual representations, such as colors, symbols, or line styles to guide data interpretation. The legend accompanies the chart or graph and is either positioned within the graphic or adjacent to it. Treat the legend as nondata ink and apply the previous suggestions.

Amount of Information

When analyzing large volumes of information, it's tempting to squeeze a lot of data into a single chart or graph. For example, Figure 20-3 compares learning activity data (registrations, no-shows, and dropouts) across two learning types (vILT and ILT) and four business units. However, with so much data in a single chart—24 data points—it's difficult to uncover the underlying story.

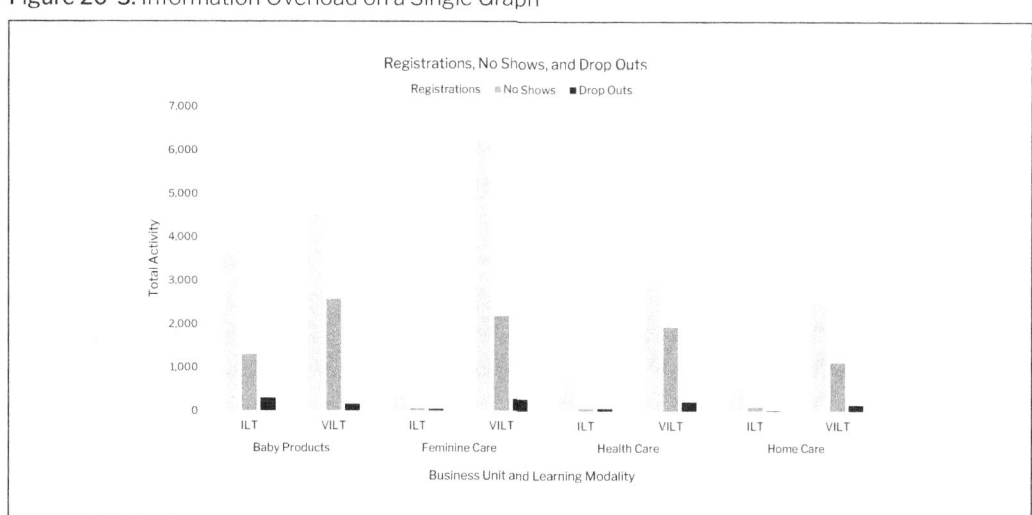

Figure 20-3. Information Overload on a Single Graph

285

CHAPTER 20

The alternative is to convert the data into percentages; for example, the percent of no-shows relative to the number of registrants and the percent of dropouts relative to the number of attendees. This simple change reduces the number of data points to 16 and makes it more consumable (Figure 20-4). Rearranging the data by learning method versus business unit enables a simpler comparison and highlights the number of no-shows and dropouts for ILT as well as vILT in the baby products business unit.

If revising the data is not possible, consider using the small multiples technique, which displays multiple charts or graphs, typically of the same type, in a grid or series. This approach enables easy comparison of related datasets or variables and often reveals patterns and trends more effectively than a single chart could on its own. Figure 20-5 presents a dataset for registrations by business unit and learning method across three regions using the small multiples technique.

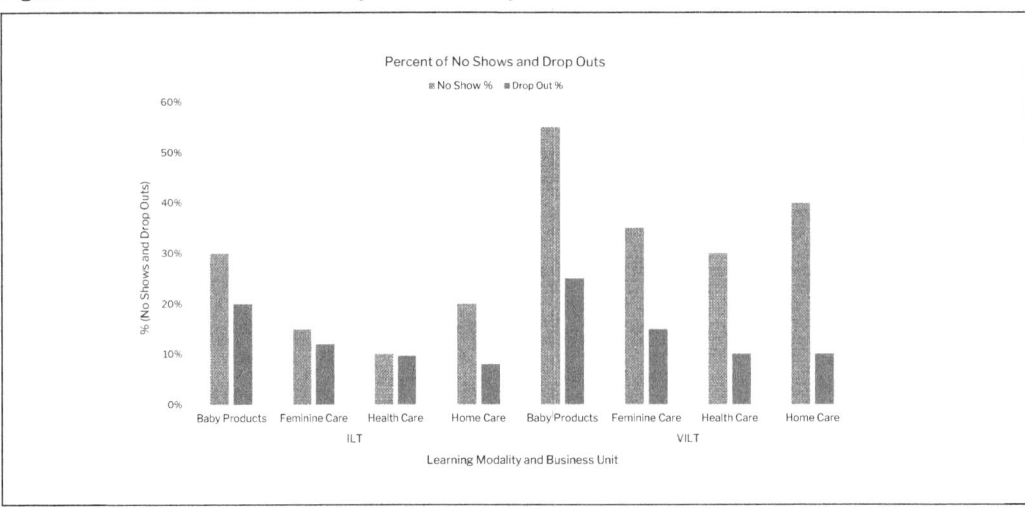

Figure 20-4. Revised Chart to Clarify the Data Story

Practitioner's Tip

Integrating design principles harmoniously can significantly enhance the effectiveness and communicative power of data visualizations.

VISUALIZING DATA

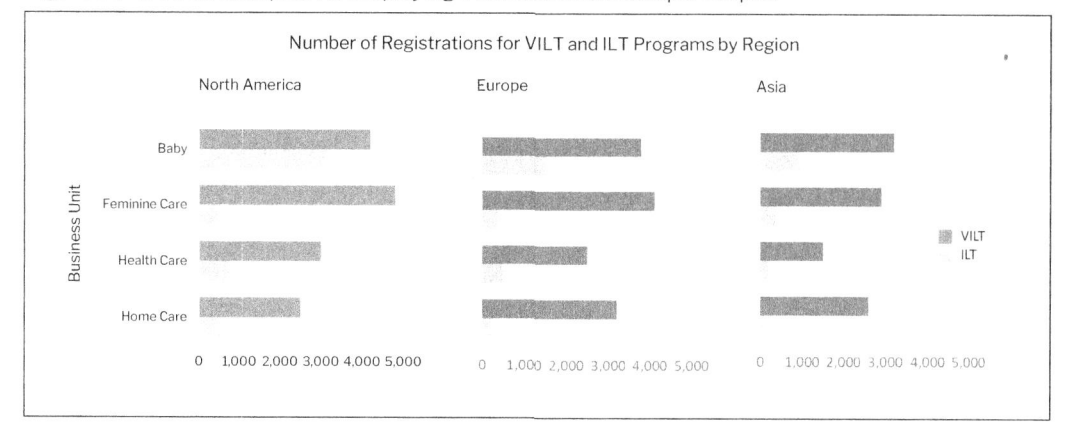

Figure 20-5. Small Multiples for Displaying Information on Multiple Graphs

What to Show in Your Visuals

While a data analyst or designer has dozens of graph and chart options, there are only four distinct categories to consider when selecting the most appropriate visual: comparison, relationship, distribution, and composition. This significantly simplifies your choices.

Comparison

Comparison visualizations contrast different data points or categories to identify similarities, differences, trends, or patterns. In Figure 20-6, for example, the bar chart on the left compares the percent favorable scores for six question categories on a post-event survey, while the line chart on the right compares scrap rates (unapplied learning) over time. The displays may be different, but both are comparison charts.

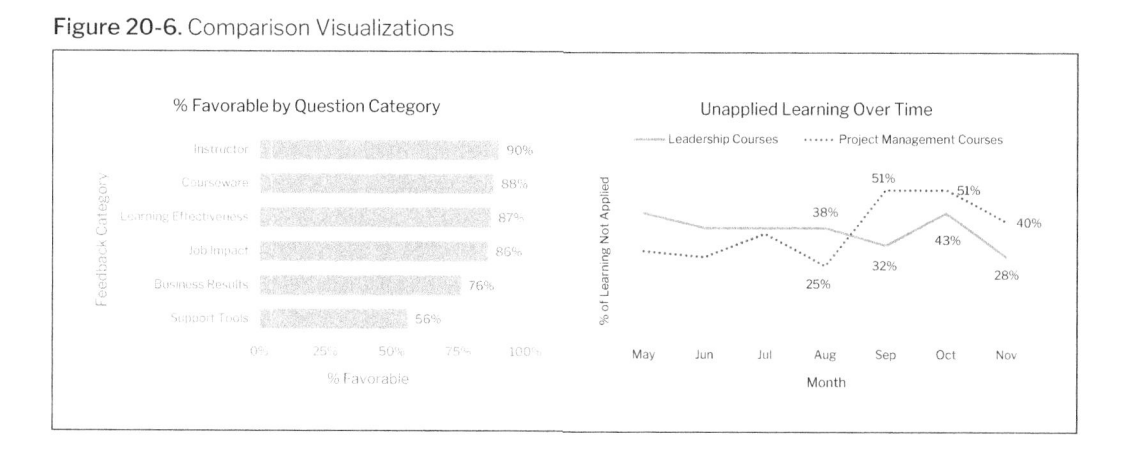

Figure 20-6. Comparison Visualizations

CHAPTER 20

Relationships

Relationship visualizations illustrate the correlation or association between two or more variables to understand how changes in one variable affect another. The scatter plot on the left in Figure 20-7 depicts the relationship between the number of attempts at completing a simulation to the score received (where the curved line depicts the best fit to the data). The chart on the right uses a heat map to visually represent data with color variations to indicate the magnitude of values within a dataset (where the lowest scores have the darkest shading and lighter shading represents higher scores).

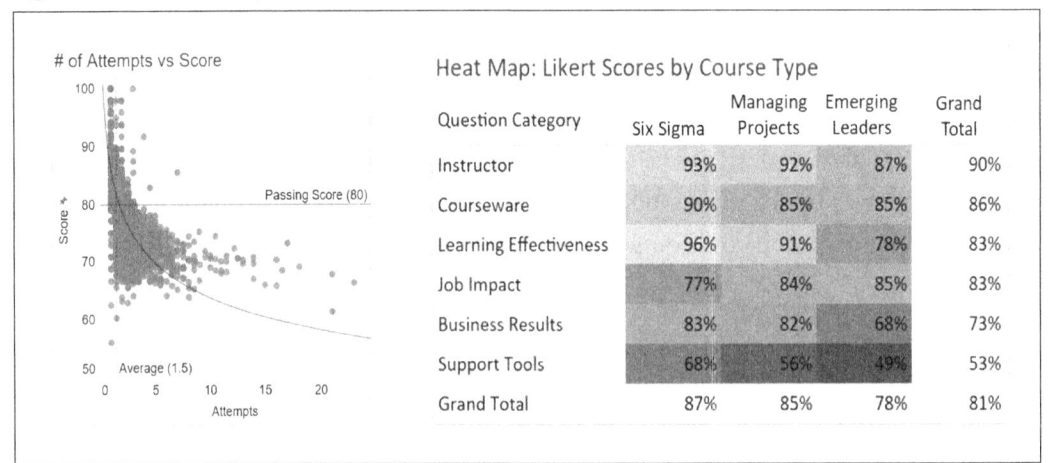

Figure 20-7. Relationship Visualizations

Question Category	Six Sigma	Managing Projects	Emerging Leaders	Grand Total
Instructor	93%	92%	87%	90%
Courseware	90%	85%	85%	86%
Learning Effectiveness	96%	91%	78%	83%
Job Impact	77%	84%	85%	83%
Business Results	83%	82%	68%	73%
Support Tools	68%	56%	49%	53%
Grand Total	87%	85%	78%	81%

Distribution

Distribution visualizations depict the spread or dispersion of data within a dataset to reveal the frequency, range, and distribution patterns. Histograms and box plots are two types of distribution charts. The bar chart on the left in Figure 20-8 shows the distribution of Likert scores; the chart on the right, called a box and whisker plot, shows the distribution of the percent favorable overall. Box plots are useful for spotting data anomalies during the data cleaning phase of analysis because they display any outliers in the data (represented by the dots above and below the box).

VISUALIZING DATA

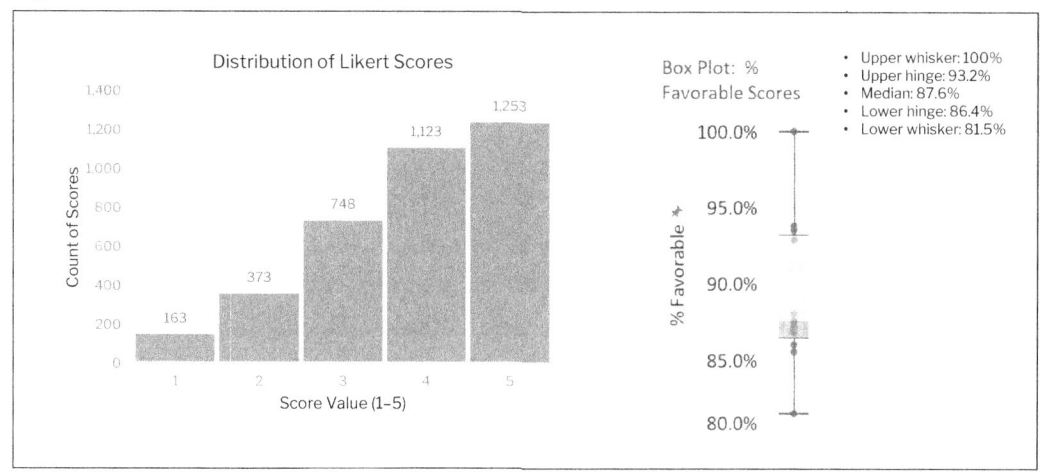

Figure 20-8. Distribution Visualizations

Composition

Composition visualizations present the parts of a whole to show the relative contribution or proportion of different components within a dataset. The most common composition chart is a pie chart, although a bar chart is another, and often better, option (Figure 20-9).

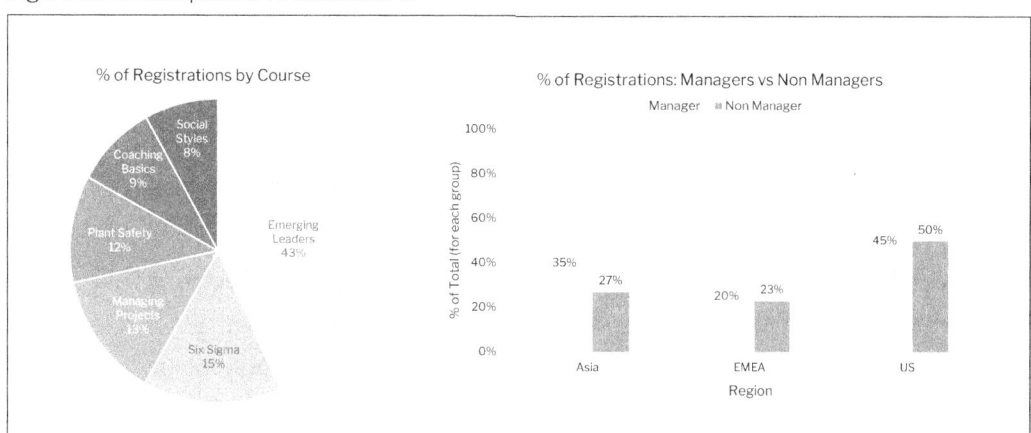

Figure 20-9. Composition Visualizations

289

CHAPTER 20

Selecting the Right Graph

The clearer you are about your objectives, the more effective the visualization. So, before creating a visualization, pause and ask yourself these questions:

1. **What is the main objective of the visualization?** A comparison, relationship, distribution, or composition?
2. **Who is the audience, and how will they interpret the visualization?** Tailor it to the audience's preferences and familiarity with chart types; for example, if the audience is not statistically savvy, opt for simpler, more intuitive visualizations.
3. **What type of data will the visualization display?** Distinguish between categorical (such as demographic data) and numerical data (such as Likert data) or qualitative data because the visualization will vary for each type.
4. **How many variables will the visual contain?** The optimal visualization depends on whether it will include one variable (such as learning investment per employee over time), two variables (such as the net promoter score of courses compared to application rates), or three variables (such as comparing course performance, course attendance, and course types).
5. **What level of granularity or detail does your audience need?** Consider whether to aggregate the data or show more detailed, granular data.

When to Use (and Not Use) a Pie Chart

Data visualization experts are not fans of pie charts. In fact, Cole Nussbaumer Knaflic, author of *Storytelling With Data* (2016), calls them "evil." Stephen Few, author of *Show Me the Numbers* (2012), says, "Allow me to make it clear without delay that I don't use pie charts, and I strongly recommend that you abandon them as well."

Despite their bad reputation, however, pie charts can be useful. However, it's important to determine when to use them and when it's best to opt for other, more effective visualizations. For example, pie charts are appropriate for:

- **Showing proportions.** Pie charts effectively communicate percentages or proportions of categories within a dataset.
- **Comparing a few categories.** Pie charts are most effective when displaying a small number of categories (fewer than seven).

On the other hand, pie charts are not appropriate for:

- **Highlighting precise values.** Pie charts are not effective at enabling comparisons of exact values of categories, especially when the slices are similar in size.
- **Comparing many categories.** A pie chart becomes cluttered and difficult to interpret with more than seven categories.
- **Showing trends over time.** Pie charts are not good at showing changes or trends over time.

When to Use a Table Instead of a Graph

While graphs and tables are both effective ways to display data, some types of data are more effectively displayed in one than the other. For example, a graph (line graph or bar chart) is best to:

- **Illustrate trends, patterns, or relationships.** Graphs are effective for showing changes over time or comparisons between distinct categories.
- **Highlight key insights or comparisons.** Graphs make complex information easier to understand at a glance.
- **Engage your audience.** Graphs are more visually appealing than tables, which makes them suitable for presentations or reports where you want to capture the audience's attention.
- **Compare multiple variables simultaneously.** Graphs allow viewers to identify trends or relationships across variables.

Tables, on the other hand, are best for:

- **Presenting detailed data.** Tables are especially effective when precise values are necessary for analysis or comparison.
- **Showing exact numerical values rather than visual trends or patterns.** Tables allow viewers to see precise numbers without any distortion.
- **Displaying data of varying types and units of measure.** Use tables to present such as raw numbers, percents, year-over-year changes, and monetary data.

Visualizing Likert Data

Learning evaluation data often comes in the form of a Likert scale with answer options ranging from strongly disagree to strongly agree. While these scales are categorical, data analysts can turn them into quantitative data by assigning a value to each point (such as 1

= strongly disagree to 5 = strongly agree). These assignments make it possible to visualize the data as quantitative rather than categorical or qualitative.

It may be tempting to treat Likert data like other quantitative data (such as registrations, attendance, test scores, or estimated performance improvement); however, it's important to recognize that Likert data is different and therefore requires other visualization choices.

Here are the five common issues with Likert data that an analyst or learning practitioner should consider when graphing it:

- **Ordinal scale.** Response options have a clear order or ranking, but the intervals aren't necessarily consistent. For example, the classic Likert scale is an ordinal scale, in which the values progress from 1 to 5. However, we cannot assume that the difference between 1 and 2 is the same as the difference between 4 and 5.
- **Subjective data.** The data captures subjective opinions, attitudes, or perceptions versus objective, concrete measurements. While Likert scale response choices are coded with numbers, the coding simply allows the analyst (whether a person or computer) to count the number of responses for each response choice.
- **Interpretation.** Consider context, item wording, and potential biases. Don't overgeneralize or misinterpret the findings.
- **Limited range.** By design, Likert scales offer a limited range of response options, which can constrain the depth of responses compared to other quantitative data.
- **Non-normal distribution.** Responses tend to skew toward extremes due to response bias or social desirability bias.

Bar charts (horizontal or vertical) are the most common choices for displaying Likert data. Consider stacked bar charts when comparing score distributions across multiple categories. For example, the two charts shown in Figure 20-10 present different stories about job impact due to three different courses. The chart on the left shows a 72 percent favorable score (percent agree and strongly agree) for each course, which suggests similar performance. However, the chart on the right shows that while the percent favorable was the same, the Six Sigma course also scored 30 percent neutral and had no unfavorable scores, while managing projects had no neutral scores (and a 30 percent unfavorable score). Consider how to display your data to provide the most information while minimizing graph clutter.

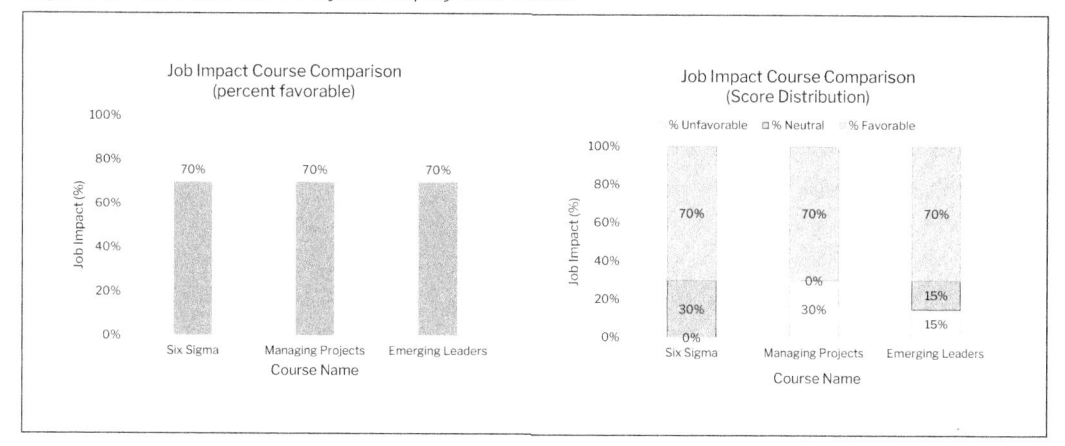

Figures 20-10. Alternative Ways to Display Likert Data

Practitioner's Tip

Likert data does not generally have a normal distribution. In most cases, respondents provide socially desirable responses, resulting in a high percentage of scores at the high end of the scale. In other cases, respondents may avoid selecting extreme response options (such as strongly agree or strongly disagree) so they appear more neutral (particularly when assessing their instructors). Histograms and box plots, mentioned earlier in the chapter, are useful visualizations for uncovering biases in the data and can guide interpretation of results.

Visualizing Non-Likert (Categorical Data)

Learning data also includes categorical data that is critical to uncovering the story. Demographic data (such as tenure, region, business unit, and role) can reveal response variations across segments of the learner population. For example, if a course designed for a global audience is found to have heavy attendance in Europe but not in Asia, the program owner can then uncover what factors might be driving differences in uptake, such as marketing, culture, or course relevance.

In addition to demographic data, learning feedback surveys often include questions that ask learners to select response options such as business results a course might affect or anticipated challenges restricting application on the job.

CHAPTER 20

Two common visualization options for this type of data are bar charts and heat maps (Figure 20-11):

- **Bar charts** are ideal for categorical data. Single or stacked bar charts can show the distribution of scores or comparisons.
- **Heat maps** display variations in results by translating the values into a color gradient.

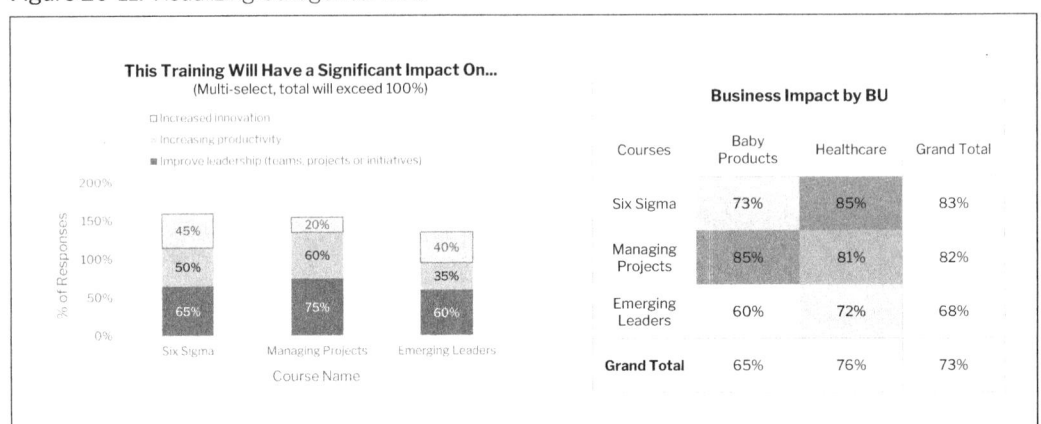

Figure 20-11. Visualizing Categorical Data

Visualizing Qualitative Data

Qualitative data can come from evaluation surveys, focus groups, and interviews when conducting ROI or business impact studies. This type of data is extremely valuable and adds context to the quantitative data. However, qualitative data can also be challenging to visualize due to three factors (Chavan 2023):

- Non-numerical data can be difficult to convert into numerical values for visualization.
- Due to its varied nature, there are no standards for visualizing qualitative data.
- Analysts will aggregate, theme, or summarize qualitative data as part of their visualizations. However, aggregation risks losing the very context that designers want to reveal.

Despite those challenges, several practices can transform qualitative data into insights through data visualization.

Hierarchical Representations

Tree maps and sunburst charts are hierarchical data visualization techniques.

- **A tree map** represents the data as a set of nested rectangles, with each rectangle corresponding to a specific category or subgroup within the dataset. The map displays the relative proportions or contributions of each category, theme, or subtheme to the overall dataset. By using proportionally sized rectangles, the visual depicts quantitative comparisons among the categories or themes. However, interpreting the relationships between themes and subthemes may require careful examination, especially with larger datasets.
- **Sunburst charts** display hierarchical relationships in a radial layout, showing parent-child relationships and nested structures. Much like tree maps, sunburst diagrams are useful for visualizing hierarchical structures with multiple levels of categorization. However, sunburst charts don't provide precise quantitative comparisons across categories or levels. In addition, they consume a lot more space than tree maps to visualize the same data.

Figure 20-12 depicts the same course feedback data in both a tree map diagram (left) and a sunburst diagram (right).

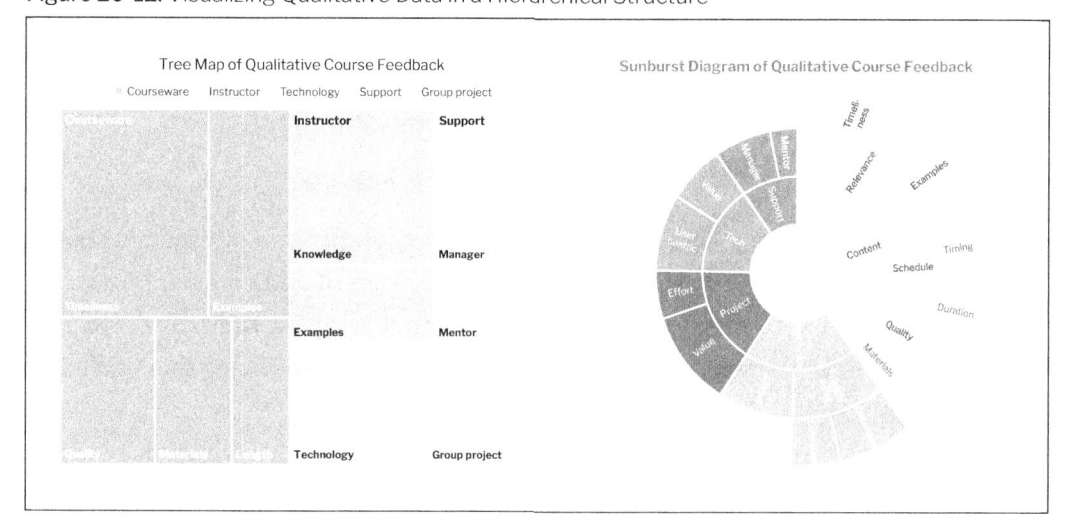

Figure 20-12. Visualizing Qualitative Data in a Hierarchical Structure

Other Forms of Visuals

There are no standards for visualizing qualitative data, so it's worth experimenting with different methods, including depicting themes and using word clouds:

Graphical Depiction of Themes

This simple method for quantifying themes from comments involves choosing a simple graphic and noting the themes and their relative prevalence (for example, 50 percent of the comments pertained to the instructor, while 20 percent pertained to courseware). Then, add relevant quotes to provide context to the graphic.

Word Clouds

Designers once regularly used word clouds to visualize qualitative data. However, use them with caution because they suffer from a number of issues:

- They prioritize words based solely on their frequency of use, which results in highlighting common, trivial, or redundant while overlooking less frequent but more meaningful ones.
- They prioritize individual words rather than capturing the text's broader themes, narratives, or structures.
- They lose context and sentiment. A word cloud from a question about what learners liked about a course may be identical to a word cloud from a question about what learners didn't like, rendering the visualizations meaningless.

Visualization Tips and Techniques

In 2023, the Learning Guild conducted a robust analysis of the state of data and analytics in learning and development. They found that 54 percent of L&D organizations used analytics in fewer than 10 percent of their projects (or not at all). In addition, 60 percent of organizations lacked data literacy skills on their L&D teams. Advancing these skills is a high priority for L&D.

While L&D requires formal training methods in analytics and data visualization, two simple informal learning methods can tap into your L&D team's innate capabilities: the notice and wonder method and data parties.

Incorporate the "Notice and Wonder" Method to Uncover the Story in a Graph or Chart

About 10 years ago, the *New York Times* launched an educational feature in its online learning network called "What's Going on in This Graph?" to help grade school students decipher graphs and uncover the data's story. Each week, a graph that appeared in the paper's content is posted in the network, along with three questions and a task. (The questions are based on Annie Fetter's Notice & Wonder method.)

1. What do you notice?
2. What do you wonder?
3. How does this relate to you and your community (or organization)?
4. Create a catchy headline that captures the graph's main idea.

This approach, although designed for grade schoolers, is equally effective for adults. It enables data visualization designers to assess whether the graph is clear and reveals the data story. The fourth step (create a catchy headline) ensures that the graph title calls out the main point. The step-wise approach simplifies the process of deciphering the graph and its meaning.

Employ Data Parties to Build Data Literacy

In addition to the Notice and Wonder approach, L&D organizations can build data and data visualization literacy through group activities that bring diverse stakeholders together to collectively review graphs or charts. This data party approach has multiple advantages:

- Diverse backgrounds, expertise, and perspectives can lead to richer discussions and uncover insights that may not have been apparent to a single person or a homogeneous group.
- Group discussions can trigger novel approaches to analyzing the data or uncovering patterns that lead to new insights or solutions.
- Participants learn from one another as they share their interpretations, questions, and analyses of the data.
- The social aspect of discussing the data with others enhances engagement and motivates participants to actively contribute to the discussion.

While data parties can have downsides (such as groupthink, dominant voices overshadowing other views, and conflicting interpretations), careful planning and facilitation can elevate not only data interpretation capabilities but also best practices in data visualization.

For L&D professionals, using a standard method (Notice and Wonder) and a collaborative review process (data party) can rapidly accelerate data visualization and graph literacy.

Summary

Data visualization is a powerful tool for converting complex datasets into easily understandable visuals, allowing stakeholders to clearly discern patterns, trends, and outliers. Learning practitioners should understand the human limitations associated with data perception to guide their visualization choices. They should also acquaint themselves with data visualization methods and techniques that can enlighten, obscure, or sometimes inadvertently mislead their audiences. Becoming proficient in designing high-quality visualizations enables learning analysts, designers, and practitioners to construct visuals that engage their audiences and prompt decisive action.

Knowledge Check

Elena Varga, chief learning officer of Your Electronic Store, has heard, anecdotally, that employees are not applying what they've learned in training courses on the job. Learners have reported that their managers are not reinforcing the knowledge and skills or even setting expectations that they will do something with the content. Based on this information, Elena initiated a program to clarify managers' roles in the learning process. She engaged Andre Ricci, the learning evaluation manager, to deploy postevent evaluations to measure satisfaction as well as manager support levels and application of content to the job.

Table 20-2 presents Andre's learning evaluation data, which he wants to display for Elena. Use the table to answer the following questions, then check your answers in appendix B.

1. What category of visualization is appropriate for this data?
2. Create two different visualizations with the data provided.
3. What are the pros and cons of each visualization method?
4. What can you conclude after viewing the visualization?
5. What effect does sample size (number of evaluations) have on your conclusions and recommendations?

6. Based on your visualizations, what is your recommendation about the value of Elena's manager support initiative? Should she continue it or stop?

Table 20-2. Data for Knowledge Check

Support Level (High or Low)	Difficult Discussions	Emerging Leaders	Managing Projects	Six Sigma	Social Styles	Grand Total
High	30%	30%	31%	36%	32%	31%
Low	42%	42%	53%	39%	42%	42%
Number of evaluations	100	90	225	25	75	515

Unapplied Learning for Courses With High and Low Manager Support

CHAPTER 21

Implementing the ISO Standards for L&D Metrics

DAVID VANCE

IN THIS CHAPTER

This chapter employs ISO standard TS 30437:2023 Human Resource Management—Learning and Development Metrics to help practitioners create a measurement and reporting strategy for their L&D measures. After reading it, you will be able to:

- Use the ISO framework to classify five types of users, four broad reasons for measuring, three types of measures, and four types of reports.
- Select the best metrics for your programs and the department.
- Select the most appropriate reports to share the metrics.

The ISO Standard for L&D Metrics

ISO, the International Organization for Standardization, brings global experts together to agree on the best way of doing things—for anything from making a product to managing a process. ISO standards combine the best thinking of global experts on processes and frameworks, including a common language with standard names, definitions, and formulas. This not only provides much-needed standard guidance for practitioners but also facilitates better communication within the industry and significantly improves the value of benchmarking because the data can be calculated with standard formulas.

Since 1946, ISO has published more than 25,000 standards through the work of 830 technical committees made up of members from 170 countries. TC260 Human Resource Management is the technical committee charged with setting standards for human capital that developed ISO TS 30437:2023 more than two years, with publication in June 2023. (TS 30437:2023 Human Resource Management—Learning and Development Metrics can be purchased from ISO by searching for TS 30437 or learning and development metrics.)

TS 30437:2023 defines L&D standards for users, broad reasons to measure, types of metrics, and types of reports, all of which you can use to build your measurement and evaluation strategy.

Five Types of Users

The starting point for a department-wide measurement strategy is identifying users. In other words, who are the customers for the data? Because there are many potential users, both inside and outside L&D, a framework or classification scheme is helpful for providing a common language.

The ISO standard includes five types of users:

- **Senior organization leader.** These high-level leaders include the CEO, CFO, head of HR, and organizational goal owners (for example, the head of sales).
- **Group or team leader.** These leaders are one level down from the senior organization leaders and include business unit, region, or department heads.
- **Head of learning.** This is the CLO or VP of training in a medium-to-large organization. In smaller organizations, this is likely the person with part or full-time responsibility for learning programs.
- **Program manager.** This person is responsible for the needs analysis, performance consulting, design, development, and delivery of a learning program. (Note that a learning program may consist of a single course or multiple, related courses.)
- **Learner.** This would be the individual learner.

Because the ISO standard is for voluntary adoption, a practitioner may adopt all, some, or none of these recommendations. So, add or subtract categories to better meet your needs; just keep in mind that the recommendations for measurement selection are based on these five user types.

Four Broad Reasons to Measure

A framework is also useful for providing a common language for why you're measuring results and to help process the answers from the users.

The ISO standard recommends four broad reasons to measure:
- **Inform.** This is the most common reason to measure—someone has asked a question about quantity, and measurement is undertaken to answer it. The most common questions are about number of participants, courses, hours, completion rates, and costs.
- **Monitor.** In this case, the user has a threshold in mind based on historical data and wants to know if the metric is above or below it. For example, if the application rate for a program has historically been 55 percent, then that's where the threshold would be set. Or, they may want to know if the value of a metric is within a historically acceptable range.
- **Evaluate.** This helps the user determine how effective a program was.
- **Manage.** This the highest-level reason to measure and consequently the least used. Managing takes monitoring to a higher level by setting a target or plan beyond what has been accomplished historically. It requires considerable effort and ability to set a realistic, achievable target and then execute a plan with discipline throughout the year to achieve the target.

Understanding the reason to measure is also important because the recommended report depends on the reason to measure.

Practitioner's Tip

Meet at least annually with all the users of your data. This includes those within and outside the department. Ask if the data they are currently receiving is meeting their needs and how they're using it. Depending on their answers, you may be able to recommend better metrics or a better report format. If it is a new user, ask why they want the data (why they want to measure), what they will do with it, and how they would like it shared.

Three Types of Metrics

The ISO standard recommends three types of metrics as a framework to organize the more than 100 available metrics to L&D professionals. While metrics could be organized alphabetically, it is much more useful to organize by common type.

The three types of metrics are:
- **Efficiency metrics.** These metrics measure quantity. The most common are the number of participants, number of courses, number of hours, completion rates, percentage of courses delivered on time, reach, and cost.
- **Effectiveness metrics.** These metrics measure quality and are adopted directly from the Katzel, Kirkpatrick, and Phillips levels of evaluation. In this framework, effectiveness metrics include Level 1 participant reaction, Level 1 objective owner satisfaction, Level 2 learning, Level 3 application (intent to apply and actual application), and Level 5 ROI, BCR, and net benefit. This metric does not address Level 4.
- **Outcome metrics.** These metrics measure Level 4, the impact or results of the learning program. They are separated from the effectiveness metrics due to research by Jack and Patti Phillips (2010), which found that while CEOs most want to see Level 4, they seldom get it from their L&D departments. In other words, the L&D profession has a great opportunity to focus more on Level 4 and share it with senior organization leaders. Breaking this metric out into its own category also makes it simpler to recommend.

As always with ISO, this information represents the best thinking of global experts, but users are free to modify it. Some may wish to keep Level 4 in the effectiveness category.

Guidance for Selecting Metrics

The ISO standard recommends 52 metrics by type of user for large organizations and 19 metrics for small and medium organizations. (Both tables are withheld from this chapter due to copyright protection.) The metrics are organized by the three types (efficiency, effectiveness, and outcome) and further categorized by formal and informal learning.

While sizes are not defined in the standard, a large organization would typically have a good-sized L&D department with full-time measurement specialists. A medium organization would have several L&D staff but no one dedicated full time to measurement. A small organization may not have a L&D department and certainly no one dedicated to measurement. Recognizing that large organizations have a much greater capacity for measurement, more metrics are recommended.

These metrics provide a starting point for your consideration. If a senior leader, group leader, chief learning officer (CLO), or program manager is interested in seeing L&D metrics and asks for your recommendations, use the table in the standard to develop a draft list, adding or subtracting metrics as appropriate.

In preparation for an annual visit with current users, ask about any recommended metrics not currently in use. For new users, list the recommended metrics and ask if they would be interested.

Four Types of Reports

Once the metrics have been selected and their values measured, the next question is how best to share the data with the user. While a simple question may be answered by a simple answer (for example, a single number), users typically prefer to see multiple metrics or time periods, which requires a report.

The ISO standard recommends four types of reports (examples are provided in the standard's appendix):

- **Scorecard.** This is the oldest form of report and is often presented in an Excel spreadsheet. A scorecard contains actual results, with columns typically showing time periods and rows showing metrics.
- **Dashboard.** Dashboards have grown in popularity as advances in software have made their creation easier. A dashboard contains actual results, as well as visual elements such as pie charts, bar graphs, or line graphs. It typically contains aggregate data such as year-to-date totals and may allow for interactivity so the user can drill down for more detail.
- **Program evaluation report.** A program evaluation report or briefing is designed to share the results of a learning program upon its completion. Many organizations have their own version of this, but common elements include the need or issue to be addressed through the learning program, the plan for the learning program, the results, and any lessons learned. This is often presented as a PowerPoint deck but may also be a Word document.
- **Management report.** The final type of report is a management report. The program has been planned in great detail and a report is needed to manage its execution monthly to ensure planned results are delivered. The management report for a learning program has the same design as a management report for sales and manufacturing. It contains columns for the plan, year-to-date (YTD) results, YTD results compared to the plan, the forecast, and the forecast compared to the plan.

Guidance for Selecting the Right Report

The ISO standard recommends that you choose a report based on the reasons to measure:

- **Use a scorecard or dashboard to inform.** A scorecard is best if the user wants to see detailed monthly or quarterly data, while users who want to see less detail and a more visual display will prefer a dashboard.
- **Use a scorecard or dashboard with a threshold and legend to monitor.** Both reports show changes in data over time.
- **Use a program evaluation report to evaluate.** This type of report is specifically designed for a briefing that focuses on results and how they compared to the plan.
- **Use a management report to manage.** This type of report is used to manage programs to a successful conclusion.

Note, however, that management reports and managing are only necessary if the program manager or the head of learning seeks to achieve specific, measurable targets, often surpassing what has been achieved historically. If the target value has been achieved before, a dashboard for monitoring may suffice. And, if there is no desired target or plan for improvement, you can use a simple scorecard or dashboard.

Application of the Standard in Practice

Application of the standard begins with general adoption; from there, it includes selecting metrics for specific programs, selecting metrics at the departmental level, and selecting the most appropriate reports for the purpose and audience. This section addresses each area of application in more detail.

Adopting the ISO TS 30437 Framework

There are four steps for adopting the ISO TS 30437 framework:
1. Use the ISO framework and language.
2. Use the ISO metric names and definitions.
3. Use the ISO guidance for selecting metrics.
4. Use the ISO guidance for selecting reports.

Step 1. Use the ISO Framework and Language

The first step is to adopt the framework and language contained in the standard. Within your own L&D department, start using the framework and language for the three types of metrics (efficiency, effectiveness, and outcome) and four types of reports (scorecard, dashboard, program evaluation, and management). Then, start using the framework and language for the four broad reasons to measure (inform, monitor, evaluate, and manage). Within your group, discuss and agree on the types of users that make sense for your organization, which may differ from those in the standard (senior leader, group leader, head of learning, program manager, and learner), so feel free to rename, add, or subtract them.

You don't need to purchase the ISO standard for this first step, but you do need the head of learning to endorse it and serve as the champion. The head of learning needs to let all L&D employees know that the ISO standard language and frameworks will be employed going forward. Then, they need to personally demonstrate the importance by using the language and framework themselves.

Step 2. Use the ISO Metric Names and Definitions

To progress to this step, you'll need to purchase ISO TS 30437 to access the recommended metric names and definitions. The standard contains the 52 most common metrics, which should more than address the needs of small and medium organizations and provide an excellent starting point for large organizations. The CLO should insist that all L&D staff use these recommended names and definitions and refrain from making up names or definitions on the fly. By purchasing this standard, you'll be able to save hours of metric research because the ISO has already done that work.

Practitioner's Tip

Build a measures library to catalog any important information about the metrics your organization's L&D team uses. This provides the safe source for metrics storage and should survive staff turnover. Imagine a large Excel spreadsheet in which the rows are metrics (organized by efficiency, effectiveness, and outcome) and the columns are the key characteristics of the metrics (such as definition, data source, date in the month when available, owner, and key users).

Step 3. Use the ISO Guidance for Selecting Metrics

Create an inventory of your existing metrics, noting the metric, type of metric, and user. Then, talk with users inside and outside L&D to discover their reasons for measuring. Compare your metrics against those recommended by the standard for small and medium organizations by type of user. Are there gaps or opportunities to add metrics? You may decide that you don't need some of the recommended metrics, which is fine because the standard is meant to be a starting place, not an ending place. If you follow this process, you will have at least considered those in the standard.

Next, especially if you are in a large organization or a very mature small or medium organization, repeat the process for the 52 metrics recommended for large organizations. Identify any gaps or opportunities to add metrics and discuss them within your department. Adding metrics may be a multiyear process that requires prioritization, depending on your goals.

Step 4. Use the ISO Guidance for Selecting Reports

Create an inventory of your existing reports and compare them with the four report types recommended in the standard. Most organizations have scorecards and dashboards for informing. If you also use scorecards and dashboards for monitoring, do you include the required threshold or acceptable range? Do you have a program evaluation report or its equivalent—some standard template for briefing results at the end of a program? These are all basic reports, and every organization should have them.

Talk with your users to determine whether the current reports are meeting their needs and aligned to their reason for measuring. Identify opportunities for additional or reformatted reports.

Practitioner's Tip

Maintain a reports inventory, similar to the measures library, that includes the name of the report, the users, the purpose (inform, monitor, evaluate, or manage), the person responsible for preparing the report, the data source, the frequency, and the publication date (for example, the 10th of each month).

Selecting Metrics for Programs

The ISO standard is designed to help you select metrics both at the program and department levels. The natural starting point is the program level. (Refer to the program manager column of Table 1 in ISO TS 30437 for this information.)

Recommended Metrics for Strategic Learning Programs

Strategic learning programs are designed to help achieve a high-level organizational goal. By definition, the goals of the CEO and head of HR fall in this category, which can also include programs in support of other senior and group leaders. Examples of high-level organizational goals include increasing sales by 10 percent, increasing productivity by 5 percent, and increasing retention by 5 points. Strategic learning programs are designed following a needs analysis or performance consulting engagement.

Use the following metrics as a starting point for strategic learning programs:
- **Efficiency metrics:**
  - Number of participants
  - Completion date
  - Completion rate
  - Cost
- **Effectiveness metrics:**
  - Level 1 Participant Reaction
  - Level 1 Objective Owner Satisfaction
  - Level 2 Learning
  - Level 3 Application
  - Level 5 ROI
- **Outcome metrics:**
  - Level 4 Results or Impact of Learning
  - Improvement in workforce competency rate

Recommended Metrics for Nonstrategic Learning Programs

Although the majority of learning programs are nonstrategic, they're very important. Examples include onboarding, compliance, basic skills, reskilling, and upskilling, when they're not components of strategic learning. Unlike strategic learning, these programs

CHAPTER 21

typically do not have outcome metrics because they're lacking any specific, measurable, high-level organizational goals. Instead, the focus is on meeting the organizational need as efficiently and effectively as possible.

The metrics recommended as a starting point for nonstrategic learning programs are the same as those for strategic learning programs, with the exception of organizational outcome measures and ROI.

> **Practitioner's Tip**
>
> Strategic and nonstrategic learning programs should both contain a balance of efficiency and effectiveness metrics. The target should include at least three or four efficiency metrics and at least three effectiveness metrics. If only efficiency metrics are selected, it signals to staff that quality is not important. Conversely, selecting only effectiveness metrics signals that efficiency is not important (for example, delivering on time). For strategic learning, you'll also need an outcome metric to establish the impact on the organizational goal.

Selecting Measures for the Department

There are two kinds of metrics for consideration at the department level: the individual program metrics aggregated across all the programs and nonprogram efficiency metrics. (Refer to the head of learning column of Table 1 in ISO TS 30437 for this information.)

Recommended Aggregate Program Metrics

You can aggregate all recommended program metrics for analysis and presentation at an enterprise and department-wide level.

These metrics are recommended for reporting at the department level:
- **Efficiency metrics:**
  - Number of total participants can be summed.
  - Number of total unique participants cannot be summed due to overlap, but can be generated by any LMS.
  - The accounting cost of each program and the opportunity cost of the participant's time can both be summed.
  - Completion rate can be averaged across all courses.
  - Completion dates need to be converted to percentage on-time completion. Score each course as completed on time or not. Sum those completed

on-time and divide by the total number of courses to calculate the on-time completion percentage.
- **Effectiveness metrics:**
  - Levels 1, 2, and 3 can be averaged across all courses. A weighted average should be used based on the number of total participants.
  - Level 5 net benefits can be summed across all courses, but individual course ROIs should simply be listed—not averaged. If the ROI percentages are averaged, use a weighted average based on the total cost.
- **Outcome metrics:**
  - Improvement in competency or skill levels can be averaged across all courses. Use a weighted average by number of total participants.
  - The isolated percentage contribution from learning and the resulting impact on the organizational goal should be listed by program or course—not averaged.

Recommended Nonprogram Metrics

This category includes efficiency metrics such as the number of courses and hours, reach (percentage of employees who have taken at least one course), and the percentage of employees with a development plan. They don't make sense at a course level and are only calculated across the department.

Here are the recommended efficiency metrics:
- Percentage of employees reached by learning
- Percentage of employees with development plans
- Total department cost
- Average formal training hours
- Percentage of employees who participated in formal learning
- Percentage of courses developed on time
- Percentage of courses delivered on time
- Courses available
- Courses used
- Total hours used

Nonprogram metrics also are recommended for informal learning if offered by your L&D department. Typically, you'll include several usage metrics for each type of informal learning program and at least one effectiveness metric. While the effectiveness metric will likely be survey-based, it's often used quarterly or biannually, rather than each time someone uses informal learning. If the respondent has used informal learning, ask how much and whether they were satisfied with the process or tool.

Selecting Reports

The standard makes it easy to select the appropriate report for each user once you've determined why they want to measure. Let's quickly review:
- If the user wants detailed, monthly historical data on efficiency or effectiveness metrics, provide a scorecard to inform.
- If the user wants summary data on efficiency or effectiveness metrics and a more visual display, provide a dashboard to inform.
- If the user wants to know if the value of a metric is within an acceptable range or above or below a certain threshold, provide a scorecard or dashboard with a legend identifying the thresholds and possibly color coding to monitor.
- If the user wants to share the results of a program evaluation, provide a program evaluation report to share results.
- If the user wants to manage a metric or a collection of metrics to a certain level, especially levels higher than historically achieved, provide a management report showing the plan, year-to-date results, and forecast to manage.

Practitioner's Tip

Share samples of reports when users first ask for data and during your annual review with them. Most users don't know what is available and or which report is best for them. Provide several examples of reports that match their reason for measuring and let them choose their preferred format.

Summary

The ISO TS 30437:2023 Human Resource Management—Learning and Development Metrics is the first comprehensive standard for L&D metrics published by ISO and provides names and definitions for 52 of the most commonly used L&D metrics. Moreover, the standard provides guidance for selecting metrics by type of user and for selecting the most appropriate report by reason to measure. The standard provides a framework and common language for L&D measurement, including three types of metrics, five types of users, four broad reasons to measure, and four types of reports. This chapter offered guidance on how to apply the standard through organization-wide adoption and metric and report selection.

Knowledge Check

Answer the following questions and check your work in appendix B.

1. What are the three types of metrics?
2. What are the four types of reports?
3. What are the five types of users?
4. What are the four broad reasons to measure?

CHAPTER 22

Using Black Box Thinking To Optimize Training Outcomes
RACHELL BAGHELAI

IN THIS CHAPTER

This chapter explores how learning professionals can use black box thinking in evaluation to create a culture of continuous improvement and results optimization. After reading it, you will be able to:

♦ Describe black box thinking and how it relates to continuous improvement.

♦ Identify different techniques to incorporate black box thinking into your evaluation methods.

♦ Use evaluation findings to make data-driven decisions to maximize training effectiveness.

The Value in Black Box Thinking

Imagine a pilot who can flawlessly navigate emergencies during rigorous flight simulator training. However, when faced with a real-life crisis, their performance falters and the airplane crashes. This scenario underscores a critical (although extreme) limitation in traditional training evaluation methods: They often focus solely on measuring the acquisition of new knowledge or skills within a controlled environment.

Attending training can be invigorating, and learners often leave feeling motivated to apply what they have learned. However, that can be much harder than anticipated once they're back to their day-to-day job. Learners may encounter competing priorities that interfere with application, unexpected situations that they were not trained on, or the need to collaborate with others who didn't attend the training. These unforeseen factors can make it challenging to successfully apply what they learned, leading to frustration or a sense that the training was not valuable.

As organizations struggle to manage costs and maintain profitability, it is more important than ever to maximize the impact of training. A robust evaluation process can help organizations create and run better programs and reduce the amount of *scrap learning*—content that is never applied back on the job (Mattox 2011). In fact, research has found that most organizations have a scrap learning rate of 60 percent, which means that more than half of the content TD professionals design and deliver is never actually applied (Phillips 2020). This can happen for several reasons, such as when content is not relevant to the learner's current job duties or conducive to the organization's current processes. However, it is impossible to know what causes scrap learning without consistently evaluating training practices.

So, how do we maximize training application and bridge the gap between a controlled learning environment and the messy reality of applying new knowledge and skills on the job? Enter black box thinking, a concept inspired by the aviation industry and popularized by Matthew Syed (2016) in his book *Black Box Thinking: Marginal Gains and the Secrets of High Performance*. Flight data recorders (black boxes) provide invaluable insights into airplane accidents, even when the cause isn't immediately apparent. These insights are used solely for the purpose of continuous improvement. In the context of training and development, you can use black box thinking and a data-based approach to learn from mistakes, encourage innovation, and improve intended outcomes.

Black Box Thinking for Results Optimization

When investigating a plane crash, investigators meticulously analyze the black box data, not just to pinpoint the cause of the accident but also to understand what actions were successfully applied and how best to prevent similar tragedies in the future. Black box thinking borrows this concept and applies it to various fields, including business and training. It is a mindset that goes beyond simply identifying successes and failures to dive deeper and focus on understanding the why behind them.

This approach offers two key benefits:

- **It encourages organizations to learn from successes and failures.** When analyzing evaluation data, the focus is often on identifying and addressing areas that need improvement. Black box thinking, however, recognizes that even successful training programs can hold valuable lessons. By analyzing what factors enabled success, organizations can replicate those elements to ensure consistent effectiveness.
- **It fosters a culture of continuous improvement.** Black box thinking moves away from a one-size-fits-all approach and encourages ongoing evaluation and adaptation. By understanding the root causes of successes as well as failures, organizations can refine training programs to better meet learner needs, achieve desired outcomes, and reduce scrap learning. This iterative process leads to a continuous cycle of learning and improvement, ensuring training programs remain relevant and effective over time.

Practitioner's Tip

Black box thinking is a differentiator. By embedding this type of thinking into functional processes, you can create significant value through high-quality, relevant, and effective solutions that consistently get even better.

—Christopher LeBrun, Analytics Practitioner and Consultant

Maximizing Training Effectiveness

To compete in today's rapidly changing world of work, employees need to continually upskill and reskill. Training opportunities range from new-hire onboarding to technical skills development to licensure preparation, all of which are aimed at improving employee skill sets so they can be more effective in their duties. Therefore, it's crucial to evaluate training programs to understand not only whether employees acquired and applied these new skill sets, but also how to enhance the program for maximal outcomes.

At its most basic level, *evaluation* refers to the systematic process of assessing a training program or initiative's efficiency, effectiveness, and impact. Traditional evaluation methods often provide a basic understanding of training outcomes, but a deeper dive may be necessary. For example, assessing the efficacy of a pilot program or the impact and value of the organization's most strategic, visible, and costly programs may require a more detailed data analysis. This is where black box thinking comes in. By using black box thinking principles when designing and implementing the evaluation process, you can gather and analyze the necessary data to truly paint a comprehensive picture of the program and better optimize future outcomes.

Creating a Culture of Continuous Improvement

To gather the data necessary to produce insights, you'll also need to create an environment that values data, feedback, learning, and the pursuit of excellence. By fostering a culture in which feedback is constructive, timely, and actionable, organizations can empower individuals to learn from their (and others') experiences, make informed decisions, and contribute to overall organizational success. However, creating a culture of continuous improvement is a journey. It requires a shift in mindset from viewing mistakes as failures to seeing them as valuable learning opportunities. This change in mindset requires the organization to build psychological safety through consistent actions and feedback loops.

Organizations that prioritize continuous improvement actively seek feedback from stakeholders to gain valuable insights and a greater understanding of the areas that need attention, as well as the enablers for maximum success. This involves establishing open channels of communication that not only encourage feedback but also value it as a means of continuous improvement. Further, trust must be established with key stakeholders at all levels to create a safe space in which learners, their managers, and other key stakeholders are comfortable sharing their honest experiences—whether good or bad. When soliciting feedback, these organizations make it clear that the goal is not to pinpoint shortcomings or assign blame, but to learn from the experience as a whole and create more innovative, adaptable, and effective training programs.

Organizations also need to close the feedback loop with key stakeholders. This not only builds trust within the organization, but also demonstrates transparency and shows employees that their voices are heard and valued. When employees see their feedback translated into action, it can motivate them to continue providing valuable feedback in the future. When they think their voices matter, they're more likely to be active participants and contribute to positive change.

Implementing Black Box Thinking in Evaluation

By making a few changes to your current evaluation process, you can easily incorporate black box thinking principles that will result in key insights to enhance training outcomes and reduce scrap learning. The rest of this chapter will offer best practices for implementing black box thinking at different stages in the evaluation process.

Strategic Alignment

Strategic alignment is a critical precursor for results optimization in training evaluation. It involves recognizing business requirements and problems, ensuring training programs address these needs, and building a compelling business case for their implementation. To incorporate black box thinking into your strategic alignment process, first align on measures of success with your key stakeholders, regularly communicate progress, and use the data collected to drive the actions you'll take.

Align on Measures of Success

Strategic alignment, continuous improvement, and black box thinking are interconnected concepts that play a complementary role in optimizing training effectiveness. By aligning with your executive sponsor and other key stakeholders, you'll set the direction, priorities, and success measures for your evaluation project. This not only ensures that the programs are aligned and meet the business needs, but that they're constantly refined and optimized to achieve the organization's strategic goals and objectives. Further, aligning on measures of success with your executive sponsor and other key stakeholders increases accountability and awareness of the work being done, which leads to better training outcomes.

Regularly Communicate

Aligning on measures of success sets the stage for regular communication touchpoints with your executive sponsor. Use these touchpoints to summarize the feedback collected to date so that stakeholders can gain valuable insights into participant experiences, both positive and negative. Regular communication enables key stakeholders to have a deeper understanding of existing barriers, why they occur, and how to prevent similar issues in the future. It also promotes accountability and responsibility, because individuals and teams take ownership of mistakes and work collaboratively to find solutions for improvement.

Use Data to Drive Action

Data is crucial for understanding the root causes of training successes and opportunities. When planning your evaluation design, build a theory of change using a logic model, which provides a structured framework for planning, implementing, and evaluating training programs. The tool is most effective in the planning stage because it helps you determine the data needed to assess training effectiveness at key points in the delivery, application, and outcome processes. You can then use this data to diagnose opportunities for optimizing the process.

Data Collection

The foundation of black box thinking lies in asking the right questions and gathering rich data. This requires careful planning and intentionally collecting the right data to capture the full picture, fostering a space for unexpected discoveries about the training being evaluated. It is important to note that building a comprehensive data collection strategy happens concurrently with strategic alignment. To incorporate black box thinking into your data collection, include diverse perspectives in design, use a multimodal strategy, and ask insightful questions.

Include Diverse Perspectives in Design

When developing your data collection strategy and designing feedback tools, ensure that you are considering and including diverse perspectives. Operating in a silo can result in unintentional blind spots or group thinking, negatively influencing the quality of your data. Actively solicit feedback on the data collection strategy and feedback tools from key stakeholders in the business, as well as any learners who will attend the program. By intentionally engaging potential learners and other key stakeholders across the business, and with various demographic attributes, the evaluation design will better capture key nuances that may otherwise be missed. A common example of this is survey question wording. Without asking for other perspectives, survey questions that will not translate well in other languages is often a misstep in the design process.

Use a Multimodal Strategy

A key component of black box thinking is using a multimodal data collection strategy. This involves using multiple methods and sources—such as surveys, interviews, observations, performance metrics, and feedback mechanisms—to gather data. Each method provides unique insights and perspectives about the effectiveness of the training program. For example, you can use a survey to capture quantitative data on trends or preferences and interviews to offer in-depth qualitative data that provides insights on the reasons behind the numbers. Using multiple methods allows you to triangulate data and corroborate findings across different datasets, which provides a more holistic and nuanced understanding of training effectiveness. You'll then be able to discover unexpected insights and achieve better outcomes in the future. (See Part 2 for chapters on data collection methods.)

Ask Insightful Questions

Black box thinking emphasizes learning from failures, analyzing root causes, and making iterative improvements based on insights gained. Asking insightful questions allows you to probe deeper into the reasons behind training successes, failures, or suboptimal outcomes and elicit thoughtful, informative responses, providing valuable insights for analysis and decision making. When designing your evaluation surveys or interviews, move beyond asking scaled questions and focus on digging deeper. Strategically use follow-up questions to probe for specific details or scenario-based questions related to the training topic to better understand how they would respond or what factors would influence their behavior.

Data Analysis

By systematically analyzing evaluation data with black box thinking, we can glean valuable insights that illuminate the strengths and weaknesses of the experience under evaluation. This allows us to identify success factors to preserve as well as areas for improvement, which becomes the foundation for refining and optimizing future programs and leads to more effective and successful results. To practice black box thinking, analyze data by demographic, examine extreme scores, and conduct thematic analysis.

Analyze the Data by Demographic

Analyzing data holistically and then by demographic attributes (such as age, department, location, or gender) offers a comprehensive approach to understanding trends, patterns, and insights within the dataset. Holistic analysis provides an overview of general trends, patterns, and correlations that may exist across the entire dataset. However, analyzing by demographic attribute allows for the detection of variances with different subgroups of the population. Compare these demographic-based scores to your overall organization scores to better understand differences in how the training content has been received and applied. This facilitates the customization and tailoring of recommendations to optimize training impact based on specific audience characteristics and better meet the needs of diverse learners.

Examine Extreme Scores

Examining extreme scores in your dataset provides another perspective. Extreme scores represent those areas where respondents showed greater results or emotion, both positive and negative. The performance improvement field routinely assesses standard deviation across items in a dataset (for example, using Six Sigma and DMAIC). Standard deviation measures the extent to which individual responses vary from the average. In the context of training effectiveness, you can use standard deviation to assess the variability and consistency in performance outcomes among learners (see chapter 11). A low standard deviation indicates that the training program has resulted in consistent results, while a high standard deviation may signal inconsistencies in learning, application, or outcomes. Any area with a high standard deviation represents the greatest opportunity for program improvement to ensure consistent learner experiences.

Conduct Thematic Analysis

Black box thinking encourages a curious and exploratory mindset toward understanding failures, mistakes, or complex systems. Similarly, thematic analysis involves a process of coding and categorizing qualitative data into meaningful themes, categories, and patterns to capture the essence of learner experiences, perspectives, or responses. You can accomplish this using a data analysis spiral technique, in which you first get a sense of the whole database and then assign themes to the data over multiple passes (Cresswell 2007). While a manual process will lead to the most in-depth understanding of qualitative datasets, you can also use a software program to aid the process (see chapter 12).

Reporting

Black box thinking has significant relevance to reporting for results optimization, particularly in terms of fostering a culture of learning, embracing transparency, and driving continuous improvement and data-driven decision making. This is accomplished through translating data from multiple modalities into one cohesive and integrated story, crafting a narrative that resonates with stakeholders, and providing strategic recommendations to drive impact and value in the organization.

Integrate Findings

Black box thinking requires a comprehensive understanding of complex systems, processes, and phenomena, which can only be achieved by analyzing various inputs and outputs and making connections across the datasets. This holistic approach allows for a more nuanced analysis and a deeper exploration of the interactions, patterns, and trends in the data. Further, stakeholders and decision makers will have greater confidence in the results if multiple data sources independently point to the same conclusions, because it reduces uncertainty and increases trust in the analytical process.

Tell a Story

Black box thinking often involves a complex analysis of datasets to uncover patterns, trends, and actionable insights. Data storytelling involves contextualizing these insights within a narrative framework that makes them accessible, meaningful, and relevant to stakeholders. The goal is to highlight the impact of initiatives, programs, and strategies on performance outcomes. Contextualizing the findings in a story allows the findings to better resonate with key stakeholders and conveys how data-driven decisions and actions influence results and contribute to organizational success, as well as what actions should be taken next to optimize outcomes (see chapters 19 and 20).

Develop Actionable Recommendations

Developing actionable recommendations based on data is crucial for results optimization because it involves translating insights derived from data analysis into practical strategies and initiatives that drive meaningful change and improvement. By focusing on high-impact recommendations, organizations can maximize the effectiveness of their efforts and resources, leading to tangible results and improved outcomes. Additionally, this is part of an iterative process to implement, monitor, and evaluate recommendations for effectiveness. By incorporating feedback loops, measuring outcomes, and revisiting recommendations based on results, organizations can refine their strategies over time to drive continuous improvement and adaptation.

CHAPTER 22

Summary

Black box thinking is a concept inspired by the aviation industry, emphasizing the use of data to learn from mistakes, encourage innovation, and improve outcomes. In the context of training evaluation, it involves going beyond traditional methods that solely measure the acquisition and application of new knowledge or skills in a controlled environment. Instead, it delves deeper into understanding the reasons behind successes and failures, fostering a culture of continuous improvement.

To implement black box thinking in training evaluation, this chapter offered several best practices for strategic alignment, collecting and analyzing data, and reporting findings to stakeholders. By following these practices, you and your organization can maximize training effectiveness, optimize outcomes, and foster a culture of learning and improvement.

Knowledge Check

Answer the following questions. Check your answers in appendix B.

1. Why is it important for organizations to prioritize continuous improvement and results optimization in training evaluation?
2. How can organizations foster a culture of continuous improvement? Why is this essential for maximizing training effectiveness?
3. What are some best practices for incorporating black box thinking principles into the evaluation process?

CHAPTER 23

Using Financial Analysis to Compare OJT and S-OJT

RONALD L. JACOBS

IN THIS CHAPTER

This chapter explores how you can use financial analysis to determine whether your organization should switch from unplanned on-the-job training to more structured efforts. After reading it, you will be able to:

- Compare the differences between structured on-the-job training (S-OJT) and unplanned OJT.
- Assess the financial benefits of your S-OJT efforts.
- Follow a process for comparing the financial benefits of S-OJT and unplanned OJT.

What Is Structured On-the-Job Training?

Prior to the 1980s, almost all training that occurred on the job could be characterized as unplanned or unstructured in the way it was developed and carried out—with less experienced employees being assigned to learn their jobs alongside someone more senior to them. Several descriptors of unplanned on-the-job training (OJT) include "Follow Joe Training," "Watch and Learn Training," "Sit by Sally Training," and "Trial and Error Learning." These phrases characterize the nature of the learning experience, as well as the anxiety and discomfort that such experiences often evoke. In this sense, how successfully trainees were able to grasp the new information using unplanned OJT became an informal measure of their ultimate fit in the organization. Were they sufficiently resilient to learn despite the barriers that unplanned OJT presented?

However, the 1980s brought new and significant disruptions to the fore. Organizations faced increasing demands for greater levels of quality and productivity and soon discovered skills gaps across all segments of the workforce (Jacobs and McGiffin 1987; Jacobs 1992). A new, more responsive training method was needed. And so structured on-the-job training (S-OJT) emerged across a wide range of work settings and jobs as a viable way to acquire specific job skills.

S-OJT is unique among training approaches because it occurs in the actual work setting, makes use of qualified experienced employees as the trainers, is based on a careful analysis of the work to be learned, and follows a systematic planning and implementation process. No other planned training approach combines these features in the same way. As artificial intelligence and big data bring new challenges to today's workers and the workplace, OJT and particularly S-OJT remain viable training options due to their focus on job skills. They can both achieve reliable and predictable learning outcomes.

Organizations have often questioned whether S-OJT makes financial sense because it often involves a substantial investment when compared with the cost of current unplanned OJT practices. Whether S-OJT is appropriate to address a performance issue should be judged in part by the tangible financial benefits obtained from its use.

Key Features of S-OJT

S-OJT is a planned process in which experienced employees train novice employees on units of work in the actual work setting (Jacobs 2003).

Planned Process

S-OJT uses a six-phase systematic process:
1. Determine the appropriateness of using S-OJT.
2. Analyze the work to be learned.
3. Develop experienced employees to be trainers.
4. Prepare S-OJT modules.
5. Deliver S-OJT using five steps.
6. Evaluate S-OJT.

A planned process also refers to the change management process that often accompanies S-OJT implementation. Here is a brief description of the critical features of S-OJT.

Experienced Employees

S-OJT is based on principles of the 1941 project initiative Training Within Industry (TWI), which includes reliance on experienced employees to deliver training. However, these individuals must have the appropriate knowledge and skills and undergo a formal program focused on the requirements for being an S-OJT trainer. The five steps for delivering S-OJT are to prepare the trainee, deliver the training, require a response, provide feedback, and evaluate performance.

Novice Employees

The novice designation is relative to the individual's level of skill related to a particular set of work tasks. From this perspective, a novice could be an employee who is new to the job or an established employee who is doing something new. Readiness to learn is an important characteristic of a novice employee.

Units of Work or Tasks

Another foundational TWI principle is the need to document the work to be learned, often through a comprehensive job and task analysis to identify the job's duties and tasks (Jacobs 2019). The task analysis provides the basis for the training content, which is presented in the form of an S-OJT module. Today, many tasks are considered examples of knowledge work, which by itself should not be a barrier for using S-OJT and calculating its financial benefits.

In the Actual Work Setting

S-OJT occurs in the setting in which the work is being done. If this is not possible, S-OJT can also be conducted in a setting that approximates those features through the use of simulators, role play, and virtual reality. The critical aspect is ensuring that these alternate environments adequately represent the features of the actual work setting.

CHAPTER 23

Comparing the Financial Benefits of S-OJT

Terry McGriffin and I conducted the first study to address the financial impacts of S-OJT in 1987. Our research focused on the learning outcomes of lab technicians in a quality control laboratory. While the company wanted to use video clips to demonstrate how to perform lab tests, McGiffin, who was also the company's training manager, realized that these clips would prevent the lab technicians from having a hands-on learning experience. Thus, he wanted to shift the emphasis from seeing how to use the technology to actually learning how to use it through training from experienced lab technicians. The results showed a dramatic reduction in learning time.

Since then, numerous published and unpublished studies have sought to verify and support the principle that planned training is superior to unplanned training and that the results within each situation differ due to the particular aspects of each workplace setting. These studies used established standards from past performance data and estimates based on the consultants' own experiences, all of which required agreement and consensus among stakeholders about the accuracy of the information.

To conduct your own comparison of unplanned OJT and S-OJT, first calculate the training costs, which are the expenses required to achieve each training option and may include analysis, delivery, evaluation, and management. Then, you'll need to determine the performance value costs. Depending on the measures of interest, performance value can be operationalized (a higher figure indicates increases in sales or productivity, while a lower figure indicates reductions in waste or lost wages). When the results show a reduction of some financial burden on the organization, such as a reduced amount of rework or defects, you might substitute the term *benefit* for *burden*.

Finally, compare the financial benefits or burdens of S-OJT and unplanned OJT. The costs and performance values of unplanned OJT and S-OJT are almost always different; for example, the cost for unplanned OJT is almost always shown as zero.

Logically, if the performance value exceeds the cost, then this would be desirable. If the cost exceeds the performance value leading to a negative benefit, then this would be undesirable. It could signify a poor selection choice was made on the part of decision-makers.

Two major questions have emerged to guide unplanned OJT and S-OJT comparison studies: training efficiency and training effectiveness. *Training efficiency* addresses the amount of time required to learn the task and whether the cost to achieve the learning was greater or less than the performance value. Michael J. Jones, Sue Neil, and I (1992) addressed this issue while studying trainee learning times across three work areas in a truck assembly plant. Thanks to this and similar studies comparing unplanned OJT and S-OJT, the industry has developed these training efficiency standards:

- Trainees across a wide range of organizational settings and jobs are able to learn tasks faster through S-OJT than unplanned OJT.
- It takes trainees four times longer on average to learn a task using unplanned OJT than S-OJT.
- Investing $1 in S-OJT typically leads to a financial benefit of between $4 and $8 in return.
- S-OJT is more efficient.

Training effectiveness addresses the relative value of the work outcomes achieved through each training option. For example, I addressed training effectiveness when I compared the number of water leaks that were observed in the windshields of assembled trucks and the value of the rework to address the leaky windshields. The results are reported as the cost of the rework when using S-OJT and included in the costs for each training option. Here are some of the other industry standards that have been established for training effectiveness of S-OJT:

- The performance value for using S-OJT typically exceeds the cost to achieve the performance value. The performance value cost of unplanned OJT is always more than the performance value.
- When subtracting the respective costs from the performance values, the benefit was greater for S-OJT than unplanned OJT.
- S-OJT had between twice the amount and 10 times the amount of financial benefits than unplanned OJT.

Case Study

The following case study compares the costs, performance value, and financial benefit or burden of unplanned OJT and S-OJT. We'll review in more detail the four phases required to carry out this comparison.

A national construction company recently implemented a new S-OJT program for its assistant construction superintendent position, which requires individuals to perform technical construction work while also overseeing the work of others at job sites. This critical

CHAPTER 23

on-site job serves as an essential link between the workers who do the work and the project managers who plan the work to be done. The company wanted to determine how effective the program was when compared with past unplanned OJT efforts.

1. Select Which Tasks to Compare

The talent development team had already conducted a job analysis for the assistant construction superintendent position and worked with stakeholders to determine which tasks to include in the comparison. The goal was to identify the tasks with the highest consequence in terms of rework cost when done incorrectly. Other potential criteria for task selection includes tasks that:

- Are associated with high error rates
- Lead to high consequences if an error is made
- Are difficult to perform
- Have undergone recent change
- Are critical for ensuring service delivery or smooth operations

The duty statement and the list of associated tasks are shown in Figure 23-1.

Figure 23-1. Tasks to Be Learned Through S-OJT

Job Title
Assistant Construction Superintendent
Duty of Focus
Conducting pre-pour activities on a commercial project
Tasks Identified for S-OJT
A.1. Conduct a pre-pour meeting with site workers. A.2. Inform workers of their individual assignments during the pour. A.3. Inspect concrete pour plan. A.4. Inspect for unwanted objects in the pour area. **A.5. Inspect rebar connections and steel placement.** A.6. Troubleshoot rebar and reinforcing steel placement problems. A.7. Provide coaching to workers on placement of rebar and reinforcing steel. A.8. Build the wooden forms per the placement plan A.9. Build a working platform. A.10. Inspect the wooden forms. A.11. Collect equipment, tools, and materials in the staging area. A.12. Conduct a final inspection of pour site before arrival of concrete.

USING FINANCIAL ANALYSIS TO COMPARE OJT AND S-OJT

For the purposes of this case study, we're focusing on task A.5—inspect rebar connections and steel placement—which is very representative of this job. Assistant construction superintendents are expected to oversee the work of others and correct any situations in which the work is not done properly. In the case of rebar connections, if the concrete is poured on incorrectly placed rebar, it will require costly rework to correct. The consequences of errors related to this task are future cracking and weakening of the concrete.

The talent development manager had never done an upfront analysis before, which made it quite challenging. However, he realized that job analysis was fundamental for calculating the financial benefits as well as other uses.

2. Calculate the Cost, Performance Value, and Financial Burden of Unplanned OJT

No training costs were required for the unplanned OJT, and the performance value was $40,000, based on 10 instances of rework, with a conservative cost estimate of $4,000 for each rework. The results showed that using unplanned OJT added an additional $40,000 in avoidable financial burden to the organization.

3. Calculate the Cost, Performance Value, and Financial Burden of S-OJT

The cost, performance value, and financial burden of S-OJT were calculated as part of the program's evaluation after the two-month implementation was over. The eight individuals who participated in the study received S-OJT in the form of a training guide delivered through a hand-held device, as well as additional S-OJT delivered by an experienced construction superintendent at the job site.

The cost per trainee was $1,200 for a total cost of $9,600; this number included the cost of the task analysis, trainer time, materials, and other costs associated with the delivery. The performance value was $4,000, because one instance of rework occurred across all eight individuals during the two months. Thus, the S-OJT program's total financial burden to the organization was $13,600.

4. Decide What Action to Take

The final phase of the analysis was to compare the results for the two training options and decide whether to continue using the S-OJT program or return to unplanned OJT. Table

CHAPTER 23

23-1 shows the training cost, performance value, and the resulting financial burden of these two training methods.

Table 23-1. Comparison of Unplanned OJT and S-OJT

	Unplanned OJT	S-OJT
Performance Value	$40,000 (10 instances of rework @ $4,000)	$4,000 (1 instance of rework)
Training Cost	$0	$9,600 (Eight trainees x $1,200 per S-OJT session)
Financial Burden (Performance Value + Training Cost)	$40,000	$13,600
Benefits of S-OJT (Financial Burden of OJT − S-OJT)		$26,400
Result	Using S-OJT saved the organization $26,400 in avoidable financial burden. The benefit-cost ratio is approximately 2.75:1. That is, for every $1 invested, the return is $2.75 or a 175% return on investment.	

The difference in financial burden between unplanned OJT and S-OJT was $26,400. In other words, the $9,600 investment in S-OJT resulted in $26,400 financial benefits. The benefit-cost ratio was 2.75:1, indicating that every $1 invested resulted in $2.75 returned. Another way to express these results is that the S-OJT investment delivered an ROI of 175 percent—for every $1 invested, the organization gained an additional $1.75 over and beyond that investment. This information was presented to management as a positive return, worthy of recommending continued use of S-OJT for tasks that have a high consequence of error. Of note, comparing the returns from this analysis with an organization's typical capital investments—which often have a return of 15 to 18 percent (Phillips and Phillips 2019)—further supports the relative importance of using S-OJT.

When conducting the analysis, the construction company and talent development manager considered three points:

- **The performance value for unplanned OJT was intentionally conservative to ensure the credibility of the results.** In this case, it did not account for the cost of project delays when the rework was being done, which would have increased the burden of unplanned OJT rework considerably.

- **The analysis occurred over a limited period of time (two months).** They knew that fully implementing the S-OJT program should lead to a greater reduction in the burden. Further, the analysis was conducted on one task alone, without considering the other tasks selected for the project.
- **The construction company realized S-OJT could have a nonfinancial benefit if it led clients to view the company as being more professional and exhibiting sound management practices.** The company could mention using S-OJT as part of project bids to demonstrate its concern for quality work and employee development.

Summary

This chapter described S-OJT and offered advice for comparing the financial benefits of S-OJT and unplanned OJT. Undertaking such an analysis may appear complicated at first glance, due to the additional professional knowledge and skills needed to complete it. In addition, the analysis requires involving managers who understand the importance of making informed decisions related to training and are willing to participate in the process. All of this takes time and effort and possibly an adjustment of role expectations.

However, you should also consider what you can gain from undertaking such a study: The results should help you move from a role that is exclusively focused on training design and delivery to one that's seen as a business partner. The calculations themselves are relatively rudimentary, but the results represent an understanding of actual work performance in the organization, not simply measures of perceptions of training programs, and they demonstrate the importance of training as a means to influence that performance.

Knowledge Check

Take a minute to reflect on these questions:

1. What new areas of professional knowledge and skills might be necessary to implement S-OJT?
2. How can L&D professionals express concerns about using unplanned OJT when most of their work is done away from the work setting of their organization?

3. It is possible to conduct a financial analysis of S-OJT when the tasks involve professional employees?
4. How should L&D professionals present the findings of an analysis to management in a convincing manner without seeming like an overbearing advocate?
5. How can L&D professionals shift current perceptions that their role only involves the design and delivery of training programs?
6. How could L&D professionals integrate AI and big data, two new topics being discussed within the community, into discussions about calculating the financial benefits of training?

Practitioner's Tip

Readers of this chapter may realize that implementing S-OJT requires some L&D skills that they may not now possess. In particular, L&D professionals may not have much experience in conducting a job analysis and then further analyzing the identified tasks for the S-OJT training guides. When done correctly, this information is fundamental for accurately calculating the financial impacts later on. Unfortunately, many L&D professionals mistakenly believe that because they likely don't have knowledge of the work, they should simply ask individuals in the field to generate this information, resulting in information that might not be entirely useful for the S-OJT program. Related to this misperception is the view that conducting a job and task analysis can be overly complicated and requires special skills, and may even result in situations in which employees openly disagree with one another about how some aspect of the work is done.

Regardless, the tip here is the necessity of embracing, not rejecting, the need to add new skills to your professional toolkit, even if the new skills challenge the boundaries of your existing mindset about L&D practice. And new skills may simply build upon existing ones, such as facilitation skills, for instance, which are considered an important part of conducting a job and task analysis with a group of subject matter experts.

PART 5

Make Measurement and Evaluation Work

As the introductory chapter mentions, the fifth part of the evaluation puzzle is implementation. It is this part that ensures a sustainable measurement practice. Part 5 of this book focuses on that issue.

To consistently and effectively create, deliver, and demonstrate value through training, systems must be in place to support measurement and evaluation implementation. This does not mean that evaluation should wait until those systems are in place—never let the need for perfection stand in the way of progress. However, it does mean that there should be an effort to ensure that assessment, measurement, and evaluation are seamlessly integrated into learning operations and the talent development ecosystem. This requires getting stakeholder buy-in, becoming consistent in the approach by following standards, and leveraging technology to more easily access measures, create objectives, collect and analyze data, and report and use results.

Part 5 will provide you insights about how you can:
- Implement a sustainable measurement and evaluation practice.
- Secure stakeholder buy-in.
- Follow evaluation standards.
- Leverage artificial intelligence.

You will also read how the world's leading innovator and manufacturer of chip-making machines, ASML, is approaching the development of a sustainable practice of measuring and evaluating training.

CHAPTER 24

Implementing a Sustainable Measurement Practice

HOLLY BURKETT

IN THIS CHAPTER

Implementing a measurement project is one thing; implementing a sustainable practice is another. After reading this chapter, you will be able to:

♦ Describe proven strategies for sustainable ROI implementation.
♦ Define the characteristics of a sustainable M&E practice.
♦ Identify six essentials for sustained success.
♦ Assess the maturity of your own M&E practice.

The What and Why of Sustainable Practice

Does this sound familiar? Janice, the corporate training director for a global banking institution, returned from an ROI Certification program after the senior vice president of people management said he wanted all talent management processes to be evaluated with the program's signature tools and techniques. Janice and her team planned to introduce the ROI Methodology during a pilot coaching initiative for 50 managers before rolling out the process to the entire enterprise.

As the pilot project unfolded and the team identified action planning and data collection processes, the pilot group members and their managers got nervous and voiced fears about negative consequences if they couldn't show positive behavioral results. That fear led to barriers," Janice explained.

CHAPTER 24

"It led to a lack of support from the operations folks who were directly affected by the coaching program as well as their operational directors. Instructional designers tasked with customizing coaching scenarios had trouble getting input from subject matter experts. The sponsor assigned key managers to help with the pilot effort, but the initiative was eventually abandoned because it never got off the ground or had the right internal support. One of the biggest barriers was the human resources department, which claimed that integrating program data with current talent development processes was too complex, despite the fact that another senior VP was our main sponsor."

If you've had similar experiences, you know that ensuring participation from diverse stakeholders with complex reporting relationships is a special implementation challenge. Gaining stakeholder support for a single ROI project is often an effort in and of itself. Sustaining that support beyond the life cycle of an isolated effort is even *more* challenging, and it's an aspect of implementation that TD professionals and organizations often overlook. After all, it's not enough to have one high-impact program if there aren't sustainable processes for ensuring that all projects and programs consistently contribute, in some way, to performance results over time.

Sustaining a durable, results-based M&E practice is especially difficult in today's fast-paced business climate with advancing technology, leaner organizational structures, and growing talent shortages. In many ways, maintaining measurement momentum is like changing tires on a moving car. As with any process improvement effort, you must maintain consistent attention, dedicated focus, and perpetual motion to go the distance. To address these challenges, you need to start with a strong foundation.

Laying the Foundation

A sustainable ROI process is one that's blended into an organization's routine and is fully endorsed at all levels by those who must make it work. You gained guidelines for aligning your measurement purpose with strategic objectives when implementing a single project or series of programs in chapter 1. However, once you've decided to introduce the ROI process into an existing training effort, it's important to step back and look at where you're planning to go with measurement practices as a whole, what you want to do with measurement results, and who needs to know and why. For sustained success, work with stakeholders to create purpose and policy statements that frame results-based measurement as a process improvement strategy and not a performance management approach.

Consider two examples of strong evaluation policy statements:

- **The Gates Foundation:** "Our evaluation policy is intended to help foundation staff and our partners align their expectations in determining why, when, and how to use evaluation."
- **The Children and Families Commission:** "Evaluation will be approached as a continuous learning opportunity to improve services and outcomes. This will be done in a partnership between the Children and Families Commission (CFC) and its Partner Network in order to discover the best approaches to achieving and sustaining comprehensive child, family, and community outcomes rather than as a means to control or coerce services delivery partners."

In addition to policy statements, laying the foundation includes working with stakeholders to establish specific targets and defining the percentage of programs planned for each level of evaluation. For example, 90 to 100 percent of programs will likely be measured at Level 1, with 10 to 20 percent typically targeted for Level 4. Many organizations set annual evaluation targets and schedule timetables for transitioning percentages to progressively higher levels of evaluation as indicated.

Maintaining Momentum

As with any process improvement endeavor, you must maintain a consistent line of sight to keep the ROI process from becoming a passing fad. To best integrate the ROI Methodology into the DNA of your organization, focus your implementation efforts on a systemic big-picture (such as the work, workplace, or worker) approach that incorporates six essentials (Figure 24-1):

1. Value creation
2. Partnerships
3. Capability
4. Sound execution
5. Change readiness
6. Innovation

CHAPTER 24

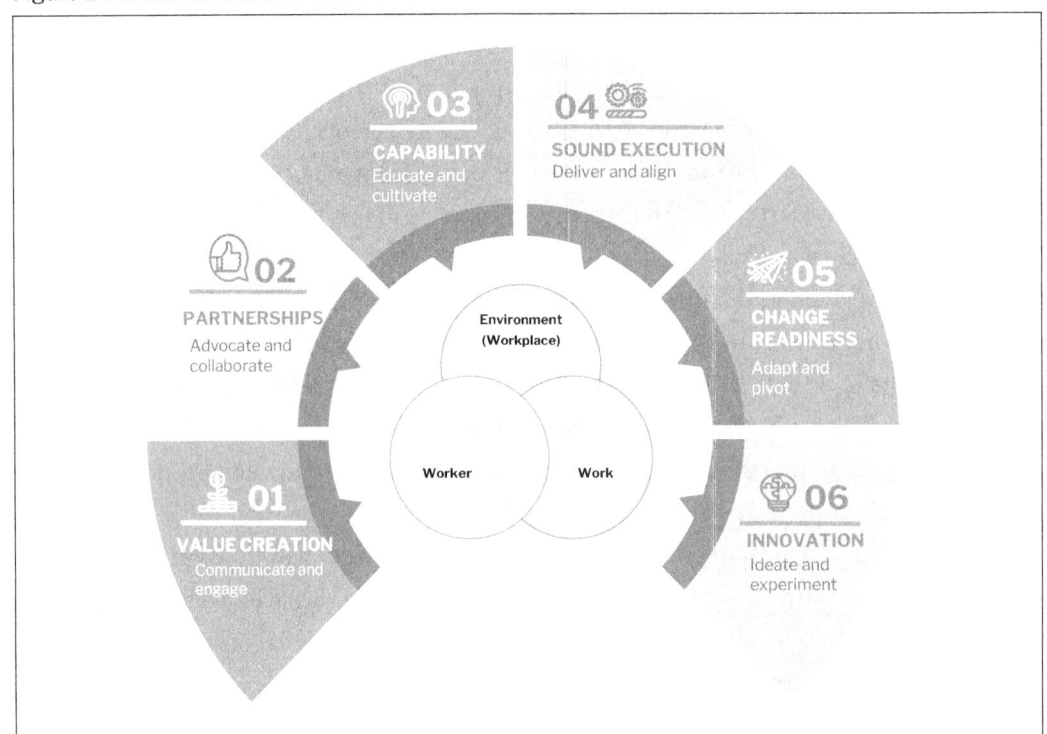

Figure 24-1. Six Essentials for a Sustainable M&E Practice

*[Diagram: A circular arrangement showing six essentials around a central "Environment (Workplace)" with "Worker" and "Work" circles:
- 01 VALUE CREATION — Communicate and engage
- 02 PARTNERSHIPS — Advocate and collaborate
- 03 CAPABILITY — Educate and cultivate
- 04 SOUND EXECUTION — Deliver and align
- 05 CHANGE READINESS — Adapt and pivot
- 06 INNOVATION — Ideate and experiment]*

Add and Create Value

When first adopting the ROI process, the focus tends to be on showing the value of a specific training program or talent development initiative. But sustainable value is more about the ROI of the ROI—the payoff of the complete process rather than the impact achieved by a single program. Value creation occurs when ROI is well-integrated and viewed as a value-added *business process* rather than a stand-alone training or evaluation process. Creating value is one of the best ways to sustain implementation support. Here's how some TD professionals enhance their value proposition.

Make It Useful

Results data that is not seen or used will have little perceived value to the organization or the stakeholders responsible for supporting and funding the ROI process over time. This means that you must ensure stakeholders obtain the information they need at the time they need it to make informed decisions. TD professionals must anticipate multiple uses and users of performance data and should not only report on results achieved but also present findings about poor outcomes, which helps expose problems and presents lessons learned for continuous improvement purposes. Indicators of utility include the capacity to provide real-world value through improved quality, effectiveness, and efficiency measures.

Continuously Improve

As you standardize the implementation of the ROI process and make it more visible, and as the competition for M&E resources becomes more intense, continuous improvement mechanisms will help ensure that the results generated from the methodology are still adding value. Many practitioners use tools like after-action reviews or L&D dashboards to communicate results or lessons learned for continuous improvement purposes. According to one seasoned ROI professional, "You have to be able to demonstrate lessons learned about a study that can be brought back into the organization and replicated. In other words, if people see a study as a one-off kind of thing, it will die."

Communicate, Communicate, Communicate

How will stakeholders know your value unless you communicate it? Provide targeted communications showing how the ROI process has helped solve real business issues and achieved critical performance outcomes. "Constant, continual communication of results" is commonly cited by professionals who have successfully integrated the ROI process for five years or longer. This includes sharing success stories throughout the organization in the form of case studies, project reports, or testimonials. Similarly, another ROI professional says, "We keep it alive and visible within our organization and in front of our leaders so they can then, in turn, be champions from an organizational perspective."

Strengthen Partnerships

While it's important to actively collaborate with managers in all phases of evaluation planning and implementation, the best time to establish support is before you need it. Take time to build allies, develop partnerships, and understand the needs of your business and its stakeholders. Develop profiles, process maps, project histories, and organizational charts for your client organizations. Cultivate a working relationship with each group.

Be inclusive. Create opportunities for middle managers, frontline leaders, and individual contributors to engage and express what they think, feel, and experience during evaluation projects.

Partnerships are enhanced when people are clear about their roles and responsibilities to support implementation. Engage your target groups and help prepare them for what to expect.

> **Practitioner's Tip**
>
> Successful, sustainable implementation is 20 percent evaluation work and 80 percent soft skills. It's lots of conversations, client relationship building, and understanding that the person in front of you is not necessarily the client.
>
> —Dan McLinden, EdD, CRP, Idea Networks

Sponsors

Ideally, your sponsor will be a CEO or CFO who can approve the resources needed to initiate, maintain, and sustain evaluation projects, especially beyond the life cycle of a single impact study. In general, you need credible sponsors to provide direction and convey a results orientation in both action and words. Sponsors also provide a critical chain of accountability. For example, when managers do not support M&E practices as assigned, the sponsor must communicate a resolve for stakeholders to uphold their responsibilities. Unfortunately, many executives are not aware of the importance of their role and often don't understand what effective sponsorship looks like. TD professionals can use executive and management briefings, conversation guides, peer networks, and coaching forums to educate sponsors about their role in driving and sustaining a results-based L&D focus.

Steering Committee

Sponsors often establish a steering committee to oversee comprehensive ROI projects and provide a governance structure. Steering committee members may help kick off management briefings about an ROI effort, provide access to operational or business data, hold managers accountable for supporting on-the-job application, ensure that managers help participants make time for learning, and assist in interpreting results data.

Managers

An effective way to enhance commitment to the ROI process is to ask for what you want! Invite managers to serve on an internal advisory committee or an impact study team. Emphasize their role in helping to:

- Define business needs.
- Support the use of new knowledge on the job.
- Identify and remove barriers to application.
- Recognize and reward performance improvement.
- Collect, analyze, and report results data.

ROI Champions

ROI champions are typically individuals who are most familiar with the ROI process and are credible messengers about its value. They can help:

- Organize technical resources.
- Provide staff support, coaching, and training.
- Facilitate communication across departments.
- Oversee system-wide processes for measuring, analyzing, and reporting results to ensure uniformity and consistency.
- Represent the organization by working with suppliers or presenting data to other companies or stakeholders.

Practitioner's Tip

Having an internal ROI champion can help you get the most out of a supplier. For example, a nonprofit children's research hospital selected a supplier to deliver a leadership development program targeting women researchers. The program curriculum was already in place, and the evaluation focused solely on Levels 1 and 2. To better assess the program's business impact, L&D's ROI champion (who was also a Certified ROI Professional) met with the supplier to establish measurable objectives for collecting results data at Levels 3, 4, and 5. Together, they developed six individual impact measures and five institutional impact measures, including intangible benefits, for the study, which ultimately reported an ROI of 117 percent.

—Organization Development Consultant at a leading pediatric and research facility

ROI Project Teams

ROI project teams typically represent a designated, cross-functional task force of advocates who are responsible for ensuring that people, processes, and systems are effectively aligned and in place to implement an evaluation effort. Project team members usually wear many different hats and can act as internal and external business partners, educators, data gatherers, advisors, coaches, peer leaders, or meeting facilitators.

Finally, when strengthening partnerships, consider this—the more you help other people get the results they want, the more likely they'll be to help you get the results you want.

Grow Capability

Developing the capability of available resources is especially critical because many organizations have turned to core teams of subject matter experts to initiate and lead ROI implementation efforts. Building capability across silos and functions helps conserve scarce resources, foster a common language around M&E, align processes and tools, and promote shared ownership for results. Keep in mind, however, that growing capability is not a one-and-done event focused simply on better evaluation efforts with isolated projects, leaders, or teams. You must continually cultivate measurement capability at both the individual and organizational levels. Let's review some enabling strategies.

Prioritize Continuous Learning

Leaders must partner with L&D professionals to create an environment that celebrates learning and links learning to opportunity. To that end, leaders across all levels should actively demonstrate a commitment to their own continuous learning and development and make learning conversations part of their everyday work. Because employees frequently complain that managers do not allow enough time for learning, best practice companies supplement managers' performance measures to include "time to learn."

Provide Performance Support

Employees across all levels need considerable support when adjusting to their evaluation roles and responsibilities because working with evaluation is generally a new endeavor. For sustained success, build measurement competencies and accountabilities into the talent management processes of these groups:

- **Senior leaders.** Educate and brief senior leaders about the value of the process. Provide special workshops like the "Executive's Role in Driving Results," and create self-directed and peer-to-peer development options. Engage them in setting evaluation targets and serving as steering committee members, advocates, coaches, or mentors.
- **Managers**. Managers can make or break the results of an evaluation effort. Engage, coach, and support them through every phase of implementation. "Our goal is to have all managers comfortable with the ROI process," says one seasoned ROI professional. "We assist department managers in all business units to conduct front-end needs assessments, we provide learning opportunities on the ROI process, and we partner with them on subsequent ROI projects. Accountability for adding value is now considered the responsibility of everyone in the organization, and ROI is a system-wide philosophy."
- **Project participants and teams.** In general, project participants and teams lack understanding about the ROI process, may have pre-existing baggage about evaluation, and fear how results data will be used; these concerns can all be partially countered by continuing education. One ROI professional approaches continuing education this way: "We have shifted from working with individual projects in the field to talking about the ROI process on a more strategic level and in higher-level committees and planning." Another says, "Now we are holding the business units accountable for doing studies and we have a two-year plan mapped out to try to institutionalize this."
- **TD professionals.** As an L&D expert and ROI champion, don't neglect your own need to continually reskill and upskill to be a more effective business partner. For example, people analytics has been consistently cited as one of the biggest capability gaps among TD and HR practitioners. While it may take time (up to several years) and ongoing investments to develop talent analytic skills, along with supporting technologies, it's important for TD professionals to embrace analytics for what it is and what it can do to revolutionize the value of learning.

Manage Resistance

Specific change responses associated with implementing a measurement and evaluation framework like the ROI Methodology include fear of accountability, fear about learning new evaluation techniques, and fear of consequences about how performance data will be used. To counter resistance, ensure that evaluation is framed as a collaborative process improvement approach instead of a corrective or fault-finding tool. Some ROI professionals invite select participants into executive briefings or management review meetings for projects that met some resistance. These face-to-face testimonials have a powerful influence because they put a face to the numbers and provide a human-interest element to your evidence-based storytelling.

Execute Well

In many organizations, translating a measurement strategy into execution involves stalled initiatives, politically charged turf battles, moving targets, and lost opportunities. While there are several approaches for closing the gap between strategy and execution, this section outlines some proven best practices.

Build and Maintain Infrastructures

Underestimating the lead time needed to create compatible support structures is a common factor in the failure of sustainable ROI implementation. "Our biggest initial barrier was that we were almost too early for our own good," one ROI professional says. "What I mean by that is we jumped to ROI without really having a solid base of measurement and evaluation within our organization."

To add sustainable value, L&D professionals need to ensure that the organization's structural processes remain adaptive, resilient, and responsive to changing needs. This means advising leaders to replace archaic systems that are poorly aligned, too complicated, or too isolated with technology-enabled, adaptive structures.

Use Effective Project Management

Collaborate with stakeholders early on to identify and prioritize key performance indicators (KPIs) that are specific, measurable, achievable, and appropriately aligned with identified business needs. Recommendations include being realistic and starting small. As an ROI professional at a global banking institution says, "I think, off the bat, if I look back, selecting five programs for ROI evaluation was probably too much." Partner with project managers to coordinate measurement milestones, tools, and methods.

Proactively Manage Risks

Regardless of how mature the ROI process may be, risk issues can occur at any stage of implementation. Risk assessment should take place during evaluation planning and revisited whenever a substantive change occurs that may alter the project's course or projected results. Managers use risk management information to assess whether an evaluation effort is on target with business goals and whether it is worth the risk of continued investment. Electing to continue an evaluation project should be an informed and conscious choice based on risk assessment. Table 24-1 highlights how to address common implementation risks and roadblocks.

Table 24-1. Addressing Implementation Roadblocks

Risks and Roadblocks	Ideas for Managing Risks and Overcoming Roadblocks
Limited internal support	• Engage a credible sponsor to provide leadership and direction. • Collaborate to solve real business issues and create value. • Build evaluation capability across all organizational levels.
Competing business demands	• Develop a protocol for prioritizing projects and resource allocations. • Proactively anticipate and manage risks. • Be ready to adapt, scale back, or change course as conditions demand.
Unrealistic expectations	• Educate stakeholders about their roles and responsibilities. • Regularly review and level expectations throughout implementation. • Show the value and utility of results data (positive or negative).
Insufficient resources	• Use cost-savings approaches to consolidate steps and conserve resources. • Ensure project plans are realistic, feasible, and scalable. • Leverage project teams and networks for cross-functional collaboration.
Flawed implementation	• Plan and deploy well. Use effective project and risk management. • Cascade overlapping projects to minimize negative impacts or fatigue. • Engage stakeholders in defining schedule, scope, and resource requirements.

Adapted from Burkett (2013)

Integrate Cost-Saving Methods

Some of the more common concerns from both internal staff and managers about ROI implementation are around the cost, time, and human resources necessary to fully implement the process. For practitioners tasked with showing value while doing more with less, here are some cost-saving approaches that provide sound, credible data with significantly fewer resources:
- Plan for evaluation early in the process.
- Build evaluation into the training process.

- Share the responsibilities for evaluation.
- Require participants to conduct major steps.
- Use short-cut methods for major steps.
- Use sampling to select the most appropriate programs for ROI analysis.
- Use estimates in the collection and analysis of data.
- Develop internal capability to implement the ROI process.
- Streamline the reporting process.
- Use technology.

Recognize Effort and Reward Progress

Recognition boosts individual motivation, fosters the development of high-performance teams, and leads to increased engagement, productivity, and quality, as well as decreased turnover and absenteeism. In addition, when project teams receive frequent recognition, they believe their work is valued and are more likely to maintain higher levels of discretionary effort throughout the year. Include both manager and peer-to-peer recognition for a variety of big and small wins, milestone achievements, and individual and team efforts.

Build Change Readiness

Implementing and sustaining a comprehensive evaluation process means transforming your role from order taker to business partner, transforming an activity-based function to a results-based function, and transforming old ways of collecting, analyzing, and reporting training results with new evidence-based measures of training success. It also means transforming systems, policies, or processes for increased accountability and transparency around performance results. In essence, implementing and sustaining a mature ROI process is nothing short of a transformational change process.

Like any transformation effort, implementing a sustainable measurement practice involves a perpetually renewing evolution of growth, in which small, evolutionary stages—rather than revolutionary ones—form the basis for continuous improvement. These stages are often likened to maturity levels because development processes are transformed from ad hoc, undisciplined states to disciplined practices capable of predictable, sustainable results. As shown in Figure 24-2, these processes build on the infrastructures established at earlier maturity levels and, subsequently, become the foundation for more sophisticated processes at the next level.

IMPLEMENTING A SUSTAINABLE MEASUREMENT PRACTICE

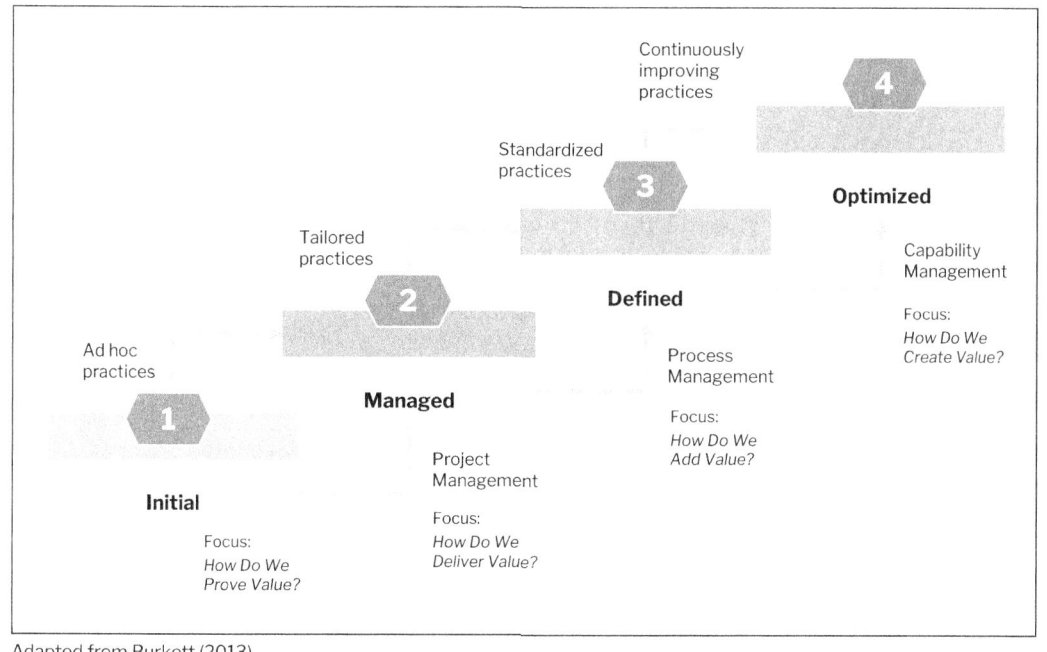

Figure 24-2. Maturity Model for a Sustainable M&E Practice

```
                                    Continuously
                                     improving
                                     practices          ┌─4─┐
                                                        Optimized
                      Standardized
                       practices      ┌─3─┐
        Tailored                                        Capability
        practices                     Defined           Management
                   ┌─2─┐                                Focus:
                                      Process          How Do We
Ad hoc                                Management       Create Value?
practices          Managed            Focus:
        ┌─1─┐                         How Do We
                   Project            Add Value?
                   Management
Initial            Focus:
                   How Do We
Focus:             Deliver Value?
How Do We
Prove Value?
```

Adapted from Burkett (2013)

The rest of this section describes how to facilitate M&E development from one stage to the next.

Continually Assess Readiness

Change is at the center of every learning and performance improvement strategy, talent development efforts are designed to drive organizational change, and today's learning leader plays a vital role as a change agent. Change readiness is about being responsive and able to act during ambiguous, complex, or unexpected circumstances. Failure to adapt to change is one of the biggest barriers to successful implementation and the overall sustainability of any M&E practice. Build readiness assessments into every implementation effort. Help leaders identify how much disruption is happening at any time and how the volume and complexity of existing changes may help or hurt the success of any planned evaluation effort.

Here are some guidelines for building change readiness:
- Assign priority levels to changes taking place.
- Allow for a learning curve after change is introduced.

- Build employees' confidence in meeting change expectations.
- Provide resource support right after a change to reduce performance dips and boost proficiency.
- Reimagine resistance as a performance anxiety or change fatigue issue.
- Cascade change in smaller launches to reduce the degree and duration of stress during each change.
- Leverage change-ready teams, networks, and communities of practice to increase success.
- Increase involvement to increase engagement.
- Monitor biases toward a hustle-and-grind mentality.
- Emphasize the role of rest and recovery in achieving peak performance.

Monitor Change (and Survey) Fatigue

Change fatigue sets in when employees feel pressured to make too many transitions at once or when initiatives have been rolled out too quickly without enough preparation. This fatigue is tied to the *cumulative* effect of change over time—not just the size or scope of any given change. Fatigue makes it harder for employees to absorb new information, perform tasks, and fully engage. And chronic fatigue leads to brain fog, burnout, and mental distance from one's job—which are also often seen as signs of resistance. After all, the message of a perfectly aligned, designed, and delivered evaluation strategy is meaningless if employees are too exhausted to hear it or apply it. To that end, remember that training or coaching support, action plan development, and follow-up survey requests—no matter how relevant or well-intended—are often perceived as just one more unmanageable demand when employees are overworked, overwhelmed, or burned out.

Enhance Management Support

Employees depend on managers to help them balance workloads, manage burnout, and navigate change. Yet today's managers are also vulnerable to high levels of stress and burnout since their responsibilities, workloads, and spans of control have doubled, post-pandemic (Klinghoffer and Kirkpatrick-Husk 2023). Ensure managers have a safe place to gain support and share their unique challenges so they're better able to shape the conditions needed for learning and performance results to occur.

Embrace the Art of Innovation

What sets sustainable M&E practices apart is their commitment to continual innovation—their ability to renew or reinvent themselves and their organizations as new conditions and demands emerge (Burkett 2017). Yet many M&E functions lack strategies or systems that foster innovation and are not up to speed with innovative technologies. Talent development professionals cannot expect to help drive innovation within the business if their own practices are stagnant and out of touch. To boost innovation with your M&E practice, consider the tips outlined in this section.

Foster Learning Agility

To survive and thrive in today's volatile and unpredictable business climate, organizations need employees with resilience and agile learning abilities. *Learning agility* is the ability and willingness to learn, unlearn, and relearn, with flexibility and speed being the two main drivers. *Flexibility* refers to the ability to give up old habits or behaviors for new behaviors that better meet the needs of the future. *Speed* has more to do with how quickly an individual can read a situation and change their behaviors, adapt, and respond with a plan of action. To foster learning agility, create space for project teams to embrace experimentation and risk to learn from both failures and successes. Make it safe to fail.

Leverage Technology

Talent development professionals depend more on digital learning solutions than ever before—not only to deliver content but to provide social learning networks and measure learning success. For instance, Unilever uses an AI-enabled talent marketplace, known as FLEX experiences, to automatically connect workers with training, mentorships, and projects that are aligned with their personal and organizational goals (Gloat n.d.). When technology is fully integrated into a learning culture and an M&E practice, organizations see improved engagement, eNPS Promoter scores, and customer service, as well as decreased incidences of burnout.

To best leverage technology, follow these tips (O.C. Tanner 2021):
- Develop and follow a change management plan for any new technology. Without such plans, adoption drops by 51 percent, and the overall employee experience decreases by 32 percent.

- Don't assume employees will easily adopt new technology. Even those who show open acceptance may push back if it disrupts their flow of work.
- Use nudge versus nag reminders to help learners apply new knowledge or provide evaluation feedback.

Focus on Futureproofing

More than 87 percent of executives report the presence of skills gaps in their organization, and more than 25 percent of organizations increased their spending on reskilling in response to the COVID-19 pandemic (McKinsey 2020). In a rapidly advancing AI economy with looming talent shortages, becoming an agile, skills-first organization is a strategic priority for more than 84 percent of leaders wishing to tip the scale toward a more futureproofed talent pipeline. Practices promoting an upskilled workforce help employees successfully redeploy to new roles and help businesses increase productivity, improve morale, lower hiring costs, and enhance their brand reputation. L&D professionals can add sustainable value by continually assessing, managing, and measuring upskilling needs and gaps.

Summary

A sustainable M&E practice implies a long-term, future focus and the capacity to endure. In a business climate of constant churn and change, building a durable measurement practice is one of biggest challenges in implementation. Successful evaluators know that there are no shortcuts to sustainability. It takes time, focused intention, and a dedicated commitment to the long haul. While the effort might seem daunting, the key is to focus on manageable, achievable actions that will keep you moving and going the distance.

This chapter looked at sustainable ROI implementation as a systemic, iterative change process and identified six key essentials for moving toward long-term integration and process maturity. The best-designed tools and techniques for ROI process implementation are meaningless unless you integrate them into the fabric of your organization and gain acceptance by those responsible for making it work. Recognize your own role as an evaluation champion and change agent. Use the self-assessment job aid in appendix A to see where you are in your journey toward creating a sustainable M&E practice; then, refer back to the tips, tactics, and examples from this chapter to support your progress.

Knowledge Check

There are six essential parts of a sustainable M&E practice. Match each action in the table with the corresponding essential part. Check your answers in appendix B.

1. Value creation
2. Partnerships
3. Capability
4. Sound execution
5. Change readiness
6. Innovation

Action	Essential Number
Ensure implementation plans are flexible, scalable, and appropriately aligned to business needs.	
Show the ROI of the ROI.	
Engage sponsors as steering committee members, coaches, or mentors.	
Create space for project teams to experiment, take risks, and learn from their failures as well as their successes.	
Consider employee workloads when requesting support for evaluation activities, like survey follow-ups or action planning.	
Continually reskill and upskill to build your business acumen and strategic partnership skills.	

CHAPTER 25

Getting Stakeholder Buy-In for Measurement and Evaluation

BRENDA SUGRUE

IN THIS CHAPTER

The need for rapid upskilling and reskilling, as well as advances in technology, provide new opportunities to revisit the value proposition for investment in training and related measurement. This chapter focuses on winning over senior executives as stakeholders because, if they buy in, others will follow. After reading it, you will be able to:

♦ Assess your current state with respect to measurement and buy-in.
♦ Increase stakeholder buy-in.
♦ Prepare for stakeholder conversations with buy-in in mind.

Why Stakeholder Buy-In Matters

Measurement and evaluation are increasingly important due to the heightened demand for training and retraining to meet growing skills gaps. Stakeholders want to know more about the value and impact of their investments. This group includes the individuals who want to build skills and advance their careers, the organizational leaders who want to maintain a workforce with the right skills, and the government agencies that monitor labor market trends and educational opportunities.

Different stakeholders expect and accept different types of evidence for their decisions and conclusions about the value of training. An individual employee may want to know which programs and certifications lead to better jobs. Corporate executives may want to know whether training on critical new skills is being consumed and is contributing to business growth and success in the market. As part of environment, social, and governance (ESG) goals, government agencies want to know whether companies are investing adequately in training and if employees have equal opportunities to build their skills.

While most companies (95 percent) measure consumption, satisfaction, and learning (or Levels 0, 1, and 2 in the Kirkpatrick and Phillips evaluation models), only 50 percent measure application of training to the job, 38 percent measure impact, and 16 percent measure return on investment (ATD 2023). This suggests that while buy-in is high for measurement that relies on data from learning management systems, it drops as measurement becomes more labor intensive and time consuming. In many cases, if training is well aligned to the skill needs of the business and consumption and ratings are high, there is less pressure from executives to formally measure impact.

It doesn't help that new requirements for disclosing training data in corporate reports are focused on input such as spend and training hours per employee rather than impact (WEF 2020). However, there is also an expectation that organizations provide a narrative about their investment in training and its impact. This is a lever you can use to get buy-in for more rigorous impact evaluation.

Advances in technology are making it easier to go beyond consumption, ratings, and assessment of learning at the end of training. Learning assessments—such as tests or self-reports of skill before and after training—are being replaced by data from skills intelligence systems that track skills gaps and gains, which can be associated with training. Automation of surveys makes it possible to follow up on the application of training and observed impact at scale. Integration of talent and business systems makes it easier to perform big data correlational studies of relationships among training, talent, and business variables.

In the context of increased external requirements and better internal sources of data, talent development professionals are well positioned to showcase and gain more buy-in for measurement and evaluation activities.

Assessing Your Current State

Different organizations and training functions are at different stages of maturity in implementing measurement and evaluation strategies, which means they'll have different levels of buy-in from senior executives.

Some organizations measure all levels, but in ad hoc and manual ways. Others have fully automated the collection and reporting of consumption and satisfaction data, but don't include any controlled studies of impact. Some organizations have stakeholders who expect every discussion about training to start with data, while others have stakeholders who are happy with anecdotes. Some organizations have a dedicated training measurement team, whereas others rely on part-time resources or consultants.

The first step is to take stock of your current state. What are the processes and scope of your current measurement activities? What would you like to do more of or improve? Is your stakeholder buy-in high or low? From there, you can work to increase support for your measurement goals.

Table 25-1 presents a framework for assessing the scope and efficiency of your current measurement strategy. Are you measuring all content or a subset? Are you tracking all employees or a subset? How efficient is your data collection and reporting for each level of evaluation?

Table 25-1. Current State: Scope and Efficiency of Levels

Measurement Levels	Scope		Efficiency	
	Content	Employees	Data	Reporting
Level 0. Consumption				
Level 1. Satisfaction				
Level 2. Skills gain				
Level 3. Application				
Level 4. Impact				
Level 5. ROI				

Table 25-2 shows another way to look at your current state. Use it to identify gaps in the chain of evidence from consumption to impact for single programs, multiple programs, and all training content in your portfolio.

CHAPTER 25

Table 25-2. Current State: Chain of Evidence

Metric	One Program	Multiple Programs	All Training
Consumption (n and %)			
Satisfaction (average rating; % favorable)			
Intent to apply (%)			
Skill gain (% before and after)			
Application (% who have applied)			
Observed impact (% who have observed impact)			
Actual impact (increase in business outcomes)			

These frameworks can help you identify specific goals, such as

- Increasing automation of data for Level 1
- Increasing filters in your reporting dashboards to select subsets of programs and employees
- Adding an automated survey to measure application and observed impact
- Aggregating data from multiple impact or ROI studies

You might also have more general goals, such as adding measurement resources to your team, increasing the amount of funding for measurement, integrating sources of data, standardizing reporting, or including more data in discussions and presentations about training.

To determine whether existing buy-in for training measurement and evaluation is high or low, look at your stakeholder's behavior. Table 25-3 shows some stakeholder behaviors and what they may indicate about the level of buy-in (low to high) you have.

Table 25-3. Assessing Level of Buy-In

Indicators of Stakeholder Buy-In	Level of Buy-In		
	Low	Moderate	High
They actively discourage it.	X		
They don't prevent it but are indifferent.	X		
They appreciate data when you share it even if they have not asked for it.		X	
They expect data and ask for it.			X
They use your data and insights in their own communications.			X
They respond positively when you suggest additional measurement activities.			X
They approve funding for measurement resources and infrastructure.			X

You want to move your stakeholders up the buy-in levels to gain implicit and explicit support for your goals.

Increasing Buy-In

You can use principles from the psychology of selling to get stakeholders to expect, appreciate, use, and approve more measurement and evaluation practices (Hoffeld 2016). You must understand their values, needs, expectations, and emotions so you can connect the benefits of measurement back to those values and needs.

How you apply these principles depends on your starting point and goals. You can use a stakeholder's questions and requests for data to highlight gaps in your measurement activities and get support to do more. You could also proactively integrate measurement into your team, processes, systems, and projects without explicitly asking for permission; for example:

- Appointing a measurement lead on your team
- Making measurement part of your end-to-end training process
- Allocating a portion of all development project budgets for measurement
- Turning on all the functionality you have for data collection and automation in your learning management system
- Creating templates for reporting and populating them with data (you might do this manually at first)
- Designing a dashboard of key metrics with filters

Instead of explaining the value of measurement, demonstrate it by bringing data to discussions and getting your stakeholders to want more.

Let's take a look at some sample conversations that illustrate how to increase stakeholder buy-in from different starting points.

Sample Conversation 1: From Consumption to Buy-In for Application

Learning: As you know, we are about to launch our new curations of learning content on generative AI. What would you like to know about its impact?

Business: We really need to get people skilled in AI. It will be important to track consumption and use it in communications to build momentum. I'd like to know what courses are most popular and most highly rated.

Learning: Would you like to know how people are using their new knowledge on the job?

Business: Yes, but how would you do that?

Learning: We could do a survey or interview a sample of employees.

Business: Let's not overengineer it. Interviews sound easier.

Learning: Actually, interviews are more work, especially the analysis! I've been wanting to set up a short survey in our LMS that we could use to check the application of any of our training programs. The survey would ask if they applied it. If they said no, they'd be asked, why not? If they said yes, they'd be asked if they were seeing an impact and to share an example. We would be able to give you the percentage of people who applied the knowledge, the percentage who observed impact, the top three barriers to application, and some sample impact cases.

Business: I like that. It would be a more complete success story than just reporting consumption.

Learning: Can you approve the survey set up as a priority project?

Business: Yes, go ahead.

Learning: Thank you. I'll send you consumption updates weekly and come back with first application results in a few months.

Sample Conversation 2: From One Impact Study to Buy-In for More

Learning: I want to share with you the results of a study we did on the impact of the technical certification program we launched last year. The results are great; you might be able to use them in your upcoming presentation to the board.

Business: I didn't know we did those kinds of studies. I'm always looking for good data to show that our business strategies are working.

Learning: Well, we allocated some of the certification program budget to measurement, so we hired a consultant to help us design the study and our HR analytics team did the analysis. If you like the results, we can do more.

Business: I've always wondered if we could look at the impact of our training programs on metrics like retention.

Learning: As you know, the certification uptake has been very high—50 percent of our technicians now have at least one. With such a critical mass, we had a big enough sample to reliably compare the retention of people with at least one certification to retention of those with no certifications. We found that retention was 4 percentage points higher for technicians with certifications. That is saving us hundreds of thousands in hiring costs.

Business: This is great information. Can you create a slide that describes the program, along with the consumption and retention numbers, and send it to Chris, who is putting together the board presentation? Can you also provide the skills gap data and show how it has been reduced since we launched the training programs? It would also be helpful if you could calculate how much we saved last year with that 4 percentage point increase in retention.

Learning: Yes. Would you also support allocating additional funding in next year's training budget for more of these kinds of studies?

Business: Yes, definitely.

Sample Conversation 3: From Satisfaction to Buy-In for Correlational Impact Study

Business: It's great to see so many of our leaders participating in the new leadership program and rating it highly. Let's mention that in our next town hall and maybe get a couple of participants to talk about it.

Learning: What else would you like to know about the impact of the program?

Business: I'd love to know if it is changing how our leaders are interacting with their teams and if we're seeing improvement in their teams' engagement scores.

Learning: We could study that in a couple ways. We could compare the engagement scores of the teams of participants with those of teams of nonparticipants before and after the program. Or we could correlate consumption patterns across the company with engagement scores.

Business: I like both! Which would be faster?

Learning: In either case, we need to wait for next year's engagement scores. It will take more effort to set up the samples for the controlled study, but it will be more conclusive.

Business: I don't think we need scientific precision, just some indication that the training is making a difference.

Learning: OK. Let's do the correlational study. I'll need to get our data analytics team involved. Do I have your support to make this a priority?

Business: Yes, go ahead.

CHAPTER 25

Sample Conversation 4: From Question to Buy-In for Controlled Impact Study

Business: I know we moved a lot of our training content to virtual platforms during the COVID-19 pandemic, but I think we need to go back to in-person classes. People learn better when they are together in person.

Learning: Actually, current research suggests that the delivery medium doesn't matter as long as the content is well designed.

Business: I think it is different in this organization. I've heard from many people that they want to go back to live classes.

Learning: We've collected a lot of data for both the in-person and virtual versions of our basic sales training program. We can do a comparison and see whether the delivery medium affects program success. I'll need to allocate some funding for a consultant to help us.

Business: Yes, go ahead. This is an important decision and we need internal data.

Three months later

Learning: Last time we met, I said that I would compare the data from the in-person and virtual versions of our basic sales training program to help determine whether to return to in-person training. My analysis found similar satisfaction levels and test scores between the two—in fact, satisfaction was higher for the virtual version. And it was less expensive.

Business: That's interesting. Do we know if the impact on sales was the same?

Learning: No, but satisfaction generally predicts impact. We'd have to do a study comparing the sales pipelines and actual revenue of people who took the training program with those who didn't for one or both versions.

Business: Let's do it.

Learning: We have run out of funds. Can we charge it to one of your budget codes?

Business: Yes. Talk to Lee in my finance team to get a code.

Sample Conversation 5: From Question to Buy-In for Automation

Email from CEO's office: We need data for our quarterly internal business report. In addition, we will be monitoring functional metrics quarterly going forward.

Can you start providing the data you're gathering annually on a quarterly basis instead? We want to monitor hours of training to make sure we maintain at least the same per person hours as last year. We also want to be able to see data by rank and geography.

Learning: It is a lot of work to pull that data together for the annual report. If we start doing it quarterly, we should set up a more automated process to generate the data.

CEO's office: Yes, we are going to need even more data for new external reporting requirements. Our competitors are going beyond what is asked and including data on the value of their training. We need to expand what we put in the annual report and show that we are ahead.

Learning: I'll need to dedicate at least one person to this activity and have them work with the IT and analytics teams to plan and generate the data we'll need on a regular basis.

CEO's office: Yes, there is a business case for another person on your team. Share this email with the talent function budget team, and it will be approved.

Sample Conversation 6: From Gap to Buy-In

Business: We need to review our strategy for external awards. Our organization is in the top 10 for brand and a great place to work. We also have a great learning culture and function. Are there any awards we could win to validate this?

Learning: Yes, there are a number of awards available. However, we have reviewed the criteria and they require a lot of data demonstrating the impact of training. They also want to see a mature and sustainable measurement approach. Frankly, we don't currently have the resources to go beyond very basic measurement.

Business: What do you need to get us ready to apply for awards?

Learning: I need a couple people dedicated to measurement who can work with IT and analytics to improve our infrastructure and conduct some studies of our flagship programs.

Business: Can you put together a proposal for what you need and a timeline for when we can apply for the awards?

Learning: Yes. I will also document what we already have because we won't be starting from scratch.

CHAPTER 25

Beyond Buy-In

You want to get to a place where measurement and evaluation of training is expected and embedded in the culture and where stakeholders trust your decisions about what and how to measure. Imagine a day when any data you want is at your fingertips, and you have the team to continuously improve systems, dashboards, and reports, as well as design and execute sophisticated studies. A day when every meeting with a stakeholder starts with data and you can answer any question by mining and using existing data and results.

You will reach a point where you have done so many impact and ROI studies that you can refer to the results of past studies as evidence that any new training solution will be effective because it is aligned to skill needs and follows the same principles of instructional design.

You know you have gone beyond buy-in when business leaders use and reuse your data in their presentations without even asking or telling you. You will be surprised and gratified when you see content in a presentation or communication by your CEO or other business leader that features training data and insight. It is the ultimate validation that your efforts to get buy-in for each step on the way to comprehensive sustainable measurement paid off. The next conversation illustrates that point where you have earned your stakeholders' trust.

Sample Conversation 7: From Consumption and ROI to Trust

Learning: We are seeing incredible consumption of the new external content library for which we now have an enterprise license. We are integrating the content into our learning paths for different roles and skills, and people are also searching the catalog and taking courses in areas of personal interest to them.

Business: Is this decreasing the amount of training we need to build ourselves?

Learning: Yes. We are getting the general content from the external library and focusing what we build on examples and practice in the context of our business. With the same budget and resources, we are increasing the quality and impact of our training.

Business: Can we quantify the impact and compare it to the additional cost of the content license?

Learning: Yes. Even without doing any calculations, I can tell that the return on investment is significant. Do you want us to put a team together to do a full analysis. We did a similar study last year on the impact and ROI of adding a simulation platform.

Business: No. I remember that study, and I don't think we need that level of analysis for this investment. I trust you!

> **Practitioner's Tip**
>
> Give your stakeholders data and insights that make them look good. When deciding what to share with stakeholders, think of your audience as your stakeholders' stakeholders, and then, take whatever data you have and turn it into a headline; for example, "Learning hours per person increased by 10 percent this year," or "The new sales training program increased the sales pipeline by 50 percent," or "The number of internal candidates with AI skills who could fill new roles in manufacturing doubled six months after new training program launched."

Summary

This chapter described how to increase stakeholder buy-in for training measurement and evaluation by starting where you are and applying the principles of selling to get buy-in for more. You should proactively do as much as you can without explicit buy-in and use the results to demonstrate the value or measurement. By demonstrating what's possible, you can convince them to want and approve more.

Knowledge Check

Take a minute to reflect on these questions:

1. How would you like to improve your training measurement and evaluation?
2. What can you do proactively to achieve that goal?
3. What existing data can you bring to stakeholders to get their buy-in for more?

CHAPTER 26

Developing and Using Professional Standards for Evaluation

MICHAEL A. LAWSON

IN THIS CHAPTER

This chapter examines how professional standards can guide the daily work of evaluators and talent development professionals. After reading it, you will be able to:

- Explain why standards matter for evaluation practice.
- Apply the ROI Methodology as a framework for culturally responsive, standards-driven evaluations.
- Adopt a set of guiding principles to govern your work in measuring and evaluating training programs.

Why Standards Matter in Evaluation Work

Professional standards exist for many job roles in today's workplace—from the American Bar Association's Model Rules of Professional Conduct for lawyers to the Project Management Institute's Foundational Standards for those responsible for project management. This chapter focuses on the use and importance of standards in evaluation practice with implications for changing evaluator responsibilities, tasks, and roles. Standards are vital to the credibility, viability, and sustainability of any profession. They are especially important for professional evaluators because—unlike other professions that serve specific people, sectors, or interests—evaluation is central to nearly every business, organization, community, and social policy (Phillips et al. 2019). Indeed, because evaluation has become a universal profession that touches just about everyone, it now represents a primary mechanism from which society can better understand the efficacy, effectiveness, and efficiency of its policies and practices as well as the problems they are designed to solve (Patton 2016).

For this reason, an evaluator's commitment and capacity to uphold professional standards enhances the likelihood that others will also engage in quality work. Standards therefore represent the evaluator's efforts to fulfill their professional and ethical obligations to the industry as well as the diverse audiences and interests affected by the work.

The work of professional evaluators is always challenging because, to do the job effectively, evaluators have to recognize and then attend to the ways in which their work influences different people and populations (Askew, Beverly, and Jay 2012). For example, most project-oriented work in the private sector typically involves or implicates at least four different interest groups (Phillips et al. 2019):

1. The people or teams who are developing the project, product, or innovation
2. The leadership or organization charged with supervising or resourcing the team or effort
3. The board of directors or investors in the project, product, or innovation
4. The intended user or consumer of the project or product

In the public sector, these audiences can become even more diverse and complex. For instance, evaluating a typical grant-funded project in the social and health services field typically invites the participation of (Patton 1998):

- The designers and directors of the program
- Their staff
- The host organization and its board of directors
- The funder and its board of directors
- Policy makers (who could be federal, state, or local)
- Community partners
- The targeted users or recipients of the funded project, program, or service

Regardless of the context, each audience or stakeholder group typically has their own unique interests and agendas. In turn, those agendas can significantly influence the actions, orientations, and expectations of evaluators (Patton 2016). For example:

- Funders and boards of directors typically direct their questions about evaluation to issues of program effectiveness and cost.
- Project staff and leadership often want evaluators to focus on issues of project effectiveness as well as feasibility and efficiency of program products or services.
- Consumers and users of targeted projects typically want evaluations to focus on and demonstrate project or product effectiveness, accessibility, and usability.
- Policy makers and private investors typically want evaluators to focus on and document issues of project or program effectiveness and cost. When possible and relevant, they'll also want to understand replicability and scalability (Bryk et al. 2014; Phillips et al. 1999).

Moreover, because these audiences and interests have different levels of influence, it can be quite tempting to shape the scope of an evaluation to fit the interests, questions, or priorities of a particular audience, perhaps at the expense of others (Patton 2016).

Practitioner's Tip

Professional standards can provide evaluators with a set of guideposts and guardrails for practice that help them better recognize, attend to, and honor the diversity of stakeholders and constituencies affected by the work.

Supporting the Increasing Complexity of the Evaluator Role

Beyond professional and ethical imperatives, evaluation standards are important for other important reasons. One of them is to help evaluators responsibly attend to and respond to rapid changes to the field, society, and the world of work. For example, program evaluation was once largely a technical enterprise in which evaluators typically kept their clients at arm's length (Weiss 1995). The impartial evaluator's role was to serve as an independent agent and help organizations verify their compliance to organizational or regulatory policies while providing an impartial analysis of program or product effectiveness (Phillips and Phillips 2014).

CHAPTER 26

The Technical and Linear Approach

In the compliance-oriented evaluation model and role, the evaluator's work was typically linear and sequential. The first task was to help stakeholders document the connection between project resources (or input) and services (outputs; Weiss 1995). Once the relationships between project input and outputs were established and verified, program evaluators would shift their focus to analyzing implementation fidelity (Patton 1998). This formative or process-oriented evaluation paved the way for a more rigorous evaluation of the service, project, or product's effectiveness and outcomes (Patton 2016).

Importantly, this technical and linear approach to program evaluation was typically guided by a conceptual tool called a logic model (Phillips et al. 2019; Weiss 1995). Beyond just a technical exercise, logic models have long represented a prized tool of program evaluators because, when designed effectively, they help organizations, project managers, and staff better understand the theories of action that guide the development, delivery, use, and dissemination of products and services (Argyris and Shon 1996). This effort to highlight the assumptions and theories of daily work helped organizations better align their resources with products and services; they also helped organizational leaders forge tighter connections between product services and outcomes (Phillips et al. 2019). For this reason, the technical-linear approach to program evaluation is useful for helping organizations become more accountable for results by enhancing coherence and alignment between stated work processes and goals (Phillips et al. 2014).

Adapting to a Changing World

Of course, the world of work continues to change dramatically, and with that, so does our understanding of work and society. Two developments have been especially important for evaluators—the rise of the internet and the increasing need for organizations to operate efficiently and effectively.

The first development relates to the internet and its role in knowledge generation and dissemination. Depending on the field, the knowledge of what works or what can work for programs and evaluations may already be available for public consumption. When what works is already known, the focus of evaluators and organizational leaders can shift away from basic questions related to "What should I do?" and "How should I do it?" to deeper questions involving how to best transfer and adapt a service, product, or technology from one organizational or community context to another (Bryk 2015). This profound shift in focus has invited, and at times required, evaluators to extend beyond a narrow focus on accountability and compliance to include collaborative work with organizations around complex issues of problem identification, organizational (and community) capacity building, product and services innovation, integration, adaptability, and adaptation, and later, enhanced efficiency (Bryk et al. 2015).

For example, evaluators are now tasked with helping organizations in the private and public sectors tackle adaptive challenges and wicked problems. *Adaptive challenges* are evident when an arising issue, condition, or circumstance exceeds an organization's expertise and know-how about how to fix it (Heifetz et al. 2015). *Wicked problems*—like climate change, global warming, homelessness, and childhood poverty—occur because of the complexity involved in addressing, changing, and monitoring multiple moving parts at the same time. This is especially evident when the work requires collaboration between and among different organizations and service sectors to design solutions that best fit the problem or challenge facing the organization and build the capacity needed to perform each function at the same time (Phillips, Phillips, and Ray 2015).

Evaluators as Agents of Co-Design

The second development for evaluators in the context of the rapidly changing landscape of society and work is that organizations across public and private sectors now must consistently and robustly engage in efforts to improve the efficiency and effectiveness of their work (Phillips and Phillips 2022). Some of these efforts may be internal, such as efforts to improve hiring and screening practices in support of worker retention and organizational productivity (Phillips and Phillips 2019). But most organizational work remains directed toward external constituencies by way of developing new products and services. Examples include the development and design of new technologies that support consumer engagement and satisfaction, as well as the development and delivery of improved practices that support individual, family, or community health and well-being (Bryson, Crosby, and Stone 2015).

Regardless of their intended audience or use, developing and delivering new products, services, and innovations requires most organizations to engage in a complex, problem-solving methodology known as *design thinking*, which typically begins by engaging the people who are closest to the problem (the users) in dialogues about how to solve it (Lewis 2014, Lawson and Alameda-Lawson 2012). Once these users help identify the problem or opportunity, program designers engage in an iterative process of ideation (challenging assumptions and creating ideas), prototyping (creating solutions), testing (implementing and evaluating), and scaling their innovations to different users (Langley et al. 2009). This process frames the design ethos of developing products and services that are user-centered and problem specific (Bryk et al. 2015).

Design thinking has now permeated the evaluation field (Phillips and Phillips 2022). As it expands in reach, design thinking brings significant implications for evaluators and their professional responsibilities and roles, including the need for evaluators to engage consistently and relationally with the product or service's users. This deep engagement can be challenging because, depending on the context, the targeted users of a newly designed product or service may be socially, psychologically, medically, or economically vulnerable, and may come from social, economic, or cultural backgrounds that are qualitatively different from the evaluator (Askew et al. 2012; Patton 2016).

> **Practitioner's Tip**
>
> Regardless of profile or background, the engagement of diverse stakeholders in design thinking requires evaluators to develop considerable knowledge of diverse people, community contexts, and cultures, as well as the skills to engage them in culturally responsive ways.

Another implication of design thinking centers on how it changes the evaluator's role relative to the program, project, or product they are evaluating. As already discussed, evaluators in the past were typically positioned as agents who were external to the program, product, or service they were evaluating (Weiss 1995). Today, however, the boundaries between project management and evaluation are often far less clear, and this ambiguity mounts when evaluators are asked to take lead roles in engaging users and clients, conducting organizational needs assessments and root cause analyses, facilitating the ideation of new products and innovations relative to stakeholders' identified needs and concerns, and identifying processes and needs for testing and organizational capacity when building support (Patton 2016; Phillips and Phillips 2022).

To perform these complex roles and functions effectively, evaluators and organizational leaders need guideposts, road maps, and clear boundaries for undertaking these tasks. This is why professional evaluation standards are increasingly paramount to the work of today's evaluator.

What Are the Different Evaluation Standards?

Evaluation involves people and organizations across different sectors, which means that there are several different evaluation standards available. In the interest of summary, most of them were developed by large umbrella organizations and professional associations (UN Evaluation Group 2016; Joint Committee on Standards for Educational Evaluation 2011; American Evaluation Association 2019). These standards are offered in service of the evaluator's social, moral, and professional obligation to pursue quality work and avoid causing harm.

Domains of Standards

Although each organization or association labels its standards differently, they all have several common elements. Most professional associations organize their evaluation standards into discrete domains that address the different issues, responsibilities, and requirements of professional program evaluations. For example, the Joint Committee for Standards for Evaluation (JCSE) standards are anchored within five domains of evaluation work (Yarborough et al. 2011):

- Utility standards (evaluator credibility and stakeholder responsiveness)
- Feasibility standards (contextual viability and project management)
- Propriety standards (clarity, fairness, and conflicts of interest)
- Accuracy standards (validity and reliability)
- Accountability standards (standards for documentation)

The American Evaluation Association's 49 standards are anchored within five domains (AEA 2019):

- **Professional practice** aims at enhancing the quality and uniqueness of the evaluator's role. This domain includes nine standards that emphasize professional ethics, professional development, and the need for evaluators to respond appropriately and responsively to cultural and organizational diversity.
- **Methodology** covers the technical aspects of an evaluation's systematic, evidence-based inquiry. Similar to the accuracy standards published by JCSE, this domain includes 14 standards that champions needs for rigorous and purposeful evaluation design, data collection and analysis, and dissemination strategies.

- **Context** offers detailed guidance on the values and principles not covered in the professional practice domain. Its eight standards emphasize the evaluator's need to engage a diverse range of users throughout the evaluation process, facilitate a shared understanding of the program and its evaluation with diverse stakeholders, and clarify diverse stakeholder interests, perspectives, and assumptions.
- **Planning and management** helps evaluators better manage the complexity of evaluation work. The 10 standards under this domain emphasize the importance of developing an evaluation plan that is feasible and resourced, addresses organizational culture appropriately, and engages stakeholders collaboratively in the development and design of evaluation work.
- **Interpersonal centers** on the relational aspects of the evaluation role, focusing on the social interactions that ground professional practices. The eight standards under this domain emphasize the importance of evaluator efforts to engage in shared decision making, trust building, and culturally responsive interactions.

Limitations for Practice and Action

AEA's 49 evaluation standards provide important guideposts for effective evaluation practices as well as a culturally responsive service, product, project, and organizational design. These standards are important because they reveal the values that undergird evaluation as a profession while also addressing the endemic complexity of evaluative work.

The issue or challenge surrounding evaluation standards, then, is not the standards themselves, nor the values they reflect. Rather, there appears to be a missing translational link that can help bridge the gap between professional values, standards, and ethics and the design, development, and delivery of evaluation best practices. Without such an explicit link or framework, evaluation standards may become disconnected from the complex choices evaluators need to make in terms of who they should engage with, in what way, at what time, and for what purpose or end.

Indeed, given the increased complexity of their role, evaluators need a value-oriented framework that integrates professional standards, ethics, evaluation design, methodology, and stakeholder engagement into a single coherent and actionable model. It would provide a detailed picture of what evaluators should strive to achieve through their work (that is, the standards) as well as how to realize those standards and values through effective evaluation practice.

The rest of this chapter explores how ROI Institute's ROI Methodology provides this type of framework for evaluation.

ROI Methodology: A Framework for Culturally Responsive and Standards-Driven Evaluations

The ROI Methodology framework fits the complex roles faced by today's evaluators. As noted earlier, evaluation has gradually changed from a distanced technical, linear, and compliance-oriented enterprise to a participatory one that emphasizes assessment and problem identification; product, program, and service development and improvement; and organizational design and capacity building (Grunow 2015; Phillips et al. 2022). Moreover, increasing public demand for transparency and fiscal accountability further requires evaluators to deepen their understanding and use of models and strategies for determining program and product effectiveness and efficiency (Phillips et al. 2019). The ROI Methodology helps evaluators meaningfully attend to these important and complex priorities.

Integrating Steps and Standards

The ROI Methodology follows 12 steps anchored in firm value commitments for how evaluators should pursue their work. Each step emphasizes a different aspect for making the evaluation responsive to its users and product or program developers. Thus, it's possible to view the ROI Methodology as a domain-level standard for what evaluations should achieve while also providing a clear and actionable sequence for achieving that standard (Phillips et al. 2014). This marriage of standards and method is an important and unique strength of the ROI Methodology.

ROI Methodology Step 1

Step 1 in the ROI Methodology (align programs with the business) focuses on the importance of making the work problem-specific and user-centered (Bryk et al. 2015). This starts when evaluators work with organizational stakeholders to define whether the focus of the work is to solve a problem or capitalize on an important opportunity (Phillips et al. 2019). Once the purpose is clarified, the evaluator works with diverse stakeholder groups to align the targeted evaluation goals with related impact measures. This effort effectively aligns services with outcomes and provides a guardrail against "solutionitis"—a condition whereby products, services, and programs are not aligned with the problems they're intended to solve (Lewis 2014). Nearly all of the standards in AEA's context domain are addressed by this initial step of the ROI Methodology.

ROI Methodology Step 2

Feasibility presents a long-standing challenge and boundary-setting exercise for evaluators and evaluation teams. Because evaluators are often asked to wear multiple hats and fulfill multiple roles simultaneously, it is easy to formulate evaluation plans without having adequate resources to achieve the project's goals (Phillips et al. 2019). It is also common for evaluators to agree on the scope of an evaluation only to learn about the organization's longstanding history of pursuing projects that outstrip existing capacity and resources (Askew et al. 2012).

Step 2 in the ROI Methodology (select the right solution) underscores the need and responsibility to develop solutions and evaluation plans that fit the problem to be solved, while also staying aligned with available resources (Phillips and Phillips 2022). This second step is important because it emphasizes the ethical imperative for evaluators to help organizations position themselves for success by way of detailed planning. In this way, evaluators can meaningfully realize the standards that fall under AEA's planning and management domain.

ROI Methodology Step 3

Step 3 in the ROI Methodology (design for results) emphasizes the need to engage stakeholders in the development and identification of success measures. Evaluators begin designing for results by engaging service or product users as they identify what project success looks like (Phillips et al. 2019). This emphasis on user engagement is important because it is a key strategy for increasing the likelihood that evaluations will be culturally responsive for diverse groups (Yarbrough et al. 2011).

Evaluators also design for results by stating up-front which methods they'll use and specifying in detail what project staff will do to make the program effective (Phillips et al. 2019). This effort to help organizations better specify their intended roles and desired processes enables evaluators to adopt a uniquely responsive and participatory approach to ensure implementation fidelity (Askew et al. 2012).

The final way evaluators design for results is by engaging in a collaborative planning process with the host organization. Here, the evaluator works with project stakeholders to develop a feasible plan for collecting data around issues of program fidelity and implementation, while also creating a plan for evaluating and analyzing the ROI (Phillips et al. 2019).

The third step of the ROI Methodology addresses several of the standards related to AEA's context domain and nearly all of the methodology domain's standards.

ROI Methodology Steps 4 and 5

Steps 4 and 5 of the ROI Methodology (design for input, reaction, and learning; design for application and impact) are firmly anchored in the process of design thinking, specifically in ideation, prototyping, and testing (Phillips and Phillips 2018). These two steps position the evaluator as a facilitator of stakeholder engagement and organizational learning and development. The latter emphasis is critical because many projects, especially those focused on design, do not initially proceed as planned (Lewis 2015). Organizations and design teams need to be able to access the information and strategies that will help them adapt and quickly respond to unanticipated challenges, opportunities, and product deficiencies (Bryk et al. 2015).

These two steps are important because they provide a process for creating meaningful feedback loops between product development, design, and user preferences and needs. By pursuing and integrating these steps and opportunities, evaluators can successfully foster the development of learning organizations. This allows ROI evaluators to attend to nearly every standard in AEA's interpersonal domain.

ROI Methodology Steps 6 Through 10

Steps 6 through 10 in the ROI Methodology (isolate the effects of the program; convert data to monetary value; identify intangible measures; capture program costs; and calculate ROI) focus on data analysis and outcome evaluation. Credible outcomes studies are critical (Patton 2016). As a general rule, they are considered credible when they are devoid of error and provide confidence that the relationship between the service or product and outcome is valid (Yarborough et al. 2011).

There are two primary threats to the credibility of any evaluation:
- **The first threat occurs if an evaluation yields a positive result when it shouldn't have.** These type 1 errors (or false positives) lead to suboptimal results. For example, ineffective or inefficient services and products may be allowed to continue if the host organization thinks that they are working as planned

when, in fact, they are not. In turn, continuing to use suboptimal practices can cause additional harm to the organization and its stakeholder groups by slowing or impeding the development of alternative solutions, which would have been pursued if the evaluation was credible.
- **The second threat occurs when an outcome evaluation yields a false negative**—incorrectly labeling a program, product, or service as ineffective, when a credible evaluation would have yielded a positive result. Thus, type 2 errors deprive users of services and resources that could have improved their lives and limit the organizational improvement that might have followed a positive result (Bryk et al. 2015; Patton 2016).

The five interrelated steps of ROI data analysis detail a rigorous and pragmatic process for helping evaluators design outcomes studies that are credible and devoid of type 1 and 2 errors.

ROI as an Antidote for Type 1 Errors

The primary way the ROI Methodology helps evaluators avoid false positives is by reducing *attribution error*, which occurs when evaluators misrepresent the impact of the service or product on its intended outcomes target (Phillips et al. 2019; Patton 2016). The ROI process helps evaluators reduce the probability of attribution error in three primary ways:
- It provides multiple, rigorous, and theoretically sound measures for converting outcomes to monetary value (Phillips and Phillips 2022).
- It offers a rigorous template for identifying and calculating the full cost of product development and service delivery, thus avoiding the pitfalls of underestimating cost and overestimating value (Buzachero et al. 2013).
- It provides a process for using stakeholder judgments as a means of adjusting down the benefits calculation for a product or program (Phillips and Phillips 2018). This downward estimation strategy ensures that ROI outcomes studies reflect conservative estimates of program effect, which, in turn, minimizes Type 1 errors.

ROI as an Antidote for Type 2 Errors

Steps 8 and 10 of the ROI Methodology—identifying intangibles and calculating the ROI—help minimize the chance that ROI evaluations will yield false negatives. Intangible outcome measures reflect program success but are not measured by money or cost; they are especially critical for programs that promise to yield long-term cost savings but struggle to do so in the short term (Phillips and Phillips 2022; APA Task Force 2008).

Consider a state-funded literacy program for elementary school students, which has a long-term goal of reducing school dropout rates and the costs associated with lost economic productivity and reliance on social services (Stroh 2014). In the short term, this program may yield strong gains in reading scores, but a negative ROI due to increased investment in instruction. Including intangibles in an outcomes study for this program can serve as a critical safeguard against type 2 errors, even among programs that are funded ultimately to produce cost savings.

There are other ways that ROI can promote evaluation credibility and avoid false negatives. Consider a recent evaluation of a substance use prevention program that provided screening and early intervention services around substance use and mental health issues to patients in primary care settings. This effort was offered in service of the goal of reducing problematic behaviors related to alcohol and substance use. The outcome evaluation that focused on intangibles could not demonstrate a significant association between program participation and significant reductions in alcohol or substance use. However, a cost analysis revealed that the program was able to significantly increase patient use of mental health services without adding any appreciable cost to the hospital's overall operations (English et al. 2023). Thus, using ROI, even when the program is cost neutral, can provide important, credible evidence of program impact while avoiding the pitfalls posed by false negatives.

Steps 6 through 10 in the ROI Methodology provide clear measures and steps for reducing error in outcomes evaluations and provide a meaningful and robust methodology for attending to the standards in AEA's accuracy domain.

ROI Methodology Steps 11 and 12

Steps 11 and 12 are the final two steps of the ROI Methodology (communicate results to stakeholders; use black box thinking). These steps center on stakeholder engagement around two areas of focus:

- Communicating project results through storytelling
- Helping stakeholders identify the necessary resources for further product development and scaling

These activities are facilitated and anchored by the findings and lessons learned from the first 10 steps of the ROI Methodology (Phillips et al. 2019). When combined, these steps provide evaluators with a process for meeting five of the seven standards in AEA's propriety domain.

CHAPTER 26

Guiding Principles

Since the ROI Methodology was first published more than 40 years ago, additional standards have been implemented based on three specific issues:

- **To conserve resources whenever possible.** The backdrop for the standards is that the time, money, and other resources devoted to evaluation are usually limited and constrained.
- **To improve the reliability and validity of the process.** If all of the data collected for an ROI evaluation (including reaction, learning, application, impact, ROI, and intangibles) is shared with different evaluators, the results should yield the same or similar ROI calculations. If not, the process is not reliable. This requires standardizing some decisions and assumptions about the process to increase the likelihood of reliability. If the evaluation system is not reliable, it's not valid.
- **To increase the credibility of the results and achieve buy-in from key stakeholders.** Being credible and conservative with the assumptions and rules will enable buy-in from sponsors, supporters, funders, and donors. Without their buy-in, it's all a waste of time.

With this in mind, new operational standards—which ROI Institute refers to as guiding principles—are continuously proposed and voted on by different groups, including users. Throughout its 30-year history, ROI Institute has used a special process to add these new standards. First, the internal ROI Institute team must approve the standard. Then, ROI Institute's global partners (representing more than 70 countries) must approve it. Third, and most important, the new standard has to be approved by 75 percent of the users.

Let's look at the current list of guiding principles and the rationale for each.

1. When Conducting a Higher-Level Evaluation, Collect Data at Lower Levels

This guiding principle ensures that all stakeholders understand how the results are developed and delivered. Key stakeholders, particularly those who sponsor, support, or fund the program or project, may be tempted to just look for the impact and ROI. In the ROI Methodology, however, evaluators present all levels of data to show the logical flow of the data. When results are delivered as expected, this shows how they were achieved. If the results are disappointing, the cause is usually visible at the lower levels. Some executives won't want to see all the data, so it's best to make the presentation very brief but still remind the audience how the success was achieved (or not).

2. When Planning a Higher-Level Evaluation, the Previous Level of Evaluation Doesn't Need to Be Comprehensive

This guiding principle could be controversial, but it builds on the issue of limited resources. The focus remains on the highest level of evaluation measured along the logic value chain. For example, if the evaluation stops at Level 4, the Level 3 evaluation doesn't have to be comprehensive. However, the evaluation will still need to provide evidence that the process was used properly. Here, an evaluator might take shortcuts and use self assessment reporting for Level 3, for example, but they would still need to include all the steps to ensure that the data is credible, reliable, and unbiased. Note that a comprehensive evaluation can still be conducted throughout the process if resources are unlimited. But, if limitations require shortcuts, evaluators should make sure activities at lower levels are conducted and documented.

3. When Collecting and Analyzing Data, Use Only the Most Credible Sources

This guiding principle asks evaluators to reflect on every action they take to collect or analyze data. Is this data source the most credible source? Would other sources be more credible? This helps make the process more acceptable.

4. When Analyzing Data, Select the Most Conservative Alternative for Calculations

This guiding principle is in place to build acceptance and buy-in for the methodology. It's important to note that Guiding Principle 3 trumps Guiding Principle 4—evaluators should always use the most credible source or process in the analysis. However, if there are two credible data to input, choose the one that leads to a lower ROI calculation. (For example, if it is in the numerator of the calculation, take the lowest number. If it is a cost item in the denominator, use the highest number. Either option will lower the ROI.) This approach is useful for securing buy-in, particularly from those who fund, sponsor, or support programs or projects.

5. Use At Least One Method to Isolate the Effects of a Project

This guiding principle addresses the attribution issue, which is critical in today's environment. Failure to comply with this guidance decreases the credibility of the evaluation and most sponsors, donors, and funders demand it. While the ideal techniques are control groups, trend line analysis, and mathematical modeling, the default method of ensuring compliance and credibility is requesting estimates from the most credible source. When estimates are used, evaluators should follow Guiding Principle 7 to ensure they are acceptable.

6. If No Improvement Data Is Available, Assume That Little or No Improvement Has Occurred

This guiding principle is important because evaluators should not infer improvement or positive impact unless they have data to support that conclusion. Therefore, when participants don't respond to surveys, assume they answered with a zero. Samples are usually small and Level 4 impact data often has a high variance. The variance of the data determines the number of responses needed to be statistically significant and make an inference about the missing data. However, if the sample size isn't large enough, the data variance will be too high for you to make any assumptions about missing data. Incomplete or missing data hurts the evaluation, so if this is an issue, consider focusing on how to improve the data collection responses.

7. Adjust Estimates of Improvement for Potential Errors of Estimation

When an estimate is provided for a measure or value, the next request focuses on the error in that estimate: "What is the organization's and evaluator's confidence in that data?" Confidence is usually expressed on a scale of zero to 100 percent, where a 100 percent confidence is no error (usually not the case), a 90 percent confidence suggests 10 percent error, an 80 percent confidence means 20 percent error, and so on. The confidence adjustment reduces the amount of error in the data by multiplying the estimate by the confidence.

This guiding principle is in place to secure more buy-in with stakeholders, particularly those at the executive level who want to know that your evaluation is very credible.

8. Avoid Using Extreme Data Items and Unsupported Claims When Calculating ROI

This guiding principle points toward how to handle baseless claims. If someone (such as a survey respondent) claims results but doesn't explain how they were achieved, leave that data out of the analysis. Extreme data items should also be removed. This is a judgment call for the evaluators because there is no easy way to define what is extreme—it's not as simple as two standard deviations from the mean. It's a gesture. Extreme data items are taken out of the analysis for nearly every study. When the data removal is explained to stakeholders, it helps build credibility with the evaluation results.

9. Use Only the First Year of Annual Benefits in ROI Analysis of Short-Term Solutions

This guiding principle involves whether a program delivers short-term or long-term benefits. This issue is decided upfront as part of the evaluation planning by asking, "How long will the program realize benefits?" Once the timeframe is determined, it is agreed to by key stakeholders and sometimes even a financial officer.

If it is a short-term program that involves very few resources, calculating one year of benefits is likely accurate and enough to justify the program. If the program involves a heavy investment and will take a long time to see success, then it is a long-term program. In this case, the calculation would include one to five years of data, depending on the nature of the program.

10. Fully Load All Costs of a Solution, Project, or Program When Analyzing ROI

This guiding principle is straightforward and involves ensuring all the costs (direct and indirect) are included in the ROI calculation. Direct costs include items that are allocated, paid for, and often a clearly visible cost to the project. Indirect costs are less obvious (such as taking time away from work to be involved in the project or program) and may be prorated to the sample size. For example, if the solution requires the use of software that is purchased, and that software has more applications beyond the sample, then the cost is divided by the number of users for the life of the software to find the cost per user. That amount is then multiplied by the number of the sample size for the ROI calculation. This is an attempt to make sure that all the costs are covered.

11. Intangible Measures Are Purposely Not Converted to Monetary Values

The philosophy behind this guiding principle is simple: The evaluator wants to convert as much data as possible to monetary values. However, if an impact measure cannot be credibly converted to money within a reasonable amount of time and at a reasonable cost, it should be left as an intangible. The good news is that classic intangibles are often converted to money at the request of the executive team. Intangibles are important—they should be treated with respect and connected directly to the program. This is the credibility part of this standard.

12. Communicate the Results of ROI Methodology to All Key Stakeholders

Many different stakeholders are involved in a program evaluation, but four are always considered key:

- The sponsor, funder, or donor wants to see the value.
- The program participants who provide data about project success want to see what you do with that data.
- The participants' managers (in an organization) or spouse or parent (in a private program) make up another key stakeholder group.
- The team members in the function area where the evaluation is conducted want to understand these studies and the value of this process.

Determining which stakeholders will receive the program results is part of the planning process.

Summary

This chapter highlighted the importance of standards for today's evaluation enterprise due to the increasing responsibilities, scope, scale, and influence of evaluation and evaluators. As the field grows, the profession and its associations will need to provide better clarity about how to realize the values of the field, maximize its potential benefits, and clarify its boundaries. To accomplish these goals, evaluators need the tools, theories, and, by extension, methodologies that enable them to realize their values by way of best practice models and related exemplars.

The ROI Methodology provides an important foundation, framework, and set of tools and strategies for this purpose. By effectively using ROI, evaluators can strengthen their work with organizations to implement well, learn quickly, and improve the practices and products of tomorrow's work for society's gain.

Knowledge Check

Take a minute to reflect on these questions:

1. How are evaluation standards represented and how do they relate to best practices in evaluation?
2. What evaluation methods can be useful for helping evaluators realize evaluation standards in pursuit of best practices?

CHAPTER 27

Leveraging Artificial Intelligence

TRISH UHL

IN THIS CHAPTER

This chapter offers ideas for how to unlock the transformative potential of generative AI in reshaping how talent development professionals approach measurement and evaluation. After reading it, you will be able to:

- Leverage generative AI to enhance data analysis, create visualizations, and gain actionable insights.
- Apply AI-driven quantitative methods, such as paired t-tests, to assess training impact on knowledge acquisition and retention.
- Build your AI literacy skills using generative AI as an interactive tutor, with a focus on ethical use and deepening your understanding of statistical methods.

Leveraging Generative AI for Training Measurement and Evaluation

Generative AI has had and will continue to have a profound influence on learning measurement and evaluation. It's incumbent on all talent development professionals to understand how they can collaborate with AI to perform statistical analyses, interpret findings, and drive data-informed decisions. By embracing this AI-powered paradigm shift, you not only enhance the effectiveness of your learning initiatives but also position yourself as an evidence-based strategic partner in shaping the workforce of today and tomorrow.

Generative AI goes beyond automating text, images, and video content—it's a catalyst for innovation. According to the *2024 PwC Global CEO Survey*, 70 percent of CEOs expect generative AI to significantly change how their companies create, deliver, and capture value within the next three years. This shows that AI isn't just about increasing speed; it's about making smarter decisions and fundamentally reshaping business models. And as business models evolve, so too must the workforce.

However, as noted by experts like Marco Iansiti and Satya Nadella (2022) in *Harvard Business Review*, simply investing in AI technology isn't enough. Success depends on a workforce that can intelligently apply these tools. This presents a unique opportunity for talent development professionals to leverage generative AI in evaluating training effectiveness, ensuring that our efforts cultivate the essential skills needed in this new era. But this opportunity goes even further: To address the demands of the present, we must use AI not only to develop an intelligent workforce but also to ensure the workforce is equipped to effectively use AI.

The Measurement Challenge

Yet, as organizations strive to build these capabilities, they often encounter a significant challenge: measuring the impact of training initiatives. Even though we know how important it is to develop human capabilities, many organizations still find it hard to measure the true impact of their training programs.

According to the *2021 LinkedIn Workplace Learning Report*, the majority of impact measurements rely heavily on qualitative feedback, satisfaction scores, and engagement metrics. While these methods provide valuable insights into participant reactions and immediate engagement, they often fall short when it comes to quantifying the true impact of training on knowledge acquisition, behavior change, and performance improvement.

This gap between understanding and action highlights the need for a more robust, data-enabled approach to measurement and evaluation. Unfortunately, many talent development professionals are ill-equipped to implement this type of approach because they lack expertise in more rigorous disciplines such as data science and statistics.

The Measurement Solution

Generative AI offers a practical solution that enables talent development professionals to adopt a more defensible, data-enabled approach without needing advanced expertise in data science and statistics. By integrating AI into your measurement and evaluation practices, you can significantly enhance the precision of your assessments and make more informed decisions based on robust quantitative methods.

There are many different potential applications for generative AI in measurement and evaluation. This technology has remarkable superpowers for overcoming even long-standing measurement and evaluation obstacles and challenges. Let's review seven practical ways to integrate generative AI into measurement and evaluation practices.

1. Align Training Objectives With Business Needs

To ensure talent development initiatives deliver measurable results, it's vital to align training objectives with business needs (as covered in chapter 1). Generative AI can help by offering a starting point for strategies to make training more relevant and effective, which you can then tailor to your specific situation. This approach can help ensure your training is directly linked to crucial business outcomes, like compliance. For example, you can prompt AI with, "Our company needs to achieve a 100 percent compliance rate with new industry regulations by the end of the year. Suggest five ways our compliance training program could be aligned to ensure we meet this target."

2. Tailor Surveys to Specific Stakeholder Needs at Scale

Understanding and addressing the unique needs of different stakeholder groups is key to successful talent development. Generative AI can streamline this process by creating customized surveys to gather targeted insights from specific groups—efficiently and at scale.

For example, you might prompt AI with, "We're launching a new-manager training program aimed at improving team communication. Create a 10-question survey specifically for first-time managers to assess their communication challenges and identify the support they need most." Using this survey as a starting point, you can further refine the questions based on the objectives and the actual needs of your stakeholders.

3. Develop a Comprehensive Evaluation Plan

Measuring training effectiveness at multiple levels is crucial for understanding the true impact of your programs. Generative AI can simplify this process by helping you design a thorough evaluation plan that covers all key areas.

For example, you might prompt AI with, "We want to evaluate the effectiveness of our leadership development program over the next year. Design an evaluation plan that measures impact at the reaction, learning, behavior, and results levels, including how we can track leadership growth and team performance improvements six months after the program." You can then customize this AI-generated draft plan to your workplace, your business partners, and your program. This approach ensures you are implementing a robust evaluation that covers immediate reactions to long-term outcomes and provides a clear picture of the program's effectiveness.

4. Integrate Evaluation Throughout the Training Design Process

Embedding evaluation into every phase of the training design process is essential for continuously monitoring and improving effectiveness. Generative AI can help you seamlessly integrate evaluation mechanisms from start to finish.

For example, you might prompt AI with, "Our organization is rolling out a compliance training series. Suggest five ways to embed evaluation into each phase of the training program, from initial knowledge assessments to post-training audits, ensuring we can continuously monitor and improve compliance adherence." You may then need to adjust the AI-generated strategies to fit your program, but this approach can help ensure that evaluation is integrated into the training design process and provides ongoing insights and drives continuous improvement.

5. Ensure Ethical Review of Your Measurement and Evaluation Plan

Designing and conducting measurement and evaluation processes in an ethical, fair, and transparent manner is essential to maintaining trust and integrity. Generative AI can assist in reviewing and enhancing these processes to meet the highest ethical standards.

For instance, you might prompt AI with, "We are preparing to evaluate our manager development program. Review the proposed measurement and evaluation plan for ethical considerations, focusing on data privacy management, the fairness of assessment methods, and transparency in reporting. Provide recommendations to ensure it adheres to the highest ethical standards." This approach ensures that your evaluation processes are not only effective but also responsible and protect the integrity of your data and the rights of your participants.

6. Create Data Visualizations to Aid in Analysis

Generative AI can create visual tools—such as histograms and interactive dashboards—that simplify the interpretation of statistical data. By visualizing your data, you can quickly identify patterns and trends, leading to more accurate evaluations and better training outcomes.

For instance, you might prompt AI to "Create a visualization that illustrates the relationship between employee engagement, customer satisfaction, and revenue growth. Use the data provided to show how varying levels of employee engagement correlate with customer satisfaction scores and how both affect overall revenue. Include a line graph or scatter plot to depict these trends over time, along with labeled data points for each metric. Use different colors or markers to clearly distinguish between high, medium, and low levels of engagement and their corresponding effects on satisfaction and revenue. Aim to identify any patterns or trends that highlight the impact of employee engagement on business outcomes."

7. Distinguish Between Immediate Learning Outcomes and Long-Term Training Results

For a comprehensive evaluation of training effectiveness, it's essential to differentiate between short-term learning outcomes and long-term training impacts. Generative AI can assist in analyzing these distinct dimensions to provide a complete picture of your training program's success.

For instance, you might prompt AI with, "Our leadership development program aims to increase the number of internal promotions to senior roles. Suggest methods to analyze the short-term learning outcomes and the long-term impact on leadership effectiveness and promotion rates within the company over the next year." This approach ensures that your evaluation captures both the immediate benefits of training and its sustained effect on organizational performance.

Note: While other applications are mentioned briefly, this seventh use case is explored in-depth through a hands-on exercise later in the chapter. This exercise will guide you in using AI to analyze learning outcomes and evaluate training results, offering practical experience that complements the theory.

CHAPTER 27

Developing Essential AI Literacy And Decision-Making Skills

The power of generative AI extends far beyond its computational and analytical capabilities. When you engage with these AI systems—by providing data and context—a valuable learning experience unfolds. And you don't need to be an AI expert to start benefiting from its application in your day-to-day work. In fact, using AI presents an opportunity to immediately apply the key skills and attitudes that are becoming more important in today's digital landscape, including (AI Unplugged 2020):

- **Critical thinking.** Use your critical thinking skills to evaluate AI's performance. Identify any limitations or issues that arise during its use and troubleshoot accordingly. This ensures that AI is applied effectively and appropriately in your work.
- **Human and AI collaboration.** Work closely with AI tools to deepen your understanding of the analysis process. While AI can process data and generate insights, your judgment is crucial in validating these outputs and applying them in context.
- **Curiosity**. Approach AI with a mindset of curiosity. Explore its capabilities and limitations, ask questions, and seek to understand how to apply it to various aspects of your work. Curiosity drives continuous learning and helps you discover new ways to leverage AI.
- **Adaptability**. Be open to adapting your processes based on the insights and outputs provided by AI. As AI technologies evolve, maintain a flexible mindset to incorporate new capabilities and practices into your work.
- **Experimentation**. Don't be afraid to test different approaches when working with AI. Refine your prompts, explore various features, and experiment with how AI can assist in different tasks. This hands-on experimentation is key to mastering AI tools.
- **Responsible AI use.** Understanding the ethical implications and potential biases of AI is crucial. Cultivate the ability to identify and address biases, ensuring that your AI-supported decisions are fair, transparent, and align with ethical standards. This includes respecting data privacy and maintaining accountability in AI use.

By cultivating these skills and attitudes, you'll be better equipped to use AI effectively, making you a more informed and capable professional in the digital age.

Using AI Responsibly, Ethically, and Inclusively

As you incorporate AI into your work, it's essential to prioritize responsible and ethical practices. This involves not only adhering to ethical standards but also actively ensuring that your AI applications are fair, transparent, and inclusive. Here are key considerations to guide you:

- **Holistic risk assessment.** Consider the broader context in which AI is used. Assess potential risks and anticipate unintended consequences before incorporating AI into your processes. This holistic approach helps prevent issues and ensures that AI applications are safe and beneficial.
- **Ethical procurement and governance.** When selecting AI tools, ensure they align with your organization's ethical standards. Establish clear accountability for AI use and create an ongoing ethical review process to monitor AI's impact and performance.
- **Data privacy and security.** Protect participant data by implementing robust privacy measures. Ensure that data is collected, stored, and processed securely, and that participants are fully informed about how their data will be used.
- **Fairness, equity, and inclusion.** AI should promote fairness across all demographic groups. Strive to identify and minimize any biases in AI systems and ensure that the outputs from the tools you use are culturally sensitive and inclusive.
- **Transparency and explainability.** Use AI models that are interpretable and maintain clear documentation of your processes. This transparency allows others to understand and audit any AI-assisted decisions, building trust in your outcomes.
- **Human-centered AI integration.** Balance AI capabilities with human expertise, focusing on optimal outcomes. Use AI to enhance efficiency and accuracy, replacing human processes where beneficial, while ensuring the overall system serves human needs and values.
- **Continuous monitoring and improvement.** Regularly assess AI's performance and gather feedback from stakeholders. Be proactive in addressing any emerging ethical challenges, and continuously refine your AI systems to improve their effectiveness and fairness.

- **Regulatory compliance and responsible use.** Stay informed about relevant regulations governing AI use. Provide ethical AI training to users within your organization and foster a culture of responsibility in AI implementation.
- **Sustainable and responsible implementation.** Consider the environmental impact of AI systems and plan for their responsible decommissioning when necessary. Maintain version control to ensure long-term sustainability and accountability.

> **Practitioner's Tip**
>
> Responsible AI use isn't just about compliance—it's about creating value responsibly. Regularly ask yourself: "How does this AI solution improve outcomes for all stakeholders?" This will guide you toward more thoughtful, inclusive, and, ultimately, successful AI implementations.

Choosing the Right Generative AI Tool

Before beginning any work with generative AI, it's important to understand that not all AI tools are created equally. The tool you choose must align with your specific needs; for example, the exercise at the end of this chapter involves statistical analysis of training measurement data based on participant test scores. To serve as an effective tool for statistical analysis and tutoring, the generative AI tool should be able to:

- **Perform statistical analysis.** Execute robust statistical tests and models.
- **Guide you through the analysis process.** Act as a knowledgeable guide, explaining each step.
- **Provide examples and analogies.** Illustrate concepts with practical examples.
- **Answer follow-up questions.** Be responsive to queries during the process.
- **Offer feedback and suggestions.** Provide insights to enhance your understanding.

Refer to the checklist in Table 27-1 for additional details on how to select an appropriate generative AI tool. Remember, the right tool will not only perform the tasks you need but also support your learning and professional development.

Table 27-1. Guidelines for Using AI as a Tool and Tutor

☐	**Verify the Generative AI Tool's Capabilities**
	Have you confirmed that the AI tool you're using can perform the necessary statistical analyses for evaluating training program effectiveness? Tip: Some versions of OpenAI's, ChatGPT's, and Anthropic Claude's are capable of conducting statistical analysis, including paired t-tests on participant test score data.
☐	**Customize Your Prompts**
	How can you continually adapt and refine your interaction with the AI tutor to ensure it provides the most relevant guidance and insights for your specific needs in analyzing training program effectiveness?
☐	**Watch for Potential Biases**
	What steps can you take to identify and mitigate any biases in an AI tool's analysis that might influence the evaluation of your training program?
☐	**Be Vigilant About Confabulation Risks**
	How will you identify and mitigate the risk of the AI tutor producing incorrect but plausible facts when analyzing student test scores and evaluating training program effectiveness, especially when asking it to provide quotes, sources, citations, or other detailed information?
☐	**Validate AI Outputs**
	Use familiar statistical analysis tools, such as Microsoft Excel or Google Sheets, to perform the same analysis on the dataset and compare the results with the AI tutor's output. This cross-validation process can help you identify any discrepancies and verify the reliability of the AI tool's analysis.
☐	**Protect Data Privacy**
	When applying these techniques to real-world data, how will you ensure that you've selected an AI tool with data privacy and use policies that align with your organization's requirements and protect sensitive information? What measures will you put in place to protect the privacy of student test scores and other sensitive data when using the AI tutor?
☐	**Supplement, Not Replace**
	How will you ensure that the AI tutor's insights are used to complement, rather than replace, established and well-tested or validated authoritative resources for the use of statistics in evaluating training program effectiveness?
☐	**Interpret the Analysis Critically**
	How will you apply your own expertise and critical thinking skills to interpret and contextualize the insights provided by the AI tutor?
☐	**Iterate and Refine Your Approach**
	What processes will you put in place to continuously experiment, learn, and improve your use of the AI tutor for evaluating training program effectiveness over time?

Equally important in the selection process is understanding how the AI tool handles your data. Before integrating any AI solution, ensure you know where your data will be stored, how it is processed, and whether it will be used to train the AI further. Some AI tools may store your data in the cloud or on external servers, which could raise concerns about confidentiality and data privacy.

Ask these key questions before making a choice:

- Does the AI tool comply with relevant data protection regulations (such as GDPR or CCPA)?
- Is there transparency about how the tool uses and stores your data?
- Can you control or limit AI's access to sensitive information?
- What measures are in place to secure your data against unauthorized access?

By considering these aspects, you can ensure that the AI tool not only meets your analytical and instructional needs but also upholds the integrity and confidentiality of your data. This responsible approach safeguards not only your organization but also the participants whose data you are analyzing.

Hands-On Application: AI-Powered Measurement and Evaluation

Now that you have the guiding principles and a selected tool in place, let's go through an application exercise using generative AI to analyze workplace training data, focusing on measuring learning outcomes and evaluating training effectiveness.

Key elements of our analysis include:

- **Learning outcomes.** The specific knowledge and skills that participants gain from training, which are typically measured immediately after the training program.
- **Training results.** The broader impacts that occur because of the training program, including how learning outcomes translate into improved workplace performance, behavioral changes, or the development of new skills and capabilities.

For these elements to be meaningful, certain conditions must be met. Specifically, participants must acquire new knowledge, retain it over time, and be able to apply it in practical contexts. This is where the concepts of knowledge acquisition and retention come into play:

- **Knowledge acquisition.** The process by which participants absorb new information during training, which is typically assessed through post-training

tests. Effective learning occurs when new knowledge is acquired, processed, and retained in memory for later use (AERO 2023).
- **Knowledge retention.** The ability to recall and use the information learned during training at a later time, which is often measured by follow-up tests conducted, for example, 30 days post-training. The true value of training lies not just in knowledge acquisition, but in its retention and application in critical situations (Bransford et al. 2000).

Testing Conditions for Learning and the Importance of Statistical Analysis

To assess training effectiveness, we will use paired t-tests to compare pretraining, post-training, and 30-day follow-up scores for knowledge acquisition and retention. Generative AI streamlines this analysis, providing deeper insights into how well the training program is achieving its goals.

When conducting paired t-tests, it's important to understand both the immediate and long-term influences on participants. In a 2019 blog post on measuring learning effectiveness, Tracey Smith and I discussed how paired t-tests can be a simple yet powerful tool for evaluating workshop outcomes. By comparing pre- and post-training scores, as well as follow-up assessments, we can gain valuable insights into how well participants retain and apply the knowledge they've acquired.

Preparing and Loading the Data

To continue, we'll need to prepare our dataset for analysis. This dataset includes the scores from the pretests, post-tests, and 30-day follow-up assessments for each participant in the training program.

Follow these steps to prepare your data:
1. **Organize the dataset.** Ensure that the dataset is well-organized, with each participant's scores correctly recorded for all three assessment points (pretest, post-test, and 30-day follow-up test).
2. **Refer to the example dataset.** Table 27-2 provides a partial example of the types of data you'll be working with, which will help ensure that your data is structured correctly.

CHAPTER 27

3. **Format your data for AI compatibility.** To ensure compatibility with most generative AI systems that perform data analysis, save your dataset as a CSV (comma-separated values) file. This format is widely accepted and easy to use across different platforms. If your generative AI tool supports file attachments, you can upload the CSV directly. If not, you may need to copy and paste the data into the AI tool's interface.
4. **Load the data into the AI tool.** Once your data is prepared and saved in the correct format, load it into your chosen generative AI tool. In an upcoming step, you'll confirm with the AI tool that the data loaded correctly.

Table 27-2. Partial Data Table for Exercise

Participant ID	Pretest Score	Post-Test Score	30-Day Score
1	75	83	77
2	69	82	76
3	76	89	82
4	85	96	89
5	68	82	80

Practitioner's Tip

Performing statistical analysis effectively ensures that your measurements of learning outcomes and training results are valid, reliable, trustworthy, and credible. By using AI-powered tools to perform complex calculations and interpret results, you can:

- Ensure the validity of your evaluations using appropriate statistical methods and tests tailored to your specific data and research questions.
- Enhance the reliability of your findings by automating data analysis processes, reducing the risk of human error, and ensuring consistency across multiple analyses.
- Increase the trustworthiness of your insights by leveraging AI's ability to process large volumes of data, identify patterns, and provide objective, data-informed recommendations.
- Boost the credibility of your training evaluation results using widely accepted, robust statistical methods and clearly communicating the AI-assisted methodology to stakeholders.

Conducting a Statistical Analysis of Learning Outcomes and Training Results

It's time to put AI to the test and see what insights it can reveal about this training program. Follow these steps, using the recommended prompts as they are or modifying them to suit your preferences and needs. Remember, your goal is to both deepen your understanding of statistical methods applied to measurement and evaluation and enhance your AI literacy through practical application.

Step 1. Data Overview and Initial Exploration

Understand the data's structure and quality before performing a paired t-test. It is crucial to ensure there are no significant issues (such as missing values or outliers), because this data will inform all subsequent analyses.

1. **Confirm that the data loaded properly:**
   - Prompt: "Can you confirm that you have successfully loaded the dataset containing pretraining, post-training, and 30-day follow-up assessment scores for 20 training program participants? Please provide a brief summary of the data structure, including the number of participants, variables, and any missing data."
2. **Explore the data using descriptive statistics:**
   - Prompt: "What basic descriptive statistics should I calculate for each set of assessment scores? How will these help me prepare for statistical analyses of knowledge acquisition and retention?"

Step 2. Checking for Normal Distribution and Visualizing the Data

Ensure the data is normally distributed and use visual tools to assess this distribution, which is required for a paired t-test.

1. **Understand the importance of normal distribution:**
   - Prompt: "Why is normal distribution important for our analysis of learning outcomes? What are the consequences of violating this assumption?"
2. **Learn methods for checking normal distribution:**
   - Prompt: "What are some ways I can check whether the assessment score data follows normal distribution? Can you explain how to interpret the results of these methods? What should I do if the data is not normally distributed?"

CHAPTER 27

3. **Create and interpret histograms:**
   - Prompt: "Can you explain how to create histograms for each set of assessment scores? How can I use histograms to visually assess whether the data is normally distributed?"
4. **Evaluate normality and plan next steps:**
   - Prompt: "Based on the histogram descriptions provided, which datasets appear to be normally distributed? How does this inform my choice of statistical tests for analyzing learning outcomes? What actions should I consider if the data is not normally distributed?"

Practitioner's Tip

Normal distribution is an assumption for many statistical tests, including the paired t-test. If your data does not meet this assumption, consider using nonparametric tests (such as the Wilcoxon Signed Rank test) or transforming the data to better fit a normal distribution.

Step 3. Conducting Paired T-Tests

Perform and interpret paired t-tests to analyze learning outcomes.

1. **Understand the paired t-test:**
   - Prompt: "Can you explain what a paired t-test is and why it's appropriate for statistically analyzing knowledge acquisition and retention in a training program? How does this test help me determine if desired learning outcomes will likely be achieved?"
2. **Conduct paired t-tests for different comparisons:**
   - *Comparison 1:* Pretraining vs. post-training scores
     - Prompt: "Please conduct a paired t-test comparing the pretraining scores with the post-training scores. What do the results suggest about immediate knowledge acquisition?"
   - *Comparison 2:* Pretraining versus 30-day follow-up assessment scores
     - Prompt: "Now, conduct a paired t-test comparing the pretraining scores with the 30-day follow-up assessment scores. How do the results differ from the pretraining to post-training comparison? What does this indicate about knowledge retention over time?"

LEVERAGING ARTIFICIAL INTELLIGENCE

3. **Interpret paired t-test results:**
   - Prompt: "Based on the paired t-test results for both comparisons (pretraining versus post-training and pretraining versus 30-day follow-up), what conclusions can you draw about knowledge acquisition and retention? Is the training program effective both immediately and over the longer term?"

Practitioner's Tip

When starting with generative AI tools for statistical analysis, it's wise to validate the outputs using Excel or Google Sheets. By replicating the AI-generated results, such as paired t-tests, in these familiar platforms, you can compare and confirm their accuracy. This cross-check not only ensures reliability but also helps you better understand the analysis process, building confidence in the AI tools as you learn. When interpreting paired t-test results, consider both the p-value and the effect size. A significant p-value indicates a difference, but the effect size will tell you how substantial that difference is. Always report both for a complete picture of your training's impact.

Step 4. Addressing Common Misconceptions

Understand and avoid common mistakes in interpreting training program results.

1. **Request an explanation of common misconceptions:**
   - Prompt: "What are some common mistakes or misconceptions when interpreting training program results? How can I avoid these pitfalls in my analysis of learning outcomes and training effectiveness?"

Step 5. Communicating Results

Learn how to accurately communicate findings to stakeholders, with a focus on distinguishing between short-term knowledge gains and true learning outcomes.

1. **Ask for strategies to accurately communicate findings:**
   - Prompt: "How can I clearly communicate these findings to stakeholders, making sure they understand the difference between short-term knowledge gains and true learning outcomes that contribute to positive training results?"

Step 6. Analyzing Training Results and Aligning With Business Outcomes

Understand how statistical test results connect to overall training results, performance enhancement, and alignment with business goals.

1. **Ask for an explanation of how statistical test results relate to training results:**
   - Prompt: "How do the paired t-test results for pretraining versus post-training and pretraining versus 30-day follow-up relate to knowledge acquisition and retention? Which results indicate positive training results?"
2. **Request an interpretation of your statistical test results in terms of training results:**
   - Prompt: "Based on the paired t-test results, can I conclude that the training had a positive impact on workplace performance or the development of new skills and capabilities? Why or why not?"
3. **Ask how these analyses help align training outcomes with business objectives:**
   - Prompt: "How do these analyses help align the training results with the desired business outcomes? What evidence should I present to demonstrate that the training has contributed to achieving key business goals?"

Summary

Generative AI is changing how we measure and evaluate training programs and other talent development initiatives. It can automate data analysis, create helpful visualizations, and apply methods like paired t-tests to assess learning outcomes. These capabilities enable talent development professionals to conduct more precise and meaningful evaluations that align with organizational goals.

Beyond its technical functions, an AI tool can serve as an interactive tutor, guiding practitioners through complex analyses and enhancing their AI literacy. By simplifying the interpretation of statistical data with tools like histograms, AI not only streamlines the evaluation process but also deepens your understanding of the results. However, ethical use of AI and thoughtful human oversight are essential to fully harness its potential responsibly. Prioritize data privacy, security, and transparency, and handle the data you collect and analyze with strict compliance to relevant data protection regulations. This includes anonymizing sensitive information, securely storing data, and clearly communicating to participants how their data will be used.

This chapter provided a hands-on example of how you can use AI to measure the impact of a training program, offering practical prompts to help uncover insights and develop data literacy. As AI continues to evolve, your ability to critically evaluate its outputs and integrate these insights into your organizational context will be key to driving success. And remember, these insights are just the starting point. Your expertise, interpretation, and deep understanding of your organization's unique context are key to making informed and effective decisions.

In this evolving landscape, AI is redefining evaluation practices, creating critical capabilities for today and tomorrow—where the synergy between human expertise and AI collaboration creates a world that works better.

Practice Exercise

1. **Organize the data.** Each row in your data table should represent a training participant, and each column should contain relevant participant test scores.
2. **Capture the data table.** Use your smartphone's camera to take a clear photo of Table 27-3 (on the next page). Ensure good lighting and focus.
    - If you're using an iPhone (iOS 15 and higher), use the Live Text feature to capture and copy the text directly from the photo.
    - On Android devices, Google Lens can capture the table and extract the text.
3. **Transfer the data to a spreadsheet.** Once you've captured the data, paste it into a spreadsheet application. Ensure that the data is still organized correctly in rows and columns.
4. **Verify and clean the data.** Review the data, adjust formatting, and save the spreadsheet in a CSV format.
5. **Input for generative AI.** Use this CSV file as the input for your chosen generative AI tool.

Table 27-3. Data Table for Exercise

participant_id	pre_score	post_score	day30_score
PARTICIPANT_001	75	83	77
PARTICIPANT_002	69	82	76
PARTICIPANT_003	76	89	82
PARTICIPANT_004	85	96	89
PARTICIPANT_005	68	82	80
PARTICIPANT_006	68	85	82
PARTICIPANT_007	86	100	94
PARTICIPANT_008	78	94	88
PARTICIPANT_009	65	81	75
PARTICIPANT_010	75	90	77
PARTICIPANT_011	65	70	64
PARTICIPANT_012	65	80	73
PARTICIPANT_013	72	87	80
PARTICIPANT_014	51	78	72
PARTICIPANT_015	53	67	63
PARTICIPANT_016	64	81	74
PARTICIPANT_017	60	75	72
PARTICIPANT_018	73	82	77
PARTICIPANT_019	61	82	78
PARTICIPANT_020	56	75	70

Knowledge Check

Take a minute to reflect on these questions:

1. How might you use generative AI as a tool and tutor for other measurement and evaluation topics and tasks?

2. How does an AI-driven approach to analyzing learning outcomes compare with the traditional methods you've used in the past? What new perspectives has it offered?

3. What strategies will you implement to ensure that your AI-driven interpretations of training results are accurate and avoid common pitfalls?

4. How do you envision the role of AI evolving in your measurement and evaluation practices? What new skills or knowledge will you need to develop to maximize its potential and enhance your effectiveness?

CHAPTER 28

Building a Measurement and Evaluation Strategy
A REAL-LIFE EXAMPLE AT ASML

ROBIN DIJKE AND KLAAS TOES

IN THIS CHAPTER

This chapter describes a real-life example of building a measurement and evaluation strategy in a corporate learning environment at ASML—one of the world's leading innovators and manufacturers of chip-making machines. After reading this chapter, you will be able to:

- Describe the measurement and evaluation challenges ASML was facing.
- Understand the significance of having a robust measurement and evaluation strategy.
- Explain what it takes to build an integrated measurement and evaluation strategy and its components.
- Understand how to implement, embed, and continuously improve a measurement and evaluation strategy.

In today's fast-paced world, top leaders and clients are asking for more detailed information about how learning solutions work and their impact on business success. They want to know not just what people think of a learning activity, but how it's being used to make real changes and whether it provides good value for the money spent. To give these leaders the information they need, companies must upgrade their measurement and evaluation methods to better track and share these advanced results. The best way to answer these demands is to create an integrated measurement and evaluation strategy to measure and check the effectiveness of learning. Ignoring these requests could lead to problems, while responding well can bring big benefits for everyone involved.

ASML in a Nutshell

ASML is one of the world's leading innovators and manufacturers of chip-making machines. All the world's top chipmakers—including Intel, Samsung, and TSMC—use ASML machines to produce the microchips that are eventually placed in smartphones and laptops, as well as more advanced equipment like medical systems and satellites. A 2021 *New York Times* article called these machines "the most complicated machines humans have built" (Clark 2021). Innovation is an important driver for enabling chipmakers to produce smaller, faster, cheaper, and more energy-efficient microchips, and ASML is pushing technology to new limits to help solve some of humanity's toughest challenges. As a result, the company has been experiencing high growth rates over the past several years, which is expected to continue in the upcoming period. By the end of 2024, ASML employed more than 44,000 people (including payroll and flexible contracts) spread across offices in more than 60 locations worldwide and had a net sales of almost US $30 billion.

Understanding the Challenge

Measuring and evaluating corporate learning activities can be complex because it requires linking learning outcomes to real-world performance and organizational goals. ROI emerges as a crucial metric in this process, because it translates learning outcomes into financial value. This quantitative approach is critical for validating the efficiency and effectiveness of learning activities and justifying the investment in them. By using established ROI methodologies, organizations can track the direct and indirect benefits of learning activities to ensure learning objectives are aligned with the business and contributing to individual growth and organizational success. ASML embarked on a journey to structurally improve specific challenges around the measurement and evaluation of its learning solutions.

ASML employees require very specific knowledge and skills to be able to design and build these highly complex machines. The combination of such specific learning needs with a fast-growing workforce (from around 26,500 employees in 2020 to more than 44,000 employees in 2024) has made learning and knowledge management among the highest strategic priorities for the company. Bringing large amounts of new hires up to speed as soon as possible is a key enabler for ASML to continue its growth. To address this challenge, ASML initiated a transformation program in 2021 to professionalize its learning function and transform it from a decentralized operating model to a hybrid operating model with both central and decentralized elements (Gartner 2023).

Before the transformation, various parts of the business had established their own training centers, which operated independently from one another and used their own ways of working to run the end-to-end learning process. As a result, each training center used their own methods and metrics for measurement and evaluation, including having their own definitions, evaluation surveys, and data storage locations. It was impossible to present metrics around the adoption and quality of learning solutions that were used consistently across the whole of ASML, let alone shared metrics on the overall business impact of the large investments in learning across ASML.

At the same time—because learning was a key strategic priority for the company—investments in learning programs were increasing, and so was attention from senior leadership. Measurement and evaluation was an area in which it made sense and added value to create a common way of working across ASML in the new hybrid operating model. This would require a solid measurement and evaluation strategy that brought actionable insights to continuously improve learning solutions and data-driven evidence of the business impact.

ASML's Approach for Building a Measurement and Evaluation (M&E) Strategy

As one of the first steps in this journey, ASML selected an industry standard methodology that could serve as a foundational framework for all measurement and evaluation practices across the company: the ROI Methodology. ASML used concise workshops to introduce the ROI Methodology to its learning professionals in 2022 at its first Global Learning Summit. Within a year, approximately 40 employees were pursuing ROI Certification. While learning professionals typically possess a wealth of knowledge about L&D trajectories,

CHAPTER 28

they're often less comfortable with data collection, analysis, and reporting to stakeholders. Therefore, these initial capability building efforts were an important part of the foundation for developing ASML's measurement and evaluation toolkit and integrating the ROI Methodology into the learning dashboard (which we'll discuss later in this chapter).

Building an Integrated, Scalable, and Balanced Measurement and Evaluation Strategy

Building and implementing a measurement and evaluation strategy requires an integrated approach (Figure 28-1).

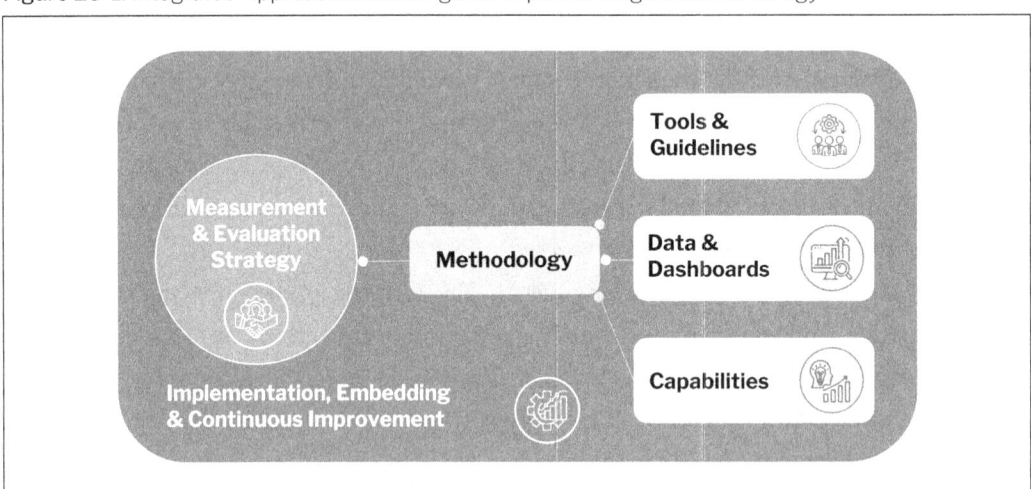

Figure 28-1. Integrated Approach to Building and Implementing an M&E Strategy

For ASML, selecting a methodology and building capabilities helped shape a more concrete measurement and evaluation strategy. Five key pillars (which touch each element in Figure 28-1) form the basis of this measurement and evaluation strategy:

1. **Solid methodology.** The measurement and evaluation process is based on a solid methodology and framework.
2. **Common way of working.** The steps in the measurement and evaluation process are consistent across ASML Academy.
3. **Enable learning professionals.** Learning professionals understand their role and responsibilities in the measurement and evaluation process and have the

knowledge, skills, and attitude (as well as the tools and data they need) to execute the tasks in the process.
4. **Scalable.** Measurement and evaluation efforts need to be scalable across the whole organization.
5. **Balanced efforts.** Measurement and evaluation efforts need to be in balance with the importance and the current performance of the learning solution.

Making Measurement and Evaluation Efforts Balanced and Scalable

The ROI Methodology provides a solid approach for performing an ROI case study tailored to a specific learning solution. While ROI case studies provide the most in-depth and accurate insights, they also require time and effort to set up and execute. The ASML Academy manages and maintains more than 15,000 learning solutions (excluding content from third-party content providers), so its staff knew that the effort put into evaluating the solutions and communicating results should be proportional to their strategic relevance and investment. It would not be appropriate to perform an ROI case study for each of these learning solutions. (For example, would you make the effort to calculate the ROI of buying a new pair of jeans? Probably not, because a pair of jeans doesn't have much strategic relevance in your life and the investment is rather low.) Moreover, if the current learning solution doesn't show any red flags, it may be sufficient to use a less in-depth method for monitoring its performance. (For example, while most people schedule an annual physical, they don't do an in-depth health check annually unless they have new complaints or symptoms.)

A lighter approach to measurement and evaluation would be particularly appealing if it still provided *indications* on the higher levels of the ROI framework (Levels 3, 4, and 5). If the right set of key parameters are selected, indications can come quite close to reality. For example, to determine the value of your real estate property, you could hire a professional to come inspect your house and write a detailed valuation report; this will probably give the most accurate value. However, a lighter way to do this is to visit a specialized website that calculates an indication of the value based on a few key parameters (such as the address, housing type, construction year, overall maintenance status, and living area and plot area in square meters). If you provide sufficient data points and relevant parameters, you might be surprised by how realistic the indications can be, and with a very limited investment of resources.

CHAPTER 28

ASML translated these principles into their measurement and evaluation strategy by creating three different routes: A, B, and C (Table 28-1).

Table 28-1. Different Routes to Go Through the Measurement and Evaluation Process

Route	Description	Effort	Outcomes
Route A	Parameters are selected from a set of key standard parameters that use standardized and readily available data collection methods and fixed definitions.	Low	Indications on key standard parameters
Route B	Where relevant, indications on key standard parameters (available in Route A) are supplemented with further investigation using custom data collection methods and a selection of these standard parameters or additional (nonstandard) parameters.	Medium	Indications on key standard parameters and further investigation
Route C	A Certified ROI Professional performs an in-depth ROI case study using the ROI Methodology, with (nonstandard) parameters and custom data collection methods where relevant.	High	In-depth ROI case study

Route A, which takes the least effort, provides indications on a set of key standard parameters. Route C is the most complex and involves a full ROI case study tailored to the unique context of the learning solution. This option provides more depth and certainty about the accuracy of the measurements. Route B sits in between and is used to investigate standard parameters in more detail through custom data collection methods; it also provides a way to investigate new, nonstandard parameters.

The starting point of any measurement and evaluation effort is selecting the appropriate route. Based on only three criteria, ASML created a route selection tool, which uses three criteria to help learning professionals determine which route to take and ROI level to measure (Figure 28-2). The three criteria are:
- Estimated annual spend on the learning solution
- Type of learning solution (such as classroom training, e-learning, or on-the-job learning activity)
- Strategic relevance of the learning solution

The route selection tool is very easy to use because learning professionals are given a fixed set of answer options for each criterion. Additional guidance is provided for a few of the combinations based on the annual learning consumption of the learning solution in terms

BUILDING A MEASUREMENT AND EVALUATION STRATEGY

of learning hours or number of unique users. The tool recommends avoiding the use of the measurement and evaluation process at learning solution level if the strategic relevance and investments are too low or the learning solution type is evaluated at vendor level instead of learning solution level (for example, in case of small learning solutions from third-party content providers). The tool helps ensure that measurement and evaluation efforts are in balance with the importance of the learning solution, and therefore remain scalable (points 4 and 5 of the measurement and evaluation strategy).

Figure 28-2. The Route Selection Tool

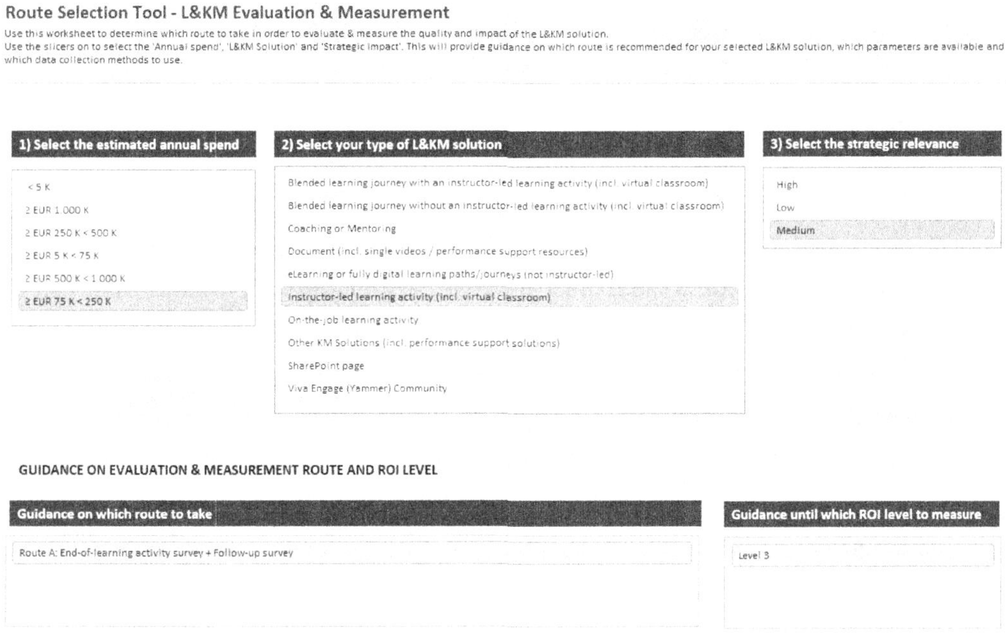

In total, ASML defined a set of 26 standard parameters to measure and evaluate learning solutions in Route A. Because not all parameters are available for each type of learning solution, the route selection tool only presents the standard parameters available for the selected type of learning solution, as well as the associated standard data collection method for measuring the parameter. The only thing learning professionals need to do is select the appropriate standard parameters and activate the standard data collection method for the learning solution.

411

CHAPTER 28

For ASML, creating a set of standardized evaluation surveys was an important step for Route A indications on key standard parameters. These results are then displayed in the learning dashboard. Depending on the survey, data is collected on ROI Levels 1 and 2 or Levels 3 and 4. The Level 4 data can also be used to calculate Level 5 ROI indications using a standardized calculation and key standardized business impact data from within ASML. The use of key standard parameters, associated standard data collection methods, and immediate access to real-time data and visualizations in the learning dashboard truly make the measurement and evaluation efforts scalable across the whole organization.

Another important element was the introduction of guidelines for minimum standards on the standard parameters (where relevant and possible). It is also possible to set targets and ambition levels that are higher than the minimum standards, but the minimum standards identify any "red flags" and ensure that measurement and evaluation efforts are in balance with the current performance, and therefore more scalable (point 4 and 5 of the measurement and evaluation strategy). As long as the standard parameter scores stay above the minimum standards, it is OK to use Route A rather than investing more efforts in the measurement and evaluation process. If the standard parameter scores go below the minimum standard, L&D should take a closer look at the context and possible root cause of the score. Then, they'll decide whether to move the measurement and evaluation to Route B for further investigation using custom data collection methods (such as interviews or focus groups) or additional non-standard parameters. Thus, Route B has two possible entry points—direct guidance based on the route selection tool or via Route A when standard parameters fail to meet the minimum standards and further investigation is needed to reveal the root causes and define follow-up actions for improvement.

Developing Tools and Guidelines and Providing Access to Data and Dashboards

Having a strategy and building capabilities through training efforts are not sufficient for embedding new ways of working. So, ASML created two tools to help learning professionals operationalize the measurement and evaluation strategy and ROI Methodology: the measurement and evaluation toolkit and a global learning dashboard.

The Measurement and Evaluation Toolkit

The measurement and evaluation toolkit is a practical performance support solution for all learning professionals involved in the process. For Routes A and B, the toolkit includes:

- **Process flows** showing who does what in the measurement and evaluation process (that is, the critical tasks and role responsibilities)
- **Quality standards and guidelines** that define what good looks like in the measurement and evaluation process (such as guidance on when to measure, what level in the ROI framework to measure, and minimum standards on evaluation results)
- **Performance support resources** that help learning professionals execute the measurement and evaluation process (including tools, templates, and best practice examples)

Route C is only intended for learning professionals with an ROI Certification. For them, the toolkit offers the performance support resources to conduct an ROI case study according to the ROI Methodology. The toolkit also explains the reasons behind key elements in the new way of working and the importance of having a solid measurement and evaluation approach in general. With this set-up, the toolkit doesn't just provide practical performance support resources, it also enhances the role and task clarity for each role in the operating model, provides quality guidance from the center of expertise, and communicates the vision and strategy behind the measurement and evaluation approach.

The toolkit is hosted on an easy-to-use intranet page and structured according to the key phases in the measurement and evaluation process (in line with the ROI Methodology) for each route (A, B, and C). It includes step-by-step guidance and supporting materials like explanatory videos, how-to guides, and practical tools and templates; for example, a reporting template to share results with stakeholders and a measurement and evaluation workbook that is used throughout the process to capture key information and decisions, as well as the actual data, insights, and follow-up actions.

The toolkit was created by representatives from all teams in the new operating model including the academies, learning shared services, and the center of expertise for learning. One design principle was to reuse what already exists in ASML as a valuable input, while another was to ensure the toolkit represented state-of-the-art quality that met industry standards. Therefore, the project team also included subject matter experts from two different consulting firms to provide an outside perspective and leverage external best practices. The design and development process used an iterative approach with all representatives participating in workshops to collect input and create a (new version of the) prototype, which was then offered for review and testing. After five iterations of the prototype, the group was able to launch the first minimal viable product (MVP).

The Learning Dashboard

Moving to a common approach for measurement and evaluation creates the opportunity to standardize how evaluation survey data is collected, centralize the storage of that data, and harmonize definitions of key metrics. Taking these steps enabled ASML to create a global learning dashboard to visualize key metrics and trends over time across the ROI framework.

While bringing all learning data to a central data warehouse and creating the learning dashboard took significant time and effort, it also made several local dashboard initiatives redundant and removed a lot of manual work for the learning professionals. They no longer had to create custom reports, use spreadsheet functionalities to generate meaningful visualizations, and copy them into slide decks to share with stakeholders. The new learning dashboard gave learning professionals immediate access to real-time data with consistent definitions and readily available visualizations, as well as filters for selecting data for specific sets of learning solutions, parts of the organization, countries and regions, employee types, and timeframes.

The learning dashboard also enabled ASML to answer the question it could not before: Show a baseline on shared metrics across the company to provide an indication of the adoption, quality, and business impact of the learning solutions. Moreover, the learning dashboard also played a key role in stimulating the implementation and use of the new measurement and evaluation process among learning professionals, because it provided such easy access to the data. This was one of the most tangible benefits.

Implementation, Embedding, and Continuous Improvement

As with all change efforts, the adoption is just as important as the quality of the designed solution. Therefore, ASML invested significant efforts in implementing and embedding the new ways of working. This started with creating a solid implementation, change, and adoption plan with a clear case for change. It also made sure to define the change impact for key stakeholders and outline how they would be involved throughout the process.

The measurement and evaluation toolkit's iterative co-creation process played an important role in this because it made the measurement and evaluation strategy tangible for learning professionals. Senior learning leaders were involved in this process through the project board and received updates in leadership meetings. The toolkit was launched during an event for all learning professionals and given additional exposure through ASML's key communication channels. After the launch event, visiting (management) team meetings for each learning team ensured that there was room to discuss the measurement and evaluation toolkit in more detail and provide support where needed.

The team also shifted their focus to ensuring the strategy, toolkit, and dashboard were fully integrated into the learning activities on the ROI Methodology for its learning professionals. The toolkit included a 35-minute digital learning path explaining key concepts and how to use the toolkit. To further enhance the capabilities of learning professionals, ASML created three (virtual) classroom training programs:

- **ROI Basics** introduces foundational ROI analysis concepts. It focuses on the alignment model (V-model) and ROI Methodology, as well as how to apply Route A from the measurement and evaluation toolkit. The interactive workshop enables participants to apply ROI analysis in their business practices effectively. They learn about the ROI Methodology and how use the route selection tool, interpret the learning dashboard, communicate with stakeholders, and apply concepts through case studies.
- **ROI Advanced** is designed for those with a basic understanding of ROI who want to enhance their knowledge and practical skills. It goes deeper into the ROI Methodology with a focus on real-world applications, aligning ROI with business goals, and enhancing skills in data collection, analysis, and effective communication of results. The course also introduces Route B from the measurement and evaluation toolkit for a comprehensive approach to ROI evaluation.
- **ROI Certification** is an advanced course designed to impart skills for conducting ROI case studies in areas like organization development and human resources. It focuses on the ROI Methodology, guiding participants through developing objectives, data collection, and converting data to monetary values, using a real learning solution for application. The course, highlighting Route C from the

toolkit, aims to make participants' initiatives more credible to leadership. It covers skills from calculating ROI to presenting results effectively, culminating in joining the ROI community.

To ensure it was continuously improving these new ways of working, ASML set up a community of Certified ROI Professionals (CRPs). This ambassador network facilitates capability building through informal learning and has monthly gatherings to exchange experiences and share feedback, which is used as input to continuously improve the process and toolkit.

The final step in embedding the measurement and evaluation strategy has been to start showing the outcomes of the measurement and evaluation process during ASML Academy's the global townhall meetings as well as reporting out to other relevant stakeholders. Periodically showing the current status helps create a more data-driven and performance-first mindset around learning and demonstrates whether improvement efforts are translating into results. When they do, it is time to celebrate that success!

Summary

This chapter detailed ASML's efforts to implement a new measurement and evaluation strategy, yielding significant insights. Central to our findings is that each component of the strategy is crucial. Leadership must make a clear, definitive choice regarding the strategy and methodology to ensure it's applicable at the workplace. The strategy emphasizes co-creation with stakeholders, dedicating ample time for capability building and the formation of an ambassador network. Furthermore, we learned that providing tangible support enhances the strategy's effectiveness, which was highlighted by the use of a learning dashboard to encourage engagement and visibility.

One lesson involved the importance of internally managing change and communications rather than outsourcing these critical functions. Taking ownership ensures that the change is more deeply integrated into the organization's fabric. Another lesson was the value of celebrating successes more openly and frequently.

The implementation underscores the necessity of a solid measurement and evaluation strategy in corporate learning. Table 28-2 presents a checklist for supporting the implementation of a measurement and evaluation strategy, which you can use to track your progress—and to ensure you're addressing all important aspects of the strategy and integrating them into your operations.

Table 28-2. Checklist for Implementing Your Measurement and Evaluation Strategy

Main Topic	Specific Actions
☐ Understand the challenges	Assess importance of evaluation and link to business success.
☐ Strategy	Define your measurement and evaluation strategy.
☐ Methodology selection	Adopt an evaluation methodology as the framework.
☐ Capability building	Engage in training and pursue certifications.
☐ Tools and guidelines	Use a measurement and evaluation toolkit.
☐ Data access	Create and use a learning dashboard.
☐ Ongoing improvement	Solicit and integrate regular feedback.
☐ Measurement route determination	Choose appropriate routes based on needs.
☐ Operational tools	Integrate the toolkit and dashboard in daily operations.
☐ Embed the process	Organize learning events and involve stakeholders.
☐ Celebrate achievements	Highlight successes in meetings and communications.

Knowledge Check

Use these three reflection questions to think about ASML's measurement and evaluation strategy:

1. What advantages does ASML gain by implementing a global standardized measurement and evaluation strategy?

2. How do Routes A, B, and C differ in their approach to measurement? What does that variation bring ASML?

3. How does the learning dashboard contribute to the success of ASML's measurement and evaluation efforts?

Acknowledgments

On August 25, 2023, ATD Press Manager Melissa Jones emailed me and Jack with an idea: "Would you have any interest in doing a second edition of *ATD's Handbook for Measuring and Evaluating Training*?" Our response was easy—yes.

Many new voices have entered the training measurement and evaluation field in the 13 years since we wrote the first edition, and many different applications have occurred. Writing a second edition seemed like the perfect way to introduce those voices and their expertise to audiences interested in building and advancing their measurement practices. We also enjoy partnering with ATD on publications, so this was a chance to do it again.

So, my first acknowledgment and expression of gratitude goes to Melissa Jones for thinking about us and offering us a chance to work with her team on another book. Thank you, Melissa.

From the beginning, we worked with Jack Harlow, developmental editor at ATD Press. Jack is a gift—easygoing, methodical, and ever-so-kind. He made this a much better book. Thank you, Jack, for your guidance, patience, and editorial expertise.

Jack (Phillips) and I met Courtney Vital Krebs when she joined ATD and managed the ROI Network. Through the years, Courtney led the creation and transformation of ATD Education, for which the ATD Measuring ROI Certificate served as the initial certificate program. From the beginning, she positioned measurement and evaluation as a central element of ATD Education and all its programs. I am thrilled that Courtney contributed to the opening chapter describing the relationship between measurement and evaluation and the Talent Development Capability Model. Thank you, Courtney, for your ongoing support and friendship. Your leadership is inspiring!

Jack and I are blessed that Hope Nicholas is on our team. Hope is our director of publications. She is our strategy. While books are not our business, we would not have a business without our books because they help us share our work and that of others with the world. But, as authors reading this know, writing a book is more complex than prompting ChatGPT. It is a lot of work—whether you are doing the writing or working with contributing authors. And it is a big responsibility. Someone reading your book may act on the information you share, so

ACKNOWLEDGMENTS

it must be accurate. Hope helps us make our work worthy of publication. She managed to get 31 contributors (including me) to deliver chapters for this book in relatively good time—it was a feat. Thank you, Hope, for your help with this book and many others.

Melissa Brown leads our marketing at ROI Institute. She also manages my travel, calendar, and email, along with our global partner network. Somehow, she is always ready to help get work done. Through the book's development (and others), Melissa jumped in whenever we needed her. Thank you, Melissa, for all you do.

And, of course, to the entire ROI Institute team, thank you for who you are and for the talents you bring to work every day.

Thank you to all those who practice training measurement and evaluation within organizations worldwide. You are the driving force behind our work as external consultants, coaches, and thought partners. Your real-life measurement challenges offer us the luxury of doing the work we love—researching, creating, and sharing—which helps us help you advance your measurement practice.

As always, my heartfelt thanks go to Jack. The terms I've heard people use when describing Jack include "famous," "guru," and "rock star." While I acknowledge he may be all of those, I prefer to describe him as "dedicated," "dependable," "funny," "inspiring," "friend," and, of course, "husband." Jack is the inspiration that drove me to embrace training measurement and evaluation. He challenges and encourages me, brings me coffee when I need it most, and makes me laugh daily. Thank you, Jack, for all you do to make our life together what it is!

Patti P. Phillips, PhD
June 2025

APPENDIX A

Evaluation Planning Workbook

Implementing a measurement practice can be challenging and starting is the hardest part. It begins by assessing your readiness for evaluation—is your focus primarily toward activity or results? What do you need to do to move results in the other direction? Do you know which programs best align with the organization's strategy and operational goals?

Your data collection, data analysis, and communication strategies lay the groundwork for what's ahead in each evaluation project. They also describe the scope of the work, which you'll need to get buy in from stakeholders from the outset. The project plan ensures all parties know their role and when to play it. And it is always helpful to determine the fully loaded costs of your programs, especially when ROI is the metric that matters.

But the real payoff of implementing a measurement practice is to implement one that will last regardless of who is at the helm of the organization. A sustainable practice that informs the decisions and actions of leaders is the ultimate testament to the value of your measurement and evaluation efforts. In this Evaluation Planning Workbook, we have compiled some frequently used tools and resources to help you get started:

- Training and Development Programs Assessment: A Survey for Managers
- Project or Program Selection Worksheet
- Data Collection Plan
- ROI Analysis Plan
- Communication Plan
- Project Plan
- Action Plan Template
- Cost Estimating Worksheet
- Self-Assessment: Characteristics of a Sustainable M&E Practice

APPENDIX A

Training and Development Programs Assessment: A Survey for Managers

Instructions: For each of the following statements, please select the response that best matches the training and development function at your organization. If none of the answers describe the situation, select the one that best fits. Please be objective with your responses.

1. The direction of the training and development function at your organization:
   A. Shifts with requests, problems, and changes as they occur.
   B. Is determined by HR and adjusted as needed.
   C. Is based on a mission and a strategic plan for the function.
2. The primary mode of operation of the training and development function is:
   A. To respond to requests by managers and other employees to deliver training programs and services.
   B. To help management react to crisis situations and reach solutions through training programs and services.
   C. To implement many training programs in collaboration with management to prevent problems and crisis situations.
3. The goals of the training and development function are:
   A. Set by the training staff based on perceived demand for programs.
   B. Developed consistent with HR plans and goals.
   C. Developed to integrate with the organization's operating goals and strategic plans.
4. Most new programs are initiated:
   A. By request of top management.
   B. When a program appears to be successful in another organization.
   C. After a needs analysis has indicated that the program is needed.
5. When a major organizational change is made:
   A. We decide only which presentations are needed, not which skills are needed.
   B. We occasionally assess what new skills and knowledge are needed.
   C. We systematically evaluate what skills and knowledge are needed.
6. To define training plans:
   A. Management is asked to choose training from a list of canned, existing courses.

B. Employees are asked about their training needs.
C. Training needs are systematically derived from a thorough analysis of performance problems.

7. When determining the timing of training and the target audiences:
   A. We have lengthy, nonspecific training courses for large audiences.
   B. We tie specific training needs to specific individuals and groups.
   C. We deliver training almost immediately before its use, and it is given only to those people who need it.

8. The responsibility for results from training:
   A. Rests primarily with the training staff to ensure that the programs are successful.
   B. Is a responsibility of the training staff and line managers, who jointly ensure that results are obtained.
   C. Is a shared responsibility of the training staff, participants, and managers all working together to ensure success.

9. Systematic, objective evaluation, designed to ensure that trainees are performing appropriately on the job:
   A. Is never accomplished. The only evaluations are during the program, and they focus on how much the participants enjoyed the program.
   B. Is occasionally accomplished. Participants are asked if the training was effective on the job.
   C. Is frequently and systematically pursued. Performance is evaluated after training is completed.

10. New programs are developed:
    A. Internally, using a staff of instructional designers and specialists.
    B. By vendors. We usually purchase programs modified to meet the organization's needs.
    C. In the most economical and practical way to meet deadlines and cost objectives using internal staff and vendors.

11. Costs for training and organization development are accumulated:
    A. On a total aggregate basis only.
    B. On a program-by-program basis.
    C. By specific process components, such as development and delivery, in addition to a specific program.

APPENDIX A

12. Management involvement in the training process is:
    A. Very low with only occasional input.
    B. Moderate, usually by request, or on an as-needed basis.
    C. Deliberately planned for all major training activities to ensure a partnership arrangement.
13. To ensure that training is transferred into performance on the job, we:
    A. Encourage participants to apply what they have learned and report results.
    B. Ask managers to support and reinforce training and report results.
    C. Use a variety of training transfer strategies appropriate for each situation.
14. The training staff's interaction with line management is:
    A. Rare; we almost never discuss issues with them.
    B. Occasional; during activities such as needs analysis or program coordination.
    C. Regular; to build relationships, as well as to develop and deliver programs.
15. Training and development's role in major change efforts is:
    A. To conduct training to support the project, as required.
    B. To provide administrative support for the program, including training.
    C. To initiate the program, coordinate the overall effort, and measure its progress (in addition to providing training).
16. Most managers view the training and development function as:
    A. A questionable function that wastes too much of employees' time.
    B. A necessary function that probably cannot be eliminated.
    C. An important resource that can be used to improve the organization.
17. Training and development programs are:
    A. Activity-oriented; all supervisors attend the "Performance Appraisal Workshop."
    B. Individual results-based; participants will reduce error rate by at least 20 percent.
    C. Organizational results-based; the cost of quality will decrease by 25 percent.
18. The investment in training and development is measured primarily by:
    A. Subjective opinions.
    B. Observations by management and reactions from participants.
    C. Dollar return through improved productivity, cost savings, or better quality.
19. The training and development effort consists of:
    A. Usually one-shot, seminar-type approaches.
    B. A full array of courses to meet individual needs.

C. A variety of training and development programs implemented to bring about change in the organization.
20. New training and development programs, without some formal method of evaluation, are implemented at my organization.
    A. Regularly.
    B. Seldom.
    C. Never.
21. The results of training programs are communicated:
    A. When requested, to those who have a need to know.
    B. Occasionally, to members of management only.
    C. Routinely, to a variety of selected target audiences.
22. Management involvement in training evaluation:
    A. Is minor, with no specific responsibilities and few requests.
    B. Consists of informal responsibilities for evaluation, with some requests for formal training.
    C. Very specific; all managers have some responsibilities in evaluation.
23. During a business decline at my organization, the training function will:
    A. Be the first to have its staff reduced.
    B. Be retained at the same staffing level.
    C. Go untouched in staff reductions and possibly beefed up.
24. Budgeting for training and development is based on:
    A. Last year's budget.
    B. Whatever the training department can "sell."
    C. A zero-based system.
25. The principal group that must justify training and development expenditures is:
    A. The training and development department.
    B. The HR or administrative function.
    C. Line management.
26. Over the last two years, the training and development budget as a percent of operating expenses has:
    A. Decreased.
    B. Remained stable.
    C. Increased.

APPENDIX A

27. Top management's involvement in the implementation of training and development programs:
    A. Is limited to sending invitations, extending congratulations, and passing out certificates.
    B. Includes monitoring progress, opening and closing speeches, and presentations on the outlook of the organization.
    C. Includes program participation to see what's covered, conducting major segments of the program, and requiring key executives to be involved.
28. Line management involvement in conducting training and development programs is:
    A. Very minor; only training and development specialists conduct programs.
    B. Limited to a few specialists conducting programs in their area of expertise.
    C. Significant; on the average, more than half of the programs are conducted by key line managers.
29. When employees complete a training program and return to the job, their supervisor is likely to:
    A. Make no reference to the program.
    B. Ask questions about the program and encourage the use of the material.
    C. Require use of the program material and give positive rewards when the material is used successfully.
30. When employees attend an outside seminar, upon return, they are required to:
    A. Do nothing.
    B. Submit a report summarizing the program.
    C. Evaluate the seminar, outline plans for implementing the material covered, and estimate the value of the program.

Assessment Scoring

Score the assessment instrument as follows. The total will be between 30 and 150 points.
- 1 point for each A response.
- 3 points for each B response.
- 5 points for each C response.

Scoring Interpretation:

Scoring interpretations are based on the input from dozens of organizations and hundreds of managers.
- **120–150: Outstanding environment** for achieving results with talent development. Great management support. A truly successful example of results-based talent development.
- **90–119: Above average** in achieving results with talent development. Good management support is effective. A solid and methodical approach to results-based talent development.
- **60–89: Needs improvement** to achieve desired results with talent development. Management support is ineffective. Talent development programs do not usually focus on results.
- **30–59: Serious problems** exist with the success and status of talent development. Management support is nonexistent. Talent development programs are not producing results.

APPENDIX A

Project or Program Selection Worksheet

Use this worksheet to determine which programs or projects are candidates for ROI evaluation. The document lists eight criteria with a scale of 1 to 5. List your programs in the left-hand column. With your team, use the drop-down list to score each program against the criteria. The column on the right will total the scores for each program. A tan bar will indicate scores in relation to each other. Once you complete the exercise, sort the programs based on the total scores, highest to lowest, to easily identify programs that rise to the top in terms of candidacy for ROI evaluation.

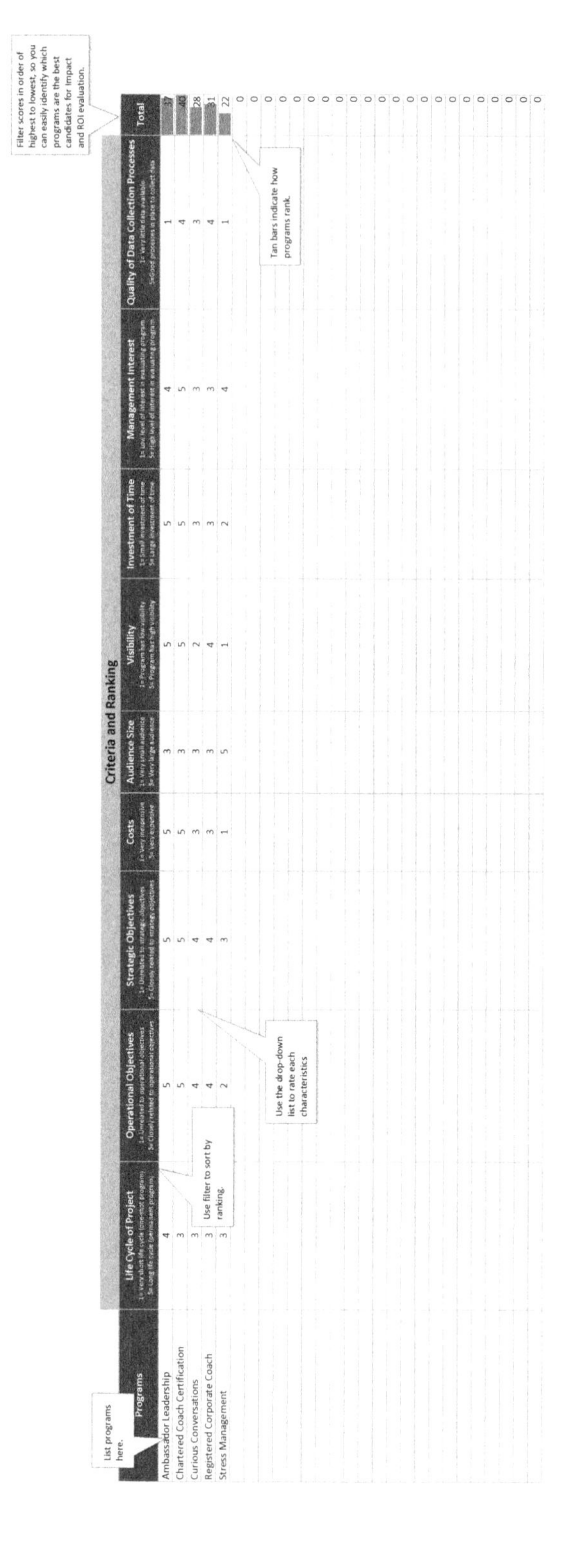

Programs	Life Cycle of Project	Operational Objectives	Strategic Objectives	Costs	Audience Size	Visibility	Investment of Time	Management Interest	Quality of Data Collection Processes	Total
Ambassador Leadership	3	5	5	5	3	5	5	4	4	39
Chartered Coach Certification	3	5	5	5	3	5	5	5	4	40
Curious Conversations	3	4	4	3	3	2	3	3	3	28
Registered Corporate Coach	3	4	4	3	3	4	3	3	4	31
Stress Management	3	2	3	1	5	1	2	4	1	22

Data Collection Plan

Program/Project: _____   Responsible Party: _____

Level	Program Objectives	Measures	Data Collection Method and Instruments	Data Sources	Timing	Responsibilities
1	Reaction and Satisfaction and Planned Action					
2	Learning					
3	Application and Implementation					
4	Business Impact					
5	ROI					

Comments:

APPENDIX A

ROI Analysis Plan

Program/Project: _____ Responsible Party: _____

Data Items (Usually Level 4)	Methods for Isolating the Effects of the Program or Process	Methods of Converting Data to Monetary Values	Cost Categories	Intangible Benefits	Communication Targets for Final Report	Other Influences and Issues During Application

Comments:

EVALUATION PLANNING WORKBOOK

Communication Plan

Program/Project: _____   Responsible Party: _____

Project Phase	Description	Recipient Action Needed?	Authors	Delivery Method	Delivery Date	Notes
Phase I: Planning						
Phase II: Data Collection						
Phase III: Data Analysis						
Phase IV: Reporting						
Phase V: Close						

APPENDIX A

Project Plan

Program/Project: _____   Responsible Party: _____

ID	Task	Start Date	Finish Date	Resources	Complete	Comments
1.0	**Planning**					
1.1	**Project Initiation**					
1.1.1	Kickoff meeting					
1.1.1.1	Finalize evaluation team members					
1.1.1.2	Validate evaluation project purpose					
1.1.1.3	Validate program objectives					
1.1.1.4	Finalize overall project timeline					
1.1.2	Finalize key milestones and deliverables					
1.2	**Data Collection Planning**					
1.2.1	Finalize measures					
1.2.2	Finalize data collection methods and instruments					
1.2.3	Finalize data sources					
1.2.4	Identify data utility					
1.2.5	Finalize data collection timing					
1.2.6	Finalize data collection responsibilities					
1.2.7	Identify baseline data					
1.3	**ROI Analysis Planning**					
1.3.1	Finalize Level 4 data items					
1.3.2	Finalize isolation methods					
1.3.3	Finalize methods for converting to monetary value					
1.3.4	Identify fully loaded costs					
1.3.5	Identify potential intangible benefits					
1.3.6	Identify other influencing factors					
1.4	**Communication Planning**					
1.4.1	Identify different communication needs					
1.4.2	Identify audiences					
1.4.3	Identify tools					
1.4.4	Develop communication plan					
1.5	**Finalize Planning Documents**					
1.5.1	**Project plan**					
1.5.2	**Data collection plan**					
1.5.3	**ROI analysis plan**					
1.5.4	**Communication plans**					
2.0	**Implementation**					
2.1	**Data Collection**					
2.1.1	Develop data collection instruments					
2.1.1.1	Create draft instruments (e.g., questionnaire)					

EVALUATION PLANNING WORKBOOK

ID	Task	Start Date	Finish Date	Resources	Complete	Comments
2.1.1.2	Test instruments					
2.1.1.3	Update based on test results					
2.1.1.4	Finalize instruments					
2.1.1.5	Develop high response strategy					
2.1.1.6	Finalize communications					
2.1.2	Implement data collection communication plan					
2.1.3	Implement data collection tools					
2.1.4	Collect data					
2.1.4.1	Level 1 data					
2.1.4.2	Level 2 data					
2.1.4.3	Level 3 data					
2.1.4.4	Level 4 data					
2.1.5	Close data collection tools					
2.2	**Data Analysis**					
2.2.1	Isolate the effects of program					
2.2.2	Convert data to monetary value					
2.2.3	Identify intangible benefits					
2.2.4	Finalize fully loaded program costs					
2.2.5	Calculate ROI					
2.2.6	Develop results					
2.2.6.1	Review with team					
2.2.6.2	Adjust based on feedback					
2.2.6.3	Finalize results					
2.3	**Reporting**					
2.3.1	Develop ROI report					
2.3.1.1	Draft final report					
2.3.1.2	Review report					
2.3.1.3	Finalize report					
2.3.2	Develop executive summary					
2.3.3	Develop initial scorecard					
2.3.3.1	Create initial scorecard					
2.3.3.2	Review with team					
2.3.3.3	Finalize initial scorecard					
3.0	**Project Close**					
3.1	**Complete Post Project Review**					
3.2	**Package Project Documents**					
3.2.1	Provide applicable project documents to client					
3.2.2	Archive documents					

APPENDIX A

Action Plan Template

Name:		Program attended:	
Your email address:			
Date completed:			
Decide	Why?	Calibration	Next Steps
What learning would you like to commit to implementing from the program? (Capture in 1 or 2 sentences.) Give your goal a title.	What will success look like for this goal? Why is this goal important to you?	What level were you at with this goal, BEFORE attending the program. (1 = low; 10 = high)	What specific actions will you take to progress this goal? In what situation can you take these actions?

Cost Estimating Worksheet

Analysis Costs		Total
Salaries and Employee Benefits (No. of People x Avg. Salary x Employee Benefits Factor x No. of Hours on Project)		$0.00
Meals, Travel, and Incidental Expenses		$0.00
Office Supplies and Expenses		$0.00
Printing and Reproduction		$0.00
Outside Services		$0.00
Equipment Expenses		$0.00
Registration Fees		$0.00
General Overhead Allocation		$0.00
Other Miscellaneous Expenses		$0.00
Total Analysis Cost		$0.00

Development Costs		Total
Salaries and Employee Benefits (No. of People x Avg. Salary x Employee Benefits Factor x No. of Hours on Project)		$0.00
Meals, Travel, and Incidental Expenses		$0.00
Office Supplies and Expenses		$0.00
Program Materials and Supplies Total		$0.00
Film	$0.00	
Videotape	$0.00	
Audiotapes	$0.00	
35mm Slides	$0.00	
Overhead Transparencies	$0.00	
Artwork	$0.00	
Manuals and Materials	$0.00	
Other	$0.00	
Printing and Reproduction		$0.00
Outside Services		$0.00
Equipment Expenses		$0.00
General Overhead Allocation		$0.00
Other Miscellaneous Expenses		$0.00
Total Development Costs		$0.00

Delivery Costs		Total
Participant Costs Total		$0.00
Salaries and Employee Benefits (No. of People x Avg. Salary x Employee Benefits Factor x No. of Hours on Project)	$0.00	
Meals, Travel, and Accommodations (No. of Participants x Avg. Daily Expenses x Days of Training)	$0.00	
Program Materials and Supplies		$0.00
Participant Replacement Costs (if applicable)		$0.00

APPENDIX A

Lost Production (Explain Basis)		$0.00
Instructor Costs Total		$0.00
Salaries and Benefits	$0.00	
Meals, Travel, and Incidental Expenses	$0.00	
Outside Services	$0.00	
Facility Costs Total		$0.00
Facilities Rental	$0.00	
Facilities Expense Allocation	$0.00	
Equipment Expenses		$0.00
General Overhead Allocation		$0.00
Other Miscellaneous Expenses		$0.00
Total Delivery Costs		**$0.00**

Evaluation Costs	Total
Salaries and Employee Benefits (No. of People x Avg. Salary x Employee Benefits Factor x No. of Hours on Project)	$0.00
Participant Costs	$0.00
Office Supplies and Expenses	$0.00
Printing and Reproduction	$0.00
Outside Services	$0.00
Equipment Expenses	$0.00
General Overhead Allocation	$0.00
Other Miscellaneous Expenses	$0.00
Total Evaluation Costs	**$0.00**
Total Program Costs	**$0.00**

EVALUATION PLANNING WORKBOOK

Self-Assessment: Characteristics of a Sustainable M&E Practice

Use this assessment tool to rate your M&E process based on the characteristics of sustainability listed below. Next, consider how members of your M&E team or your stakeholders might respond. Based on this review, identify one or two priority areas for process improvement or action planning.

Rating Scale
1 = Strongly disagree; 2 = Disagree; 3 = Neither agree nor disagree; 4 = Agree; 5 = Strongly agree

Characteristic	Description	Rating (1–5)
C-level engagement	Senior leaders are engaged as visible business partners and measurement advocates. Executives can clearly describe how results-based evaluation practices add and create organizational value.	
Efficiency	We routinely monitor time, usage, and cost indicators. A large portion of resources are used on non-training performance solutions, particularly organization development, process improvement, and job-specific initiatives.	
Effectiveness	We use a variety of qualitative and quantitative methods to evaluate our organizational impact and progress toward key outcomes. We regularly assess the business relevance and alignment of our evaluation processes.	
Investment	A percentage of the total HR, L&D, or OD budget is regularly applied toward M&E, including staffing resources and systems for effectively collecting, analyzing, and displaying results data. Also includes investment in continuing education around measurement best practices for enhanced capabilities of M&E staff and key business partners.	
Utility	M&E results are routinely used by our senior leaders, managers, and business units to track learning and performance outcomes (including negative outcomes) with L&D initiatives.	
Demand	Stakeholders across all organizational levels regularly request performance results for continuous process improvement and improved decision making. M&E processes are adapted to meet evolving demands.	
Credibility	Results data generated from our M&E process is consistently perceived as timely, trustworthy, and relevant to multiple stakeholder needs. M&E staff members are considered credible evaluation experts and organizational leaders in performance improvement.	

APPENDIX A

Characteristic	Description	Rating (1–5)
Governance	Operating policies, procedures, and standards are in place for governing measurement practice in our organization. A cross-functional steering or governance committee ensures that standards are applied in a consistent manner and that results data remains relevant and trustworthy over time.	
Continuous improvement	We use a variety of approaches to identify, share, and apply lessons learned from measuring organizational results. We use results data to drive innovation, improve practices, and experiment with new ideas.	
Resilience	We have the capacity to adapt successfully in the face of disruption or change. We use a variety of change or risk management approaches to monitor change fatigue, buffer disturbances, alter direction, and still maintain our core functioning during adversity.	

Adapted from Burkett (2013)

APPENDIX B

Answers to Knowledge Checks

Chapter 1. Aligning Training to the Needs of the Business
1. **C.** Correlate learning's performance with business KPIs to measure effectiveness
2. **D.** 50–90 percent
3. **A.** Executive commitment; **B.** Executive involvement; **E.** Executive support
4. **C.** Payoff needs
5. **A.** Business needs
6. **F.** All of the above

Chapter 2. Analyzing Performance Gaps
1. True
2. True
3. False
4. True
5. False

Chapter 3. Developing Powerful Program Objectives
As you evaluate your chosen program's objectives at each level, determine whether each objective includes:
- One area of focus per objective
- An observable outcome
- Applicable conditions
- Applicable criteria
- Absence of subjectivity

If the program you've chosen does not have objectives at Level 0 through 5, create them for the missing levels based on what you know about the program.

APPENDIX B

Chapter 4. Planning Your Evaluation Project

1. Evaluation planning is important because it defines what you will measure, how you will measure it, and who should be involved and their role. This ensures that all data is captured and activities stay on track, which establishes the integrity of the data and the credibility of the overall evaluation. Use an evaluation plan to show stakeholders a clear plan for measuring the program's effectiveness and outcomes. This gives stakeholders confidence to support and invest in the program.
2. Evaluation planning helps identify when measures will be collected and analyzed throughout the program. Establishing the timing allows you to capture key data based on when you expect to see the measures improve. Timing can also help determine how you will collect the data. Impact data should be collected based on the time it takes for business measures to improve once participants have had time to apply the skills or knowledge learned.
3. According to Guiding Principle 10, ROI analysis should be based on fully loaded costs to ensure that all costs are considered when tabulating and prorating costs for the solution.
4. When selecting your communication target audience, consider what you want to communicate and what actions you need them to take based on the evaluation results.

Chapter 5. Designing Learner Surveys

1. **C.** Data from traditional smile sheets using Likert-like scales have been shown to be virtually uncorrelated with learning results—giving us poor information.
2. **A.** While it is essential to improve learner survey questions using distinctive performance-focused questions, learner surveys are not enough. We should also be using other learning evaluation methods like measuring foundational knowledge, decision-making competence, task competence, transfer to work performance, and results.

Chapter 6. Designing Questionnaires and Surveys for Follow-Up Evaluation

1. **B.** Option A is a double-barreled question that asks the respondent to address two different topics in the same question; it also gave limited choices on how to answer.
2. **A.** Option B is a loaded question because it includes language saying how good it is (top of the line).

ANSWERS TO KNOWLEDGE CHECKS

3. **B.** Option A is not descriptive—effective could mean something different to each respondent.
4. **A.** Option B has limited answer options and doesn't provide enough details or answer options to understand the ability to use the skills (what does success look like). The question is also anchored—by including "as a result of participating in the program," the respondents will associate their behavior with the learning event.
5. **B.** Option A includes potential uncommon language—the respondents might not know what silo thinking is. By explaining the specific behaviors, they're also able to accurately rate the agreement with the statement.

Chapter 7. Designing and Delivering Tests

1. Recall, interpretation, and problem solving
2. No. It is an item targeting the problem-solving cognition level. Items like this would be more aligned with a learning outcome for a food safety manager course than a basic food handler course.
3. If written items don't match the cognitive levels in the learning outcomes, you can rewrite them to adjust their cognitive complexity using the tips in Table 7-1.
4. Because the question is negatively framed using the word "NOT" in the stem, the incorrect action (option A) is presented as the correct response. This can be confusing to test-takers and may lead to misinterpretation or selection of the wrong answer.

Chapter 8. Conducting Interviews

1. Introduced content, presuppositions, and evaluation
2. *Deductive coding* is based on the researcher's pre-existing theories or hunches about key issues or thematic areas. *Inductive coding* is based on issues emerging as important from the data itself during the analysis process.
3. Deductive coding provides a framework for interview analysis, while inductive coding allows for the emergence of unexpected themes and insights from the data.
4. *Advantages* include accuracy, it can capture details, and it is helpful in instances where the researcher is less experienced or is not as familiar with the design elements of the conceptual framework or thematic areas of interest. *Disadvantages* include time-consuming and may contain irrelevant or sensitive information, and it can be difficult to analyze due to the sheer volume of data.

APPENDIX B

5. SRIR is a qualitative research method that emphasizes the researcher's own subjectivity and how it may influence the research process. It involves ongoing reflection on the researcher's own biases, assumptions, and interpretations throughout the research process—from data collection to analysis and reporting.
6. SRIR can improve data quality by increasing researcher awareness and minimizing researcher bias.

Chapter 9. Conducting Focus Groups

1. False
2. This was a reflective question.
3. True
4. C. Before, during, or after training has taken place.

Chapter 10. Using Action Planning as a Measurement and Transfer Strategy

This chapter asked reflective questions.

Chapter 11. Using Statistics in Evaluation

1. This table outlines the measures of central tendency (mean, median, and mode), dispersion (range and IQR), and standard deviation for all four data sets.

	Preprogram	Test	Postprogram	LoE
Valid	10	10	10	10
Mode	56.004	94.756	91.366	5.674
Median	54.500	93.000	89.500	6.000
Mean	55.700	92.600	88.700	6.100
Std. Deviation	14.907	4.274	5.012	1.912
IQR	17.250	5.250	7.500	2.750
Range	48.000	13.000	15.000	6.000
Minimum	36.000	85.000	81.000	3.000
Maximum	84.000	98.000	96.000	9.000
25th percentile	45.250	90.500	84.500	5.000
50th percentile	54.500	93.000	89.500	6.000
75th percentile	62.500	95.750	92.000	7.750

2. The coefficient of variation for the test scores and LoE are:

	Test	LoE
Coefficient of variation	0.046	0.313

ANSWERS TO KNOWLEDGE CHECKS

Chapter 12. Analyzing Qualitative Data
1. True
2. The features of a grounded theory analysis are:
   - Reading transcripts
   - Consolidating labels into larger categories
   - Creating labels for language trends
3. True

Chapter 13. Isolating the Effects of the Program

The improvement in reject rates due to the program is 0.75 percent. The trend line picks up the routine noise that occurs as reject rates go down. Six months prior to the program, the reject rate was at 1.85 percent. Had the training not occurred, the reject rate probably would have been at 1.45 percent six months after the timing of the program.

Given that a program did occur, however, the actual reject rate was tracked six months after the program. The actual six months average was 0.7 percent. Had a comparison been made between the preprogram average (1.85 percent) and the actual postprogram average (0.7 percent), the amount would have reflected the pre-post difference only, not the contribution of the program.

Because a trend existed, the reject rate would have been 1.45 percent. To determine the contribution of the program, the projected reject rate six months after the program (1.45 percent) is compared with the actual six month reject rate (0.7 percent), resulting in a difference of 0.75 percent. This is the amount of change attributable to the program.

Chapter 14. Converting Measures to Monetary Value

Medicine Gelatin Manager	$36,288.00
Bill Burgess	$9,603.36
18 other participants	$54,109.00
10 other participants	0
Total Benefits	**$100,000.36**
The program costs	**$60,000**
The ROI is 66.67%	

APPENDIX B

To calculate the ROI

$$\text{ROI} = \frac{\$100,000.36 - \$60,000}{\$60,000} \times 100 = 66.67\%$$

Medicine Gelatin Manager Action Plan Analysis

1. Unit of measure: 1 kg of waste per month
   - *This is located at the top of the action plan.*
2. V: $3.60 per kg (standard value)
   - *This is located in item B.*
3. ΔP: 8,000 kgs – 2,000 kgs = 6,000 kgs × 0.20 × 0.70 = 840 kgs per month
   - *The current performance in item D from the current performance at the top of the action plan. Or, take from the text where Medicine Gelatin Manager explains the basis for the change. Also, take into account items E and F to isolate the effects of the program using estimates.*
4. AΔP: 840 kgs × 12 = 10,080 kgs per year.
   - *As shown on the action plan, this is a monthly measure. To annualize it, multiply the monthly improvement by 12.*
5. AΔP x V: 10,080 × $3.60 = $36,288
   - *Multiply the annual change in performance by the value of one unit. This amount goes in the table.*

Bill Burgess Action Plan Analysis

1. Unit of measure: 1 hour of unproductive time per month
   - *This is located at the top of the action plan.*
2. V: $52.00 per hour (standard value)
   - *This is located in item B.*
3. ΔP: 32 hours – 8 hours = 24 hours × 0.75 × 0.95 × 0.90 = 15.39 hours per month
   - *An explanation of the change in performance is in item D. They went from 32 hours to 8 hours, leaving a difference of 24 hours. Take into account items E and F to isolate the effects of the program using estimates. In this case, you'll also take into account the time saved used productively, shown in item G.*
4. AΔP: 15.39 hours × 12 = 184.68 per year.
   - *As shown on the action plan, this is a monthly measure. To annualize it, multiply the monthly improvement by 12.*

ANSWERS TO KNOWLEDGE CHECKS

5. AΔP × V: 184.68 hours × $52.00 = $9,603.36
   - *Multiply the annual change in performance by the value of one unit. This amount goes in the table.*

Chapter 15. Identifying Program Costs

1. **$1,250 per person over the life of the program**—$250,000 development costs divided by 200 participants over the life of the program.
2. **$31,250 in development costs**—$1,250 per person development cost multiplied by 225 participants in ROI study.

Chapter 16. Calculating the Return on Investment

1. **The BCR is 2.09:1**—for every dollar invested, there is $2.09 in benefits.
2. **The ROI is 109 percent**—for every dollar invested, $1.09 is returned after the investment is recovered.
3. **The PP is 0.48**—the investment will be paid back in 48% of one year, or just under six months.

Chapter 17. Measuring Intangible Benefits

1. **B.** Benefits that are difficult to measure and often not directly related to financial gain
2. **C.** By incorporating intangible benefits into the program's evaluation framework to reflect broader impacts
3. **B.** Intangible benefits are subjective and qualitative
4. **B.** Conducting extensive financial audits
5. **B.** It is crucial for making intangible benefits relatable for the audience

Chapter 18. Forecasting ROI

1. False
2. False
3. False
4. True
5. False
6. True

APPENDIX B

Chapter 19. Telling the Story

1. This is a classic example of designing a valuable training program but misusing time and resources by failing to deliver on the communication plan. The communication violated many basic principles for disseminating results:
   - Reports were not generated in an immediate fashion to allow enhancements to be implemented.
   - Communications were not tailored to the interest and needs of the unique stakeholders.
   - No consideration was given to customizing the type of media used for senior management versus the participants.
2. Here is a suggested communication plan for the marketing strategy project:

Green Goods Communication Document	Communication Target	Distribution Method
Complete report with appendices	• Program sponsor WLP staff • Selling team manager	Distribute and discuss in a special meeting
Executive summary	• Senior management in the marketing units • Senior corporate management	Distribute and discuss in regularly scheduled meeting
General interest overview and summary without the actual calculation (5 to 8 pages)	• Sales reps involved in training	Mail with letter
General interest article (1 page)	• Sales reps from all sales teams and company employees	Publish in company publication
Brochure highlighting program, objectives, and specific results	• Team leaders with an interest in the program • Prospective sponsors including all marketing teams	Include with other marketing materials

Chapter 20. Visualizing Data

1. The primary category of visualization is a relationship to demonstrate the impact of manager support on the level of unapplied learning

ANSWERS TO KNOWLEDGE CHECKS

2. Two visualizations are a bar chart and a heat map:

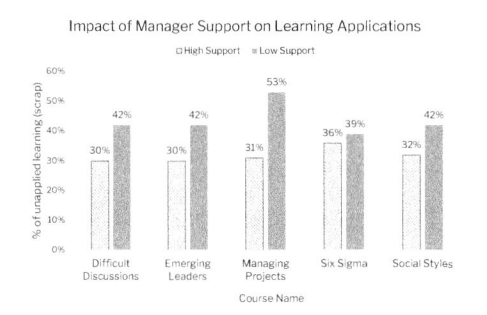

Impact of Manager Support on Learning Applications

Unapplied Learning for Courses With High and Low Manager Support

Support Level (High or Low)	Difficult Discussions	Emerging Leaders	Managing Projects	Six Sigma	Social Styles	Grand Total
High support	30%	30%	31%	36%	32%	31%
Low support	42%	42%	53%	39%	42%	42%
# evaluations	100	90	225	25	75	515

3. Pros and cons of each method:
   - Bar chart
     - Pro: Clear differences are evident for all courses, so it's easy to draw conclusions.
     - Con: It could appear cluttered if the number of course comparisons increases.
   - Heat map:
     - Pro: It provides a gradation of performance, not simply good or bad.
     - Con: It's more difficult to see the differences between high and low support scrap rates.
4. For large sample size courses, there is a big difference in scrap rates depending on manager support. The gaps range from 10 points to 21 points, suggesting that manager support highly influences scrap rates
5. Sample size appears to matter. The course with a small number of evaluations (Six Sigma) also has the smallest gap.
6. Continue the program because it appears to be working. Also, continue to gather data and determine whether the results are stable over time or if manager support is more effective for some courses than others.

Chapter 21. Implementing the ISO Standards for L&D Metrics
1. Efficiency, effectiveness, and outcome
2. Scorecard, dashboard, program evaluation, and management
3. Senior leader, group or team leader, head of learning, program manager, and learner
4. Inform, monitor, evaluate, and manage

APPENDIX B

Chapter 22. Using Black Box Thinking to Optimize Training Outcomes

1. Organizations should prioritize continuous improvement and results optimization in training evaluation for several reasons:
   - **Reduce scrap learning.** Training programs can be expensive and a high rate of scrap learning (knowledge not applied on the job) represents wasted resources. Continuous improvement helps identify and address these gaps.
   - **Maximize training effectiveness.** Traditional evaluation methods may not capture the full picture of training effectiveness. By constantly optimizing, organizations ensure programs are relevant, effective, and lead to actual behavioral changes on the job.
   - **Align training with business needs.** Business needs evolve, and training programs need to adapt with them. Continuous improvement ensures training remains aligned with strategic goals and addresses current challenges faced by the organization.
   - **Gain competitive advantage.** In today's rapidly changing world, organizations that can adapt and learn continuously gain a competitive advantage. Training evaluation provides valuable insights to inform future training initiatives and keeps employees equipped with the necessary skills.
   - **Data-driven decision making.** Continuous improvement involves using data to identify what works and what doesn't. A data-driven approach ensures training decisions are based on evidence and lead to more effective programs and greater credibility with stakeholders.

2. Fostering a culture of continuous improvement is crucial for maximizing training effectiveness because it encourages a growth mindset and open communication about challenges. Here's how organizations can achieve this:
   - **Shift mindset from blame to learning.** View mistakes as learning opportunities, not failures. Encourage employees to share feedback on training experiences, both positive and negative. This ultimately leads to better programs and better outcomes for all.
   - **Psychological safety.** Create an environment where employees believe it is safe to speak up and offer honest feedback without fear of reprisal. This fosters open and transparent, two-way communication and allows for early identification of issues.

- **Open communication channels.** Establish clear communication channels for soliciting feedback from learners, managers, and other stakeholders. Actively listen to feedback, demonstrate a commitment to addressing concerns, and take visible action.
- **Celebrate successes.** Recognize and celebrate instances where training leads to positive results. This reinforces the value of training and motivates employees to participate actively in the future.
- **Focus on actionable feedback.** Don't just collect feedback; use it to make actual improvements. Regularly update training programs based on insights gathered through evaluation.
- **Focus on learning over blame.** When discrepancies arise, focus on understanding the underlying causes rather than assigning blame. This encourages experimentation and innovation in training design.

3. The chapter outlines several best practices for incorporating black box thinking into training evaluation:

- **Strategic alignment**
    - *Align measures of success.* Collaborate with stakeholders to set clear goals and performance metrics for training programs. This ensures everyone is on the same page about what success looks like.
    - *Regular communication.* Maintain open communication with stakeholders throughout the evaluation process. Regularly share findings and insights to promote transparency and encourage buy-in.
    - *Data-driven decisions.* Use data collected during the evaluation to guide future training decisions. This data-driven approach ensures programs are relevant and effective.
- **Data collection**
    - *Diverse perspectives.* Involve stakeholders and learners in designing data collection tools. This ensures a comprehensive approach that captures what matters most to a diverse set of perspectives.
    - *Multimodal strategy.* Use multiple data collection methods—like surveys, interviews, observations, and performance metrics—to triangulate the data and gain a more holistic picture.

APPENDIX B

- ○ *Insightful questions.* Design interview and survey questions that go beyond surface level and into the why behind the desired training outcomes.
- **Data analysis**
  - ○ *Demographic analysis.* Analyze data by demographic to identify variations in training effectiveness for different groups. This allows for tailored recommendations that have greater influence.
  - ○ *Examine extremes.* Analyze data for high and low scores to understand where there are outliers and explore the reasons behind them. This can reveal areas for significant improvement.
  - ○ *Thematic analysis.* Conduct thematic analysis of qualitative data to identify patterns and trends in learner experiences and feedback. This provides in-depth insights into stakeholder experiences.
- **Reporting**
  - ○ *Integrate findings.* Present a cohesive story by integrating findings from various data sources. This strengthens the credibility of the evaluation and results.
  - ○ *Data storytelling.* Use clear and concise language to tell a compelling story about the impact of training programs. Translate data into actionable insights for stakeholders that answer the "so what."
  - ○ *Actionable recommendations.* Develop practical recommendations based on what is uncovered in the data analysis. These recommendations should be specific, measurable, achievable, relevant, and time-bound (SMART).

By incorporating these best practices, organizations can leverage black box thinking principles to optimize training effectiveness and create a continuous learning environment.

Chapter 23. Using Financial Analysis to Compare OJT and S-OJT
This chapter asked reflective questions.

Chapter 24. Implementing a Sustainable Measurement Practice

1. Value creation
2. Partnerships
3. Capability
4. Sound execution
5. Change readiness
6. Innovation

ANSWERS TO KNOWLEDGE CHECKS

Action	Essential Number
Ensure implementation plans are flexible, scalable, and appropriately aligned to business needs.	4
Show the ROI of the ROI.	1
Engage sponsors as steering committee members, coaches, or mentors.	2
Create space for project teams to experiment, take risks, and learn from their failures as well as their successes.	6
Consider employee workloads when requesting support for evaluation activities, like survey follow-ups or action planning.	5
Continually reskill and upskill to build your business acumen and strategic partnership skills.	3

Chapter 25. Getting Stakeholder Buy-In for Measurement and Evaluation
This chapter asked reflective questions.

Chapter 26. Developing and Using Professional Standards for Evaluation
This chapter asked reflective questions.

Chapter 27. Leveraging Artificial Intelligence
1. Generative AI can enhance measurement and evaluation activities beyond analyzing learning data. For example, when designing evaluation surveys, AI can help craft questions that reduce bias and improve response rates. As a tutor, it can guide practitioners through statistical concept selection, explaining when to use different methods like correlation analyses versus regression models. For qualitative analysis, AI can assist in identifying themes from open-ended responses while teaching evaluators about coding frameworks and thematic analysis approaches. The key is leveraging AI for task completion and skill development simultaneously.
2. AI-driven approaches fundamentally shift the speed and depth of learning analytics. Traditional methods often require choosing between a broad analysis of simple metrics or a deep analysis of a limited sample due to time constraints. AI enables both simultaneously—quickly analyzing large datasets while highlighting nuanced patterns that might be missed manually. For instance, while traditional methods may show overall knowledge retention rates, AI can identify specific content areas where retention varies by learner characteristics, delivery method, and application context. This richer analysis allows for more targeted program

APPENDIX B

improvements. However, AI's insights must still be validated against business context and learning objectives.
3. A multi-layered validation approach is essential for AI-driven analysis. This includes:
   - Cross-validating AI findings with traditional statistical methods
   - Establishing clear criteria for what constitutes a meaningful pattern versus statistical noise
   - Regularly testing AI outputs against known benchmarks and subject matter expert insights
   - Documenting and monitoring AI's decision-making logic for consistency
   - Maintaining human oversight, particularly for high-stakes decisions
   - Building in bias detection mechanisms and ethical guidelines
   - Most importantly, viewing AI as an augmentation tool rather than a replacement for human judgment in evaluation
4. AI's role in M&E continues to expand, actively helping analyze data and design better evaluation approaches from the start. This evolution requires developing technical and strategic skills across research and assessment methodologies. *Technical skills* include understanding AI capabilities and limitations, prompt engineering, and data validation methods. *Strategic skills* involve knowing when and how to best apply AI, integrating AI insights with business context, and maintaining ethical guidelines as capabilities expand. Additionally, *communication skills* become even more crucial—being able to explain AI-driven insights to stakeholders and translate technical findings into actionable recommendations. Success will depend on balancing technical proficiency with human-centered evaluation practices.

Chapter 28. Building a Measurement and Evaluation Strategy

1. This standardized way of working allows ASML to ensure consistency and comparability of learning KPIs across all academies, departments, and locations. This approach enables the company to centralize its data, streamline its processes, and reuse best practices. It also facilitates the aggregation and analysis of data, providing clearer insights into the effectiveness of its learning solutions on a global scale.
2. Each route offers a different level of depth and resource investment, allowing ASML to tailor its evaluation efforts to the strategic importance of the learning

ANSWERS TO KNOWLEDGE CHECKS

solution. Route A is low effort, providing basic indications with minimal resources. Route B offers a deeper investigation for more significant learning solutions, using custom data collection methods. Route C involves an in-depth analysis suitable for high-stakes learning solutions. This tiered approach helps ASML balance effort versus impact, optimizing resources while still gathering necessary data to inform decisions.

3. The learning dashboard centralizes real-time data and visualizations, making it an essential tool for monitoring and reporting on the effectiveness of learning solutions. It supports quick access to performance data across various metrics, helping learning professionals and decision makers understand trends, identify issues, and make informed adjustments to the learning strategy. The dashboard enhances transparency and accountability by providing a clear view of the KPIs related to learning investments.

References

Abbott, A. 1988. *The System of Professions: An Essay on the Division of Expert Labor*. University of Chicago Press.

Adelsberg, D., and E. Trolley. 1999. *Running Training Like a Business*. Berrett Koehler.

Agrawal, S., A. De Smet, P. Poplawski, and A. Reich. 2020. "Beyond Hiring: How Companies Are Reskilling to Address Skill Gaps." McKinsey, February 12. mckinsey.com/capabilities/people-and-organizational-performance/our-insights/beyond-hiring-how-companies-are-reskilling-to-address-talent-gaps.

Ahadi, S., and R.L. Jacobs. 2017. "A Review of the Literature on Structured On-the-Job Training and Directions for Future Research." *Human Resource Development Review* 16:323–349. doi.org/10.1177/1534484317725945.

AI Unplugged. 2020. "What is AI Literacy? Competencies and Design Considerations." AI Unplugged, Georgia Institute of Technology.

Alliger, G.M., S.I. Tannenbaum, W. Bennett Jr., H. Traver, and A. Shotland. 1997. "A Meta-Analysis of the Relations Among Training Criteria." *Personnel Psychology* 50:341–358.

Alliger, G.M., and E.A. Janak. 1989. "Kirkpatrick's Levels of Training Criteria: Thirty Years Later." *Personnel Psychology* 42:331–342.

American Educational Research Association, American Psychological Association, and National Council on Measurement in Education. 2014. *Standards for Educational and Psychological Testing*. APA.

American Evaluation Association. 2019. "AEA Standards Competency Report." eval.org/Portals/0/Docs/AEA%20Evaluator%20Competencies.pdf.

American Psychological Association Task Force on Evidence-Based Practice for Children and Adolescents. 2008. *Disseminating Evidence-Based Practice for Children and Adolescents: A Systems Approach to Enhancing Care*. APA.

Argyris, C., and D. Schon. 1996. *Organizational Learning II: Theory, Method, and Practice*. Addison Wesley.

REFERENCES

Armstrong, J., ed. 2001. *Principles of Forecasting: A Handbook for Researchers and Practitioners.* Kluwer Academic Publishers.

Askew, K., M. Beverly, and M.L. Jay. 2012. "Aligning Collaborative and Culturally Responsive Evaluation Approaches." *Evaluation and Program Planning* 35(4): 552–557.

ATD (Association for Talent Development). 2015. "ATD Master Performance Consultant Program Job Aids." Association for Talent Development.

ATD. 2023. *Measuring Impact: Using Data to Understand Learning Programs.* ATD Press.

ATD. 2024. *2024 State of the Industry.* ATD Press.

Australian Education Research Organisation (AERO). 2023. "Knowledge Is Central to Learning." Explainer. edresearch.edu.au/resources/explainer/knowledge-central-learning.

Better Evaluation. 2014. "Rainbow Framework." betterevaluation.org.

Bill and Melinda Gates Foundation. n.d. "Evaluation Policy." gatesfoundation.org/about/policies-and-resources/evaluation-policy.

Block, P. 2011. *Flawless Consulting*, 3rd ed. Pfeiffer.

Boudreau, J., and P. Ramstad. 2007. *Beyond HR: The New Science of Human Capital.* Harvard Business School Press.

Bransford, J.D., A.L. Brown, and R.R. Cocking, eds. 2000. *How People Learn: Brain, Mind, Experience, and School.* National Academies Press.

Broad, M.L., and J.W. Newstrom. 1992. *The Transfer of Training.* Basic Books.

Brown, P.C., H.L. Roediger III, and M.A. McDaniel. 2014. *Make It Stick: The Science of Successful Learning.* Belknap Press of Harvard University Press.

Bryk, A.S., L. Gomez, A. Grunow, and P. LaMahieu. 2015. *Learning to Improve: How America's Schools Can Get Better at Getting Better.* Harvard Education Press.

Bryk, A.S. 2015. "Accelerating How We Learn to Improve." *Educational Researcher* 44(9): 467–477.

Bryson, J.M., B.C. Crosby, and M.M. Stone. 2015. "Designing and Implementing Cross-Sector Collaborations: Needed and Challenging." *Public Administration Review* 75(5): 647–663.

Burkett, H. 2013. "Ten Tactics for a Sustainable Evaluation Process." *InfoLine*, ATD Press.

Burkett, H. 2017. *Learning for the Long Run: 7 Practices for Sustaining a Resilient Learning Organization.* ATD Press.

Buzachero, V.B., J. Phillips, P.P. Phillips, and Z.L. Phillips. 2013. *Measuring ROI in Healthcare: Tools and Techniques to Measure the Impact and ROI in Healthcare Improvement Projects and Programs*. McGraw Hill.

Cairns-Lee, H., J. Lawley, and P. Tosey. 2022a. "Enhancing Researcher Reflexivity About the Influence of Leading Questions in Interviews." *The Journal of Applied Behavioral Science* 58(1): 164–188.

Cairns-Lee, H., J. Lawley, and P. Tosey. 2022b. *Clean Language Interviewing*. Emerald Publishing Limited.

Chavan, S. 2023. "Data Visualization for Qualitative Data." *Medium*, February 7. thesidvizstudio.medium.com/data-visualization-for-qualitative-data-75174379a342.

Cizek, G.J., and D.S. Earnest. 2016. "Setting Performance Standards on Tests." In *Handbook of Test Development*, 2nd ed, edited by S. Lane, M.R. Raymond, and T.M. Haladyna, 212–237. Routledge.

Clark, D. 2021. "The Tech Cold War's 'Most Complicated Machine' That's Out of China's Reach." *New York Times*, July 4.

CohenMiller, A., N. Durrani, Z. Kataeva, and Z. Makhmetova. 2022. "Conducting Focus Groups in Multicultural Educational Contexts: Lessons Learned and Methodological Insights." *International Journal of Qualitative Methods* 21:1–10.

Cokins, G. 1996. *Activity-Based Cost Management: Making It Work—A Manager's Guide to Implementing and Sustaining an Effective ABC System*. McGraw-Hill.

Cresswell, J.W. 2007. *Qualitative Inquiry & Research Design: Choosing Among Five Approaches*. Sage Publications.

Crow, R., B. Hinnant-Crawford, and D. Spaulding, eds. 2019. *The Educational Leader's Guide to Improvement Science*. Myers Education Press.

Dishman, L. 2022. "Managers Have It 10 Times Harder Now—Here's How to Help Them." Fast Company, March 25. fastcompany.com/90733761/managers-have-it-10-times-harder-now-heres-how-to-help-them.

Doerr, J. 2018. *Measure What Matters: How Google, Bono, and the Gates Foundation Rock the World With OKRs*. Portfolio.

Dooley, C.R. 1945. *The Training Within Industry Report (1940-1945): A Record of the Development of Supervision-Their Use and the Results*. War Manpower Commission, Bureau of Training, Training Within Industry Service.

REFERENCES

English, T., M. Lawson, S. McIntosh, and D. Albright. 2023. "Evaluating SBIRT Outcomes in Primary Care Clinics." Research presented at Annual Meeting of Addition Health Services Research (AHSR) Conference, New York.

Eval Academy. n.d. "Grab the Cake, It's Time for a Data Party! Benefits of and How to Run Your Own." Eval Academy. evalacademy.com/articles/benefits-of-a-data-party-and-how-to-run-your-own.

Fairchild, M., J. Haag, and M. Torrance. 2023. "The State of Data & Analytics in L&D: 2023." Learning Guild. learningguild.com/insights/304/the-state-of-data-analytics-in-ld-2023.

Fetter, A. 2011. "Ever Wonder What They'd Notice?" Video, YouTube, April 15. youtube.com/watch?v=a-Fth6sOaRA.

Few, S. 2012. *Show Me the Numbers*. Analytics Press.

Fink, A. 2003. *How to Ask Survey Questions*. Sage Publications.

Franklin, S., H. Binder-Matsuo, and S. Gopal. 2023. "Extend the 'Job Honeymoon': Acknowledging It Is Hard to Start a Job Can Help." *Strategic HR Review* 22(4): 110–114.

Friedlob, G.T., and F.J. Plewa. 1996. *Understanding Return on Investment: Getting to the Bottom of Your Bottom Line*. Wiley.

Gallo, C. 2016. *The Storyteller's Secret: From TED Speakers to Business Legends, Why Some Ideas Catch On and Others Don't*. St. Martin's Press.

Garcia-Arroyo, J., and A. Osca. 2019. "Big Data Contributions to Human Resource Management: A Systematic Review." *The International Journal of Human Resource Management*. DOI: 10.1080/09585192.2019.1674357.

Gartner. 2023. "Key Considerations for L&D Structures of the Future." Gartner, March. gartner.com/document/4212799?ref=solrAll&refval=407830147&.

Gilbert, T.F. 2007. *Human Competence: Engineering Worthy Performance*. The International Society for Performance Improvement.

Glaser, B., and A. Strauss. 1967. *The Discovery of Grounded Theory: Strategies for Qualitative Research*. Aldine Transaction.

Gloat. n.d. "How Unilever Used Upskilling to Prepare for the Future." Gloat. resources.gloat.com/resources/unilever-customer-success-story.

Grunow, A. 2015. *Improvement Discipline in Practice*. Carnegie Foundation for the Advancement of Teaching. carnegiefoundation.org/blog/improvement-discipline-in-practice.

Gunawardena, C.N., N.V. Flor, and D.M. Sánchez. 2025. *Knowledge Co-Construction in Online Learning: Applying Social Learning Analytic Methods and Artificial Intelligence*. Routledge.

Guo, S., and M.W. Fraser. 2014. *Propensity Score Analysis: Statistical Methods and Applications.* Sage Publications.

Haladyna, T.M., and M.C. Rodriguez. 2013. *Developing and Validating Test Items.* Routledge.

HCM (Human Capital Media) Advisory Group. 2015. "2015 Measurement and Metrics." Chief Learning Officer Business Intelligence Board Report, Presentation. info.clomedia.com/hubfs/HCM_Research_Takeaways/2015_CLO_Research_Takeaways/2015_CLO_Measurement_and_Metrics_v4.pdf.

Heifetz, R., M. Linsky, and A. Grashow. 2009. "The Practice of Adaptive Leadership: Tools and Tactics for Changing Your Organization and the World." Harvard Business School Press.

Hinkin, T.R., and J.B. Tracey. 2000. "The Cost of Turnover." *Cornell Hotel & Restaurant Administration Quarterly*, June.

Hoffeld, D. 2016. *The Science of Selling: Proven Strategies to Make Your Pitch, Influence Decisions, and Close the Deal.* Tarcher Perigee.

Horngren, C.T. 1982. *Cost Accounting: A Managerial Emphasis*, 5th ed. Prentice-Hall.

Huggett, C., J.J. Phillips, P.P. Phillips, and E. Weber. 2023. *Designing Virtual Learning for Application and Impact: 50 Techniques to Ensure Results.* ATD Press.

Iansiti, M., and S. Nadella. 2022. "Democratizing Transformation." *Harvard Business Review*, May–June.

International Organization for Standardization (ISO). 2023. *ISO TS 30437:2023 – Human resource management – Learning and development metrics.* International Organization for Standardization.

Jacobs, R. 2019. *Work Analysis in the Knowledge Economy: Documenting What People Do in the Workplace for Human Resource Development.* Springer.

Jacobs, R.L. 1992. "Structured On-the-Job-Training." In *Handbook of Human Performance Technology*, edited by H.D. Stolovitch and E.J. Keeps, 499–512. Jossey-Bass.

Jacobs, R.L. 1994. "Comparing the Training Efficiency and Product Quality of Unstructured and Structured OJT." In *The Return on Investment in Human Resource Development*, edited by J. Phillips. ATD Press.

Jacobs, R.L., ed. 2001. "Planned Training on the Job." *Advanced in Developing Human Resources* 3(4). Sage Publications.

Jacobs, R.L. 2003. *Structured On-the-Job Training: Unleashing Employee Expertise in the Workplace*, 2nd ed. Berrett-Koehler.

REFERENCES

Jacobs, R.L. 2017. "Knowledge Work and Human Resource Development." *Human Resource Development Review* 16(2): 176–202.

Jacobs, R.L., and M.J. Bu-Rahmah. 2012. "Developing Employee Expertise Through Structured On-the-Job Training (S-OJT): An Introduction to This Training Approach and the KNPC Experience." *Industrial and Commercial Training* 44(2): 75–84.

Jacobs, R.L., and T.D. McGiffin. 1987. "A Human Performance System Using a Structured On-the-Job Training Approach." *Performance and Instruction* 25(7): 8–11.

Jacobs, R.L., and A.M. Osman-Gani. 2005. *Workplace Training & Learning: Cases From Cross-Cultural Perspectives.* Pearson Prentice Hall.

Jacobs, R.L., M.J. Jones, and S. Neil. 1992. "A Case Study in Forecasting the Financial Benefits of Unstructured and Structured On-the-Job Training." *Human Resource Development Quarterly* 3(2): 133–139.

Jacobs, R., and M. Hruby-Moore. 1998. "Comparing the Forecasted and Actual Financial Benefits of Human Resource Development Programs: Learning From Failure." *Performance Improvement Quarterly* 11(2): 93–100.

Karpicke, J.D., A.C. Butler, and H.L. Roediger III. 2009. "Metacognitive Strategies in Student Learning: Do Students Practise Retrieval When They Study on Their Own?" *Memory* 17(4): 471–479.

Kendeou, P., and P. van den Broek. 2005. "The Effects of Readers' Misconceptions on Comprehension of Scientific Text." *Journal of Educational Psychology* 97(2): 235–245.

Kirkpatrick, J., and W. Kirkpatrick. 2016. *Kirkpatrick's Four Levels of Training Evaluation.* ATD Press.

Kirschner, P.A., and J.J.G. van Merriënboer. 2013. "Do Learners Really Know Best? Urban Legends in Education." *Educational Psychologist* 48(3): 169–183.

Klinghoffer, D. and K. Kirkpatrick-Husk. 2023. "More Than 50% of Managers Feel Burned Out." *Harvard Business Review.* hbr.org/2023/05/more-than-50-of-managers-feel-burned-out.

Knaflic, C.N. 2016. *Storytelling With Data.* John Wiley & Sons.

Krippendorff, K. 1980. *Content Analysis: An Introduction to Its Methodology.* Sage.

Kvale, S. 1996. *Interviews: An Introduction to Qualitative Research Interviewing.* Sage.

Langley, G.J., R.D. Moen, K.M. Nolan, T.W. Nolan, C.L. Norman, and L.P. Provost. 2009. *The Improvement Guide: A Practical Approach to Enhancing Organizational Performance.* John Wiley & Sons.

REFERENCES

Lawson, M.A., and T. Alameda-Lawson. 2012. "A Case Study of School-Linked, Collective Parent Engagement." *American Educational Research Journal* 49:651–684.

Leberman, S.I., and A.J. Martin. 2004. "Enhancing Transfer of Learning Through Post-Course Reflection." *Journal of Adventure Education and Outdoor Learning* 4(2): 173–184.

Lewis, C. 2015. "What Is Improvement Science? Do We Need It in Education?" *Educational Researcher* 44(1): 54–61.

LinkedIn Learning. 2021. *2021 Workplace Learning Report*. learning.linkedin.com/resources/workplace-learning-report-2021.

LinkedIn Learning. 2023. "Building the Agile Future." *2023 Workplace Learning Report*. learning.linkedin.com/resources/workplace-learning-report-2023.

Loubere, N. 2017. "Questioning Transcription: The Case for Systematic and Reflexive Interviewing and Reporting Method." *Forum: Qualitative Social Research (FQS)* 18(2).

Mafi, S. 2001. "Planned On-the-Job Managerial Training." In *Planned Training On the Job*, edited by R.L. Jacobs. Sage.

Mattox, J.R. 2011. "Scrap Learning and Manager Engagement." *Chief Learning Officer* 10(4): 48–50.

Miles M.B., and A.M. Huberman. 1994. *Qualitative Data Analysis: An Expanded Source Book*, 2nd ed. Sage.

Mollick, E.R., and L. Mollick. 2023. "Assigning AI: Seven Approaches for Students, With Prompts." *SSRN*, September 23.

Mootee, I. 2013. *Design Thinking for Strategic Innovation: What They Can't Teach You at Business or Design School*. John Wiley & Sons.

Morgan, D.L. 1998. *The Focus Group Guidebook*. Sage Publications

Nas, T.F. 1996. *Cost-Benefit Analysis: Theory and Application*. Sage Publications.

Neale, J. 2016. "Iterative Categorization (IC): A Systematic Technique for Analysing Qualitative Data." In *Addiction, Methods and Techniques, 1096–1106*. Society for the Study of Addiction.

Nelson, J.W. 2021. "Using Predictive Analytics to Move From Reactive to Proactive Management of Outcomes." In *Using Predictive Analytics to Improve Healthcare Outcomes*, edited by J.W. Nelson, J. Felgen, and M.A. Hozak, 3–31. John Wiley & Sons.

New York Times. n.d. "What's Going On in this Graph?" nytimes.com/column/whats-going-on-in-this-graph.

REFERENCES

Nichols, D. n.d. "Coloring for Colorblindness." davidmathlogic.com/colorblind/#%25234D81FF-%2523B24CED-%2523FFA851-%25235FD9C5.

O.C. Tanner. 2021. "Global Culture Report 2021." octanner.com/global-culture-report/2021-technology.

O'Connell, R. 2024. "LeBron James Has Done Everything in the NBA. Except This." *Wall Street Journal*, March 13.

Patton, M.Q. 1998. "Discovering Process Use." *Evaluation* 4(2): 225–233.

Patton, M.Q. 2002. "Qualitative Evaluation Checklist." Western Michigan University. files.wmich.edu/s3fs-public/attachments/u350/2018/qual-eval-patton.pdf.

Patton, M.Q. 2016. "State of the Art and Practice of Developmental Evaluation: Answers to Common and Recurring Questions." In *Developmental Evaluation Exemplars: Principles in Practice*, edited by M.Q. Patton, K. McKegg, and N. Wehipeihana, 1–24. The Guilford Press.

Phillips, J.J. 1982. *Handbook of Training Evaluation and Measurement Methods*. Gulf Publishing.

Phillips, J.J., and P.P. Phillips. 2008. *Beyond Learning Objectives: Develop Measurable Objectives That Link to the Bottom Line*. ASTD Press.

Phillips, J.J., and P.P. Phillips. 2009. *Measuring for Success: What CEOs Really Think About Learning Investments*. ASTD Press.

Phillips, J.J., and P.P. Phillips. 2010. *Measuring for Success*. ASTD Press.

Phillips, J.J., and P.P. Phillips. 2016. *Handbook of Training Evaluation and Measurement Methods*, 4th ed. Routledge.

Phillips, J.J., and P.P. Phillips. 2016. *Real World Training Evaluation: Navigating Common Constraints for Exceptional Results*. ATD Press.

Phillips, J.J., and L. Zúñga. 2008. "Costs and ROI: Evaluating at the Ultimate Level." In *Measurement and Evaluation Series*, edited by P.P. Phillips and J. J. Phillips. Pfeiffer.

Phillips, J.J., P.P. Phillips, and R. Robinson. 2013. *Measuring the Success of Sales Training*. ASTD Press.

Phillips, K. 2016. "How Much Is Scrap Learning Costing Your Organization?" ATD blog, td.org/insights/how-much-is-scrap-learning-costing-your-organization.

Phillips, K. 2020. "Pinpointing the Underlying Causes of Scrap Learning." *Training*, July–August. trainingindustry.com/magazine/jul-aug-2020/pinpointing-the-underlying-causes-of-scrap-learning.

Phillips, P.P., and J.J. Phillips. 2008. *The Value of Learning: How Organizations Capture Value and ROI*. Pfeiffer.

Phillips, P.P., and J.J. Phillips. 2014. *Measuring ROI in Employee Relations and Compliance*. Society for Human Resource Management.

Phillips, P.P., and J.J. Phillips. 2017. *The Bottomline on ROI*, 3rd ed. HRDQ Press.

Phillips, P.P., and J.J. Phillips. 2018. *Value for Money: Measuring the Return on Non-Capital Investments*. ROI Institute.

Phillips, P.P., and J.J. Phillips. 2019. *Return on Investment Basics*, 2nd ed. ATD Press.

Phillips, P.P., and J.J. Phillips. 2022. *Show the Value of What You Do: Measuring and Achieving Success in Any Endeavor*. Berrett-Koehler.

Phillips, P.P., and C.A. Stawarski. 2008. *Measurement and Evaluation Series, Book 2 Data Collection*. Pfeiffer.

Phillips, P.P., J.J. Phillips, and B. Aaron. 2013. *Survey Basics*. ASTD Press.

Phillips, P.P., J.J. Phillips, and R. Ray. 2015. *Measuring the Success of Leadership Development*. ATD Press.

Phillips, P.P., J.J. Phillips, and K. Toes. 2024. *Return on Investment in Training and Performance Improvement Programs*. Routledge.

Phillips, J.P., and B.C. Aaron. 2008. *Isolation of Results: Defining the Impact of the Programs*. Pfeiffer.

Pollock, R.V.H., A.M. Jefferson, and C.W. Wick. 2015. *The Six Disciplines of Breakthrough Learning: How to Turn Training and Development Into Business Results*, 3rd ed. ATD Press.

Preskill, H., and T. Beer. 2012. "Evaluating Social Innovation." FSG/Center for Evaluation Innovation. groupjazz.com/evaluation/images/Evaluating_Social_Innovation.pdf.

Prinz, A., S. Golke, and J. Wittwer. 2018. "The Double Curse of Misconceptions: Misconceptions Impair Not Only Text Comprehension But Also Metacomprehension in the Domain of Statistics." *Instructional Science* 46(5): 723–765.

PwC. 2024. "Thriving in an Age of Continuous Reinvention." PwC Global CEO Survey. pwc.com/gx/en/ceo-survey/2024/download/27th-ceo-survey.pdf.

Rhodes, M.G. 2016. "Judgments of Learning: Methods, Data, Theory." In *The Oxford Handbook of Metamemory*, edited by J. Dunlosky and S.K. Tauber. Oxford University Press.

ROI Institute. 2014. ROI Certification Building Capability and Expertise With ROI Implementation, Planning Evaluation.

REFERENCES

ROI Institute. 2020. *ROI Benchmarking Study*. roiinstitute.net/wp content/uploads/2021/07/ROI Institute Benchmarking Report 2021.pdf.

ROI Institute. 2023. *Application Guide: The ROI Methodology in 12 Easy Steps*.

ROI Institute. 2023. "Measuring the Impact and ROI of the Insights Discovery Program." info.insights.com/hubfs/ROI%20Report_Final.pdf.

ROI Institute. 2024. "ROI Certification Workbook." ROI Institute.

Rucci, A.J., S.P. Kim, and R.T. Quinn. 1998. "The Employee-Customer-Profit Chain at Sears." *Harvard Business Review*, January-February.

Sabattini, L., and P.P. Phillips. 2021. "The ROI of Inclusion Toolkit." The Conference Board, April 5. conference-board.org/publications/ROI-of-inclusion-tool-kit.

Salkind, N. 2000. *Statistics for People Who (Think They) Hate Statistics*. Sage.

Seidman, E. 2012. "An Emergent Action Science of Social Settings." *American Journal of Community Psychology* 50:1–16.

Shrock, S.A., and W.C. Coscarelli. 2007. *Criterion-Referenced Test Development: Technical and Legal Guidelines for Corporate Training*. Pfeiffer.

Sitzmann, T., K.G. Brown, W.J. Casper, K. Ely, and R.D. Zimmerman. 2008. "A Review and Meta-Analysis of the Nomological Network of Trainee Reactions." *Journal of Applied Psychology* 93(2): 280–295.

Smith, P. 2012. *Lead With a Story: A Guide to Crafting Business Narratives That Captivate, Convince, and Inspire*. AMACOM.

Smith, T. and T. Uhl. 2019. "How to Measure Learning Effectiveness." Numerical Insights. numericalinsights.com/blog/how-to-measure-learning-effectiveness-a-simple-test-for-workshop-value.

Society for Industrial and Organizational Psychology. 2018. *Principles for the Validation and Use of Personnel Selection Procedures*, 5th ed. American Psychological Association.

Stein, D., and C. Valters. 2012. "Understanding Theory of Change in International Development." *Justice and Security Research Programme*, Paper 1.

Stroh, D. 2015. *Systems Thinking for Social Change: A Practical Guide to Solving Complex Problems, Avoiding Unintended Consequences, and Achieving Lasting Results*. Chelsea Green Publishing.

Surowiecki, J. 2004. *The Wisdom of Crowds: Why the Many Are Smarter Than the Few and How Collective Wisdom Shapes Business, Economies, Societies, and Nations*. Doubleday.

Syed, M. 2016. *Black Box Thinking: Marginal Gains and the Secrets of High Performance.* John Murray Publishers.

Tetlock, P.E., and D. Gardner. 2015. *Super Forecasting.* Broadway Books.

Thalheimer, W. n.d. "The Learning-Transfer Evaluation Model: Sending Messages to Enable Learning Effectiveness." worklearning.com/ltem.

Thalheimer, W. 2018. "Donald Kirkpatrick Was NOT the Originator of the Four-Level Model of Learning Evaluation." Work-Learning Research, January 30. worklearning.com/2018/01/30/donald-kirkpatrick-was-not-the-originator-of-the-four-level-model-of-learning-evaluation.

Thalheimer, W. 2022. *Performance-Focused Learner Surveys: Using Distinctive Questioning to Get Actionable Data and Guide Learning Effectiveness.* Work-Learning Press.

United Nations Evaluation Group. 2016. "Norms and Standards for Evaluation." unevaluation.org/document/detail/1914.

US Equal Employment Opportunity Commission. 1978. *Uniform Guidelines on Employee Selection Procedures.* 29 C.F.R. Part 1607.

USAID. 2015. "Evaluation Design Matrix Templates." usaidlearninglab.org/resources/evaluation-design-matrix-templates.

Uttl, B., C.A. White, and D.W. Gonzalez. 2017. "Meta-Analysis of Faculty's Teaching Effectiveness: Student Evaluation of Teaching Ratings and Student Learning Are Not Related." *Studies in Educational Evaluation* 54:22–42.

Vance, D., and P. Parskey. 2021. *Measurement Demystified: Creating Your L&D Measurement, Analytics, and Reporting Strategy.* ATD Press.

Vona, M.K., M. Woolf, and B. Sugrue. 2019. "Learning's Value in the Era of Disruption." *Training*, February 27. trainingmag.com/learnings-value-in-the-era-of-disruption.

Wang, G., Z. Dou, and N. Lee. 2002. "A Systems Approach to Measuring Return on Investment (ROI) for HRD Interventions." *Human Resource Development Quarterly* 13(2): 203–24.

Watershed. 2022. "Adopting Learning Analytics, Closing the C Suite/L&D Language Gap." watershedlrs.com/resources/research/adopting-learning-analytics-c-suite-l-and-d-language-gap.

Watershed. 2022. "Measuring the Business Impact of Learning in 2022." watershedlrs.com/resources/research/measuring-business-impact-learning-2022.

REFERENCES

Watson, J. 2001. *How to Determine a Sample Size: Tipsheet 60.* Penn State Cooperative Extension.

Weber, E. 2014. *Turning Learning Into Action: A Proven Methodology for Effective Transfer of Learning.* Kogan Page.

Weiss, C.H. 1995. "Nothing as Practical as Good Theory: Exploring Theory-Based Evaluation for Comprehensive Community Initiatives for Children and Families." In *New Approaches to Evaluating Community Initiatives: Concepts, Methods and Contexts,* edited by J.P. Connell, A.C. Kubisch, L.B. Schorr, and C.H. Weiss, 65–92. The Aspen Institute.

World Economic Forum (WEF). 2020. "Measuring Stakeholder Capitalism: Towards Common Metrics and Consistent Reporting of Sustainable Value Creation." Whitepaper. WEF, September. weforum.org/docs/WEF_IBC_Measuring_Stakeholder_Capitalism_Report_2020.pdf.

Yarbrough, D.B., L.M. Shulha, R.K. Hopson, and F.A. Caruthers. 2011. *The Program Evaluation Standards: A Guide for Evaluators and Evaluation Users.* Joint Committee on Standard for Educational Evaluation. Sage Publishing.

Zechmeister, E.B., and J.J. Shaughnessy. 1980. "When You Know That You Know and When You Think That You Know But You Don't." *Bulletin of the Psychonomic Society* 15(1): 41–44.

Additional Resources

Aiken, L. 1991. *Psychological Testing and Assessment*, 7th ed. Allyn and Bacon.

Alreck, P.L., and R.B. Settle. 1995. *The Survey Research Handbook: Guidelines and Strategies for Conducting a Survey*, 2nd ed. McGraw-Hill.

Boudreau, J.W., W.F. Cascio, and A.A. Fink. 2019. *Investing in People: Financial Impact of Human Resource Initiatives*. Society for Human Resource Management.

Bowles, M., C. Burns, J. Hixson, S.A. Jenness, and K. Tellers. 2023. *How to Tell a Story: The Essential Guide to Memorable Storytelling From the Moth*. Crown.

Brinkerhoff, R.O., and D. Dressler. 2002. "Using Evaluation to Build Organizational Performance and Learning Capability: A Strategy and a Method." *Performance Improvement*, July.

Broad, M.L. 2008. *Beyond Transfer of Training: Engaging Systems to Improve Performance*. John Wiley & Sons.

Burkett, H. 2002. "Leveraging Employee Know-How Through Structured OJT." In *Implementing On-the-Job Learning*, edited by J.J. Phillips and R. Jacobs. ASTD Press.

Burkett, H. 2005. "ROI on a Shoestring: Evaluation Strategies for Resource-Constrained Environments (Part II)." *Industrial and Commercial Training* 37(2): 97–105.

Burkett, H. 2006. "Evaluating a Career Development Initiative." In *Evaluating the Four Levels*, 3rd ed., edited by D. Kirkpatrick. Berrett-Koehler.

Burkett, H. 2010. "Action Planning as a Performance Measurement and Transfer Strategy." In *ASTD Handbook of Measuring & Evaluating Training*, edited by P.P. Phillips. ASTD Press.

Burkett, H. 2015. "Talent Managers as Change Agents." In *The Talent Management Handbook*, edited by T. Bickham. ATD Press.

Burkett, H. 2016. "From Making It Stick to Making It Last." *TD*, September. td.org/magazines/td-magazine/from-making-it-stick-to-making-it-last.

Burkett, H. 2024. "Combating Change Fatigue." *TD*, January. td.org/magazines/td-magazine/combating-change-fatigue.

ADDITIONAL RESOURCES

Burkett, H. 2012. "Case Study 5.2: Community Healthcare Association of the Dakotas." In *Fundamentals of Performance Improvement*, 3rd ed., edited by D. Van Tiem, J.L. Moseley, J.C. Dessinger. Pfeiffer.

Damodaran, A. 2017. *Narrative and Numbers: The Value of Stories in Business*. Columbia Business School Publishing.

Duarte, N. 2008. *Side:ology*. O'Reilly Media.

Earl, S., F. Carden, and T. Smutylo. 2001. "Outcome Mapping: Building Learning and Reflection Into Development Programs." betterevaluation.org/sites/default/files/Outcome_Mapping_Building_Learning_and_Reflection_into_Development_Programs.pdf.

Evergreen, S. 2019. *Effective Data Visualization: The Right Chart for the Right Data*. Sage Publications.

Few, S. 2009. *Now You See It*. Analytics Press.

Few, S. 2012. *Show Me the Numbers*. Analytics Press.

Fink, A. 2003. *The Survey Handbook*, 2nd ed. Sage Publications.

Hale, J. 2012. *Performance-Based Certification: How to Design a Valid, Defensible, Cost-Effective Program*, 2nd ed. Pfeiffer.

Hall, K. 2019. *Stories That Stick: How Storytelling Can Captivate Customers, Influence Audiences, and Transform Your Business*. HarperCollins Leadership.

Heath, C., and K. Starr. 2022. *Making Numbers Count*. Avid Reader Press.

Kaufman, R. 2002. "Resolving the (Often-Deserved) Attacks on Training." *Performances Impermanency* 41(6).

Kee, J.E. 2004. "Cost-Effectiveness and Cost-Benefit Analysis." In *Handbook of Practical Program Evaluation*, 2nd ed., edited by J.S. Wholey, H.P. Hatry, and K.E. Newcomer. Jossey-Bass.

Keuler, D. 2001. "Measuring ROI for Telephonic Customer Service Skills," In *In Action: Measuring Return on Investment*, vol. 3., edited by P.P. Phillips. ASTD Press.

Kida, T. 2006. *Don't Believe Everything You Think: The 6 Basic Mistakes We Make in Thinking*. Prometheus Books.

Knaflic, C.N. 2016. *Storytelling With Data*. John Wiley & Sons.

Koomey, J.G. 2008. *Turning Numbers Into Knowledge*. Analytics Press.

Krueger, R.A., and M.A. Casey. 2015. *Focus Group: A Practical Guide for Applied Research*, 5th ed. Sage Publishing.

Kurnoff, J., and L. Lazarus. 2021. *Everyday Business Storytelling: Create, Simplify, and Adapt a Visual Narrative for Any Audience*. Wiley.

Kusek, J.Z., and R.C. Rist. 2004. *Ten Steps to a Results-Based Monitoring and Evaluation System: A Handbook for Development Practitioners*. The World Bank.

Morgan, D.L. 1997. *Focus Groups as Qualitative Research*. Sage Publications.

Niedermann, D., and D. Boyum. 2003. *What the Numbers Say: A Field Guide to Mastering Our Numerical World*. Broadway Books.

Patton, M.Q. 2014. *Qualitative Evaluation and Research Methods*. Sage Publications.

Phillips, J.J., and P.P. Phillips. 2007. *Show Me the Money: How to Determine ROI in People, Projects, and Programs*. Berrett-Koehler.

Phillips, J.J., and W.F. Tush. 2008. *Communicating and Implementation-Sustaining the Practice*. Pfeiffer.

Phillips, J.J., and L. Zúñiga. 2008. "Costs and ROI: Evaluating at the Ultimate Level." In *Measurement and Evaluation Series*, edited by P.P. Phillips and J.J. Phillips. Pfeiffer.

Phillips, J.J., P.P. Phillips, R. Stone, and H. Burkett. 2006. *The ROI Fieldbook: Strategies for Implementing ROI in HR and Training*. Elsevier.

Phillips, P.P., and J.J. Phillips. 2002. "Evaluating the Impact of a Graduate Program in a Federal Agency." In *In Action: Measuring ROI in the Public Sector*, edited by P. Phillips, 149–172. ASTD Press.

Phillips, P.P., and J.J. Phillips. 2007. *The Value of Learning: How Organizations Capture Value and ROI and Translate Them Into Support, Improvement, and Funds*. Pfeiffer.

Phillips, P.P. and J.J. Phillips. 2007. *Proving the Value of HR: ROI Case Studies*. ROI Institute.

Phillips, P.P., and J.J. Phillips. 2019. *Proving the Value of Soft Skills: Measuring Impact and Calculating ROI*. ATD Press.

Phillips, P.P., and J.J. Phillips. 2022. *Show the Value of What You Do: Measuring and Achieving Success in Any Endeavor*. Berrett-Koehler.

Phillips, P.P., J.J. Phillips, and K. Toes. 2024. *Return on Investment in Training and Performance Improvement Programs*. Routledge.

Russ-Eft, D., and H. Preskill. 2001. *Evaluation in Organizations: A Systematic Approach to Enhancing Learning, Performance, and Change*. Basic Books.

Sunstein, C.R. 2019. *The Cost-Benefit Revolution*. MIT Press.

Tufte, E. 2001. *The Visual Display of Information*. Graphics Press.

ADDITIONAL RESOURCES

Vance, D., and P. Parskey. 2020. *Measurement Demystified: Creating Your L&D Measurement, Analytics, and Reporting Strategy.* ATD Press.

Wallace, D. 2010. "Implementing and Sustaining a Measurement and Evaluation Practice." In *ASTD Handbook of Measuring & Evaluating Training*, edited by P.P. Phillips. ASTD Press.

Walonick, D.S. 2004. *Survival Statistics.* StatPac.

Weber, E. n.d. "Action Planning Masterclass." Video. tinyurl.com/5evjd5c3.

Weber, E. n.d. "Coach M Analytics for Insights." Lever – Transfer of Learning. transferoflearning.com/insights.

Zigarmi, L., J. Diamond, and L. Mones. 2024. "A Guide for Getting Stakeholder Buy-In for Your Agenda." *Harvard Business Review*, January.

About the Contributors

Katharine Aldana, a two-time ROI Institute ROI Practitioner of the Year and 2023 Best Published ROI Article award winner, is known for her creative program improvement strategies. Katharine spent more than seven years designing learning strategies and performing program evaluations for a Fortune Top 20 organization and teaching ROI implementation both internally and externally. She continues to leverage these same skills and experiences in numerous strategic roles and projects outside L&D. In 2021, Katharine began facilitating ROI Institute's Live Virtual ROI Boot Camp, inspiring new practitioners with her passion and extensive knowledge of what it takes to manage a program from inception to execution and evaluation. Her enthusiasm for program effectiveness and real-world experience make her a dynamic facilitator and highly sought-after ROI implementation resource. In 2024, Katharine earned a master's degree in applied business analytics from Boston University.

Rachel Baghelai, PhD, is an industrial and organizational psychologist and PMP-certified project manager with more than 15 years of experience in professional services. She has methodological expertise in assessment, measurement and evaluation strategy, qualitative and quantitative research methods, statistical analyses, and research reporting. Rachel has experience as an external consultant helping her clients through their assessment and analytics journeys, as well as an internal consultant working to enable change and measurable outcomes. The key to her success has always been her ability to build relationships with others from all walks of life to understand the needs of her clients and the people who make up their organizations. Rachel has advanced degrees in business and psychology. Her dissertation research at The Chicago School of Professional Psychology was focused on optimizing the application and business outcomes of corporate training.

Nader Bechini is a partner and regional director of ROI Institute in the MENA region with a strong international reputation in measurement and evaluation. With more than

ABOUT THE CONTRIBUTORS

23 years of experience, Nader is dedicated to helping organizations and talent development professionals enhance their performance and effectiveness. Nader's mission is to empower others to inspire, influence, and create meaningful impact. He has facilitated workshops, managed talent development programs, and consulted with organizations in more than 30 countries across North and South America, Europe, Africa, Australia, and Asia. His client portfolio includes notable organizations such as Meta, Microsoft, NOAA, KPMG, IDEXX, Lululemon, 211sandiego, Alamo College, IBA University Germany, the University of Dubai, Omantel, STC, Saudi Aramco, and Bank of Georgia. His work has earned recognition, including multiple awards from ROI Institute for the best international implementation of the ROI Methodology in 2015, 2019, and 2020, as well as an award for the best African HR expert from the Moroccan Society for Human Resources in 2019. His articles on learning and development have been translated into several languages, including Korean, Russian, Chinese, French, Arabic, and Spanish. Nader has also been featured in various radio and TV programs, as well as HR magazines in Saudi Arabia, Sudan, Tunisia, France, Egypt, Russia, Jordan, Bahrain, Morocco, and Algeria. Nader is an accredited certified coach from the International Coaching Federation and a Certified Professional in Talent Development from the Association for Talent Development. He holds a master's degree in marketing and an executive leadership certificate from INSEAD Business School.

Timothy R. Brock, PhD, CRP, is the chief facilitation officer at ROI Institute, the leading source of ROI competency building, implementation support, and research. He is a former advanced doctoral programs faculty member at Capella University and a former faculty member at the United Nations Systems Staff College in Turin, Italy. Timothy has published multiple chapters and articles on performance improvement and evaluation. He retired from the US Air Force after serving in the enlisted and officer ranks, and retired from Lockheed Martin, where he led their global simulation learning and performance team. He can be reached at tim@roiinstitute.net.

Kaycee Buckley, CRP, is the global commercial talent director for core diagnostics at Abbott. She is accountable for leading best-in-class talent development programs, such as identifying competencies and measuring business impact, supporting more than 2,000 employees to institutionalize organizational initiatives and drive global standardization.

ABOUT THE CONTRIBUTORS

Kaycee has 25 years of experience in the learning and development industry and has focused on evaluation and measurement since becoming a Certified ROI Professional in 2019. Kaycee was awarded the 2019 Best Published Case Study from ROI Institute for her case study, "Measuring ROI in Coaching for Sales Managers," in *Proving the Value of Soft Skills: Measuring Impact and Calculating ROI*. She was also awarded the 2021 Practitioner of the Year award from ROI Institute. Kaycee has presented at numerous conferences on the subject of demonstrating the value of learning and development and measuring its impact on business.

Holly Burkett, PhD, SPHR, SCC, CRP, is principal of hb Consulting | Evaluation Works, a performance consultancy in Davis, California. She is an accomplished measurement specialist, talent builder, change leader, and workplace learning professional with more than 20 years' experience as a trusted business advisor to organizations such as Apple, Chevron, SEVA, and Roche Biomedical. She is passionate about helping teams show how their work adds value and helping organizations develop capabilities that foster sustained engagement, performance, and well-being. As an associate of ROI Institute and Certified ROI Professional, a Prosci change practitioner, Marshall Goldsmith Stakeholder Centered Coach, Senior Professional in HR, and Conference Board Research Fellow, Holly is a sought-after facilitator, coach, and speaker. Her publications include the award-winning book *Learning for the Long Run*, as well as contributions to *The ROI Fieldbook*, ATD's *TDBoK Guide,* and ISPI's *Fundamentals of Performance Improvement,* among others. She holds a doctorate in human capital development. Contact Holly at holly@hollyburkett.com.

Judith Cardenas is the founder and CEO of Strategies By Design. She has worked in many diverse work settings and held positions of president and vice president in higher educational institutions. She also has significant expertise in measuring results and accountability. Judith has a doctorate in education administration from Baylor University and a doctorate in training and performance improvement from Capella University. She holds a certification as an ROI Professional and has completed a variety of postdoctoral training including leadership development at Harvard University's John F. Kennedy School of Government, human performance improvement at ATD, and advanced ROI Methodology at Villanova University. In addition, she holds a Registered Corporate Coach designation. You can contact Judith at judith@strategiesbydesigngroup.com.

ABOUT THE CONTRIBUTORS

Robin Dijke is responsible for learning analytics at ASML. He has been leading the learning quality, process, and analytics team in ASML's global center of expertise for learning and knowledge management since June 2022 and has more than 18 years of experience in the fields of people and organization, learning, and change management. Before ASML, Robin was the global learning and development manager at Royal DSM N.V. and worked for the people and change practice within KPMG Management Consulting, where he served more than 50 organizations as a people and change consultant.

Cindy Hill is an industrial and organizational psychologist and has been in the measurement and research division at ACT for more than 25 years. She has spent many years developing and reviewing licensure and certification assessment programs including job analysis, the development of test content outlines, national surveys, data analysis, item writing and review, standard setting, and validating the test scores of off-the-shelf and company-specific tests. Her recent research has explored the alignment and stacking of credentials through standardized frameworks. As part of ACT's partnership with the Association for Talent Development, Cindy developed and facilitates ATD's Test Design and Delivery Certificate program.

Caroline Hubble is vice president of consulting services at ROI Institute. She facilitates various courses on the ROI Methodology and provides expert coaching to individuals working toward ROI certification. Caroline's professional background includes financial industry experience, where she managed training evaluation, analytics, and operations for business line and enterprise-wide training departments. She has successfully designed and implemented evaluation and reporting strategies for many complex programs. Her operational, project, and relationship management expertise significantly contributes to improved business practices. Caroline holds a BA in psychology from Rollins College and has a master of science in organizational development. She is also a Certified ROI Professional. She can be reached at caroline@roiinstitute.net.

Ronald L. Jacobs is principal of SiTUATE, a global consulting firm that focuses on workplace learning and performance. Ron is an emeritus professor of human resource development at The Ohio State University and The University of Illinois. He introduced S-OJT to the field in the 1980s and has implemented the training approach in national and international organizations and government agencies. Ron's research on comparing the financial benefits of unplanned versus structured on-the-job training provided a breakthrough for understanding the value of investing in S-OJT. The SiTUATE platform supports using S-OJT and includes a built-in feature to help track the financial impacts.

Katinka Koke is a specialist working in the United Nations Institute for Training and Research within the planning, performance monitoring, and evaluation unit since February 2016. Her responsibilities include evaluation, strategic planning, monitoring, and quality assurance, and she has conducted numerous focus groups as part of independent evaluations of training and capacity building projects or activities. Prior to that, Katinka worked in the College of Europe Development Office where she was responsible for planning and implementing professional training events and larger EU-funded technical assistance projects and preparing funding proposals. Katinka also gained experience through traineeships in the European Institutions, an embassy, and a regional government. Katinka holds an MA in EU international relations and diplomacy studies from the College of Europe and a bachelor of laws in comparative and European law from the Hanse Law School, and she spent an Erasmus year studying in Montpellier, France. She is a member of the United Nations Evaluation Group and the United Nations Network for Strategic Planning.

Faith Krebs is a master performance consultant and the owner of The ROI Generator. She is a trusted business advisor who coaches leaders and business owners on how to optimize and accelerate business results. Faith is a Certified ROI Professional and an associate of ROI Institute. She is passionate about measurement and evaluation and coaches her clients on how to measure the efficacy of their human capital solutions. She is a senior fellow in the Human Capital Analytics Institute of The Conference Board, as well as a certified facilitator for the Association for Talent Development, the largest global professional organization of its kind. Faith draws on decades of experience working for McDonald's as an executive in field operations, restaurant innovation, learning, talent development, and performance where she led worldwide organizational strategies and solutions that drove profitable, sustainable, and scalable business growth. While there, she led the global learning and performance organization that designed, developed, and deployed core performance-based learning solutions for 1.6 million employees spanning 118 countries.

ABOUT THE CONTRIBUTORS

Michael A. Lawson is head of the department of educational studies in the College of Education at the University of Alabama where he also serves as an associate professor of educational research and evaluation. His research focuses on student, family, and community engagement, improvement science, and organization development and redesign. His work has been published in leading academic journals such as *Review of Educational Research*, the *American Educational Research Journal*, and *Research on Social Work Practice*. Prior to his tenure in academe, Michael enjoyed a 15-year career as program designer and evaluator for complex change initiatives in Northern California. He now lives in Hoover, Alabama, with his wife, Kaye, and their three dogs, Whiskey, Lucy, and Milo.

Sardék Love is the CEO of Sardek Love International, a leading global training, speaking, and performance consultancy. Known as "the Engagement Expert" and a skilled human performance improvement practitioner, Sardék equips managers, talent development professionals, and consultants with the systems and processes to dramatically improve employee performance. As the lead facilitator among a small and elite group of experts who teach the ATD Master Performance Consultant designation program, Sardék has taught in multiple countries to ATD corporate clients such as SAP Concur, Regeneron, Nationwide Insurance, Saudi Aramco, and British Petroleum. A graduate of Virginia Tech, he has traveled to and worked in 32 countries and is a highly sought-after keynote speaker on the international speaking circuit.

David Maddock, EdD, project director for Federal Javits Grant Project GLIMPSE, is an evaluation specialist in the field of education. He has spearheaded numerous evaluations for education programs totaling more than $15 million. Many of his evaluation projects have been published in academic journals, books, and even on the websites of the programs they evaluated. David's expertise in evaluation can be seen in his application of the ROI Methodology to the field of education, a model that has been used in multiple school districts across Florida since it was first developed. This resulted in David being named the ROI Practitioner of the Year by ROI Institute, as well as UCF CCIE's Distinguished Alumni of the Year. David has an undergraduate degree in writing, a master's degree in communication from Florida State University, and an EdD in education leadership with a focus on statistics from the University of Central Florida.

ABOUT THE CONTRIBUTORS

Beryl Oldham has more than 35 years' experience in learning and organization development. Before moving into full-time L&D consulting in 2013, she held senior generalist HR, organization development, and learning and development roles in a range of government and corporate organizations. Beryl is the New Zealand business partner with ROI Institute, a Certified ROI Practitioner, and the managing director of Complete Learning Solutions, a New Zealand–based consultancy that helps its clients build organizational capability through excellence in learning design, delivery, and technology. She is passionate about evaluation and measurement and can be reached at beryl.oldham@completelearning.co.nz.

Peggy Parskey has more than 25 years of experience driving strategic change to improve organizational and individual performance. She focuses on team and organizational improvement, leveraging performance measurement methods, management of change, and organizational design to ensure sustainable capability. Her firm, Parskey Consulting, focuses on performance measurement as a lever of strategic change. She has melded her expertise in culture change with her deep experience in measurement to enable senior leaders to manage change initiatives leveraging data-informed decision making. Peggy has co-authored three books: *Learning Analytics and Using Talent Data to Improve Business Outcomes*, second edition, with John Mattox and Cristina Hall, and *Measurement Demystified* and *Measurement Demystified Field Guide* with David Vance. Peggy is certified in management of change methodologies both at the organizational and individual performer levels. She also holds a bachelor of science in mathematics from Simmons University and two master's degrees from the University of Chicago in statistics and business administration. She served as the assistant director of the Center for Talent Reporting between 2011 and 2023. She is also a past president of the Los Angeles Chapter of ATD, having also served as program director and chief financial officer.

Jack J. Phillips, PhD, chairman of ROI Institute, is a world-renowned expert on accountability, measurement, and evaluation. Jack provides consulting services for Fortune 500 companies and major global organizations and regularly consults with clients in manufacturing, service, and government organizations in 70 countries. The author or editor of more than 100 books, he conducts workshops and presents at conferences around the world. Jack's

ABOUT THE CONTRIBUTORS

expertise in measurement and evaluation is based on more than 27 years of corporate experience in the aerospace, textile, metals, construction materials, and banking industries. He has served as training and development manager at two Fortune 500 firms, as senior human resource officer at two firms, as president of a regional bank, and as a management professor at a major state university. He has undergraduate degrees in electrical engineering, physics, and mathematics; a master's degree in decision sciences from Georgia State University; and a PhD in human resource management from the University of Alabama.

Damien M. Sánchez, PhD, CRP, is the owner of Puerta Abierta Performance Consulting. He conducts evaluations and develops online learning modules for clients, including the New Mexico Department of Health. Damien is an associate with ROI Institute, where he teaches how to evaluate programs to ROI. He is also an adjunct instructor at the University of New Mexico. Damien has published several peer-reviewed articles and has received awards for academic excellence, contributions to the Latino community, and citizenship.

Suzanne Schell, CRP, is the CEO of ROI Institute Canada. She teaches the ROI Methodology to audiences across Canada and is involved in numerous program evaluation projects, including many ROI forecasts. Her role includes developing data collection and analysis strategies to identify change in behavior and barriers to implementation and impact. Suzanne has brought the ROI Methodology to many individuals and organizations in Canada through ROI certification, one- and two-day workshops, webinars, and consulting.

Brenda Sugrue, PhD, is a leader in learning innovation. She was the global chief learning officer at EY from 2014 to 2024 and was selected by *Chief Learning Officer* magazine as 2018's CLO of the Year. Her career has spanned corporate and academic roles including vice president of innovation and research at Kaplan and professor of instructional design and technology at the University of Iowa. Brenda applies learning science and measurement at scale to transform training and education. She advises organizations on strategy development and implementation to improve the efficiency, effectiveness, and experience of learning and talent management.

Will Thalheimer, PhD, MBA, is a consultant, speaker, and researcher at Work-Learning Research. He is a world-renowned thought leader focused on research-based practices for learning, work performance, presentations, and evaluation—and an advocate for learning professionals. Through Work-Learning Research (worklearning.com), Will empowers organizations to build maximally effective learning and performance solutions and strategies. He wrote the award-winning book *Performance-Focused Learner Surveys* and the *CEO's Guide to Training, eLearning & Work: Empowering Learning for a Competitive Advantage*. Will created LTEM, the Learning-Transfer Evaluation Model, and conducts popular workshops like the LTEM Boot Camp. He co-created The Learning Development Accelerator and the eLearning Manifesto.

Klaas Toes, MSc, is the vice president of global business development at ROI Institute and the European director of ROI Institute Europe. He has more than 30 years of experience in human capital strategies, leadership change, and sales across various sectors and government agencies. A skilled learning economist, Klaas founded ROI Institute Europe in 1998, pioneering people analytics in Europe by proving the financial value of learning. His collaborations with major companies like ABN AMRO, Microsoft, Peugeot, and Sodexo led to the development of a people analytics solution that is recognized by academic and business communities. Author of *De Waarde van Leren* and co-author of *Return on Investment of Training and Performance Improvement Programs*, Klaas regularly speaks about people analytics, business alignment, and return on learning. He currently serves as a member of IFTDO's Strategy, Governance, and International Relations Committee. From 2016 to 2021, he served as the European council director for people analytics at The Conference Board. His ventures in HR and L&D have had a global influence and established him as a respected leader in the field.

Trish Uhl is the founder of global consulting firm Owl's Ledge, where she provides strategic advisory to CLOs and organizational leaders, helping them build AI-fluent workforces and integrate AI-powered technologies into organizational strategies. Trish focuses on driving workforce transformation, fostering human-AI collaboration, and delivering measurable business outcomes while ensuring responsible AI deployment. In addition, Trish serves as an AI product manager at a major financial services firm, leading the AI intelligent agents portfolio and developing generative AI enterprise solutions that drive innovation, transform business processes, and support more than 54,000 associates and 8 million clients. Trish previously served as director of learning enablement and innovation. In that role, she integrated advanced technologies into enterprise learning and led the firm's first deployment of generative AI solutions. She also served as a people analytics expert-in-residence for the CIPD, co-creating the People Analytics Accredited Programme to advance HR analytical capability globally. A passionate advocate for the UN SDGs, Trish is committed to advancing AI literacy in communities, promoting inclusion, and empowering individuals to excel in an AI-driven future. She combines technical expertise with a human-centric approach to help people flourish and organizations thrive, fostering human and AI collaboration that creates a world that works better. Yay cake! Trish can be contacted at trishuhl@owls-ledge.com.

David Vance, PhD, is the author of *The Business of Learning*, now in its second edition, and co-author with Peggy Parskey of *Measurement Demystified* and *Measurement Demystified Field Guide*. He and Peggy developed the Talent Development Reporting Principles, which are described in the *Measurement Demystified* books and widely used. Dave is the founder and former executive director of the Center for Talent Reporting, which was a nonprofit, membership-based organization dedicated to the creation and implementation of standards for human capital measurement, reporting, and management. He is the former president of Caterpillar University, which he founded in 2001. Prior to this position, Dave was chief economist and head of the business intelligence group at Caterpillar. Dave teaches in the PhD program at Bellevue University and in the executive education program for chief learning officers at George Mason University. He also serves on the Metrics Working Group for the International Organization for Standardization where he led the creation of the first comprehensive standard on L&D metrics. Dave received a PhD in economics from the University of Notre Dame.

Henri van den Idsert is a monitoring and evaluation specialist with more than 15 years of experience. He currently serves as a senior evaluation specialist at the UN Refugee Agency. Throughout his diverse career spanning research firms, government institutions, NGOs, and UN agencies, Henri has tackled complex evaluations, mostly in postconflict and emergency settings in East Africa, Southern Africa, and the Middle East. His focus lies in results-based management, capacity building, strategy analysis, and systems thinking. Henri takes pride in his pivotal role in advancing data-driven approaches, ensuring informed decision making within humanitarian and development settings. Henri is of Kenyan and Dutch origin and lives with his loving wife and two children in Geneva, Switzerland. The views expressed in his chapter are done in Henri's personal capacity and do not reflect in any way the views or opinions of his employer.

Eric T. Vincent, MS ICE-CCP, is senior manager of credentialing accreditation for ANSI-ANAB's ISO/IEC 17024 and ASTM E2659 programs. Previously, he served as program director in ACT's Credentialing and Career Services group. He has designed and implemented credentialing programs across several professions and organizations. In addition to conducting job analysis studies and the creation of a variety of assessments, Eric has aligned the results with training and education initiatives. He is a facilitator of the ACT and ATD Test Design and Delivery Certificate program.

Emma Weber is the founder and CEO of Lever—Transfer of Learning. She is a learning transfer authority and has made it her mission to make a difference to learning transfer worldwide. Frustrated by the amount of learning that is wasted when it fails to make it across the knowing–doing gap, Emma developed the Turning Learning Into Action (TLA) methodology. TLA is deployed throughout 20 countries and in 12 languages by a talented team and Coach M, a conversational AI chatbot that's challenging the industry's thinking of what's possible in learning transfer. Emma shares her passion and expertise through her writing. *Turning Learning Into Action: A Proven Methodology for Effective Transfer of Learning* was published by Kogan Page in 2014. In 2023, she co-authored *Designing Virtual Learning for Application and Impact: 50 Techniques to Ensure Results* published by ATD Press. To learn more, visit transferoflearning.com.

Kevin M. Yates is known in the global training, learning, and talent development community as "the L&D Detective." He solves measurement mysteries and investigates the impact of training and learning. Having worked with world-renown brands including Grant Thornton, Kantar, McDonald's, and Meta (Facebook), Kevin leverages his experience and expertise for revealing effectiveness and impact for training and learning. The core of his L&D Detective work is using facts, clues, evidence, and data to reveal training and learning's contribution and impact on workplace performance. He is also president and founder of Meals in the Meantime, a nonprofit helping people who need food with pop-up food pantries.

Index

Page numbers followed by *f* and *t* refer to figures and tables, respectively.

A

accuracy
    in data visualization, 282–283, 283*f*
    of questionnaires, 88
actionable recommendations, 323
action planning, 139–154
    case studies of, 151–154
    example action plan for, 140–142, 141*t*
    following up on, 148–151, 148*f*–151*f*
    reasons for failure of, 143–145
    stop, start, continue format for, 142
    successful, ensuring, 146–147, 147*t*
activity-based costing (ABC), 201
adaptive challenges, 371
adding value, 340–341, 340*f*
aggregate program metrics, 310–311
aligning training to business needs, 3–18
    Alignment Process: V Model for, 10–14, 10*f*
    benefits of, 7–9
    business needs in, 10*f*, 11–12
    case study of, 14–16, 15*t*
    changing conversation with clients for, 10
    conducting conversations about, 16
    input needs in, 10*f*, 14
    learning needs in, 10*f*, 13
    leveraging generative AI for, 389
    payoff needs in, 10*f*, 11
    performance needs in, 10*f*, 12–13
    preference needs in, 10*f*, 13–14
    reasons for, 3–7, 4*t*, 5*t*
    in ROI Methodology, 375–376
alignment (generally)
    on measures of success, 319
    strategic, black box thinking for, 319–320
Alignment Process: V Model, 10–14, 10*f*
Alqarni, Arwa, 238
American Evaluation Association (AEA), xxvii, 373–374

Application and Implementation (Level 3) measures, xxv*t*, xxvi, xxix–xxx
application objectives, 42–43
artificial intelligence. *See* generative artificial intelligence (AI)
ASML, 406
    measurement and evaluation challenge for, 406–407
    measurement and evaluation strategy of, 407–416
attribution error, 378
authorship phenomenon, 117–119

B

balanced measurement and evaluation strategy, 409–412, 410*t*, 411*f*
behavioral change, in diversity and inclusion, 151–153
belonging, improving, 245–246
benefit-cost ratio (BCR), 224–225, 227*t*
bias
    in data visualization, 282–283, 283*f*
    in measuring intangible benefits, 240
Bishop, Elizabeth A., 91
black box thinking, 315–324
    to create continuous improvement culture, 318
    in data analysis, 321–322
    in data collection, 320–321
    implementation of, 319–323
    key benefits of, 317
    to maximize training effectiveness, 317–318
    in reporting, 322–323
    for results optimization, 316–317
    in ROI Methodology, 379
    for strategic alignment, 319–320
    value in, 315–316
Black Box Thinking (Syed), 316
Block, Peter, 273
Boyer, Brook, 135, 137

483

INDEX

Brinkerhoff, Robert, 140
Broad, Mary L., 8
Brown, Peter C., 69
Buckley, Kaycee, 7
Burrus, Gary, 51, 205
Business Impact (Level 4) measures, xxv$t$, xxvi, xxvi$t$
business needs, 10f, 11–12. *See also* aligning training to business needs
Butler, Andrew, 69

C

Cairns-Lee, Heather, 117–119
capability, building, 153–154, 344–346
case application and practice, xxiv, xxiv$f$, xxv$t$, xxvi, xxix–xxx
categorical measures, 158
central tendency measures, 161–164, 161t, 163f, 164f
chain of impact
 in data collection plan, 54t
 in isolating effects of programs, 187–188, 188f
 in program objectives development, 34–35, 35t
 return on investment in, 230–231, 231f
change fatigue, 350
change readiness, 348–350, 349f
Children and Families Commission (CFC), 339
cleanness rating, 118–119
Coach M, 149–154, 149f–151f
coding interview data, 122–123
coefficient of variation (CV), 166
cognitive levels, for tests, 101
comment questions, in learner surveys, 76
communicating results, 265–278
 case study of, 265–266
 communication plan for, 268–273
 media selection for, 268
 opportunities for, 273
 of ROI Methodology, 379, 384
 routine feedback on project progress, 273
 to senior leadership, 275–277, 277f
 for sustainable measurement practice, 341
 targeted, 267
 by telling a story, 274–275
 testimonials in, 268
 timing of, 267
 unbiased, 268
communication
 alignment conversations, 16
 analyzing need for, 269
 analyzing reactions to, 272–273
 black box thinking for, 319

changing conversations with clients, 10
 conversations to increase stakeholder buy-in, 359–363
 in developing program objectives, 46–47
 of intangible benefits to stakeholders, 243–244
 subjective language, 45–46
communication documents, 270–271, 271f
communication plan, 268–273
 analyzing need for communication, 269
 analyzing reactions to communication, 272–273
 delivering results, 272
 developing communication documents, 270–271, 271f
 identifying target audience, 269–270
communication targets, for final report, 59
comparison visualizations, 287, 287f
composition visualizations, 289, 289f
confirmability, in interviews, 117–119
content, questionnaire, 83–86, 85f–85f, 90
Content Analysis (Krippendorff), 175
content analysis, for qualitative data, 175
continuous improvement
 culture of, 318
 of measurement and evaluation strategy, 416
 for sustainable measurement practice, 341
continuous learning, prioritizing, 344
continuous measures, 158
control groups, in isolating effects of programs, 188–191, 189f
converting measures to monetary value, 199–213
 databases in, 204
 estimates in, 205–207, 206t
 historical costs in, 204
 intangible measures in, 208–209
 internal and external experts in, 204
 by linking measures, 204–205
 methods for, in ROI analysis plan, 58
 reasons for, 199–201
 in ROI Methodology, 377–379
 standard values in, 202–203
 steps in, 207–208
 techniques for, 201–207
correlation coefficient, 167–168, 168f
cost-benefit analysis (CBA), 224
costs
 categories of, 58–59
 of evaluation, 9
 historical, 204
 program costs, 215–222
 in ROI analysis, 383

484

cost-saving methods, integrating, 347–348
criterion-referenced tests, 104–105
culture of continuous improvement, 318
custom analysis lexicon, for qualitative data, 178, 178*t*
cut score, 103–105, 104*t*–105*t*

D

Daley, Lynne, 16
dashboards, 305, 306, 414
data
    aligning data visualization to type of, 283
    converted to monetary value (*See* converting measures to monetary value)
    in driving action, 320
    improvement, 90, 382
    in ROI analysis plan, 58
    types of, 68
    useful, 340–341
data analysis, xxviii*f*, xxxii–xxxiii, 155–156
    black box thinking in, 321–322
    for converting measures to monetary value, 199–213
    delving into, 241
    forecasting ROI, 249–262
    of intangible benefits, 235–248
    from interviews, 111–113, 113*t*, 119–123
    isolating effects of programs, 185–198
    of program costs, 215–222
    for qualitative data, 171–184
    return on investment calculation, 223–233
    in ROI Methodology, 381
    statistics in, 157–170
databases, in converting data to monetary value, 204
data categorization, xxv–xxvii, xxv*f*
data collection, xxviii*f*, xxxii, 63–64
    action plans for, 139–154
    black box thinking in, 320–321
    with focus groups, 125–138
    follow-up questionnaires and surveys design for, 79–96
    learner surveys design for, 65–77
    navigating, 241
    for qualitative data, 172–173
    in ROI Methodology, 380–381
    test design and delivery for, 97–109
    through interviews, 111–124
data collection plan, 52–57, 53*t*–55*t*
    chain of impact in, 54*t*
    data sources in, 53*t*, 56
    measures in, 52–54, 53*t*
    methods and instruments in, 53*t*, 55, 55*t*
    program objectives in, 52, 53*t*
    responsibilities in, 53*t*, 57
    timing in, 53*t*, 56–57
data ink, 284
data management, for interview data, 119–123
data parties, 297–298
data sources, in data collection plan, 53*t*, 56
data visualization(s), 279–299
    aligned to type of data, 283
    avoiding bias in, 282–283, 283*f*
    comparisons, 287, 287*f*
    composition, 289, 289*f*
    data parties for, 297–298
    design concepts for, 283–287, 283*f*, 284*f*, 286*f*
    distribution, 288–289, 289*f*
    hierarchical representations, 295, 295*f*
    and human perception of information, 280–281, 281*t*
    leveraging generative AI for, 391
    for Likert data, 291–293, 293*f*
    maintaining accuracy in, 282–283, 283*f*
    for non-Likert (categorical) data, 293–294, 294*f*
    Notice and Wonder method in, 297
    objectives of, 280
    pie charts, 290–291
    for qualitative data, 294–296, 295*f*
    relationships, 288, 288*f*
    selecting the right graph for, 290
    tables vs. graphs in, 291
    tips and techniques for, 296–298
decision-making, leveraging AI in, 392–393
deductive coding, 123
delivery methods
    for communicating results, 272
    for questionnaires, 91
    for tests, 97–109
demographics, analyzing data by, 321–322
denaturalized transcription, 120
descriptive statistics, 159–167
    coefficient of variation, 166
    distribution, 160, 160*t*
    interquartile range, 162–163
    mean, 161–164, 161*t*, 163*f*, 164*f*
    measures of central tendency, 161–164, 161*t*, 163*f*, 164*f*
    measures of dispersion, 162–163
    measures of variance, 164–167, 165*t*, 166*f*
    median, 161–164, 161*t*, 163*f*, 164*f*
    mode, 161–164, 161*t*, 163*f*, 164*f*
    range, 162

INDEX

descriptive statistics (*continued*)
    standard deviation, 164–166, 165*t*, 166*f*
    variance, 166
design
    AI in integrating evaluation into, 390
    including diverse perspectives in, 320
    in ROI Methodology, 376–377
    of tests, 97–105, 98*f*
design, development, and implementation plan, for questionnaires, 81–83, 81*t*, 82*t*
Designing Virtual Learning for Application and Impact (Huggett et al.), 143
design thinking, 371–372
The Discovery of Grounded Theory (Glaser and Strauss), 175
discrete measures, 158
dispersion measures, 162–163
distribution
    of data, 160, 160*t*
    of questionnaires, 88–91
distribution visualizations, 288–289, 289*f*
diversity, equity, and inclusion (DEI)
    case study for delivering behavioral change in, 151–153
    measures of, xxvi*t*
Doerr, John, 33

E

effectiveness metrics, 304
    for reporting at department level, 311
    for strategic learning programs, 309
effects
    of intangible benefits, isolating, 243–244
    of programs, isolating, 58 (*See also* isolating effects of programs)
efficiency metrics, 304
    nonprogram, 311
    for reporting at department level, 310–311
    for strategic learning programs, 309
Eid, Mahmoud bin, 243
employee performance assessments, 23–27, 25*t*, 26*t*
employee time, converted to monetary value, 203
estimates
    in converting data to monetary value, 205–207, 206*t*
    of improvement, in ROI Methodology, 382
    in isolating effects of programs, 195–197, 197*f*
    of training costs, 220–221, 221*t*
ethics, in use of generative AI, 393–394
evaluation, xxiii–xxx, 317

benefits of, xxiii
framework for, xxiv–xxvii, xxiv*f*, xxv*t*, xxviii*f* (*See also specific topics*)
by interviewers, 118
planning (*See* planning evaluation)
professional standards for, 367–385
program evaluation reports, 305, 306
purpose of, 66
as reason to measure, 303
technical and linear approach to, 370
of test results, 106–107
threats to credibility of, 377–378
use of term, 67
using statistics in, 157–170
evaluation plan, 52–60
    AI in ethical review of, 390–391
    data collection plan in, 52–57, 53*t*–55*t*
    leveraging generative AI in developing, 390
    project plan in, 60, 61*t*
    ROI analysis plan in, 57–60, 57*t*
evaluation standards, 367–385
    domains of, 373–374
    and evaluators as co-design agents, 371–372
    importance of, 367–369
    limitations of, 374–375
    ROI Methodology framework, 375–384
    to support complexity of evaluator role, 359–372
execution, 346–348, 347*t*
experienced employees, in S-OJT, 327
experts
    in converting data to monetary value, 204
    for forecasting ROI, 257
extreme scores, examining, 322

F

facilitation skills, 174
feedback on project progress, 273
Fetter, Annie, 297
Few, Stephen, 290
financial analysis, of OJT vs. S-OJT, 325–334
FIND (frame, initiate, navigate, delve), 240–241
Flawless Consulting (Block), 273
Flor, Nick V., 176, 179
Floyd, George, 151
focus groups, 125–138
    case example of, 130
    conducting discussions with, 132–137, 133*f*, 134*f*, 136*f*
    discussion questions for, 130–132
    facilitation skills for, 174

486

formats for, 128
method selection for, 128
objectives of, 127–128
qualitative data from, 172
question types in, 126
selecting participants for, 126
tailored to specific context or needs, 127–130, 127*f*
target audience for, 129–130
timing of, 128–129
follow-up
on action planning, 148–151, 148*f*–151*f*
questionnaires and surveys for, 79–96
forecasting from modeling, in isolating effects of programs, 191, 193–194
forecasting ROI, 249–262
after program launch, 247–259, 258*t*
case study of, 260–261
at different levels, 251–252, 251*t*
postprogram, 256
preprogram, steps in, 252–257, 253*f*
reasons for, 249–251
selecting experts for, 257
formative focus groups, 128
formats, focus group, 128
fully loaded costs, 58
futureproofing, 352

G

Gallo, Carmine, 275
Gardner, Dan, 249
Gates Foundation, 339
generative artificial intelligence (AI), xxxiv, 387–404
in aligning training objectives with business needs, 389
application exercise for, 396–402, 398*t*
choosing tools for, 395–396, 395*t*
in creating data visualizations, 391
in developing AI literacy and decision-making skills, 392–393
in developing comprehensive evaluation plan, 390
in distinguishing between immediate learning outcomes and long-term results, 391
in ethical review of measurement and evaluation plan, 390–391
in integrating evaluation in training design process, 390
leveraging, 387–388
and measurement challenge, 388
responsible, ethical, and inclusive use of, 393–394

in tailoring surveys to stakeholder needs, 389
Glaser, Barney, 175
goals
organizational, 21–22, 22*t*
SMART, 145
Golke, Stefanie, 69
graphs, 290, 291
grounded theory, 175
group leaders, 302
guiding principles, in ROI Methodology, xxiv, xxiv*f*, xxvii, xxix*t*, 380–384
Gunawardena, Charlotte Nirmalani, 179

H

head of learning, 302
hierarchical data representations, 295, 295*f*
histograms, 163–166, 163*f*, 164*f*, 166*f*
historical costs, in converting data to monetary value, 204
Howshan, Mohammed Al, 242
Huggett, Cindy, 143
human perception of information, 280–281, 281*t*
Husserl, Edmund, 117

I

Iansiti, Marco, 388
impact objectives, 43–44
impact study, 270–271, 271*f*
implementing measurement and evaluation, 335
getting stakeholder buy-in when, 355–365
leveraging artificial intelligence in, 387–404
professional evaluation standards in, 367–385 (*See also* evaluation standards)
strategy for, xxiv, xxiv*f*, xxx, 405–417
sustainable measurement practice in, 337–353
improvement data, 90, 382
inclusivity, in use of generative AI, 393–394
Indeed, 265–266
indexing interview data, 122–123
inductive coding, 123
inferential statistics, 167–168, 168*f*
influences affecting measures, in ROI analysis plan, 59
informing
as reason to measure, 303
scorecards or dashboards for, 306
infrastructures, building and maintaining, 346
innovation, embracing art of, 351–352
Input and Indicators (Level 0) measures, xxv, xxv*t*
input needs, 10*f*, 14

INDEX

input objectives, 38–40
Insights Discovery, 265–266
instruments, in data collection plan, 53t, 55, 55t
intangible benefits, 235–248
    building credibility about, 244
    case studies of, 245–246
    challenges in measuring, 239–240
    communicating, to stakeholders, 243–244
    finding, 240–241
    isolating effects of, 243–244
    laying out data on, 244
    narratives sharing importance of, 244
    in ROI analysis plan, 59
    strategies for quantifying, 241–243
    types of, 237–238
    value of, 235–237
intangible measures
    in converting data to monetary value, 208–209
    in ROI Methodology, 377–379, 384
integrated measurement and evaluation strategy, 408–409, 408f, 415
International Organization for Standardization (ISO), xxvii, 301–302. *See also* ISO standards for L&D metrics
interpretation, test items addressing, 101
interquartile range (IQR), 162–163
interval data, 68
interviews, 111–124
    analytical framework for, 111–113, 113t
    art of probing in, 116–117
    building rapport in, 115–116
    challenges with verbatim transcription of, 120–121
    coding results from, 122–123
    data management framework for, 119–120
    dealing with confirmability in, 117–119
    developing protocol for, 113–114
    qualitative data from, 172
    systematic reflexive interviewing and reporting with, 120–122
    of top and standard performers, 24–27, 25t, 26t
    transcription and analysis of, 119–123
introduced content, 117
isolating effects of intangible benefits, 243–244
isolating effects of programs, 185–198
    chain of impact in, 187–188, 188f
    with control groups, 188–191, 189f
    estimates in, 195–197, 197f
    by forecasting from modeling, 191, 193–194
    importance of, 185–186

methods for, 58
in ROI Methodology, 377–379, 382
techniques for, 186–187
with trend line analysis, 191–193, 192f
ISO standards for L&D metrics, 301–313
    adopting ISO TS 30437 framework, 306–308
    application of, 306–312
    framework and language of, 307
    metric names and definitions in, 307
    on reasons to measure, 303
    on reports, 305–306, 308
    on selecting measures, 310–312
    on selecting metrics, 304–305, 308–310
    on selecting reports, 312
    on types of metrics, 304
    on types of users, 302
iterative categorization, 122–123

J

Janahi, Ameena, 243
Jefferson, Andy, 139
Joint Commission on Standards for Evaluation Education (JCSEE), xxvii
Joint Committee for Standards for Evaluation (JDSE), 373
Jones, Michael J., 329

K

Karpicke, Jeffrey, 69
Kendeou, Panayiota, 69
key performance indicators (KPIs), 19, 23–25
Kirschner, Paul, 69
Knaflic, Cole Nussbaumer, 290
Krippendorff, Klaus, 175
Kvale, Steiner, 113–114

L

leadership capability, building, 153–154
leading questions, 117
learners, 302
learner surveys, 65–77
    comment questions in, 76
    good questions for, 69–70
    importance of, 65
    increasing response rates for, 76–77
    LTEM in discerning value of, 66–67
    performance-focused, 70–74, 71t–74t
    traditional, problems with, 67–69
    using Likert-like scales and numeric scales, 68–69
learning agility, fostering, 351

INDEX

learning dashboard, 414
Learning (Level 2) measures, xxv–xxvi, xxv*t*
learning needs, 10*f*, 13
learning objectives, 41–42
learning outcomes
    AI application exercise for, 396–402, 398*t*
    testing, 101
learning transfer, 8
Learning-Transfer Evaluation Model (LTEM), 66–67
LeBrun, Christopher, 317
Level 1 evaluations, 67
Likert data, visualizations of, 291–293, 293*f*
Likert-like scales, 68–69
logical frameworks, 111–112
Loubere, Nicholas, 120, 121

M

management
    as reason to measure, 303
    of resistance to measurement, 345–346
    using management reports for, 306
management reports, 305–306
management structure and support, performance influence of, 28
managers
    enhancing support for, 350
    in learning transfer process, 8
    providing performance support for, 345
    in sustainable measurement practice, 343
McDaniel, Mark A., 69
McGriffin, Terry, 328
McLinden, Dan, 342
mean, 161–164, 161*t*, 163*f*, 164*f*
measurement
    challenge of, 388
    data types/levels in, 158–159, 159*t*
measurement and evaluation (M&E), xxiii–xxx. *See also specific topics*
    AI in ethical review of, 390–391
    benefits of, xxiii
    implementation and sustainability of, xxxiii–xxxiv
    implementing, 335 (*See also* implementing measurement and evaluation)
    strategy for, xxiv–xxx, xxiv*f*, xxviii*f*, xxxiv
measurement and evaluation strategy, 405–417
    ASML's approach for building, 407–416
    balanced and scalable, 409–412, 410*t*, 411*f*
    challenge in developing, 406–407
    continuous improvement of, 416
    implementation of, 414–415

    integrated approach to, 408–409, 408*f*
    integration of, 415
    learning dashboard for, 414
    toolkit for, 412–415
measures
    of central tendency, 161–164, 161*t*, 163*f*, 164*f*
    converting to monetary value, 199–213 (*See also* converting measures to monetary value)
    in data collection plan, 52–54, 53*t*
    of dispersion, 162–163
    intangible, 208–209
    levels of, xxv–xxx, xxv*t*, xxvi*t*
    linking, 204–205
    of ROI, 224–230
    types of, 158
    of variance, 164–167, 165*t*, 166*f*
Measure What Matters (Doerr), 33
median, 161–164, 161*t*, 163*f*, 164*f*
Merdad, Leena, 237
methods
    in data collection plan, 53*t*, 55, 55*t*
    for focus groups selection, 128
    for isolating effects of programs, 58
    for qualitative data analysis, 175–176
metrics, ISO standards for, 301–313. *See also specific metrics*
mode, 161–164, 161*t*, 163*f*, 164*f*
momentum, maintaining, 339–340, 340*f*
monetary value
    converting measures to, 199–213 (*See also* converting measures to monetary value)
    importance of, 199–201
monitoring
    of change or survey fatigue, 350
    as reason to measure, 303
    scorecards or dashboards for, 306
Moustakas, Clark, 117
multimodal data collection strategy, 320–321
multiple-choice tests, 102–103
Murphy, Kelly, 253

N

Nadella, Satya, 388
narratives, of intangible benefits, 244
naturalized transcription, 119–120
Neale, Joanne, 122–123
Neil, Sue, 329
net present value (NPV), 227–229, 228*t*
Newstrom, John W., 8
nominal data, 68

INDEX

nominal group technique, 14–15
nondata ink, 284
non-Likert (categorical) data, visualizations for, 293–294, 294f
nonprogram metrics, 311–312
nonstrategic learning programs, metrics for, 309–310
Notice and Wonder method, 297
novice employees, in S-OJT, 327
numeric scales, 68–69

O

objectives, 2
    of data visualization, 280
    of focus groups, 127–128
    impact, 43–44
    input, 38–40
    learning, 41–42
    levels of, 34–35, 35t
    powerful, 36–38, 37t, 38t
    program, 52, 53t (*See also* program objectives)
    reaction, 40–41
    ROI, 44–45, 229–230
    value of, 33–34
on-the-job training (OJT)
    case study of S-OJT vs., 329–333, 330f, 332t
    financial analysis comparing S-OJT and, 325–334
    financial benefits of, 328–329
    unplanned, 325–326
open-ended questions, 172, 174
optimizing effectiveness, of questionnaires, 86–88
ordinal data, 68
organizational goals, defining, 21–22, 22t
outcome metrics, 304
    for reporting at department level, 311
    for strategic learning programs, 309
outcomes
    AI in distinguishing between immediate learning outcomes and long-term results, 391
    defining, for job roles, 24
    optimizing (*See* results optimization)
output data, converted to monetary value, 202–203

P

participant selection, for focus groups, 126
partnerships, strengthening, 9, 340f, 341–344
payback period (PP), 226–227, 227t
payoff, converting measures to show, 200
payoff needs, 10f, 11
performance-focused learner surveys, 70–74, 71t–74t
performance gaps, 19

performance gaps analysis, 19–32
    assessing factors that influence performance in, 27–29
    case study of, 31
    defining organization goals in, 21–22, 22t
    employee performance assessment in, 23–27, 25t, 26t
    importance of, 20
    involving key stakeholders in, 29
    process for, 20
    stakeholder project planning meetings in, 23
    summarizing performance gap in, 30, 30t
performance needs, 10f, 12–13
performance support, providing, 344–345
personal motivation, assessing performance influence of, 28
Phillips, Jack J., 143
Phillips, Patricia Pulliam, 143
pie charts, 290–291
planning evaluation, xxviiif, xxxi, 1–2, 49–62
    to align training to business needs, 3–18
    evaluation plan development, 52–60
    importance of, 49–50
    initiation of, 240–241
    performance gaps analysis for, 19–32
    program objectives development in, 33–47
    in ROI Methodology, 381
    scope of evaluation definition in, 50–52
Pollock, Roy, 139
post-course evaluations, 67
postprogram forecasting of ROI, 256
preference needs, 10f, 13–14
preprogram forecasting of ROI, 252–257, 253f
presuppositions, 117–118
Prinz, Anja, 69
probing, in interviews, 116–117
problem solving, test items addressing, 101
process model, xxiv, xxivf, xxvii, xxviiif
program benefits, normalized by money, 200
program costs, 215–222
    for acquisition, 218, 218t
    capturing, in ROI Methodology, 377–379
    categories, 217, 218t
    for delivery and implementation, 218t, 219
    for design and development, 218, 218t
    estimation of, 220–221, 221t
    for evaluation and reporting, 218t, 220
    importance of identifying, 215–216
    monitoring issues with, 216–221
    for needs assessment and analysis, 217, 218t

for overhead, 218t, 220
prorated vs. direct costs, 217
sources of, 216–217
for technological support, 218–219, 218t
program evaluation reports, 305, 306
program launch, forecasting ROI after, 247–259, 258t
program manager, 302
program objectives
application objectives, 42–43
chain of impact in, 34–35, 35t
in data collection plan, 52, 53t
developing, 33–47
impact objectives, 43–44
input objectives, 38–40
learning objectives, 41–42
pitfalls in, 45–47
powerful, 36–38, 37t, 38t
reaction objectives, 40–41
ROI objectives, 44–45
value of, 33–34
project management, 346
project participants, performance support for, 345
project plan
developing, 60, 61t
summary in, 21–22, 22t
project planning meetings, 23
projects, needs, scope, and results of, 21
project teams, performance support for, 345
propensity score match, 190
protocol, interview, 113–114
purpose
of evaluation, 66
for questionnaires, defining, 80

Q

qualitative data analysis, 171–184
collection instruments for, 172–173
content analysis in, 175
custom analysis lexicon in, 178, 178t
defining qualitative data, 171
and grounded theory, 175
improving quality of, 173–174
methods for, 175–176
sentiment analysis in, 176–177, 177t, 180–184
traditional methods for, 176
value of qualitative data, 172
visualization of, 294–296, 295f
quality, converted to monetary value, 203
quantifying intangible benefits, 241–243

quantitative data analysis, 171
questionnaires, 79–96
accuracy of, 88
clearly defined purpose for, 80
content of, 90
creating content of, 83–86, 85f–85f
delivery method for, 91
design, development, and implementation plan for, 81–83, 81t, 82t
developing questions for, 84–86, 85f–86f
distribution of, 88–91
drafts of, 87
executing, 91–92, 92f–93f
experience of completing, 88
functionality of, 87
improving response rates for, 89–91
optimizing effectiveness of, 86–88
plan for successful use of, 80–83, 81t, 82t
qualitative data from, 172
respondent population for, 88–89, 89t
scope of, 80–81
steps in developing, 79–80
structure of, 83–84
testing, 87–88
timeline for responding to, 91
using and analyzing results of, 88
questions
comment questions, 76
for focus groups, 126, 130–132
for good learner surveys, 69–70
insightful, 321
leading, 117
on Likert-like scales, 68–69
open-ended, 172, 174
for questionnaires, developing, 84–86, 85f–86f
yes-or-no, 174

R

Radtke Jil, 56
Rainbow Framework, 112
range (R), 162
rapport building, in interviews, 115–116
Reaction and Planned Action (Level 1) measures, xxv, xxvt
reaction forms, 67
reaction objectives, 40–41
recall, test items addressing, 101
recognition, 348
reflexive dialogue, 122
relationship visualizations, 288, 288f

INDEX

reporting
  black box thinking in, 322–323
  impact studies, 270–271, 271f
  ISO standards for L&D metrics on, 305–306, 308, 312
  metrics for reporting at department level, 310–311
  of program costs, 218t, 220
  in ROI analysis plan, 69
  of ROI in performance contexts, 230–231, 231f
  systematic reflexive interviewing and reporting, 120–122
resistance, managing, 345–346
respondent population, for questionnaires, 88–89, 89t
response rates
  for learner surveys, increasing, 76–77
  for questionnaires, 89–91
responsibilities
  in data collection plan, 53t, 57
  in use of generative AI, 393–394
results analysis, for questionnaires, 88
results optimization, xxviiif, xxxiii, 263
  better programs for, 9
  black box thinking for, 315–324
  financial analysis to compare OJT and S-OJT, 325–334
  ISO standards for L&D metrics, 301–313
  telling the story, 265–278 (See also communicating results)
  visualizing data, 279–299 (See also data visualization)
return on investment (ROI), 223–233
  analysis plan for, 57–60, 57t
  benefit-cost ratio, 224–225, 227t
  calculating, in ROI Methodology, 377–379, 383
  case study of, 232
  in chain of impact, 230–231, 231f
  defined, 224
  forecasting, 249–262
  formula for, xxvii
  importance of, 223–224
  in Inclusion Toolkit, xxvi, xxvit
  metrics for, 224–230
  monetary benefits in calculating, 201
  net present value for, 227–229, 228t
  objectives for, 44–45
  payback period for, 226–227, 227t
  reporting in performance contexts, 230–231, 231f
  ROI champions, 343
  ROI Methodology (See ROI Methodology)
  ROI metric for, 225–226, 227t
  selecting programs for evaluation of, 231–232
  setting targets for, 229–230
Return on Investment (ROI) (Level 5) measures, xxvt, xxvii–xxix
rewards, 348
Rhodes, Matthew, 69
risk management, 347, 347t
Roediger, Henry, 69
ROI analysis plan, 57–60, 57t
  comments in, 60
  communication targets for final report in, 59
  cost categories in, 58–59
  data items in, 58
  influences affecting measures identification in, 59
  intangible benefits in, 59
  methods for converting data to monetary value in, 58
  methods for isolating program effects in, 58
ROI champions, 343
ROI Institute, xxvii, 63, 231, 375
ROI Methodology, xxvii, xxviiif, xxx–xxi, 375–384
  designing for results in, 376–377
  guiding principles for, xxiv, xxivf, xxvii, xxixt, 380–384
  integration of standards and method in, 375
  on lack of improvement data, 90
  selecting the right solution in, 376
  steps in, 374–379
ROI project teams, 344

S

Santos, Laurie, 237
scalable measurement and evaluation strategy, 409–412, 410t, 411f
scope
  of evaluation, 50–52, 376
  of questionnaires, 80–81
scorecards, 305, 306
scrap learning, 316
SCS, 260–261, 261t
SECOR Bank, 14–16, 15t–16t
senior leadership
  communicating results to, 275–277, 277f
  ISO standard on, 302
  providing performance support for, 345
sentiment analysis
  for qualitative data, 176–177, 177t
  using R, 180–184
Shaughnessy, John, 69

Show Me the Numbers (Few), 290
The Six Disciplines of Breakthrough Learning (Pollock, Jefferson, and Wick), 139
SMART goals, 145
smile sheets, 67
Smith, Paul, 274
solutions
    annual benefits in ROI analysis of, 383
    selection of, in ROI Methodology, 376
sponsors, 342
St. Mary-Corwin Medical Center, 246
stakeholder buy-in, 355–365
    assessing current state of, 357–359, 357t, 358t
    going beyond, 365–365
    importance of, 355–356
    increasing, 359–363
stakeholder needs
    aligning training to (*See* aligning training to business needs)
    defining, 1–2
    generative AI in tailoring surveys to, 389
    and level of evaluation, 51
    types of, 11–14
stakeholders
    communicating intangible benefits to, 243–244
    communicating results of ROI Methodology to, 384
    in developing qualitative questions, 174
    framing expectations of, 240
    key, in performance gaps analysis, 29
    project planning meetings with, 23
standard deviation (SD or s), 164–166, 165t, 166f
standards, xxiv, xxivf, xxvii
    for evaluation (*See* evaluation standards)
    ISO standards for L&D metrics, 301–313
    for tests, 103–105, 104t
standard values, in converting data to monetary value, 202–203
statistics, 157–170
    in AI analysis of learning outcomes and training results, 399–402
    descriptive, 159–167 (*See also* descriptive statistics)
    inferential, 159, 167–168, 168f
    for test item performance, 106–107
    and types of measurement data, 158–159, 159t
steering committees, 342
stop, start, continue format, 142
Storytelling With Data (Knaflic), 290
strategic alignment
    black box thinking for, 319–320
    of training to business needs (*See* aligning training to business needs)
strategic learning programs, metrics for, 309
Strauss, Anselm, 175
structure
    management, performance influence of, 28
    questionnaire, 83–84
    workplace, performance influence of, 27
structured on-the-job training (S-OJT)
    case study of OJT vs., 329–333, 330f, 332t
    development of, 325–326
    financial analysis comparing OJT and, 325–334
    financial benefits of, 328–329
    six-phase systematic process of, 326–327
student response forms, 67
subjective language, in developing program objectives, 45–46
summative focus groups, 128
Superforecasting (Tetlock and Gardner), 249
survey fatigue, 350
surveys. *See also* questionnaires
    defined, 80
    generative AI in tailoring, 389
    learner, 65–77
    qualitative data from, 172
sustainable measurement practice, 337–353
    adding and creating value for, 340–341, 340f
    building change readiness for, 348–350, 349f
    embracing art of innovation for, 351–352
    executing well for, 346–348, 347t
    foundation for, 338–339
    growing capability for, 344–346
    maintaining momentum with, 339–340, 340f
    strengthening partnerships for, 340f, 341–344
Sword, Rosalyn, 70
Syed, Matthew, 316
systematic reflexive interviewing and reporting (SRIR), 120–122

T

tables, graphs vs., 291
talent acquisition, assessing performance influence of, 28
target audience
    for communicating results, 269–270
    for focus groups, 129–130
tasks
    defining, for job roles, 24
    in S-OJT, 327
TD professionals, performance support for, 345

INDEX

team leaders, 302
technology. *See also* generative artificial intelligence (AI)
   in action planning, 149–154
   assessing performance influence of, 28–29
   leveraging, 351–352
telling a story
   black box thinking for, 323
   with results, 274–275
testing, of questionnaires, 87–88
tests, 97–109
   best practices for item writing, 101–102
   case example for, 107–109
   cognitive levels for, 101
   creating items for, 100–102
   criterion-referenced, 104–105
   design of, 97–105, 98*f*
   evaluating results of, 106–107
   of learning outcomes, 101
   multiple-choice, 102–103
   number of items on, 99–100
   planning, 99
   reliability, validity, and fairness of, 97–98, 98*f*
   standard setting for, 103–105, 104*t*
   threshold scores (cut scores) on, 103–105
   using item-level data to improve item quality on, 106–107, 107*t*
Tetlock Phillip, 249
Thalheimer, Will, 3
thematic analysis, 322
theories of change, 111–112
Theory of Change (ToC) approach, 112–113, 113*t*
threshold score, 103–104
timeline, for questionnaire response, 91
timing
   in data collection plan, 53*t*, 56–57
   of focus groups, 128–129
toolkit for measurement and evaluation, 412–415
traditional learner surveys, 67–69
traditional qualitative data analysis methods, 176
training and development, performance influence of, 27
training effectiveness, 329
   AI application exercise for, 396–402, 398*t*
   black box thinking to maximize, 317–318
   effectiveness metrics, 304, 309, 311

training efficiency, 328–329
training reaction surveys, 67
Training Within Industry (TWI) initiative, 327
trend line analysis, 191–193, 192*f*
Turning Learning Into Action (TLA), 148, 148*f*, 152, 153
Type 1 errors, 378
Type 2 errors, 378–379

U

Unilever, 351
useful data, 340–341
US Office of Personnel Management (OPM), xxvii

V

value
   adding and creating, 340–341, 340*f*
   in black box thinking, 315–316
   of intangible benefits, 235–237
   of monetary contribution, 200 (*See also* converting measures to monetary value)
value creation, 340–341, 340*f*
van den Broek, Paul, 69
van Merriënboer, Jeroen, 69
variance (s^2), 166
variance measures, 164–167, 165*t*, 166*f*
Vertex, 245–246
visualizing data. *See* data visualization

W

Weber, Emma, 143
Wick, Calhoun, 139
wicked problems, 371
Wilson, Stephanie Wagner, 105
Wittwer, Jorg, 69
workplace structure and environment, performance influence of, 27
work routines, defining, 24
work units, in S-OJT, 327

Y

yes-or-no questions, 174

Z

Zechmeister, Eugene, 69
z-scores, 167

About the Editor

Patti P. Phillips, PhD, is co-founder and CEO of ROI Institute, a US-based consulting firm that serves for-profit, not-for-profit, government, and nongovernmental organizations in 70 countries as they build capability in measurement, evaluation, and human capital analytics.

An internationally recognized leader in measurement and analytics, Patti routinely speaks at industry conferences worldwide and contributes to the growing body of research in human capital and human capital analytics. Her expertise is documented in more than 70 books—including *Return on Investment in Training and Performance Improvement Programs*, third edition; *Show the Value of What You Do: Measuring and Achieving Success in Any Endeavor*; *Proving the Value of Soft Skills*; *ROI Basics*, second edition; *Making Human Capital Analytics Work*; and *Measuring ROI in Healthcare*—published by the Association for Talent Development (ATD), McGraw-Hill, Wiley, Kogan-Page, Berrett-Koehler, and other major publishing houses. Her work has been cited by CNBC, Euronews, and *National Geographic* and published in more than a dozen business journals. She is a thought partner for research organizations such as The Conference Board Human Capital Center and the Institute for Corporate Productivity People Analytics Board (i4cp).

She, along with her husband and ROI Institute co-founder Jack J. Phillips, was the recipient of the 2024 Association of Learning Providers Thought Leader Award, 2022 ATD Thought Leader Award, and the 2019 Center for Talent Reporting Distinguished Contributor Award. In 2019, she was named among the top 50 coaches globally by the Thinkers50 organization and named a finalist for the Marshall Goldsmith Distinguished Achievement Award for Coaching.

Patti has served as a board member for the UN Institute for Training and Research (UNITAR) and is currently board chair of the International Federation of Training and Development Organizations and a board member of the International Society for Performance

ABOUT THE EDITOR

Improvement. She is also the chair of the UNITAR Evaluation Advisory Board and co-chair of the Institute for Corporate Productivity People Analytics Board. She also serves on the Advisory Boards of Cognota and CoachHub.

Patti lives in Birmingham, Alabama. You can reach her at patti@roiinstitute.net or connect with her on LinkedIn (linkedin.com/in/pattipphillips).

About ATD

atd The Association for Talent Development (ATD) is the world's largest association dedicated to those who develop talent in organizations. Serving a global community of members, customers, and international business partners in more than 100 countries, ATD champions the importance of learning and training by setting standards for the talent development profession.

Our customers and members work in public and private organizations in every industry sector. Since ATD was founded in 1943, the talent development field has expanded significantly to meet the needs of global businesses and emerging industries. Through the Talent Development Capability Model, education courses, certifications and credentials, memberships, industry-leading events, research, and publications, we help talent development professionals build their personal, professional, and organizational capabilities to meet new business demands with maximum impact and effectiveness.

One of the cornerstones of ATD's intellectual foundation, ATD Press offers insightful and practical information on talent development, training, and professional growth. ATD Press publications are written by industry thought leaders and offer anyone who works with adult learners the best practices, academic theory, and guidance necessary to move the profession forward.

We invite you to join our community. Learn more at td.org.